D0990848

SPORTING GENDER

SPORTING GENDER

The History, Science, and Stories of Transgender and Intersex Athletes

Joanna Harper

ROWMAN & LITTLEFIELD
Lanham • Boulder • New York • London

Published by Rowman & Littlefield
An imprint of The Rowman & Littlefield Publishing Group, Inc.
4501 Forbes Boulevard, Suite 200, Lanham, Maryland 20706
www.rowman.com

6 Tinworth Street, London SE11 5AL

British Library Cataloguing in Publication Information Available

Library of Congress Control Number: 2019949312

∞ ™ The paper used in this publication meets the minimum requirements of American National Standard for Information Sciences Permanence of Paper for Printed Library Materials, ANSI/NISO Z39.48-1992.

CONTENTS

FOREWORD

David Epstein

In the spring of 2012, I sent the reporter's version of a message in a bottle: not a crumpled paper stuffed in wind-worn glass, but an e-mail that I figured had only a marginally better chance of getting a response. I was hoping to be put in touch with Joanna Harper.

I was, at the time, a senior writer at *Sports Illustrated*, working on a story pitch about transgender athletes with my colleague Pablo Torre. We had already made successful contact with two trans men who were college athletes—basketball and track and field—both of whom delayed medical transition from female to male while they competed on women's teams. But our pitch had a gaping hole. We hadn't found anyone who would give us a personal account of sports' true third rail: an athlete who had been born male but transitioned to female and was now competing against women. And then I came across a post by Joanna on the now-defunct site WomenRunningTogether.com.

In it, Joanna described her transition—how she had been born male and, as a man, had been an exceptional runner (2:23 marathon); how in 2004, as a forty-seven-year-old medical physicist, she had started testosterone suppression. In 2007 she began to compete as a woman, and she didn't just compete: She won the women's 50–54 age group at the USA Track & Field Club Cross Country Championships. Her post was both illuminating and disarming. She recounted having "married two very attractive women (not at the same time), bought a big beautiful house in the suburbs and lived what many people thought was a wonderful life"—but also how she was devastated by puberty, when her body changed in ways that precisely betrayed the person she wanted to become. She wrote about eventually undergoing transition surgery, and that afterward people would ask how she was doing. I remember sitting in my *SI* office and laughing out loud when I read her standard reply: "[P]retty well, I'm back at work and I'm doing a little running now. Oh yeah and my IQ is up 10 points too."

So I wrote an e-mail to the proprietor of WomenRunningTogether.com explaining who I was and asking if there was any chance my message could be forwarded to Joanna. I didn't hold out much hope. Obviously, Joanna was willing to share, or she wouldn't have written that post. But *SI* was an entirely different beast. She would not be in control of the words we chose to put in a story, or of the context in which we placed them in an article that might eventually grace a side table at her dentist's office. And she could rest assured that many thousands of readers would recoil at her story—some would consider her a cheater—no matter what the article said. The public discussion about transgender athletes had not been, shall we say, enlightened. Were I Joanna Harper, I probably would not have responded to me. Fortunately, I'm not Joanna Harper.

What began as an outside shot at a quote became much more. For starters, not only was Joanna willing to chat, but—like a good scientist—she had kept assiduous track of her race times as she underwent transition. She had lost a lot of muscle, and her allotment of oxygen-carrying red blood cells had declined; her race times followed suit. She was much slower as a woman than she had been as a man. And yet—according to performance tables that indicate how competitive a runner is compared to other athletes of the same age and sex—after one year of testosterone suppression she was precisely as relatively competitive as a woman as she had been as a man. Not only that, but she had (and was willing to share) similar data for a handful of other runners who had transitioned. One runner she tracked competed in the same 5K for fifteen straight years, eight times as a man and, after testosterone suppression, seven times as a woman. She had run under 19 minutes every single time as a man, and over 20 minutes every single time as a woman. In all the hours I'd spent perusing articles in medical journals that tried to triangulate the impact of hormone suppression on athletic performance, I had come across nothing close to that.

Joanna has since published some of that data, and it comprises the best available evidence that a year of testosterone suppression is reasonable for competitive fairness among distance runners who were born male and transition to female. But Joanna is the first to point out that the conclusion cannot be extrapolated to other sports. "For cardiovascular factors, trans women go from typical men to typical women after transition," she told me recently when I spoke with her for a *Wall Street Journal* piece. "But with strength, they go from typical men to somewhere in between typical men and typical women, and 'somewhere in between' isn't very precise."

That's the thing about Joanna: she has somehow managed to *live* this incredibly fraught topic while also maintaining an extraordinary ability to step outside of her own experience and examine the facts like the scientist she is. In my experience as a science writer—and as a human on earth (and on Twitter)—that is *incredibly* rare. Snow leopard rare—as in: we all believe it exists even though we've never actually seen it in the wild.

For me, Joanna started as the person on another shore whom I hoped to reach with my message in a bottle. Infrequently, you do that as a journalist and not only does the recipient become a source, but you start commiserating about a shared love of Irish theater, and before you know it the source has become a friend. Less frequently still, the source who became a friend then becomes an intellectual role model. That's what happened here. These days, when I try to explain a topic that is complex and emotionally fraught, I find myself asking: What would Joanna do? Her mix of lived experience, intellect, patience, rationality, and empathy are, in my experience, simply singular. This is not to say that I agree with her on everything related to transgender or intersex athletes (or Irish theater), because I don't. I couldn't possibly; I've changed my mind on certain aspects several times since she and I first connected. But that's not the point. These issues are so difficult because well-meaning people can agree on the underlying science and still disagree passionately over what should be done about it. An intellectual role model needn't be someone you always agree with, but rather someone whose approach to problems, and to other people, you wish to emulate—or someone whose approach would make the world a better place if it were adopted more widely.

I consider it one of the most important achievements of my *SI* career that I played a tiny role in helping Joanna on her way to becoming an impactful global voice on the issues in this book. I hope you will enjoy—as much as I always do—spending a little time with her formidable brain.

David Epstein is an award-winning investigative reporter and author of the New York Times *bestseller* The Sports Gene.

ACKNOWLEDGMENTS

There are several people I should thank for helping to make this book possible. I'll start with my parents, John and Barbara Harper, who instilled in me a love of learning and an ambition to succeed. This book would not exist if David Epstein hadn't entered my life. I am eternally grateful to Arne Ljungqvist with the IOC and Stéphane Bermon with the IAAF, who welcomed me with open arms, and to Alice Dreger, who made the introduction to Arne. Dorianne Coleman has taught me a lot about working successfully with diverse people. Jonathan Ospina Betancurt has become the younger brother I never had. María José Martínez-Patiño has been inspirational. Yannis Pitsiladis and Theodora Papadopoulou have opened doors for me. Ross Tucker was the first international figure who took notice of me, and I thank him for ten years of science. Eric Vilain served as a mentor to me.

Others I should thank include Suzanne Ray, Jonathan Taylor, Liz Riley, Richard Budgett, Angelica Linden Hirschberg, Richard Auchus, David Handelsman, Sid Angadi, Annabel Bennett, Gemma Whitcomb, Emma O'Donnell, Martin Ritzen, Chris Lavey, Pete Magill, and all of the athletes who have shared their data and stories with me. Last, but by no means least, editor Christen Karniski has graced me with her guidance and suggestions. I'm sure that I have left people out, but thank you everyone.

INTRODUCTION

Twenty years ago I would never have imagined that I would someday write a book. Up until that point, I had written a number of short articles for running club newsletters, school newspapers, and blogs, and I hoped to one day publish an article or short story in a real publication. That was the height of my writing ambition.

I became somewhat more serious about writing once I started my gender transition in 2004. At the time, a few people suggested that I should write a book. I demurred, as there were already many dreadful examples of transgender memoirs, and only a few that I admired, such as Jenny Boylan's *She's Not There.* I had no desire to add my name to the list of mediocre writers who had published transition-related tales.

In 2009 I began writing for a popular running website called Younger Legs for Older Runners, hosted by the well-known runner/writer Pete Magill. In the fall of that year I wrote an article for Pete on Caster Semenya, and the feedback from the article made me realize that a book on gender-diverse athletes might be possible. It wasn't, however, until David Epstein came into my life that I really got serious about creating such a book. David and I had e-mailed each other often starting in 2012, but it was the night that we first met in a Manhattan brew pub in March 2013 that really lit my flame. In the six years since, I have spent countless hours making this book a reality.

As is common with such projects, the book has had several permutations since my first tentative draft. My editor Christen Karniski is largely responsible for the current mix of history, science, and biography that you hold in your hand. I have worked with Christen for almost two years and am grateful for her input.

I should state that I have gently altered some of the details presented here, mostly in the interest of withholding confidential information but sometimes to help with the flow of the narrative. I have tried to maintain the integrity of the overall picture in any such instance. The subject matter present herein is both complicated and controversial, and I haven't shied away from the science or the conflict. I have tried to explain the salient details of the biology to the best of my ability, and to present my viewpoints while acknowledging that there are other competing beliefs on the issues.

I hope that you find this book both informative and enjoyable. I know that anything written here is not the final word on the subject, and I'm certain that there will be plenty more twists and turns in the upcoming years.

1

"PREHISTORIC" WOMEN'S SPORT

When I first decided to open this book with a chapter on the early history of women's sport, I took the standard position that sport for the "weaker sex" had languished until the twentieth century. And then I heard a talk by Mary Anne Case, a law professor at the University of Chicago. Professor Case argued that this standard history was in need of some revision, suggesting that most people started looking at women's sports in the period of the nineteenth century, a time of rigid sex roles and not indicative of the overall history of women's sport.[1] Case is an engaging speaker, and after her talk I decided that I would compare two theses: the "standard history" of women's sport and a revisionist history suggesting that women's sport has a richer history than most people think.

Let's start by looking at the ancient Greeks. It is well-known that the early Olympics were reserved for men only, and that women were not permitted to participate or even watch the games under penalty of being thrown from the cliffs of Mount Typaion. That doesn't seem very welcoming, does it?[2] On the other hand, women had their own games, called the Heraean Games or Heraia in honor of the Greek goddess Hera. The officials, organizers, and the athletes of the Heraia were all women. That fact makes the ancient Greeks seem pretty enlightened.[3] Clearly, there is a need to look more closely if one wants to resolve the dispute between the standard history of women's sport and a more revisionist approach.

The Olympic Games started in 776 BCE and initially consisted of a single race known as the stade because it ran the length of the stadium, approximately 192 meters. Starting in 724 BCE, other events were added to the program. First a double stadium or diaulos was added, and then a long-distance race of approximately 5 kilometers was added in 720 BCE. The pentathlon, wrestling, boxing, chariot races, and other events followed, and soon there was a substantial and varied athletic program for Greek men. The men also competed in the nude, so there might have been a reason to ban women.[4] And it was true that women did have a place in the ancient Olympics, as owners and/or trainers of the horses used in the chariot races and other equestrian events. But even the female owners of horses could not enter the stadium to see their horses run.[5] I do assume, however, that it was acceptable for some of the horses be female. Hence, there would have been some nonhuman female athletes included in the ancient games.

By contrast, the Heraia started a little later, probably in the sixth century BCE. Although women were allowed to compete in the Olympic stadium, the only recorded event at the Haraean Games was a footrace that was five-sixths the length of the stade.[6] Certainly, the fact that Greek women had only the one event is extremely troubling if one views the Heraia from a modernist perspective. I'd also like to look a little more closely at the length of the race, as that might prove troublesome too. First let's give the Greeks some benefit of the doubt: If we are looking strictly at the time taken to run the race, then there is some justification for making the women's race slightly shorter in distance. Men run approximately 11 percent faster than women,[7] meaning that both the men's stade and the women's five-sixths stade—hopefully they had a catchier name for the women's race—would have taken approximately the same length of time to complete. Even today the standard men's high hurdle race is 110 meters long while the women's race is 100 meters in length,[8] and no one seems to care.

On the other hand, one of the chief complaints of women runners is the fact that they have been stuck in shorter races forever. The women's marathon was not contested at the Olympics until 1984, the 10,000 meter race wasn't added until 1988, and women first got to race the steeplechase in the 2008 Olympics in Beijing.[9] And it was only in 2017 that the world cross-country championships had the same 10 kilometer race for both sexes; previously, the men had run 12 kilometers while the women covered 8 kilometers.[10] Moreover, many lower-level cross-country events still have shorter races for women than for men.

The sexist tradition of shorter races for women is not limited to running events. Female swimmers were similarly shortchanged in the modern Olympics. Women were first allowed to swim only two events in the 1912 Olympics, and it wasn't until 1968 that the longest race was bumped up to 800 meters. Despite the fact that male swimmers are allowed to swim the 1500 meters in the Olympics, women have not yet had the opportunity to do so. That will change in the 2020 Tokyo games where both men and women will have the opportunity to swim the 800 and the 1500 meters.[11] It could be argued that requiring women to compete in shorter races than men goes back to that 5/6 stade race.

So the fact that the Greeks had a separate athletic event for women really wasn't so wonderful. The Heraia was better than nothing but fell far short of equality. Furthermore, the Greeks did not generally encourage young women to participate in sports outside of the Heraean Games. There was one city-state in Greece that was more accepting of women athletes. The Spartans encouraged women to be athletic and gave women additional rights not found in other Greek city-states. And for a time, Sparta was considered the leader among the Greek city-states.

Spartan women were permitted to exercise regularly in the company of Spartan men. Just like their male counterparts, Spartan women were allowed to exercise in the buff, although the women often wore tunics during sports. Perhaps the vaunted Spartan toughness was a result of having their women run without sports bras: very Spartan indeed. Spartan women were also given public education and were allowed to own land, both of which were unheard of in the rest of Greece. Spartan women were not, however, allowed to hold jobs or earn money other than from their land ownership. And the rationale for these freedoms accorded Spartan women was that these free, fit, and educated women would quickly find mates and produce healthy and fit children. In the end, the highest role for women in Sparta was still motherhood.[12] The rest of the Greek world was not amused by the license given Spartan women, and when Sparta began to decline in the fourth century BCE, Greek women were kept in their places. Women were given their Heraia, but that was about it.

Professor Case also argued that although it was true that women's sport did not take off until the twentieth century, the same thing could be said about men's sport: Outside of the nobility, sporting opportunities for everyone were limited until recently, and the amateur system was designed to keep it that way by allowing only those with wealth and leisure time the opportunity to compete in many sports.[13] So let's take a closer look at the sporting lives of men and women in medieval times and on into the twentieth century. First off, it is true that the medieval peasantry had to work hard six days a week and had little time for fun and games. But the serfs did get the one day off out of every seven, and were, in fact, encouraged to take up certain sports on their off day. Additionally, the fact that much of the work revolved around agricultural activities meant that there were times of the year when work was less intense, and holidays often amounted to approximately eight weeks per year for the average man.[14]

The sports that were most valued in the Middle Ages were those that were seen as training for the seemingly endless wars that the nobles fought with the assistance of their peasant armies. Hence, archery was perhaps the most prized sport, and in England men were required to have bows and arrows. Jousting tournaments were popular, too, although the requirement of a horse and the inherent danger of the sport meant that only brave knights engaged each other on that particular playing field.[15] The peasants also played outdoor sports such as bowls, hammer throwing, horseshoes, wrestling, and a host of other sports, most of which would not be recognized today. Almost all of these games were designed to increase the physical capabilities of potential soldiers.

Contrary to popular belief, medieval women were given some limited opportunities to compete in sport. Noblewomen engaged in hunting and falconry, while peasant women could participate freely in footraces and ball games.[16] And there was one woman of the era whose athletic fame survives even now. In the Middle Ages, golf—which evolved from the Netherlandish game of *colf*—was a sport that was reserved for nobility. The first recorded reference to the game of golf in Scotland was in 1421, and by 1457 the game had grown so popular that it was banned by King James II, who felt that Scottish men were neglecting their archery for this new craze.[17] At first all the golfers were male, but it did not take long before there was a female golfer of note.

Mary Stuart was born in 1542, and within a week of her birth she became queen of Scotland upon her father's death. The real power, however, lay with Mary's mother, the regent, and young Mary was sent to France. Many members of the sixteenth-century Scottish royalty were keen on the game of golf, and Mary played regularly while she was growing up in France.[18] Since it would have been unbecoming for a young queen to carry her own clubs, a cadet was assigned the task of toting them for her.[19] At age fifteen Mary was married to the dauphin, or prince, of France. Within two years Mary first became queen of France, when her father-in-law died, and shortly thereafter became a widow upon the death of her husband. Since she no longer had any claim to the throne in France, she returned to Scotland to rule as queen.[20]

Once home, she resumed her passion for golf, playing at St. Andrews and other courses along the east coast of Scotland.[21] She also continued to have someone else carry her clubs, and that someone was now called a *caddy*, a word almost identical in sound to the French pronunciation of *cadet*.[22] Mary also found another husband in Henry Stuart, Lord Darnley, but the relationship quickly soured. Darnley died under suspicious circumstances, and the fact that Mary was back out on the links only days after Darnley's death was considered damning.[23] Mary abdicated her throne and fled to England, where she was placed under house arrest by her cousin Elizabeth I. Eighteen years later, Mary was beheaded for plotting against Elizabeth to seize the throne of England.[24]

Mary's son, James, was elevated to the throne of Scotland after Mary's abdication. In addition to the throne, James also inherited a love of golf from his mother. Upon the death of Elizabeth I, James became king of England. Although he might be best known for the King James Bible, he also helped the game of golf find a wider audience, making Mary the mother of golf.[25] Despite Mary Stuart's unfortunate end, she paved the way for many female golfers.

And what of the nineteenth century, that era when men and women had very rigid roles? As it turns out, one popular new sport of that century was actually played by many women who had the time and the equipment, and would eventually prove to be the most lucrative sport for women. The game of tennis evolved out of earlier handball sports that were played in medieval Europe; in the sixteenth century, rackets began to be used in Britain to play what was then called lawn tennis.[26] Many nineteenth-century pictures of the sport show stately couples playing mixed doubles on an hourglass-shaped court.

The first major men's tennis tournament was played in Wimbledon 1877, and by 1884, women had their own tennis championship on the venerable grass courts in south London. Maud Watson was the first female Wimbledon champion, taking home a prize of a silver flower basket worth 20 guineas,[27] far smaller than the $2 million Garbine Muguruza won for her straight-set victory over Venus Williams in the 2017 women's Wimbledon final. Although it is lamentable that neither golf nor tennis were played by female commoners at the time, the same could be said for men. The aristocracy had far more time on their hands for leisure activities such as sport, and the notion that sport was only pure if one did not earn money from it, was really just a front.[28] The rich could afford to play for free, but if commoners were to spend many hours on sport they would somehow still need to earn a living.

In the nineteenth century, many Europeans had a fascination with ancient Greek culture, and there were several informal athletic festivals that were touted as "Olympic Games." But it wasn't until 1892 that Baron Pierre de Coubertin suggested a major international sporting festival mimicking the ancient Greek event. The baron proposed that the modern games should be for men only, stating that women's inclusion would be "impractical, uninteresting, unaesthetic, and incorrect."[29] And so the first modern Olympic Games—held in Athens in 1896—carried on the ancient tradition of excluding women.

Women first competed in the Olympic Games in 1900 in Paris, and it is no surprise that only two sports with competition for all women at these games were held in golf and lawn tennis. There were, however, women who competed (among and against men) in equestrian events and in yachting, as well as three French women who competed in croquet.[30] Larger representation for women in the Olympic Games would have to wait another quarter century and would be tied to the rise of the women's movement, which sought a more general equality with men.

At the dawn of the twentieth century, the lives of women were still restricted in ways that would not be considered acceptable in the twenty-first century. In 1900, most women could not vote, few were educated or worked outside the home, and their lives revolved very much around their fertility. Many of these conditions would change as a result of the actions of the women's movement.[31] The most prominent of the pioneering women's activists in the early twentieth century were the suffragettes. While women all over the world were organizing for the right of universal suffrage, it was particularly in England that the movement's leaders became convinced that in order to be successful they had to be militant and radical, and they adopted tactics such as hunger strikes. The militancy of the British leaders led to the derisive name suffragettes, but the name was soon adopted by the women themselves.[32] Whether or not the tactics of the suffragettes were helpful, women all over the world began to win the right to vote. By 1920 a great many countries—including Australia, New Zealand, Great Britain, the United States, Canada, and Sweden—had amended their laws to allow women to vote.[33]

Spurred on by the success of the woman suffrage movement and unhappy about the refusal of the International Olympic Committee (IOC) to include women's athletics (track and field to North Americans) on the program, Alice Milliat, a French translator whose passion was rowing, formed the Women's Olympic Games. The first edition of these games was a one-day track meet held in Paris in 1922 attended by eighteen athletes. Four years later a substantially larger event was held in Gothenberg, Sweden, where women from ten nations gathered to run, jump, and throw. The 1926 event caught the attention of the IOC, which agreed to hold a track and field competition for women if Milliat would take the word *Olympics* out of her event's name.[34]

Rather than the full men's slate of athletics, the IOC included only five events for women in the 1928 games in Amsterdam: the 100 and 800 meter races and the 4 x 100 meter relay on the track, and the high jump and discus in the field.[35] Although four of the five events were met with general acceptance from the public and the IOC, the sight of some of the women's 800 meter runners falling to the track after the race was taken as a sign that the race was too strenuous for the fairer sex. In fact, it is a very common sight to see both male and female distance runners of all abilities and nationalities sprawled out on the tartan after completing their races; the athletes almost always get up again after a minute or two. But the IOC would not accept this normal sign of fatigue in women, and they were not allowed to run the 800 again until the 1960 Olympic Games in Rome.[36]

And this was the state of women's sport at the dawn of the fourth decade of the twentieth century. Returning to the question of whether or not to revise the early history of women's sport, I would suggest that although it is true that the standard version of the early history is lacking some nuance, it is also definitely true that women's sport was subjected to many limitations prior to 1930. The 1930s would include substantial growth of women's sport; however, that decade would also be the first in which the femininity of many women competitors would be called into question, a that trend had already begun at the 1928 Olympic Games with rumblings about some of the more successful athletes, such as 800 meter silver medalist Hitomi Kinue of Japan.[37] Interestingly enough, I have not found any corresponding references in English to the possible intersex status of the winner of the Amsterdam 800—a German runner by the name of Lina Radke who set a world record in the race that would last until 1934 and appears to have an Adam's apple in the picture of her crossing the finish line. Perhaps the fact that, unlike Hitome, Radke was married shielded the German runner from unfavorable comments. At any rate, questions over the status of the women competing in Amsterdam were very minor compared to what transpired in the 1930s.

Many of the women who had their femininity questioned in the early twentieth century were probably intersex individuals, and the 1930s would be the launching pad for a debate over intersex women in sports that continues today. Before we get to the events of the 1930s, we should look at the science of intersex conditions, as that science sheds much light on what transpired during that decade.

2

THE SCIENCE OF INTERSEX CONDITIONS

There are people who have physical and/or chromosomal characteristics that blur the line between male and female, and there are many controversies surrounding this small segment of humanity. The first controversy is the question, exactly what do we call these people? I use the term *intersex*, and I feel comfortable doing so since the Organisation Intersex International (OII)—the largest international organization run by and for intersex people—incorporates the term into its name, as do most other similar organizations. There is, however, far from universal agreement about the optimal terminology.

Until the twenty-first century, intersex people were generally called hermaphrodites. The term comes from Hermaphroditus, the mythical son of Hermes and Aphrodite. Hermes, the winged messenger of the gods, is always portrayed with the face of an angel and the body of a Greek god. Aphrodite was the most beautiful of all the goddesses, and so you can imagine that their progeny would rival those of Brad Pitt and Angelina Jolie for looks. In fact, Hermaphroditus was so good looking that a nymph named Salmacis, who was mightily smitten, prayed to the gods that she could be united forever with him. Although the nymph was undoubtedly imagining a sexual union, the Greek gods had an interesting sense of humor. One day, as Hermaphroditus was bathing in the fountain where Salmacis lived, she embraced him and dragged him underwater. Instead of granting the nymph sex, however, the gods fused Hermaphroditus and Salmacis into one body; "[t]he result was a person with the figure and breasts of a woman but with the sex organs of a man."[1]

At the beginning of the nineteenth century, the term *hermaphrodite* was used for anyone with atypical genitalia and/or secondary sex characteristics, such as the bearded ladies one could find at many carnivals; however, as doctors and scientists of the period studied these "monstrosities"[2] they came up with a specific taxonomy based on the gonads hermaphrodites possessed. At the time, anyone with testes was considered male, while anyone with ovaries was considered female. Historian Alice Dreger refers to this period as the age of gonads.[3] Hence, those hermaphrodites with breasts and other female characteristics but whose bodies held testes were called male pseudohermaphrodites, while those with a male phenotype but possessing ovaries were called female pseudohermaphrodites. Only those extremely rare individuals with both ovarian and testicular tissue—the term *ovotestes* is used today—were considered true hermaphrodites.

During the twentieth century, medical people also started to use the term *intersexual* to describe hermaphrodites. By the end of the twentieth century, intersex people were starting to band together and form support groups. One of the first of these groups was the Intersex Society of North America (ISNA), which was founded in 1993 by an intersex woman named Cheryl Chase.[4] Chase was invited to the International Consensus Conference on Intersex in 2005 that was convened in order to update many aspects of care for intersex people;[5] this meeting resulted in a set of consensus statements that were published in 2006. One recommendation was to separate the person from their specific medical condition and to refer to intersex conditions as disorders of sex development (DSDs).[6] Although the intentions of the committee were honorable, and it is true that many intersex conditions result in infertility and sometimes even life-threatening issues, the use of the word *disorder* is problematic. I work in cancer therapy, and unfortunately it is all too common to refer to our patients by their disease—that is, we often say that we are treating a prostate, when we mean that we are treating a patient with prostate cancer. Hence, when we use the term *disorder* it is far too easy to think of the people involved as being disordered. In reality, many intersex people lead perfectly healthy lives with no medical interventions at all. As a result of the controversy over the use of the word *disorder*, the term *DSD* was met with disdain by many intersex people. Other intersex people and their allies tried to roll with the punches, deciding that they would keep the initialism while changing the fuller term to differences of sexual development.[7] I align myself with the latter group, and throughout this book I will use DSD to refer to intersex conditions with the proviso that the first *D* should always stand for *difference*. Intersex people are not, per se, disordered, merely atypical.

If people with DSDs are atypical, then what exactly is typical? All fetuses have the same physical appearance for the first six weeks or so after conception. External genitalia, the most obvious marker of sex, are essentially identical at that point in development. Anatomically speaking, all fetuses look mostly female at this time, except that the genital tubercle present at this stage is larger than a "normal" clitoris.[8]

At least 99 percent of all living human beings have either an XX or XY pair of sex chromosomes.[9] In general, those people who are male have the XY pair and those who are female have the XX pair. Our individual sex chromosome pattern causes almost all of the differences between men and women, and this differentiation starts sometime around the sixth week of development. At this point in time, the male fetus gets a signal from the Y chromosome on a gene called the SRY gene, and testosterone floods the embryo, causing it to head down the male developmental path. The skin that forms the labia changes to become the scrotal sack, and the genital tubercle grows to be the length of a penis. Those children without a Y chromosome don't undergo as much outward change; the genital tubercle does not experience the same amount of growth and ends up as a clitoris.[10]

The undifferentiated fetus also has gonads and two sets of ducts, the Müllerian and the Wolffian ducts, which can become the respective internal sex organs of female and male children. In the male fetus, the Y chromosome causes the secretion of a protein called the anti-Müllerian hormone (AMH). This protein inhibits the development of the Müllerian ducts, preventing the growth of the internal female organs. The gonads, stimulated by testosterone, become testes, and the Wolffian ducts become the seminal vesicles and other structures connecting the testes to the prostate. The testes will eventually descend into the scrotal sac. On the other hand, a fetus without a Y chromosome won't receive any AMH, so the Müllerian ducts become the fallopian tubes, uterus, and upper portion of the vagina. Without testosterone, the gonads will develop as ovaries and reside adjacent to the fallopian tubes. All of these sex-based physical changes start to take place in the first trimester after conception.[11] Those embryos with a DSD, however, often have markedly different development. The majority of DSDs are autosomal recessive conditions, and understanding the implications of this statement requires some knowledge of genetics.

Genes are DNA chunks that fulfill some purpose. Since human DNA is diploid in nature, there are two versions of each gene that we carry, and these are called alleles. Often the alleles are identical, but sometimes the two alleles for the same gene are different. If the two alleles vary, one of them will dominate, and the gene will function according to the dominant allele. The other allele is called recessive. In order for a gene to function according to a recessive allele, both alleles must be identical. Since we inherit our DNA from our parents, we have an equal chance to have four possible alleles for each gene. Thus, we get a recessive condition only if (a) both our parents carry the recessive allele and (b) we get one copy of the recessive allele from each parent. Recessive conditions are much more likely to occur when the parents are related, since the likelihood of each parent having the same recessive allele is much higher.[12] People who have one copy of an allele for a recessive condition are called carriers. If both of one's parents are carriers of a recessive condition, then one has a 50 percent chance of being a carrier, a 25 percent chance of having the recessive condition, and a 25 percent chance of neither carrying nor having the condition.

Many intersex conditions are rare in the general population but are much more common in certain isolated communities where the recessive allele is carried by a significant percentage of the population and where consanguinity—colloquially known as inbreeding—is the norm. Perhaps it is because most of us are familiar with the term *hermaphrodite*, or perhaps it is because of the human fascination with genitalia, but most people tend to think of intersex people as those with atypical genitalia. This is not always the case, at least for those who subscribe to a broader definition of what constitutes an intersex person. And perhaps it is because most people feel that there is something wrong with having atypical genitals that the largest controversy over intersex people has ensued. As surgical techniques were refined over the course of the twentieth century, it became common to perform "normalizing" surgeries on intersex people with the goal of making the genitals of the intersex patient look as much like other human beings as possible. Largely because "it is easier to dig a hole than to make a pole," most of these surgeries have been feminizing surgeries.[13]

Furthermore, it was theorized by intersex pioneer John Money and others in the middle of the twentieth century that it was important to develop a gender identity consistent with the sex assigned at birth. Hence, many feminizing surgeries were performed very early in life.[14] There are some intersex people who require early surgery in order to ensure health or even survival, but no two-year-old girl needs to have a vagina. And yet, in many cases, intersex toddlers have been given vaginoplasties by well-meaning surgeons trying to appease anxious parents.[15]

The most serious problem with early surgeries on intersex patients is that these operations are performed on the most personal of areas without authorization by the patients themselves. It wasn't until intersex people began to organize that there was any meaningful pushback against such surgeries. Even today, there are still a great many feminizing surgeries performed on very young intersex patients, but at least there is a more nuanced discussion around the serious ramifications of such surgery.[16]

There are entire books devoted to the controversies surrounding intersex people, but I should talk about the DSDs themselves. I will start with congenital adrenal hyperplasia (CAH), one of the more common DSDs, with an approximate prevalence of 1 in 15,000 worldwide but much more common in certain ethnic groups. Excessive cell growth (hyperplasia) of the adrenal glands is problematic since these glands produce the essential steroid hormones cortisol and aldosterone as well as androgenic hormones. Testosterone (T) is the most common androgen, and the typical female receives roughly half of her T from her adrenal glands. Cortisol helps regulate blood sugar, the immune system, and the metabolism, while aldosterone is central in electrolyte regulation in the blood. In 95 percent of people with CAH there is a deficiency of an enzyme called 21-hydroxylase. This enzyme is necessary to produce cortisol, hence 21-hydroxylase deficiency results in reduced cortisol output as well as reduced aldosterone production. The pituitary gland senses the deficit in cortisol and signals the adrenal glands to work harder. Unfortunately, this means the adrenal glands pump out too many androgens. Even with increased adrenal activity, cortisol levels will be low due to the enzyme deficiency. People with

CAH require lifelong daily cortisone-type medication to restore the body's endocrine balance.[17]

Children with both XX and XY patterns can be born with CAH; symptoms can range from life-threatening salt wasting (in severe cases) to reduced adult height (in mild cases). The excess androgens associated with CAH in females can cause virilization, often resulting in atypical genitalia, including an enlarged clitoris. According to Dreger, "CAH is, in fact the most common cause of congenital ambiguous genitalia in genetic females."[18] Virilized CAH girls have typical female internal sex organs, since no AMH is released in utero because they have two X chromosomes. In some cases, infant virilization is so pronounced that XX CAH individuals are declared male at birth. XX CAH babies who are assigned male at birth would have been described as female pseudohermaphrodites under the older taxonomy.[19]

Girls with CAH often have different psychosocial development as well. It is common for CAH women to exhibit traits typically associated with a more masculine persona, including a greater interest in sports and sexual attraction to other women. It has been reported that approximately 5 percent of CAH genetic women identify as male, a rate approximately ten times higher than average.[20] Imagine how horrible it would be for a male-identified XX person with CAH to have their penis reduced to the size of a typical clitoris in infancy just because of their genetic makeup.

I would next like to look at a couple of relatively common DSDs that come into play in the determination of eligibility for women's sport. These two conditions result in atypical chromosomes, so it would be beneficial to first talk a little more about typical chromosome patterns. Most people have twenty-three pairs of chromosomes, with twenty-two pairs being classified as autosomal chromosomes. The twenty-third pair is typically the XX or XY sex chromosomes, hence typical humans can be described as 46,XY or 46,XX individuals. But not everyone is born with this chromosome pattern.

Approximately 1 in 2,500 females is born with Turner syndrome, a condition in which a female has one typical X chromosome and one missing, partially missing, or rearranged X chromosome. Babies born with Turner syndrome do not have twenty-three pairs of chromosomes in each cell, and the resulting pattern can be described as 45,X or 45,XO. The missing X chromosome affects fetal and childhood development, with shorter stature often evident by age five. Most girls with Turner syndrome have nonfunctioning ovaries and it is rare for them to undergo puberty. It is not uncommon for girls with Turner syndrome to have heart and/or kidney problems that can occasionally be life threatening. Unlike CAH, Turner syndrome is not an inherited condition; rather, it is the result of atypical cell division.[21]

In a similar fashion, atypical cell division during the reproductive process can result in males having two or more X chromosomes; a condition known as Klinefelter syndrome. Klinefelter syndrome is relatively common, affecting as many as 1 in 500 newborn males, and the karyotype of people with the syndrome can be described as 47,XXY. Variations on Klinfelter syndrome include 48,XXXY and 49,XXXXY karytopes. Men with Klinfelter syndrome often have small and/or undescended testes that produce lower than typical amounts of testosterone. As a result of this syndrome, these men often have delayed or incomplete puberty, breast enlargement, infertility, and reduced body hair. It is not uncommon for Klinefelter men to have a small penis, sometimes with hypospadias (a condition in which the urethral opening is on the underside of the penis). Men with Klinefelter syndrome tend to be less boisterous and more sensitive than others, and developmental delays are not uncommon.[22]

Although Turner and Klinefelter syndromes are considered sex chromosome DSDs, the resulting individuals are not always considered intersex people; most people with these syndromes do not have obviously atypical genitalia, nor do they generally exhibit gender dysphoria. Others would argue that of course these syndromes produce intersex people because, after all, the subjects have atypical chromosomes and physical presentations. If one considers people with Klinefelter and Turner syndrome to be intersex, then the overall frequency of intersex people is much higher than it is usually understood to be, due to the relatively high frequency of these two syndromes. I cannot provide a definitive answer to this controversy, but I do believe that both Turner and Klinfelter syndromes definitely belong in a book devoted to gender-diverse athletes.

Beginning in the middle of the twentieth century, officials began to look for a method to determine who exactly should be competing in women's sport. In the 1960s it was decided to allow only those athletes with two X chromosomes to compete as women.[23] And therein lies the issue with both Klinefelter men and Turner women: If two X chromosomes are required to classify as a female athlete, then Klinefelter men would be identified as women because they have two (or more) X chromosomes, while Turner women would be identified as men because they have a single X chromosome.

A similar problem arises if one looks at the cells of a person with a mosaic of sex chromosomes. Mosaicism arises when any of the twenty-three pairs of chromosomes have differing composition, but only when there is a mosaic of sex chromosomes is mosaicism thought of as an intersex condition.[24] There are mosaic variants of both Klinfelter and Turner syndromes. The former results in a mosaic of 46,XY/47,XXY chromosomes, while the latter results in a mosaic of 46,XX/45,X chromosomes. There can also be a mosaic of 46,XY/46,XX chromosomes. In all cases of mosaicism, there can be large variances in the individual's phenotype depending upon the percentage of cells that display the typical sex chromosomes for the individual's assigned sex compared to the percentage of cells containing atypical sex chromosomes. It can be very challenging to determine the appropriate sports category for individuals with mosaicism if one uses chromosome pattern as the basis for that decision.

Those intersex people of most interest to the sports world are ones with XY DSDs—that is, conditions resulting in people with testes being identified as female at birth. XY DSDs comprise only a very small portion of the overall intersex population. The occurrence rate of all XY DSDs combined is approximately 1 in 20,000 live births, much lower than the occurrence rates of CAH, Klinefelter syndrome, or Turner syndrome.[25] Despite the infrequency of XY DSDs in the general population, many prominent female athletes were likely born with these conditions.

The first XY DSD that I would like to discuss is androgen insensitivity syndrome (AIS), which occurs when XY people have a mutation that prevents them from making a protein called an androgen receptor. There are two standard subdivisions: those with complete androgen insensitivity syndrome (CAIS) are unable to absorb and use any testosterone their bodies make, while those with partial androgen insensitivity syndrome (PAIS) have an impaired sensitivity to testosterone.[26] I found this standard division of AIS into two distinct subcategories to be artificial and unsatisfactory. Generally speaking, biology tends to operate on a continuum, and I thought it was more likely that androgen sensitivity would, too. So I asked Eric Vilain, director of genetic research at George Washington University and one of the world's leading intersex experts, whether androgen sensitivity existed on a spectrum, and he confirmed my speculation. Despite this, however, it is still useful to refer to CAIS and PAIS, and I will continue to do so.

Children with CAIS do not develop typical male external genitalia, as their bodies do not heed the call of testosterone that occurs early in fetal development. Their gonads, however, develop as testes, since AMH is secreted by the gonads of virtually every fetus with a Y chromosome. Many of these infants are born with typical female external genitals; the rest have atypical ones. More often than not, CAIS children have no idea that they are different from other girls until they reach puberty and fail to menstruate. CAIS women usually have almost hairless bodies and are taller than average; it has been reported that they are overrepresented in both modelling and sports.[27] The former can easily be explained by their greater height and their usually willowy limbs, but the latter is much more difficult to understand. CAIS women might gain some athletic superiority from a partial adaptation to the testosterone in their systems, but there is no easily explained mechanism of how they process the T. Some scientists propose a non–hormonally mediated effect from the Y chromosome as the cause of increased athletic capabilities.[28] Regardless of the cause, the overrepresentation of CAIS women in sports is small, as is any possible athletic advantage.

Individuals with CAIS almost universally identify as female and have typical female psychosocial development. PAIS women, on the other hand, have varying gender identity and psychosocial development. The degree to which a person with PAIS is advantaged over other female athletes depends upon both their sensitivity to testosterone and to the level of T in their blood. Serum T levels for PAIS individuals can range from the upper female level up to typical male levels; by contrast, those with CAIS can have serum T levels at the upper end of the male range, since none of their T gets taken up by their cells.[29]

It would be instructive to look next at a DSD known as 5-α reductase type 2 deficiency (5-ARD). Individuals with 5-ARD have an XY chromosome pair, but because of a mutation in the 5-α reductase type 2 gene, the body is deficient in the enzyme 5-α reductase. In turn, this enzyme deficiency means that testosterone produced by the fetus cannot be converted into dihydrotestosterone (DHT). DHT is a more potent androgen than testosterone, although DHT is only produced in those tissues that express the 5-ARD type 2 enzyme, including the prostate gland, skin, hair follicles, and external genitalia. Infants with 5-ARD are usually born with undescended testes and internal sex organs typical of those people with a Y chromosome. There is a wide variation in the appearance of the external genitals of neonates with 5-ARD, ranging from near-typical male to typical female. When these children reach puberty, they usually go through virilization, including hirsutism, descending testicles, and enlargement of the phallus. These changes can result from increasing testosterone levels finding alternate pathways to produce DHT, or the higher T levels can act directly to produce virilization. It is not uncommon for those with 5-ARD to produce sperm, and they can often father children with the assistance of in vitro fertilization.[30] The prevalence of 5-ARD is much higher in those remote areas where the allele for the DSD is present, and there is a high incidence of consanguinity. Despite the fact that the worldwide incidence of 5-ARD is as small as 1 in 100,000, pockets of much higher concentration exist. In a small village in the Dominican Republic, the incidence of 5-ARD is greater than 1 percent of those born with XY chromosomes.[31]

Unlike those born with CAIS, 5-ARD athletes have typical sensitivity to androgens, meaning that they benefit greatly from their serum T levels, which usually fall well within the typical male range. Their T levels and androgen sensitivity means that athletes with 5-ARD have almost the full male advantage over other athletes who were assigned female at birth. It is therefore no surprise that despite the low overall incidence of 5-ARD within the general population, this DSD is extremely overrepresented among elite female athletes. The most recent DSD regulations proposed by the International Association of Athletics Federations (IAAF) in 2018 lists a series of restricted DSDs, and 5-ARD is at the head of list, presumably because it is the most common DSD among world-class track stars.[32]

Another XY DSD of note is 17β-hydroxysteroid dehydrogenase 3 deficiency. This enzyme deficiency causes the testes to produce androstenedione instead of testosterone. Some of the androstenedione in the bodies of these people is converted to T, but there is little conversion to

DHT, often resulting in female-appearing genitalia at birth. During puberty, testosterone production increases and these individuals go through a marked virilization.[33] Male gender identity is common in both 5-ARD and 17β-HSD3, with as many as 50 percent of those assigned female at birth undergoing gender transition as adults.[34] The uncertainty of the gender identity of many intersex people is but one reason that Dr. Katrina Karkazis suggests in her book *Fixing Sex* that "all gender assignments are provisional."[35]

If all of the above information seems complex, that is because sex is complicated. The notion that there is one bright line that separates males from females is clearly fantasy; however, if one is concerned about elite sports, then it is important to find an appropriate method to separate male athletes from female athletes; one that allows for meaningful competition within the women's category.

Unfortunately, almost none of the scientific information listed above was known in the first half of the twentieth century, although the existence of hermaphrodites was widely recognized. A small but growing movement to establish competitive sports for women was in existence at this time, and there was also a relatively high prevalence of hermaphrodites in Europe and America. The growth of women's sport in the 1930s, coupled with the number of intersex athletes, gave rise to a decade rife with tension surrounding female athletes, with reverberations that continue today. This is why I will next examine women's sports during the fourth decade of the twentieth century.

3

INTERSEX ATHLETES IN THE 1930s

There were several prominent female athletes in the 1930s who were probably hermaphrodites, or intersex as we would say today. Consanguinity (literally "shared blood"; in other words, descending from the same ancestor) was much more prevalent in Europe and North America in the nineteenth and early twentieth centuries than it is today, and frequent inbreeding was one cause of the DSDs found in these athletes. As an example of the banality of inbreeding at the time, Charles Darwin and his wife, Emma, were first cousins.[1] Although there is nothing morally wrong with marrying one's cousin, there are negative genetic consequences—such as hemophilia—of doing so.[2] The kings and queens of Europe were all interrelated for hundreds of years, and they suffered many devastating health problems because of this practice.[3] The health problems resulting from consanguinity are one reason that much of the world has constructed taboos around the practice of inbreeding. There are, however, parts of the world where consanguinity is still the rule today.[4]

Most DSDs are autosomal recessive conditions; hence these conditions will occur more frequently in times and places where consanguinity is common.[5] Given the athletic advantages of higher testosterone levels, it would follow that performance-enhancing DSDs were likely present in many female sports stars in the early twentieth century.

Stella Walsh was born Stanislawa Walasiewczowna in a tiny village in Russian-occupied Poland in 1911. There is little genealogical information available about Walsh's parents, and I don't know if they were related in any way. It is unlikely that there was a doctor present when the future star was born, and if her genitalia were atypical no one noted it. Stella's father was not present at the birth; he had moved to Cleveland, Ohio, in search of work. In 1912 Stella and her mother also immigrated to the United States.[6]

Walsh grew up in the heart of Cleveland's Slavic Village and soon found out that she could outsprint all the girls and boys in her neighborhood. Before long she was training with the local Polish sports club, which would become a second home for her. People who grew up with Walsh understood that she was different from other girls. Some spoke of a "birth defect" or "mutation" when describing her atypical genitals. Others understood that she was a hermaphrodite. Walsh had to put up with quite a bit of teasing from her contemporaries at school. Perhaps it was the teasing or perhaps it was the shame of knowing she was different, but Walsh was very shy in social situations. Once she began competing in elite sport, she never changed with other women, nor did she ever want to share a room with any of the other female athletes. Certainly this behavior was noted by her competitors and led to a certain amount of isolation from the women she lined up against on the track.[7]

Walsh was not the only female athlete of note who first saw the light of day in 1911. That same year, the great Babe Didrikson was also born to immigrant parents; Didrikson's parents had moved from their native Norway to Port Arthur, Texas, in 1908. The couple brought three children with them and conceived four more after reaching US shores. Mildred, the sixth of the seven children, was first called "Baby," and then "Babe" after the seventh child arrived. The name stuck when she showed an early aptitude for sports, as Babe Ruth was the premier baseball player of the era.[8]

Back in Cleveland, Walsh had grown to 5 feet, 6 inches tall by the time she started high school in 1926—she would finally reach a height of 5-foot-9—dwarfing her mother and even topping her father. It was in high school that she was also given the name we recognize, as her non-Polish teachers had difficulty pronouncing her given name. By 1927 she was winning sprint races throughout Cleveland. Walsh competed in the 1928 US Olympic trials, earning a spot as an alternate on the 4x100 meter relay, but once her Polish citizenship was revealed she was cut from the US team.[9]

By 1929 Stella Walsh had blossomed into one of the best sprinters in the world, winning a number of sprint races that summer while representing Poland in dual meets against other European countries. In the 1930 Millrose Games indoor track meet at Madison Square Garden, Walsh won the 50-yard sprint in a world record time of 6.0 seconds. The second, third, and fourth place women were all Canadian, and Walsh was lauded for defending American honor even though she wasn't American. That year saw Walsh, at the age of nineteen, establish herself as the world's number one female sprinter. She became the first woman in history to break the 11-second barrier in the 100-yard dash, running 10.8 seconds. She won the 60, 100, and 200 meters at Alice Milliat's Women's World (formerly Olympic) Games in Prague, Czechoslovakia, and was named the World's Greatest Women's Athlete.[10] One of the women Walsh was repeatedly matched against that summer of 1930 was the Japanese star Hitomi Kinue, who had won the silver medal in the ill-fated 800 meter race in the 1928 Olympic Games and was also one of the track stars of the era whose femininity was questioned. Hitome fell seriously ill later in 1930 and died of respiratory failure on August 2, 1931, at the age of twenty-four.[11]

The year 1930 was also a watershed for Didrikson. A junior in high school, that year she led her team to the Texas state high school championships. She was spotted by the manager of the athletic program for a Dallas insurance company, who convinced her to drop out of school and join the company basketball team. That spring Babe led the team to the finals of the Amateur Athletic Union (AAU) championships and was named an all-American. Later that spring she took up track and field, and soon was excelling in that sport too. The following year, 1931, saw Babe lead her team to the national title in basketball and blossom into a world-class athlete in track and field. Her favorite events were the hurdles and the javelin, but she was good at many other events, too. Babe was boastful, disdained feminine attire, and wore her hair closely cropped; she displayed no sense of the femininity that was expected of women of the South. As a result of her behavior, Babe was not well liked by the other women athletes. But Babe didn't care about being popular; she had set her sights on making the US Olympic team for the 1932 games.[12]

Everyone in America assumed that Stella Walsh would also be a member of Team USA, as she could become a naturalized US citizen upon her twenty-first birthday in April 1932. It didn't quite work out that way. By 1932 the Great Depression had greatly dimmed the financial prospects of many companies, including the New York Central Railroad, Walsh's employer. The NYCRR had hired her in 1930 in an attempt to capitalize on her notoriety, but the company's declining revenue made keeping her on an impossibility; Walsh was downsized, along with many other employees. At the same time, the Polish government offered her a job and a free university education if she competed for Poland in the 1932 Olympic Games. At the time, Olympic sports were still officially strictly amateur, and Walsh was prohibited from taking a job in a sports-related field, as it could be seen as compensation for her athletic success. Walsh needed to support herself and help her family out, so she agreed to the Polish government's offer.[13]

The Depression, along with the distance separating Los Angeles from Europe, resulted in a sizable reduction in the number of athletes competing in the 1932 games compared to 1928. Amsterdam had witnessed a total of 2,883 athletes, including 277 women, while the Los Angeles games only had 1,332 total and 126 female athletes.[14] But what the LA games lacked in numbers, it made up for in splash. Hollywood had become the world's entertainment capital, and the local organizing committee recognized spectacle when they saw it. The 1932 games featured the 104,000-seat Los Angeles Memorial Coliseum, the first appearance of the Olympic flame, and the first Olympic athlete village.[15]

The three favorites in the 100 meters were Walsh, American Billie Von Bremen, and Canadian Hilde Strike. Walsh had the fastest heat and semifinal times, and her 11.9-second finish in the latter was a new world record. No one else ran faster than 12.2 heading into the final, and Walsh was the prohibitive favorite. The final didn't go according script, however, as Strike got a fabulous start while Walsh was last off the starting line. By 50 meters Walsh had caught her much smaller rival but couldn't pass her, and both women hit the finish line in 11.9 seconds, tying the new record. Walsh was given the win in part because of a finish line camera photo. The 1932 Olympics were the first time that such cameras were used, but the phrase *photo finish* would become ubiquitous in the sport. The Polish people were delighted with the victory of Stanislawa Walasiewicz, as she was listed in the results. The Polish press took no notice of the fact that Walsh had lived in the

United States since her first birthday. Walsh's gold medal marked the only women's track and field event that was not won by an American. But many people outside of Poland were less than thrilled with Walsh's victory. Her height, musculature, and masculine facial features combined to draw unwelcome attention. American Mary Carew, who was part of the gold medal–winning 4x100 meter relay team, called Walsh "this manly woman." Strike faulted Walsh for seldom staying at the hotel with the other women and for wearing her sweat suit all the time, and the Canadian team manager called Walsh the "big husky Polish girl with the mannish frame."[16]

Although Walsh won the premier event in the 1932 Olympic Games, she was outshone by the Babe in LA. Here's how it happened: Didrikson entered eight events at the national track championships in Evanston, Illinois, earlier in 1932, setting world records in the javelin and 80 meter hurdles, and tying Jean Shiley for the world record in the high jump. At the Olympic Games in Los Angeles, Didrikson shattered her world record in her first javelin throw but injured her shoulder in the act. Fortunately, her first throw held up for the gold medal, and she didn't need a healthy shoulder for her other two events. Shoulder problems or not, Didrikson faced close battles with her American teammates. Didrikson and Evelyne Hall both ran a new world record time of 11.7 seconds in the 80 meter hurdles, but Didrikson won what the *New York Times* called an "eyelash" victory. She tied Shiley with a new world record of 5 feet, 5 inches in the high jump but lost the jump-off to Shiley when she was called for a foul for clearing the bar headfirst in her western roll style.[17]

The Associated Press named Babe the outstanding woman athlete of 1932. Didrikson decided that she could help her family financially by turning pro, and she did so at the end of 1932. In those days, professionals were barred from competing in most sports, instead making their living by giving exhibitions. After two years on the exhibition circuit, Didrikson decided she wanted to return to competitive sports, so she took up golf, one of the few sports with legitimate outlets for pros. She also learned to wear more feminine clothing and tone down her boasting. Furthermore, she found a husband—the noted wrestler George Zaharias—through her new sport. They met on the golf course when she was 26 and he was 29. The handsome, strapping athlete was the first man in whom Babe had shown any romantic interest.[18]

Up until Didrikson's transformation, she, too, had been the subject of rumors about her status as a "real woman." For instance, in 1932, sports reporter Paul Gallico said, "Everybody in Los Angeles was talking about the Babe. Was she all boy?"[19] Gallico also made unkind statements about Didrikson's facial features. Marriage, more feminine attire, and a new sport that was considered more ladylike put an end to the suggestions that she was not 100 percent female. Given the fact that Didrikson was very media savvy, it has been suggested than at least some of the changes were undertaken "to tamp down criticism of her masculine mien."[20] At 5 feet, 7 inches tall and possessing taut but not overly imposing musculature, Didrikson's phenotype was not as masculine as the other "muscle molls" of the era, but in family photos she is much bigger than her mother and in fact looks like a slightly taller, longer haired, younger version of her father.

Didrikson may have turned pro, but Stella Walsh continued to race as an amateur, winning many sprint titles over the next couple of years. She was, however, beaten a few times by other athletes. An ankle injury in 1933 caused Walsh to lose a couple of races, and she was beaten in both the 100 and 200 meter races at the last Women's World Games in London in 1934 by German sprinter Kathe Krauss, whose physique was even more masculine-appearing than Walsh's. Krauss also took home the bronze medal in the discus throw at those games. Walsh did win the 60-meter dash at the meet and placed second in the 100 and 200. Regardless of these few blemishes on her record, Walsh was still regarded as the world's best female sprinter during the period stretching from 1932 until 1935.[21]

That year, a tall young American farm girl would wrest the mantle of world's fastest woman from Walsh. Helen Stephens was born in the small town of Fulton, Missouri, on February 3, 1918. Stephens's mother, Bertie Mae, was from a family that had enough money to send Bertie to William Woods College, a local, private two-year finishing school. Very little is known about the family of Helen's father, Frank, other than that they were poor dirt famers in the area.[22] Hence it is possible that there was some degree of consanguinity between her parents, who were both from the same relatively small gene pool, but there is no proof of this. Stephens's cousin Howard McAllister was a state high school hurdles champion, and Helen used to join him as he did informal track and field training. Stephens identified McAllister as her brother in a local newspaper clipping.[23] It is not clear whether this was a slip of the tongue or indicates some inbreeding. By 1934, when Stephens was fifteen, she had nearly reached her adult height of 6 feet, and she spoke with a low gravelly voice. She was also unusually strong, lean, muscular, and fast. That year, track coach W. Burton Moore timed Stephens in 5.8 seconds in a 50 yard dash in a PE class. Although the accuracy of the school's cinder track or the coach's hand timing might have been questionable, Stephens had just tied the outdoor world record for the distance. Her feat was reported in the school newspaper.[24]

Despite her obvious talent, Stephens did not seriously begin to train for track until early in 1935. While Moore scheduled six meets for the boys on his team that season, there were no high school girls' meets for Stephens. There was, however, a unique opportunity nearby: The Amateur Athletic Union (AAU) indoor meet would be held in St. Louis in March 1935. Moore entered Stephens in the shot put, the standing broad jump, and the 50-meter sprint. Moore and his wife, Mary, who was the chaperone, drove Stephens to the meet on the morning of March 22. Stephens had borrowed track spikes and sweats from boys on the team, as she had none of her own.[25] She won her two field events, but the real test would come when she faced Stella Walsh in the 50-meter dash.

Stephens won her heat in 6.6 seconds and repeated that time in the final, dusting Walsh and everyone else. She had just broken the American record for the distance and became a national star at her very first track meet. Stephens also created a heated rivalry when she answered a reporter's question about Stella Walsh with the witty reply "Stella Who?"[26] Stephens was joking, of course—she knew very well who Stella Walsh was—but Walsh was not amused. Stephens returned home to a heroine's welcome: There was a Helen Stephens day, a parade, multiple college scholarship offers, and nationwide press attention. "That greenie from the sticks," as Walsh called her,[27] was quickly becoming a confident and self-assured young woman.

The AAU indoor meet was the beginning of two years of dominance for the "Fulton Flash." In the summer of 1935, Stephens won both the 100- and 200-meter sprints at the AAU national championship.[28] As an American resident, Walsh could have run the AAU meet, but instead she chose to compete for Poland. From her base in her native country,

Walsh had an impressive summer, winning races and setting world records at odd distances such as 80, 250, and 500 meters. Walsh returned to Cleveland in the fall, but ducked out of the 1936 indoor AAU meet, where Stephens set a world record of 6.6 seconds for the 50 meters. Walsh would not race Stephens again until the Berlin games.[29]

The IOC had awarded the 1936 Olympic Games to Berlin in 1931, but that decision became suspect in 1933 when Adolf Hitler rose to power. Many countries considered boycotting the games, and the 1935 AAU vote on the boycott question was quite close, but in the end all of the major nations sent teams to the 1936 games. A handful of Jewish American athletes stayed home, but most of the stars—including Jesse Owens and Helen Stephens—made the journey to Germany for the games.[30] Stella Walsh and her Polish team never seriously considered boycotting,[31] and the matchup between the two sprinters was on.

The Germans had assembled a strong team befitting their determination to use the games to display the superiority of the Aryan race. In their stable were two of best female sprinters in the world: Kathe Krauss, who had twice beaten Walsh in 1934, and Marie Dollinger.[32]

The heats were held on August 3, and Stephens ran a wind-aided 11.4 seconds in her heat; no woman would run faster for more than thirty years.[33] All of the favorites advanced to the final, with Stephens matching the world record of 11.5 in her semifinal, trailed by Krauss. Walsh and Dollinger both ran 11.7 in the other semi, with the German edging out the Pole.[34] Stephens ran away from her rivals in the final, again running 11.5, with Walsh second in 11.7, and Kraus and Dollinger taking third and fourth places, both in 11.9.[35] After the race, Dollinger suggested that all three of the medalists were of questionable femininity, stating that she was "the only woman in the race."[36] Questions had swirled about Stephen's femininity prior to the Olympics, but there is nothing like an Olympic gold medal to focus attention on an athlete. Other female athletes were surprised to share living quarters with the tall, muscular, deep-voiced American sprinter, and the Polish press questioned whether she was really a woman.[37]

Stephens's response was that she had been tested by an IOC physician "who sex-tested all athletes prior to competition."[38] In his 1941 book *A Farewell to Sport*, author Paul Gallico claimed that the AAU had confirmed the IOC test.[39] It most definitely was *not* true that the IOC sex-tested all female athletes in 1936—Stella Walsh would have failed any such test—but perhaps Stephens was tested in some manner. Certainly she would have been given the standard, probably cursory, examination by an AAU physician prior to the games. The truth regarding Stephens's claim of a sex test will likely never be known. The controversy didn't end there, as the American magazine *Look* ran an article featuring a less-than-flattering picture of Stephens in its January 1937 issue, captioned "Is This a Man or a Woman?" Stephens lawyered up, sued, and won a judgment of $5,500.

Stephens was named the most outstanding American woman athlete of 1936 by the Associated Press. She turned pro in 1937, formed a basketball touring group, and gave many paid exhibitions of her running and throwing talents. Even after Stephens retired from professional sports, she continued to engage in sports such as bowling, golf, and swimming. She later returned to track and field in her sixties, participating in several senior Olympics competitions. Stephens lived as a closeted lesbian and had a forty-year marriage-equivalent relationship with Mabel Robbe.[40] Stephens passed away after a stroke in 1994.

Although Stephens achieved modest success as a professional athlete, hers was nothing like the career of Babe Didrikson. By the 1940s, women's professional golf was gaining notoriety, and Didrikson was the star. As Babe's golf career gained steam, Zaharias quit his sport to manage her. Although he excelled at his task as his wife's manager, his lack of a sporting outlet and his robust eating habits caused his weight to balloon to a peak of almost 400 pounds. The couple who had seemed so in love were now just cohabiting. They were, however, living in style as Didrikson had grown quite prosperous. In 1950 she met fellow golfer Betty Dodd, who said "the minute I saw her, I knew that had to be the Babe." Before long, the two women were constant companions, and it wasn't long before Dodd moved into the Zaharias household. Although they were not public about their relationship, there was little doubt in the golf world that Babe and Betty were a couple. Didrikson continued to be the world's best female golfer until her career was derailed by colon cancer; she died at the shockingly young age of forty-five on September 27, 1956. She was named the outstanding American woman athlete six times by the Associated Press, a record that stands today.[41] Didrikson would later be named the greatest female American athlete of the twentieth century.[42]

Unlike Didrikson and Stephens, Walsh never turned pro, but she continued to compete in amateur sports for the rest of her life. She returned to Cleveland after World War II and became an American citizen in 1947. At the time, Olympic rules forbade athletes from competing for a second nation once they had already been in the games. Walsh was still running well and would have made the 1948 US Olympic team for the London games, the first games held since 1936 due to the war. In fact, the 100 meter winner in London, Fanny Blankers-Koen, ran slower than either Walsh or Stephens had run in 1936.[43]

Walsh endured an arranged marriage, some legal problems, and other difficulties, but she maintained her love of sports well into her sixties. On December 4, 1980, Walsh was out doing some shopping when she was accosted by two thugs who demanded her purse. When she resisted, they shot her in the stomach and fled. Walsh was taken to the hospital but died on the operating table.[44]

As she had been killed in a crime, an autopsy was required. The local TV station broadcast the details from the autopsy report, including the fact that Walsh had no uterus, an abnormal urethra, and a nonfunctioning, underdeveloped penis. When released, the actual report stated that "the majority of her cells had a normal X and Y chromosome, and a minority of her cells contained a single X chromosome" and the doctor later described her condition as mosaicism (the sole X chromosome indicated Turner syndrome). He also confirmed that she had male genitalia.[45] There was a stream of negative publicity once the autopsy results were released. The tagline "Stella was a fella" was used over and over again. From that time onward, Walsh was often listed among the most notorious cheaters in sport. Although Walsh certainly would have known that she was different from other women, she competed under the rules that existed at the time. There was no cheating involved in her athletic career, and Walsh was undoubtedly not the only intersex woman competing in the 1930s.

Let's look a little more closely at some of the other so-called muscle molls of the era. I previously mentioned that the Japanese sprinter Hitomi Kinue and the German 100 meter bronze medal winner Kathe Kraus were accused of being somewhat less than 100 percent female. But beyond mere accusations, there were three European athletic stars of the 1930s who were almost undoubtedly intersex.

Mark (neé Mary Louise Edith) Weston competed as a thrower, winning several British national championships in the late 1920 and the 1930s. He competed in the Women's World Games in 1928, and it was there that he first started to feel that he wasn't a woman. In 1929 he won the national title in the shot put, discus, and javelin. He won an international shot put title in 1934, although not at the Women's World Games. It wasn't until 1936 that Weston had the courage to seek out medical assistance. Weston had atypical genitalia and was advised to have surgery.[46] In 1936 Weston had two operations at Charring Cross Hospital in London, emerging as Mark. Mark gave up sports and married Alberta Bray, with whom he had three children.

Zdenka Koubkova was a Czech runner who set a world record in the women's 800 in 1934 and had earlier set national records for other distances and both the long and high jump. In the 1934 Women's World Games, Koubkova won the 800-meter race (and apparently all of the other competitors survived the ordeal of racing twice around the oval). Koubkova, too, had atypical genitalia and was given the option of living as either male or female.[47] He chose male. Prior to the 1936 Berlin Olympic Games, he asked to be recognized as male, changed his name to Zdenek Koubek, and retired from sport. Koubek and Hitomi (and maybe Radke) were early examples of probable intersex athletes to excel at the 800 meter distance; they would not be the last.

Avery Brundage and others used the stories of Weston and Koubek to push for compulsory sex testing.[48] The cases of the British thrower and the Czech 800 meter star were proof that women who weren't entirely female were competing successfully in high-level women's sport. Furthermore, the speculation around athletes such as Walsh, Didrikson, Stephens, and Krauss fanned the flames of gender controversy. The fact that Brundage was attempting to introduce sex testing in 1936 strongly suggests that Helen Stephens was not tested at the Berlin games. Upon returning from the Berlin Olympic Games, Stephens apparently considered undergoing surgery similar to that of Koubek and Weston, telling an Olympic coach that she had always "felt out of joint as a girl." It was also true that many people in Stephens's life assumed that she was not "truly male or female." Her penchant for dressing as a man, down to wearing a tie,[49] and her sexual orientation—lesbian behavior is common among intersex women—also support the suggestion that she probably manifested some DSD.

Of all of the stories of intersex athletes of the 1930s, surely none is stranger than the story of Heinrich Ratjen. Ratjen, then called Dora, competed in the women's high jump in the Berlin Olympics, finishing fourth. When Ratjen was born, the midwife was indecisive about the baby's sex but eventually settled on female. Raised female, Ratjen decided he was really male at age ten or eleven but continued to live as female.[50] Ratjen started competing in sports in his teens and was immediately successful. In 1935 Ratjen and fellow German high jumper Gretel Bergmann shared a room while attending at a German training camp in the Black Forest.[51] Bergmann noted that Ratjen always took a bath in private rather than using the communal shower facilities. It was not long before Ratjen bumped Bergmann off of the 1936 German Olympic team. The Germans had three women who had cleared 1.60 meters, and all were medal threats, but were allowed to enter only two of them in the games. Unsurprisingly, the Germans kept the two Aryan jumpers and dismissed the Jew from the team. The third German high jumper, Elfriede Kaun, shared living space with Ratjen at the games and also noted that he had to shave his face and that he had a very deep voice.[52] Kaun cleared 1.60 meters, placing third in a three way jump-off for the Berlin medals, while Ratjen placed fourth in 1.58 meters.

After the 1936 games, Ratjen continued to mature, and he jumped higher. He set the world record of 1.70 meters in 1938, in winning the European Championships. Ratjen's appearance had become even more masculine at this point. On his way home from the European Championships, a train conductor ordered him to get off the train, and he was accused of impersonating a woman and was questioned by police. A doctor was summoned who declared Ratjen male, but with some reservation. Shortly thereafter, Ratjen took the name Heinrich and returned his European gold medal. His world record was stricken from the books.[53]

Ratjen's story took an even more unusual turn in 1966, when *Time* magazine reported that Ratjen had confessed that he had been forced by the Nazis to compete as female. He reportedly said that "for three years I lived the life of a girl. It was most dull."[54] He gave no more interviews after 1966, and his tale was accepted as the truth for the rest of his life; there was even a movie made based on this fictional life history. Ratjen died in 2008, and the following year the German news magazine *Der Spiegel* ran the true story of Ratjen's life, debunking the mythology that had grown up around the German high jump star.

It seems difficult to believe that Ratjen's story would be taken at face value for all of those years, but the idea that he was the Nazi's "secret weapon" in the 1936 games became pervasive. The reality was that the Germans already had two female high jumpers capable of winning medals in Berlin. If the Nazis were really looking for a man to disguise as a woman, why wouldn't they have picked an athlete who was going to win an event—and specifically, an event in which German women had no medal prospects?

The list of probable intersex athletes in the 1930s is undoubtedly longer than I have documented here. It was a common belief that "hermaphrodites [were] passing themselves off as female,"[55] ignoring the fact that these women had been declared female at birth. No one can control the circumstances of their birth. Furthermore, the rules at the time permitted anyone born and raised as female to compete in women's sport. It was, however, true that these 1930-era rules led to a stunning over-representation of probable intersex athletes at the apex of women's sports, as epitomized by the sweep of the podium in the 100 meter race at the 1936 Olympic Games. Eighty years later, a similar lack of restrictions upon intersex athletes would lead to another stunning Olympic-podium sweep.

We are unlikely to ever know whether athletes such as Helen Stephens, Babe Didrikson, and others were simply masculine-appearing women or if they manifested some DSD. Since the double helix structure of DNA was not determined until the 1950s,[56] it would not have been possible to identify which DSDs these women might have had during their sporting careers. Thus, from eighty years away, it is impossible to know just how much of an advantage was gained by those athletes who were intersex.

One thing, however, seems clear to me. The rise of women's sport in the 1930s, combined with the prevalence of consanguineous marriages in the early twentieth century, resulted in substantial tension. Unfortunately, success in women's sport at the time became associated with being less than fully feminine. It is disingenuous when we laud only those successful female athletes who aren't too masculine appearing, since the musculature needed for strength and speed creates a more masculine appearance. It is an exercise fraught with futility to separate success in women's sport from "excessive" masculinity. On the other hand, if we are to have equitable and meaningful competition for women, we must draw a line between male and female athletes. It is reasonable to question whether the virilizing nature of the puberty that many intersex athletes undergo should disqualify them from women's sports. The question of how to deal with hermaphrodites was first raised in the 1930s, and more than eighty years later there is still not a universally accepted solution. In fact, questions over intersex athletes remain among the most contentious issues in all of sports even today.

It would also be wrong to place blame on those who practiced inbreeding in the early twentieth century. They were merely following customs that were common at the time. As the twentieth century progressed, there was a decrease in consanguineous marriages in the Western world, largely due to increased urbanization and the gradual shift to smaller family sizes.[57] At the same time, early medication intervention in the lives of intersex people became more common, and these two factors gradually reduced the number of athletes with DSDs in Europe and the Americas as the century wore on. But despite the downward trend in the frequency of intersex athletes in the Western world, there were several prominent intersex athletes who turned up after World War II.

4

POSTWAR SEX TESTING

There were no Olympic Games in 1940 or in 1944 as a result of the upheaval caused by World War II, but with the cessation of hostilities in 1945, the era's athletes got back to the sports that they loved. And it wasn't long before issues of gender and sport once again were raised. In 1946 the IAAF introduced regulations mandating that all female athletes obtain a certificate from a physician in order to participate in the European Athletics Championships held in Oslo, Norway. French sprinter Léa Caurla became the first casualty of this new rule. Caurla won the bronze medal in the 200 meter dash and was a member of the French 4x100 meter relay team that took second place at those championships. Caurla, who later underwent surgery to transition to Léon, refused to undergo an examination at the meet and was banned by the French Athletic Association.[1]

Caurla's surgery was probably similar to that performed on Mark Weston and Zdenek Koubek in the 1930s. It was not uncommon at the time for intersex persons who were declared female at birth but later realized that they possessed male gender identities to have operations to create more male-appearing genitalia. Weston's surgeon referred to the procedure as "corrective."[2] Although I was unable to ascertain the exact details of the surgical procedures performed at the time, it is not difficult to speculate on their nature. An individual with inguinal testes could have the skin surrounding the testes reshaped to look more like a scrotal sac, and one with an enlarged clitoris could have the surrounding hooding removed so that their phallus would more closely resemble a typical penis. Today, surgery designed to create a more male-typical phallus is called metoidioplasty, and surgery to replicate a scrotum is called scrotoplasty.[3] Caurla was not the only member of the French 4x100 meter team in 1946 to undergo such an operation. Claire Brésolles also underwent surgical transition, emerging as Pierre and apparently later fathering a child, although details are sparse.[4] The German athlete Helga Cordes transitioned to male in 1952 and lived incognito thereafter. Cordes was determined to be an "underdeveloped male,"[5] at age 17 leading one to believe that he might well have had 5-ARD.

The best known case of an intersex athlete running afoul of the IAAF in the first few years after World War II was Foekje Dillema, a Dutch athlete born in the remote village of Burum in the Friesland region of the Netherlands and formally registered as a female at birth.[6] Dillema later became an important rival of her countrywoman Fanny Blankers-Koen, who had won four gold medals—in the 100 and 200 meter dash, the 80 meter hurdles and in the 4x100 meter relay—at the 1948 Olympic Games in London, England. Blankers-Koen was a thirty-year-old mother of two, and her victories helped erase the myth that motherhood and athletic success were not compatible.[7] It was also in 1948 that twenty-year-old Dillema started competing in athletics. It did not take long for Dillema to attain world-class stature. On June 18, 1950, Dillema ran 24.1 seconds for the 200 meter race in front of 60,000 spectators at a meet in Amsterdam taking the national 200 meter record from the "Flying Housewife," as Blankers-Koen was known. Blankers-Koen did not participate in the race, and it was said that she refused to race Dillema over the longer sprint distance. At the 1950 European Athletics Championships in Brussels, the IAAF once again required a gynecologic exam of female athletes, and Dillema was banned as a result. In Brussels in 1950, Blankers-Koen went on to win gold medals in three of the same four events that she had won in London in 1948, including the 200 meters, all by large margins. In 1952 Dillema had an unspecified operation on "her glands"—perhaps a gonadectomy—and lived out the rest of her life in her hometown village of Friesland. After her death in 2007 an autopsy revealed that she had a mosaic of chromosomes with approximately 30 percent of her cells bearing the Y chromosome.[8]

Although Dillema and other probable intersex women in Western Europe caused something of a stir in the world of athletics, it was nothing compared to the storm that would soon engulf several athletes from the Eastern Bloc countries. The Soviet Union first competed in the Olympics in the 1952 games in Helsinki and was immediately successful, wining seventy-one total medals; twenty-three of them were won by their female athletes, even though there were far fewer sports for women at the games. By comparison, the United States won seventy-six total medals with only eight of their medals coming from the distaff side. Soviet women were particularly successful in athletics, winning eleven of the twenty-seven available medals in the nine events open to women. The only medal won by the US women's track team was the gold in the 4x100 meter relay.[9] Many of the Russian women were quite masculine appearing, leading to speculation that they were either hermaphrodites or men masquerading as women. In hindsight, there is also the possibility these women were early users of anabolic steroids. The inherent distrust between the West and the Soviets only exacerbated the situation. One of the most prominent Soviet athletes to appear in the 1950s was Maria Itkina, who ran 54.0 seconds in 1957 to beat the world record in the 400 meter sprint by a hefty 1.2 seconds. She would hold the record for five more years, bringing her time down to 53.4 seconds in 1962. Itkina stood five feet, five inches tall and weighed in at a very muscular but lean 137 pounds.[10]

Easily the most prominent of the masculine-appearing Soviet athletics stars of the early 1960s were sisters Tamara and Irina Press. They were born in Kharkiv, Ukraine, in 1937 and 1939, respectively.[11] It was not long after World War II that the two young Press sisters began to show athletic promise. By the 1960 Olympic Games in Rome, the sisters were dominant. Tamara won the silver in the discus and took gold in the shot put, while Irina won gold in the 80 meter hurdles. The pair became the first sisters to claim gold medals at the same Olympic Games.[12] Rather than becoming celebrities, however, the two were mocked by Western news outlets for their masculine appearance, with some wags dubbing them the "Press brothers." Many people publicly speculated that the two were, in fact, men masquerading as women. Tamara's full adult size of five-foot-eleven and 225 pounds was gigantic for a woman the time. Although Irina was smaller by comparison, she was no waif at five-foot-six and 165 pounds.[13] Both sisters displayed obvious breast development, a fact that should have ended the masquerade rumors, but did not.

At the 1964 Olympic Games in Tokyo, the Press sisters captured even more honors than in 1960, with Tamara setting Olympic records in both her shot put and discus victories, and Irina also setting a new world record as she won the gold medal in the first Olympic women's pentathlon. All told, the sisters set twenty-six world records in the 1960s.[14] The speculation over the Press sisters' sex only increased with their accumulation of victories and was one of the main reasons for the change determining eligibility for women's sports that occurred in the 1960s. The sporting careers of the Press sisters, Itkina, and other Eastern Bloc women would soon end, however, due to the instigation of mandatory sex testing by the IAAF in 1966. The retirement of the many of these athletes in 1966 only increased the speculation that they were men.[15] A far more logical explanation is offered by Thomas Murray in his book *Good Sport*; he suggests that the Press sisters "probably manifested a DSD" and retired to avoid being flagged due to their atypical anatomy.[16]

From 1946 until 1966 the IAAF, and the IOC, relied on physicians to certify that their nation's female competitors were "really" women. With the ongoing mistrust of the Eastern Bloc officials and athletes, it was decided to remove the testing from the realm of the individual nations and replace the tests with an inspection undertaken by doctors at the sporting festivals. The IAAF first undertook sex testing at the 1966 British Empire Games in Kingston, Jamaica. At these games, female athletes were both visually observed and manually manipulated in order to determine the presence of the required female organs. This practice was quickly modified; two weeks later at the European Athletics Championships in Budapest, Hungary, the testing procedure was strictly visual.[17] At the Budapest championships, three female doctors inspected each of the 243 women participating. Although the inspection of each athlete was carried out in private, the overall testing procedure was described as a nude parade, since each athlete was required to "parade naked in front of a panel of doctors."[18] Once female athletes passed their sex test, they were given a femininity card that they could bring to subsequent events to avoid further testing.

One athlete who was banned as a result of the visual inspection method was the Polish sprinter Ewa Klobukowska. The sprinter had earned a bronze medal in the 100 meter race and a gold in the 4x100 at the Tokyo Olympics in 1964. She later set a world record of 11.1 seconds over the 100 meter distance.[19] At the European Cup athletics meet in Kiev in 1967, Klobukowska was flagged due to the appearance of her genitalia. Further testing revealed that Klobukowska possessed a mosaic of XX/XXY chromosomes. The sprinter was done in by the Y chromosomes she possessed in a mosaic of mostly X ones. Klobukowska was banned from the sport and her records were annulled by the IAAF. It was reported that she gave birth to a son in 1968,[20] but another report states that Klobukowska was born with testes that had been surgically excised prior to 1967.[21] The latter report would be consistent with her Y chromosome and would mean that she was incapable of bearing children. Regardless of her gravida stage, Klobukowska never competed again.

It is hardly surprising that visual testing proved very unpopular with the female athletes, and the IAAF quickly found itself looking for another method. Although the visual inspections were replaced by the IAAF after 1967, this very short era illustrates one of the most contentious methods of determining female eligibility in sporting history. Scientific developments soon presented the opportunity to replace the visual inspections with a more sophisticated method. In order to properly characterize this new testing modality, it is necessary to backtrack a few years.

In 1948, University of Western Ontario scientist Murray Barr discovered that the neurons of female cats looked different than those of male cats. The nucleus of the female cats' neurons contained a darkly stained mark. This dark stain was caused by the second of the two X chromosomes the female cats possessed and became known as the Barr body or sex chromatin.[22] The Barr body was also plainly visible in human females and became the anchor of a simple method to determine whether or not a subject had the typical female XX sex chromosomes. Barr himself was not thrilled by the subsequent usage of his discovery to separate men from women, stating that the "presence or absence of sex chromatin . . . is a minor detail in the femaleness or maleness of the whole person."[23] The use of sex chromatin as a gatekeeper would fail in several instances with regard to athletes with DSDs. Any woman with Turner syndrome would fail to register a Barr body as there is no second X chromosome in the nuclei of her cells. Turner syndrome certainly does not impart any athletic advantage onto those it affects; in fact, women with Turner syndrome are less likely to become elite athletes than other women. Additionally, in the unlikely event that a man with Klinefelter syndrome was tested for sex chromatin, he would be judged female due to his second X chromosome. For the same reason, a phenotypically male athlete with a 46,XX karyotype and CAH would also be mischaracterized as female by the Barr body test. As an illustration of the inadequacies of Barr body testing, the method probably would have failed to note the mosaic nature of the chromosomes in Klobukowska's cells, as all of her cells did in fact have two X chromosomes. A simple test for sex chromatin would have come back positive on the Polish sprinter and she probably would have been spared the more detailed analysis indicating that she had both XXY and XX chromosomes.[24]

Another important component of the next phase of sex testing was the founding of the IOC Medical and Scientific Commission. The commission was created largely as a response to the death of Danish cyclist Knud Enemark Jensen at the 1960 Olympics in Rome. Jensen and two of his Danish teammates were hospitalized for heat exhaustion after competing in temperatures that reached 104 degrees. The Danish team doctor admitted to administering a vasodilator drug to the riders, and traces of amphetamines were found in Jensen's blood upon his autopsy.[25] The IOC was concerned about possible widespread amphetamine usage, so IOC president Avery Brundage created a four-person medical commission in 1961. All of the members were physicians. By 1967 the medical commission was headed by Prince Albert de Merode, despite the fact that he had no medical background, was very concerned with doping. He would head up the IOC medical commission until his death in 2002. The commission was also assigned the task of determining an effective sex testing methodology for the 1968 Olympic Games.

The IOC decided to use a buccal smear test to gather DNA from the mouths of female athletes and to test the samples for the presence of the Barr body. The method was relatively inexpensive and was intended to ensure that only those women with the XX chromosome pattern would be competing in the female category. The medical commission implemented the Barr body test at the 1968 winter and summer games in Grenoble, France, and Mexico City, respectively. To minimize the costs of testing, the IOC randomly selected 20 percent of the female athletes at the Grenoble Winter Games to undergo the buccal smear. This decision was not well received, and even the IOC admitted that instead of random athletes, the top finishers in each event should have been tested.[26]

Although no athlete failed her test in Grenoble, Austrian downhill ski champion Erika Schinegger was missing from the Winter Games as a result of sex testing. Schinegger was born into a farming family in the small town of Agsdorf in the Kaernten Mountains in 1948. She was labeled a girl by the midwife who delivered her, although her mother had doubts about the infant's anatomy and her father would have preferred a son to help with the farm work. The young skier showed early promise, winning her first ski race at the age of twelve after walking 14 kilometers to the race and starting from the 314th—and last—spot. It is a disadvantage to start after the course has been chewed up by other skiers, so her victory under these circumstances is quite remarkable.[27] By the time she was sixteen, Schinegger had been invited to join the Austrian national youth team. In 1965, at the age of seventeen, she won a downhill ski race at Sun Valley, Idaho, and was soon bumped up to the adult team. Schinegger also picked up adult habits like smoking and drinking, and was gregarious and well-liked by her teammates. It was noted by many that she spoke with a deep voice, and Schinegger herself was troubled by the fact that she never got her period or grew breasts. She was also teased by her teammates for her tomboy ways, her unfeminine haircut, and her refusal to shower with her female teammates.[28] A major event in Schinegger's growing unease with her upbringing as a female was the time when her pretty roommate undressed in front of her as they were preparing for bed. "I started trembling as if an earthquake had freed something in me."[29]

In 1966 Schinegger was named to the Austrian team that would compete in the World Alpine Ski Championships in the Andes Mountains of Chile. The course was treacherous, and Canadian champion Nancy Greene suffered a horrific fall in which she broke her coccyx. Schinegger, possessing the fearlessness of youth, launched herself down the brutally steep slope and wound up edging out Frenchwoman Marielle Goitschel by an eighth of a second. Schinegger was named the female Austrian athlete of the year, and her equipment suppliers rewarded her handsomely enough that the so-called amateur was able to buy herself a Porsche. She was showered with many other gifts, including marriage proposals. She was growing increasingly troubled by feelings that she didn't belong in a woman's life, but she did her best to bury such doubts as she began to prepare for the 1968 Olympic Games in Grenoble.[30] She would never make it to the starting line.

Late in 1967, the entire female Austrian ski team underwent the buccal smear test in Innsbruck. The team then headed to the slopes for their pre-Olympic training camp. Schinegger was soon called back to Innsbruck by herself, where she was confronted by a six-man tribunal of physicians and ski officials (the Austrian Ski Federation or ÖSV). The tribunal told her that she had a male chromosome pattern and that she should resign from the sport citing unspecified personal reasons. The ski federation would pay for a long foreign vacation where she could avoid the press until the resulting publicity blew over. Schinegger signed the resignation letter but requested that she be allowed to return to the clinic under an assumed name for further testing.[31] The more extensive tests confirmed the results of the Barr body test; she did indeed have male chromosomes, which accounted for the presence of testes in her abdomen.[32] The urologist presented Schinegger with two choices. Her first option was surgery and hormone therapy in order to continue her life as a woman—"Medicine can make you a woman," he explained, "but never a real woman."[33] The other option was to undergo more extensive surgery that would reshape the flesh around the internal testes and genital tuber to resemble the anatomy of other men. Schinegger's parents, ski sponsor, and the ÖSV all advised the first option, but by this point Schinegger had decided that he was really a man.[34]

On January 2, 1968, Schinegger checked into the clinic in Innsbruck under an assumed name, wearing female clothing, to begin a six-month regimen of four surgeries to remake his genital region. He did so without any family or friends to support him. Although Schinegger suffered from loneliness and despair during that time, he persevered. He used the downtime to study male skiing technique on TV and boned up on male etiquette by reading books. He ordered men's clothing from a catalog using his cousin's name. After he recovered from surgery, he exited the hospital using the name Erik and driving his Porsche.[35] Within days of his release from the hospital, Erik competed in a local cycling race. It was here that he revealed what he had been doing for the last six months. In the documentary film *Erik(A)* by Kurt Mayer, Schinegger described the process as "not a transformation. It was a correction." Press reports at the time were mixed, with some newspapers being supportive and some of the national papers, which had lionized the young skier, now making fun of him.[36] The reaction from his hometown was almost uniformly negative. Many people avoided him entirely or stared at him as he sat on the men's side of the church. The town of Agsdrof had given Schinegger a two-acre plot after the 1966 World Cup victory, but now it reneged on the deal, claiming that the contract had stipulated Erika, not Erik, Schinegger.[37]

The ÖSV also treated Erik poorly after he resumed racing in the men's category. He won three races in the Europa Cup series in the 1968–69 season and applied to represent Austria in the men's championship division. Although Erik's personal coach welcomed him back, the Austrian team coach rebuffed Schinegger, calling him an "embarrassment." The ÖSV not only forbade him from representing Austria, they also blocked him from competing for any another country. At the age of twenty-one, when Erik should have been coming into his own as a skier, he saw no option but to retire from competitive skiing.[38] Erik did not, however, give up on life. He passed his ski school certification in 1973 and started running a ski school in 1975. He also married a pretty young woman in 1975, and in 1978 the couple welcomed a daughter into their lives. Fathering a child was an important milestone for Schinegger. In 1988 Schinegger published his book, *Victory over Myself*, which went on to sell more than one hundred thousand copies. That same year, he gave Marielle Goitschel the gold medal from the 1966 World Cup downhill championship in a public ceremony. In 1996, on the thirtieth anniversary of the event, the International Ski Federation (FIS) gave Goitschel another gold medal; in return, Goitschel returned Schinegger's original medal to him on live TV in Paris.[39] His graciousness over the 1966 medal, along with the publicity from the televised event, earned Schinegger much praise in France, and his book was translated into French.

Although Schinegger was shunned by many when he was young, he has been treated very well in the twenty-first century. The 2005 documentary and a 2017 German film told his story. He was a contestant on the German version of *Dancing with the Stars* in 2014. His second marriage has been a success; he and his wife run the very successful Schischule Schinegger and two inns. They retired from operating a restaurant in 2015. Nancy Greene, who went on to win a World Cup Championship and become one of Canada's most recognized sports heroines, recalls fondly that Schinegger was "generous, fun-loving and outgoing" whether presenting as male or female.[40]

After the Grenoble winter games, the IOC announced that it would test all of the women competing in 1968 summer games in Mexico City. A total of 803 women were tested, and although no one officially failed, one IOC medical team member claimed that the testing was successful because some women dropped out rather than undergo the testing procedure.[41] The IOC medical commission also tested for drugs, and two athletes failed drug testing. That number likely would have been much higher had there been a test for anabolic steroids, which were rumored to be in widespread use by the athletes competing in the games. Drug testing would get more sophisticated as the 1970s unfolded, and steroids would be banned and tested for in subsequent Olympic Games. On the other hand, sex-testing methodology wouldn't change for another twenty years, despite the obvious limitations of the Barr body test and the opposition of several important scientists.

The four Olympic competitions in the 1970s—summer games in Munich and Montreal, winter games in Sapporo and Innsbruck—all featured the buccal smear method of gathering DNA with the goal of ensuring that only those athletes with the XX chromosome pattern competed in women's events. Unlike the previous decade, the 1970s featured no prominent cases of intersex athletes. There were no Press sisters, Schineggers, or Klobukowskas during this period. In all probability, any intersex athlete who was discovered by the testing regimen took the option of quiet retirement over any more public option. In 1972 the South Korean volleyball team claimed that their North Korean counterparts were using a man masquerading as a woman, but this claim was unfounded.[42] The 1970s also saw the rise of the great East German sports team featuring many women who had been rendered quite masculine-appearing by the excessive steroid use that was required for all of the nation's aspiring athletes. During the 1976 Olympic Games in Montreal, the East German swim coach was asked about the broad shoulders and deep voices of his athletes. He responded that "we came here to swim, not to sing."[43] And they did swim and run and throw with great success. Despite having a population of fewer than 20 million people, the German Democratic Republic (DDR) earned almost as many Olympic medals in Montreal as the United States and was not far behind the mighty USSR. (The medal tally was DDR 90; USA

94; USSR 125).[44] There was, however, little doubt that the masculine appearance of the East German athletes sowed suspicion in the minds of many sports fans regarding the correlation between masculine characteristics and gender variance among elite female competitors.

There is no official tally of the number of athletes who failed the Barr body test during the 1972 and 1976 Olympics, but one source suggests that there were three failures in Munich.[45] Those women who failed were told to fake an injury, go home, and retire from sport. As far as we can tell, all of the women who were so flagged agreed to this stipulation and disappeared from history. It was not until the 1980s that one very brave young woman would challenge this paradigm.

Up until this point, this book has focused entirely on intersex athletes, but it is time to widen that focus. In 1970 it was unthinkable that any transgender athlete would be allowed to compete in women's sports. Yet it was only a few years later that the first openly transgender athlete would break through that barrier. Before getting to her story, however, it would be appropriate to examine some aspects of the larger transgender experience.

5

TRANSGENDER 101

In North America in the twenty-first century, most of the discussion around gender-variant athletes revolves around transgender athletes. This has not always been the case. From the 1930s until the 1970s, the controversy centered on the role of hermaphrodites in sport. That narrative first began to change in the seventies. Before tackling the subject of transgender athletes, it would be appropriate to talk about some general transgender terminology, science, and history. Distinguishing sex from gender would be a good place to start. Although I will sometimes use the word *sex* to refer to activities such as intercourse, most of the time I use the word to describe those biological qualities that make us male, female, or somewhere in between. There are different ways one can subdivide biological sex into its component pieces. I prefer to use seven categories: gonads, external genitalia, internal genitalia, chromosomes, hormones, secondary sex characteristics, and gender identity.[1] Others would use different divisions,[2] and some experts would argue that gender identity is not biologically based, but no expert would claim that biological sex is simple.

Gender can be defined as the state of being male or female, but it can also be defined as a nonbinary social construct. Almost everyone has some characteristics that are more typically male and some that are more typically female. The majority of people, however, tend to consistently express their gender in a manner that is most often either typically male or typically female. Others could be described as genderfluid. It is often implied that gender is a one-dimensional continuum between male and female.[3] I prefer to think of gender as a two-dimensional plane, with male and female at either end of a lengthy vertical axis and various gender aspects along a horizontal axis. In particular, I would like to highlight four gender aspects in this book: gender assigned at birth, social gender, legal gender, and a concept that I have dubbed athletic gender. It is very possible, for instance, to have a social gender that differs from one's athletic gender, and this idea will become important later. Throughout this book I will use the terms *trans man* and *trans woman* as opposed to *female-to-male* or *male-to-female*.

If gender identity is indeed biologically based, then exactly how does incongruity between gender identity and other biological components of sex occur? When discussing fetal development in chapter 2, I wrote about the differentiation between male and female embryos that occurs within the first trimester of life. Testosterone spikes, or lack thereof, are responsible for the two different development paths that male and female fetuses travel. These spikes occur in the first trimester of life. Most human embryonic brain development, including all higher functions, does not occur until late in the second trimester. Not only is it true that brain structure is different for men and women, but it has also been observed that the brains of transgender people often have physical similarities to the brains of others with whom they share gender identity. In other words, in some (but not all) ways the brains of trans men, for example, would be more like the brains of cisgender men than the brains of cisgender women.[4]

These facts have given rise to the theory that testosterone spikes at the end of the second trimester are responsible for sex-based brain differences, and that incongruent gender identity results from a lack of second-trimester testosterone spikes in trans women or the presence of second-trimester testosterone spikes in trans men. Although this theory currently remains unproven, the majority of experts in transgender science agree that there is a biological foundation for gender identity.[5]

Regardless of the exact causes of transgender identity, it is certainly true that trans people have walked the earth since the beginning of time, and in certain cultures transgender people have long been recognized and even prized. The *hijra* of India are one of the most prominent examples of historical recognition of transgender people. Traditionally, the word *hijra* is used in India to refer to those people who were declared male at birth but later underwent the removal of their external genitalia. Historically, this removal was carried out with a very crude form of surgery called *nirvan*, which involved two diagonal cuts to remove the offending organs. It was understood that there would be substantial blood loss with *nirvan*, and the loss was considered important to cleanse the *hijra* of her male life. Assuming that the *hijra* survived *nirvan*, she was ready for her new life.[6]

References to *hijra* are found in many ancient texts, including the epic Sanskrit poem *Ramayana*, or the story of Rama. In that poem, Rama is exiled to the forest, but since he is beloved most of his townsfolk follow him. He exhorts all "men and women turn back," but those who were "neither men nor women" didn't know what to do and so stayed put. Years later Rama returned from exile and found the third-gender people still camped out in the forest waiting for him. Rama blessed the *hijra* and told them they would someday rule the world (probably right after the meek inherit it).[7] It was felt that the *hijra* had the power to bestow fertility on brides, and so the *hijra* were invited to sing and dance at weddings. *Hijra* also traditionally were invited to the births of male children. Traditionally, the *hijra* earned their living by asking for alms at weddings and births, but the demand for their services has shrunk in recent times, forcing more and more *hijra* to resort to sex work for their welfare.[8] When India became a British colony, the British rulers were disgusted by the social acceptance of the *hijra* and stripped them of any legal protection. In modern India, the *hijra* live in a state of marginalized acceptance.[9] It is only very recently that the *hijra* have been allowed to gain permanent employment, obtain education, and generally participate in the modern society that India has become. In 2014, India granted the *hijra* the legal right to be recognized as a third gender.[10]

The Samoan *fa'afafine* are another example of a traditional third gender. Like the *hijra*, the *fa'afafine* are biological males who undertake a female role in society. The *fa'afafine* do not, however, require surgical initiation into their roles. Traditionally, boys were assigned as *fa'afafine* when their families had too many boys and not enough girls to fulfill the female roles in the household. These boys would be dressed in traditional female attire. As time went on, *fa'afafine* were increasingly likely to be chosen because they expressed more feminine than masculine characters. Modern Samoan boys who prefer to dress in women's clothes are not discouraged from doing so. Rather, the *fa'afafine* are raised as one would raise a daughter. Most of these boys would be described as gay in Western society, but the *fa'afafine* are not burdened with this sort of label. Instead they are accepted as part of Samoan society.[11] Other Polynesian islands have their own version of the *fa'afafine*, and the entire region is very accepting of gender diversity.

Another Asian nation that has a long history with the notion of a third gender is Thailand. The Thai notion of *phet* or sex/gender/sexuality has long had three main varieties: *ying* (female), *chai* (male), and *kathoey* (intersex or transgender).[12] In ancient Thai culture, the meaning of *kathoey* was probably a mix of the modern notions of intersex and genderqueer. Although the *kathoey* were accepted in traditional Thai society, they were not revered. Instead, it was assumed that the *kathoey* were enduring karmic punishment for past-life sins and were to be pitied but not hated.[13] The ancient Thai ideas about the *kathoey* were not affected by Western notions of homosexual sin until the middle of the twentieth century, and by this time the Western world was beginning to accept gay and transgender culture. Until the twentieth century, Thai people were mostly androgynous in appearance, hence the differences in the three Thai *phets* were subtle. After World War II, there began to be greater Western influence upon Thai culture, resulting in greater feminization of female Thai couture. Modern Thai dress has a marked differentiation between male and female styles, and hence the *kathoey*, who had always existed, were much more noted by European visitors to the country—so much so that after World War II the *kathoey* became one of the most prevalent features of Thai life as seen from the Western point of view. It was this Western attention to the *kathoey* that resulted in the well-known English translation of the word as "ladyboy."[14] Unfortunately, there has been little modernization in the treatment of the *kathoey*. They cannot serve in the armed forces or change their legal gender recognition from that assigned to them at birth (although that may change soon);[15] hence it is not surprising that modern day transgender Thai people prefer to use terms other than the traditional Thai term *kathoey*.[16]

Many Native American cultures accepted a third and sometimes a fourth gender role. The four gender roles could be summarized as masculine men, feminine men, feminine women, and masculine women.[17] Those people whose spirit deviated from the spirit generally associated with their sex were called different names in each of the individual tribal languages; today they are called by the pan-Indian expression two-spirit.[18] It is important, however, to not conflate traditional Western terms with actual indigenous ideas; the two-spirit concept is not akin to being gay or even to being transgender. Two-spirit people were simply different than the majority of the native people, and this difference was usually accepted and often celebrated. Given the tradition of oral record keeping among the Native Americans and the multiplicity of cultures within the various tribes, it is far too easy to make facile statements about what did or did not happen to two-spirit people, but it would appear that many tribes honored their two-spirit members for being more spiritually gifted than the rest of the tribe.[19] Hence it was not uncommon for a two-spirit tribe member to assume the role of religious leader or teacher.[20] Just as with the *hijra* in India, the respect for two-spirit people within Native American tribes diminished once European notions of homophobia began to filter into the traditional indigenous culture. In more recent times, there has been an LGBT-fueled resurgence of the traditional acceptance of two-spirit people.[21]

European society wasn't as accepting of transgender identity as other parts of the world, but transgender people still existed. If we accept the Williams Institute estimate that 0.6 percent of the population is trans,[22] then roughly 1 in every 200 historic personages was transgender. Of course, given the lack of acceptance, most transgender people in Western society did everything they could to hide. If one is looking for historical transgender figures, one can examine gender expression. For instance, if someone assigned female at birth consistently expressed herself in a masculine manner, then it is not unreasonable to suggest (but is also not proven) that this person might have been a closeted trans man. One powerful way a female-bodied person could express a masculine gender is by going to war.

According to Colby College history professor Elizabeth Leonard, "there have [been] women serving in men's dress in armies since the beginning of wars."[23] In the US Civil War alone, at least 250 women served on both sides. Some of them were in it for the money or the adventure; however, some of the soldiers who had been assigned female at birth would be described as transgender men today. One such soldier was Albert Cashier, who had been born Jennie Hodges in Ireland. After immigrating to America, Cashier adopted male dress and worked as a man under that name before enlisting in the war. Cashier continued to live "as a man"[24] after the war, so I will use the male name and assign him male pronouns for the remainder of his story. Cashier enlisted in the military on August 6, 1862. At the time, the standard military medical examination required only that recruits show their hands and feet. Both the Union and Confederate armies were desperate for soldiers, hence Cashier and other female-bodied soldiers would not have been inspected too closely. As long as they could pull a trigger, they would have been welcome to fight and die alongside the men. Once he joined the 95th Illinois Infantry, Cashier proved to be a brave and able soldier. He fought in at least forty campaigns, escaped enemy capture, performed a heroic flag rescue, and suffered only one wound that required a brief hospital visit. At the end of the war, he was given an honorable discharge and sent on his way. After the war, Cashier worked as a handyman, farm laborer, and janitor. He never married, but there are letters that seem to indicate that he had a female "sweetheart" at one time. He turned down a military pension because it would have required him to undergo a full medical examination.[25]

It wasn't until he was old, feeble, and suffering from dementia that his secret was discovered. He was admitted to an asylum in 1914, and after he was examined, he was required to dress as a woman for the short remainder of his life. He fell and broke a hip, and his condition went downhill quickly. He died on October 10, 1915. His fellow soldiers rallied to his support, and he was buried with full military honors despite the fact that he was not a cisgender man. It is possible to argue that Cashier lived his life the way he did because, as an illiterate person, he would have little economic opportunity if he lived as a woman. As a man he could earn his living without needing to read or write.[26] Given his persistent male gender expression, however, and his utterly consistent lifelong male lifestyle, it appears appropriate to describe Albert Cashier as a trans man.

One way in which trans women could historically have expressed their gender was on the stage. Until relatively recently, it was common for acting on stage to be restricted to male-bodied persons, and thus men (often older boys) assumed all of the female roles in theatrical productions. Of interest, in many Shakespeare plays the female characters (played by young men) cross-dress as men within the plays.[27] Some of the male actors would have been in it for the work, but some of them were undoubtedly closeted trans women.

It wasn't until the twentieth century that transgender people began to live more public lives. One of the first openly transgender persons was a Danish painter christened Einar Wegener, but who became known as Lili Elbe. Wegener was born on December 28, 1882, in rural Denmark, but moved to Copenhagen to attend the Royal Danish Academy of Fine Arts. Einer studied painting and he met fellow painter Gerda Gottlieb at the academy. They were married in 1904 and began their life together as working artists. Einer painted landscapes while Gerda was a successful illustrator of books and fashion magazines. One of Gerda's most frequent models was in fact her husband, who adored being transformed into a woman for Gerda's portraits.[28] It wasn't long before Wegener was living part-time as a woman known as Lili Elbe. Conservative Copenhagen was not the best place for Lili and Gerda, and they began a nomadic few years looking for a future home. In 1912 they settled in Paris, largely because Lili could live openly as herself. Lili lived the rest of her life as a woman.[29] In 1919 Dr. Magnus Hirschfield founded the German Institute for Sexual Science in Berlin; he coined the term *transexualism* in 1923. Lili learned of the work of Hirschfield and others in Germany, and in 1930 and 1931 she had four surgeries, including orchiectomy, penectomy, and transplantation of human ovarian tissue. These surgeries allowed her to change her legal name and gender in Denmark, although her legal gender change meant that she and Gerda had to divorce. Unfortunately, Lili died from heart paralysis after her final surgery in 1931. She was forty-eight years old.[30] Lili's personal diaries were published in 1933 as the book *Man into Woman*. This was one of the first and most influential books ever written about a transgender person. Her story was retold in the 2000 novel *The Danish Girl*, which was later made into a feature film starring Eddie Redmayne as Lili and Alicia Vikander as Gerda.

Another important trans pioneer was Christine Jorgensen, who was born on Manhattan Island on May 30, 1926, and christened George William Jorgensen. She admired her older sister Dolly's long blond hair and dresses, but was denied both.[31] Jorgensen always manifested feminine affects and was often teased and castigated for her girly ways. She took no interest in sports, nor did she have any romantic interest in girls. Jorgensen did, however, develop an interest and aptitude in photography. Jorgensen served in the US Army, performing clerical work for the latter part of 1945 and almost all of 1946. Jorgensen never fired a weapon, engaged in combat, or otherwise fulfilled any of the usual armed forces duties. She did, however, perform her clerical duties as required, and she received an honorable discharge.[32] Jorgensen knew that she was different from other biological men and sought answers to her questions. Although she was rebuffed by the first physician she sought out, her search led her to an insightful book on endocrinology. Jorgensen managed to obtain a supply of estradiol and began to self-administer the hormone. Later she found a more sympathetic doctor through a college classmate.[33] Jorgensen learned that sex change procedures were being performed in Scandinavia, so in the spring of 1950 she spent most of her meager savings on a one-way trip to Norway, her ancestral home. Within a few months Jorgensen had become the patient of Dr. Christian Hamburger, an endocrinologist who was willing to supervise hormonal therapy to make her more feminine, and by the end of the year she had also received approval for surgery from Dr. Georg Sturup, a leading Danish psychiatrist.[34] She also started to sell photographs to various European magazines, earning enough money to keep herself afloat.

Jorgensen had an orchiectomy on September 21, 1951, and a penectomy in November 1952. In May 1952 she changed her name to Christine on her passport; the name was chosen to honor Dr. Hamburger. After she got her new passport, Christine began to dress publicly in women's clothing, and she wrote her parents to tell them of her new life. She was also visited by two aunts who welcomed her new version of herself.[35] Christine was recovering from her penectomy and contemplating her return the United States when her gender change made the front page of the *New York Daily News*. On February 13, 1953, Christine Jorgensen returned to New York, arriving to a new life of celebrity.[36] In 1954 she had a vaginoplasty operation in New Jersey, completing her surgical transition.[37]

Although Christine was not happy being showered with so much attention, her celebrity allowed her to advocate powerfully for acceptance of transgender people. She also become a friend and collaborator of Dr. Harry Benjamin. Thirteen years later, Dr. Benjamin published his highly regarded book *The Transsexual Phenomenon*, which would make him the world's leading authority on the subject. Benjamin would later suggest, "Indeed Christine, without you, probably none of this would have happened."[38] She also collaborated with medical researchers such as Alfred Kinsey. Jorgensen's celebrity was a double-edged sword. She capitalized on her fame by engaging in a very successful nightclub act and took meetings with many of the biggest names of her era. On the other hand, she learned that being a famous transgender person was not as good for her romantic prospects. Although she had several boyfriends over the subsequent years, she never married. She was denied the right to marry a man due to her male birth certificate.[39] After Christine's parents passed away in 1967, she moved to California, where she lived the rest of her life. She continued to perform until 1982 and passed away in 1989 from cancer at the age of sixty-two.[40] She left an enduring legacy as one of first advocates for a broader understanding of the notion that gender was not tied to biological sex.

In general, transgender men have received less publicity and notoriety than transgender women, largely because of their ability to "pass" as cisgender men. One well-known twentieth-century case is that of jazz musician Billy Tipton, who managed to conceal his birth sex from almost everyone in his life for over forty years. Tipton was born Dorothy Lucille Tipton in Oklahoma City on December 19, 1914, and was sent to live with an aunt in Kansas City upon her parents' divorce when she was four. In high school she studied piano and saxophone, and took the gender neutral name of Tippy Tipton.[41] She discovered early on that her opportunities to play in public would be very limited as a girl, so she began to dress as a man in 1934, binding her breasts and wearing a prosthetic penis. At first Tipton cross-dressed only when performing, but by 1940 Billy Lee Tipton was living full-time as a man with a common-law wife. A total of five different women would call themselves Mrs. Tipton over the next thirty years.[42]

Tipton worked steadily, if unspectacularly, as a jazz pianist for many years, first in other musicians' bands and, starting in 1951, with the Billy Tipton Trio in the state of Washington, where he had settled. The trio recorded two albums in the 1950s, selling a respectable 17,678 copies in 1957 alone. The Billy Tipton Trio was offered the lucrative position in 1958 as the house band for a new casino in Reno, Nevada, where they would have backed Liberace, but Billy declined the offer, perhaps fearing the greater renown the new position would entail. In the 1960s Tipton settled in Spokane with his fifth wife, Kitty, and their three adopted children. He told his wife that he had lost his virility and damaged his ribs in a car wreck years earlier, hence the binding and the inability to consummate their marriage.[43] The couple slept in separate beds, and their sex life was probably minimal. Tipton continued to perform into the 1970s, when his career was ended by arthritic fingers and changing musical tastes. Kitty and Billy split in 1981 and the boys lived with Billy from that point onward. For obvious reasons, Tipton avoided medical care, ignoring a bleeding ulcer until it killed him in 1989. It was only upon his death that his children and former wife learned about his anatomy. After his death, there were plenty of articles and one book written about his life.[44] Many speculated that his choice to live as a man was more about economic necessity than gender identity, but that is not known for certain.

At the dawn of the eighth decade of the twentieth century there was beginning to be a public acknowledgment of the lives of trans people. For instance, two of the leaders of the 1969 Stonewall riots were trans women. There were not, however, any transgender athletes of note at the time. That would change soon enough with a pioneering tennis player named Renée Richards and a couple of sport stars who would later become transgender celebrities.

6

EARLY TRANSGENDER ATHLETES

The first transgender athlete of note was a tennis player who took the name Renée Richards—Renée is French for "reborn"—after she transitioned. Renée was first born as Richard Raskind, and since she referred to herself as Dick in her pretransition years, I will, too. Dick Raskind grew up in an overachieving family; his mother, father, and older sister all preceded him into careers in medicine. Dick started wearing his sister's clothes at age six, and at eight or nine he was routinely venturing out into his Forest Heights neighborhood dressed as a girl. When dressed this way, Dick took the name Renée.[1] It was not unusual for Renée to spend two or three hours at a time wandering the streets, attending movies, or window shopping in her upscale surroundings. The young Raskind was a standout athlete in baseball and football, but it was when he started taking tennis lessons at age ten that he found his sport.[2] Dick won his first club championship tournament within a year of taking up the game. When Dick was a junior in high school, he won the Eastern States Boys Tennis Championship, and he repeated that victory as a senior.

One important revelation happened when Dick was in West Point, New York, for a tennis tournament. He was browsing a rack of books in the hotel stationery shop when he discovered one with the title *Man into Woman*, the story of Lili Elbe. Dick now realized that his fantasy about becoming Renée could actually come true. Dick followed in his father's footsteps by matriculating at Yale University. Both tennis and cross-dressing continued to be staples of the young Raskind's life. Dick reached the semifinals of the US national junior tourney during his freshman year, while Renée had her first sexual experience with a man. Richards felt strangely unfulfilled in both worlds.[3] As Dick progressed through Yale, he became the star of the tennis team, excelled as a student, and found himself a beautiful girlfriend. None of these achievements could keep him from fantasizing about becoming Renée. Upon graduation, Dick wanted to become a tennis professional; his parents pressed him to go to medical school, and he acquiesced.

For the next several years, Raskind balanced medicine, tennis, and transgender life. There were abortive periods of hormones and one close call with surgery. Marriage and fatherhood couldn't dim the siren call of Renée, and the marriage dissolved. Renée restarted hormones and finally had her long-delayed vaginoplasty, the medical term for gender reassignment surgery.[4] Although Renée returned to work as Dick after the surgery, she began to make plans to move to California. Renée changed all of her identification, then went out to California to interview. The interview went well, and in February 1976 Renée moved to Newport Beach. Although she had not been forthcoming about her past during the interview, it soon became necessary for her to open up to her colleagues. Her medical peers accepted her easily.[5] Tennis would be another matter.

Renée joined the John Wayne Tennis Club, at first playing only recreationally, but she soon decided to play in a tournament in La Jolla. The day after she won the tournament, a San Diego–based reporter called her up and confronted her with her past. At first she denied her history, but the reporter had too many details to ignore, and Renée finally admitted the truth. The cat was out of the bag. Although much of the world was in shock over the news, Renée got thousands of pieces of mail urging her to continue to play, so when she received an invitation to a tournament in New Jersey in August, she decided to accept. Twenty-one other women boycotted the tournament in protest. Although Renée had to endure a plague of reporters, she made it to the semifinals before losing.[6] The US Open was only weeks away.

The United States Tennis Association (USTA) and the Women's Tennis Association (WTA) refused to let Renée play at her old stomping grounds in Forest Heights unless she could pass a chromosome test. Renee did not take the test, nor did she quit. Instead, she spent the next few months playing in those tournaments that allowed her to play. Renée also decided to take to the legal courts, and she found a willing lawyer in the infamous Roy Cohn. In the summer of 1977 Renée won the right to compete against other women.[7] It was a precedent-setting victory for transgender athletes. Renée played in the 1977 US Open, losing to Virginia Wade in the first round; however, she and her doubles partner, Betty Stuart, reached the finals before losing to Martina Navratilova and Betty Stove. Renée continued to play until 1981, when she retired from professional play. She was ranked as high as 19th on the WTA rankings, but it was in doubles play that she truly shone. She and partner Ilie Nastase twice reached the semifinals of the US Open in mixed doubles.[8] Renée faced a cruel double standard on the courts: When she won, her opponents claimed she had an unfair advantage, but if she lost, it was said that she had tanked the match.

After Richards retired from active play, she coached Navratilova to two Wimbledon titles and was inducted into the USTA Eastern Tennis Hall of Fame in 2000. Later in life, Richards expressed a fair bit of regret, not over her decision to transition but about the consequences of doing so. She also stated that she didn't believe that trans women should be competing with other women. She claimed, "I know if I'd had surgery at the age of 22, and then at 24 went on the tour, no genetic woman in the world would have been able to come close to me. And so I've reconsidered my opinion. There is one thing that a transsexual woman unfortunately cannot expect to be allowed to do, and that is to play professional sports in her chosen field."[9] I doubt that Renée would have been as dominant as she claims. Although it is true that her height and strength would have given her an advantage over cisgender women, I am also convinced that transgender women are disadvantaged in terms of quickness with respect to other women. Richards stated in 1983 that "I was moving the skeleton of a man my size with the muscle mass appropriate to a woman of my size."[10] I believe it is this combination that results in the quickness disadvantage. There is a complex interaction of advantages and disadvantages when transgender athletes compete against cisgender female athletes, just as there is when any two different population groups compete against one another. It is foolhardy for Richards, or anyone else, to reflexively suggest that trans women will dominate sports simply because they have some advantages.

Renée Richards might have been the first openly transgender athlete of note, but other successful athletes of the period were secretly transgender. Most of the stories of these secretive trans athletes will never be known; however, two trans athletes from the period would go on to become celebrities in the twenty-first century. The first of these two athletes was given the name William Bruce Jenner at birth, and I will use the name Bruce when I describe her pretransition life. Jenner was born on October 28, 1949. In high school, he was a star on the football and basketball teams, but his true passion was the pole vault. Jenner's dad made a vaulting pit for him in the backyard, and Jenner's skill and determination resulted in a Connecticut state championship in the event. The pole vault was only one of several track and field events in which Jenner was successful, a precursor to his ultimate athletic success as a decathlete.[11]

The decathlon is an athletics competition consisting of ten separate events spread out over two days. The events on the first day are the 100 meter dash, the long jump, the shot put, the high jump, and the 400 meter dash. After resting overnight, the athletes come back the next day to compete in the 110 meter hurdles, discus throw, pole vault, javelin throw, and 1500 meter race. Each event is scored against a point table, and the points are added up for total score that determines the final placing of each competitor. The scoring system means that rather than compete directly against one another, the decathletes are competing against a scoring table.[12] The indirect competition and the grueling nature of the event combine to create a feeling of comradery within the multievent fraternity. All the men who test themselves over the ten-event competition have a bond that no one else can quite fathom.

Jenner went to college on a football scholarship but was more successful on the track team. His coach at Graceland encouraged him to tackle the decathlon, and Jenner took to the challenge immediately, scoring a school record 6,991 points in his very first attempt in the spring of 1970 as part of the Drake Relays. Later that spring Jenner would finish third in the National Association of Intercollegiate Athletics (NAIA) national championship decathlon. By 1972 Jenner had improved enough to qualify for the US Olympic Trials in Eugene, Oregon. After the first day he was in eleventh place, but Jenner was always strong over the last four events, and he started to move up as the second day went along. He had moved up to fifth by the start of the 1500, and he used a massive personal best of 4:16.9 to claim third place—and one of the slots on the US Olympic team.[13] It was a dream come true for the twenty-two-year-old college senior to make the Olympic team, but the games in Munich took a nightmare turn on September 5, just prior to the scheduled start of the decathlon. Eleven Israeli athletes and coaches were taken prisoner by the Palestinian terror group Black September. Wrestling coach Moshe Weinberg and weightlifter Yossef Romano were shot early in the attack as they fought back against the intruders. The following day the terrorists killed the remaining nine Israeli hostages when the German police tried to rescue them. Five of the eight terrorists were killed in the attempted rescue and the other three were captured.[14]

The decathlon was delayed by the attack and the funeral, but eventually held. Jenner finished tenth with a score of 7,722 points. Jenner decided that he would devote the next four years of his life to becoming the best decathlete he could. After marriage and graduation, Jenner moved to San Jose, California, in the spring of 1973 to begin his quest for gold in Montreal.[15] In those years San Jose was a training mecca, especially for throwers. Future discus world record holders John Powell and Mac Wilkins as well as world-class shot putter Al Feuerbach all wound up there. Much later on, Jenner would call her quest for decathlon greatness "The Grand Diversion."[16] Jenner's first year in San Jose did not go well as he dealt with injuries and had trouble adapting to his new life.

By 1974, however, Jenner saw the fruits of his increased training. He scored 8,240 points to open his season at the Kansas Relays; no one had scored more since Russian Nikolay Avilov's world record of 8,454 to win the 1972 Olympics. Later in the year, in Estonia, Jenner would score 8,308 to beat Munich silver medalist Leonid Lytvynenko by more than 450 points. At year's end, *Track and Field News* would rank Jenner as the number one decathlete in the entire world. In two years he had vaulted from number ten in the Olympics to number one in the world.[17] He had arrived at the top of his event. Years later, I had the opportunity to ask Jenner about this remarkable improvement and the answer I was given is: "I was not a speed-gifted athlete like 2016 gold medalist Ashton Eaton, so I had to work at other events in order to gain points. One way was to work on endurance. In the off season I would run five miles twice a day totaling up to seventy miles per week."[18] This running would be part of six-to-eight-hour training days that Jenner put in, week after week, for multiple years. Jenner's weight routine was to work one day on upper body, one day on lower body, and rest from weights every third day. As the season approached, Jenner would cut down on the running distance and increase the amount of speed work, until he was training more like a sprinter for the last six to eight weeks before the big race. It was this combination training that allowed Jenner to maximize speed event points without sacrificing either the strength to succeed in throwing events or the endurance to be good at the 1500 meters.[19]

Jenner upped the ante in the 1975 United States versus Russia meet. During the first day, Jenner put up personal bests in the 100 meters, long jump, and high jump, finishing the day in second place to another American, Fred Dixon. Despite standing second, Jenner was on world record pace due to his excellence in the second-day events. Jenner not only broke the world record but became the first man to ever score 8,500 points. Jenner was once again ranked number one in the world for 1975, setting him up as the favorite for the gold medal in Montreal.[20] The first hurdle was to place in the top three at the United States Olympic Trials. It is relatively easy to not make a legal mark in several of the ten disciplines, and a zero score in any event would doom Jenner's gold medal attempt before it began. Jenner was also dealing with an injured tendon on his throwing hand—Jenner is left-handed—that prevented him from putting the shot well. Additionally, Dixon had blossomed into a medal threat and would battle Jenner for a spot on the team. It would seem prudent to play it safe at the trials in order to make the team. That's not the way it worked out.

By the end of the first day, Jenner was in third place, 141 points behind Dixon and 72 points behind his record pace from August 1975. Given his second-day excellence, Jenner was sitting pretty for the team. He knew that he could be 150 to 200 points down to a competitor and make it up over those four events. And his opponents knew it, too, putting enormous pressure on them to score points early in the decathlon knowing that Jenner's strength was at the end. And that is exactly how the trials worked out. Although Jenner's pole vault was nothing special, he uncorked enormous throws in the discus and javelin, and ran a terrific time of 4:16 for the 1500; his resulting total of 8,538 just edged out his previous world record.[21] The Montreal Olympic Games were just six weeks away. Although Jenner's life at the time was entirely devoted to the task at hand, she would later say, "[I]t was all just a game. Just sports."[22]

The Olympic decathlon started well for Jenner as he ran an autotimed 10.94 hundred meters, marginally better than Dixon and three-tenths of a second faster than the defending champion Avilov. West Germany's Guido Kratschmer was the fastest of all entrants at 10.66, putting him into the mix for the gold. Avilov won the long jump with 24′ 8″, Kratschmer jumped 24′ 3″, and Jenner had his second-longest jump ever at 23′ 8.25″, but Dixon jumped 22′ 8″, two feet short of his personal best, effectively knocking him out of medal contention. After two events Kratschmer led, Jenner was sixth, and Avilov was eighth. Jenner's injured hand had healed by this time, and he put the shot over 50 feet for a personal best to make up ground on Kratschmer and Avilov, who both throw in the 48-foot range. After three events Kratschmer still led, but Jenner had moved up to second while Avilov was in fifth. Both Kratschmer and Jenner cleared 6′ 8″ in the high jump, but Avilov had a monster day, topping 7 feet and displacing Jenner for second place. Jenner sat third while the German continued to lead. Jenner ran a very strong 400, clocking 47.5—half a second ahead of his two main rivals. Jenner remained in third, but only 35 points separated the three athletes at the end of the first day. If Jenner had his normal second day, it wouldn't be close.

The next morning Avilov won the hurdles, moving into the lead almost a hundred points ahead of Jenner. Jenner unleashed a monster throw in the discus to win the competition and move into second, only nine points behind Avilov. Kratschmer also threw the discus well and was only 27 points down on the Russian. Jenner equaled his personal best in the pole vault, crushing his rivals, and moved into the lead by 66 points. Given his strength in the last two events, it was apparent he had just won the gold medal. Kratschmer passed Avilov, but only 10 points separated them. Jenner threw the javelin 224′ 10″, virtually ensuring a new world record and ballooning his lead to almost 200 points. Kratshmer put more ground on Avilov in the battle for second. The Russian Lytvynenko was well down in the overall standings, but was a superb 1500 meter runner for a multievent guy, and he opened up a good lead by the 800 meter mark of the final event. Undeterred, Jenner almost ran Lytvynenko down in the last lap and recorded another personal best of 4:12, giving him a new world and Olympic record of 8,618 points.

Kratschmer finished second with 8,411 points while Avilov wound up in third with 8,369 points.[23]

Jenner was handed a small American flag and ran with it on his victory lap, setting a trend that would become the standard for medal winners everywhere. Jenner had decided that Montreal would be his last track meet, and he was so sure of his intentions that he left his vaulting poles in the stadium. They were a nuisance to travel with, and Jenner knew that he would never need them again.[24] Jenner went on to Wheaties box fame and fortune, a lucrative broadcast and speaking career, and he lived happily ever after. Well, not quite on that last part. All the while Jenner had been living the American dream, he had been dealing with a terrible secret. Bruce Jenner, the world's greatest athlete and the perfect example of virility, was transgender. He had started cross-dressing at ten years old, sneaking clothes out of his mother's closet and using one of her scarfs to simulate hair longer than his brush cut. At first, his mother's shoes were too big, so he used his older sister's shoes. Once dressed, Jenner would go for walks in the neighborhood after dark. The feeling Jenner had at those moments was a sense of belonging.[25]

Nearly forty years after the glory of Montreal, Jenner would undergo a very public transition to become Caitlyn Jenner, one of the biggest transgender celebrities of all time. After her transition, I had the opportunity to interview Jenner for this book. Among other things, I asked Caitlyn if she thought her gender dysphoria had any role in her athletic success. She replied that success in sports depends upon God-given athletic talent combined with what she called the mental side of the sport. She said that the fortitude to perform well was also a God-given talent. Jenner witnessed many athletes who possessed either the talent or the determination to perform well, but few who possessed both the physical and mental traits needed to be a champion. Although not denigrating her physical talents, Jenner said that her determination to succeed at sports was her greatest asset. She cites the fact that before Montreal her personal bests in the ten events totaled fewer than 8,700 points, but over the two days of the 1976 Olympic decathlon she managed to score 8,634 points. A large part of Jenner's determination came from the fact that she suffered both from dyslexia and from gender dysphoria. She felt a constant inferiority as a result of her twin maladies, and success in sports was her way of overcoming her feelings of inadequacy. She felt like she needed to prove her manhood, and this drove her harder than anyone else. She says that she is grateful for her disadvantages in life, as they fueled her athletic success.[26] It is not unreasonable to suggest that without her transgender makeup Jenner might never had become an Olympic champion.

Caitlyn Jenner was not the only champion athlete from the period to later come out as transgender. The other secretive transgender athletic hero of the era is a British cyclist who earned fame first as Robert Millar and later as Philippa York. Sticking with my convention for this chapter, I will refer to York's cycling triumphs using her birth name. Robert Millar was born in Glasgow on September 13, 1958, and by the age of five he understood that he was different from other children. Millar's epiphany came at age five when he and his classmates were asked to line up on one side of the playground or the other depending on whether they were a boy or girl. Millar knew that he was moving to the wrong side with the boys, "but there was no way to communicate that."[27] Instead of focusing on his gender dysphoria, he put his energy into sports, and soon found that he excelled at cycling. As Robert Millar, he established himself as a leading Scottish cyclist in 1976 and later won the British amateur road race championship in 1978. Millar's small stature made him perfect for climbing, and he moved to France in 1979 to pursue a career as a cyclist. Millar turned pro in 1980 with the Peugeot cycling team, and it wasn't long before he became one of the best mountain cyclists in the world.

In 1983 Millar debuted in the Tour de France, winning a stage in the Pyrenees and finishing fourteenth overall and third in the mountain classification. It was an impressive debut on the grandest stage of professional cycling. In 1984 Millar would be better, not just winning another Pyrenean stage, but—even more impressively—winning the polka-dot jersey awarded to the king of the mountains. Millar also finished fourth overall behind three of cycling's greatest legends: Lauren Fignon, Bernard Hinault, and Greg Lemond. Millar was the first English-speaking cyclist to win the mountain classification, and his performance at the Tour that year stamped his as one of the world's best cyclists of his time.[28] The year 1985 would see the most infamous chapter in Millar's cycling career. He was leading the Vuelta a España at the start of the penultimate day of cycling but suffered a flat tire at the foot of the second of three climbs that day. As Millar worked his way back up to the leaders, Spanish climber Pedro Delgado, who had started the day six minutes behind Millar, launched a breakaway with José Recio. By the time Millar caught the lead group, Delgado was seven minutes ahead of the pack. Rather than trying to chase Delgado, the rest of the pack was content to allow a Spaniard to win the tour, and none of Millar's teammates were in the pack to let him know of the true situation. Millar was under the impression he had won the Vuelta until he crossed the finish line. The last day was a ceremonial ride, and there was nothing Millar could do. The scandal became known as the stolen Vuelta. Despite being incensed over the trickery, Millar returned to the Vuelta in 1986 and repeated his runner-up finish.[29]

In 1987 Millar was second in the Giro d'Italia; no British rider has ever matched that feat. This meant that Millar had reached the podium in all three of the world's great cycling tours. He was to that point the greatest British rider ever, and still sits third on the all-time list of British cyclists.[30] Although Millar would never again reach such heights, he remained one of the world's best climbers and a formidable presence in the world of cycling throughout the rest of the 1980s and into the 1990s. Millar was famously reserved and private in his personal life. He would marry a Frenchwoman in 1985, although none of his family or teammates attended the wedding. The couple had a son named Edward, but the marriage did not last.[31] Millar met his current partner, Linda, in the early 1990s, and they had a daughter named Liddy.[32]

Around the dawn of the twenty-first century, Millar disappeared from public life altogether. Although there were rumors of a gender transition, these were generally dismissed, and it was assumed that the former great cyclist had simply become a hermit. It wasn't until 2017 that Millar appeared publicly as Philippa York, confirming that she was indeed transgender.[33]

These transition stories will be covered later, but for now I'd like to mention that Jenner met the openly transgender Renée Richards at a now-forgotten celebrity event in 1987.[34] I asked Caitlyn about the meeting, and she noted that she was aware that the two shared a common issue but "I never could have said, 'Hey Renée, we need to talk.'"[35] Despite her inability to open up to the tennis star, Jenner said she had great admiration for Richards's courage.

There was another connection between Jenner and Richards. Both are left-handed. It is an interesting coincidence, as many people have compared southpaws to transgender people. Sociologically, both groups have faced discrimination for their differences. Only a hundred years ago, left-handed people were forced to use their right hands, even to the point of having their left hand bound. The Romans quite literally thought lefties were evil, evinced by the fact that our word *sinister* evolved from the Roman word for left. Beyond sociology, the left-handed nature of both athletes is interesting because being a southpaw is an advantage in many sports, including tennis. Obviously, Renée Richards possessed this advantage whether playing against men before her transition or facing women opponents afterward. No one would have suggested that she be forbidden to play because of her left-handed advantage, but many suggested that whatever advantages she possessed as a transgender athlete should have prevented her from competing. There were many who predicted that a flood of transgender athletes would follow in the wake of Renée Richards, driving "normal" women out of sports.[36] That didn't happen, of course. In fact, there was only a trickle of other trans athletes in the twentieth century, and I will cover a few memorable cases soon. By contrast, the 1980s and 1990s would provide a stage for some of the most significant events in the history of intersex athletes. One of the major catalysts for these changes was an intersex athlete who would, much later in life, become one of my friends. This athlete would change the way gender-variant athletes would be treated, and her story is very much worth telling.

7

NOT THE END OF SEX TESTING

Throughout the 1970s, the Barr body test continued to be used to determine eligibility for women's sport, but there were scientists who were opposed to the practice, realizing that biological sex was far more complex than the presence or absence of sex chromatin. One of these scientists was Finnish geneticist Albert de la Chapelle. While he did believe in using a scientific method to separate male from female athletes, de la Chapelle did not think the Barr body test was the correct method.[1] Despite his persistent opposition to the use of sex chromatin in gender testing, de la Chapelle made little impact on Albert de Merode and other leaders of the IOC's medical commission. What de la Chapelle and the other opponents of the test needed was a case they could rally around, and eventually they found one in the form of Spanish hurdler María José Martínez-Patiño.

In a 2015 presentation to the IOC, Eric Vilain (discussed in chapter 2) stated that he felt the history of intersex athletes in sport could be divided into eras that corresponded with the rise of three intersex women. María was the first of Eric's three women. Until María's story came to light, the human cost of sex testing was not appreciated by many people. Once people saw what befell María, attitudes toward intersex women began to change. María José Martínez-Patiño was born on July 10, 1961, and raised in the northwestern corner of Spain in a region known as Galicia. The region has some lovely scenery and hosts the world-famous Cathedral de Santiago in Santiago de Compestella. The cathedral is said to house the remains of St. James and is the primary destination of El Camino de Santiago, also known as the Way of St. James. Thousands of pilgrims walk to the cathedral every year from several different starting places in Spain, France, and Portugal. The region is also somewhat remote, and the Romans quite literally thought of it as the end of the world. In fact, the finger of land in Galicia jutting farthest out into the Atlantic is still known as Finisterra.

María had "an affinity for running and jumping" as a child, and she gravitated into athletics, where she found her greatest talent lay in the 100 meter hurdles. She was named to the Spanish team for the very first IAAF World Track and Field Championships held in Helsinki Finland in 1983. Although the IAAF had hosted many important meets prior to 1983, there was no true world athletics championships except for the Olympic Games, which were held every four years. Initially the IAAF world championships were intended to be held every four years, but the meet proved so popular with athletes and fans that starting with the 1991 meet in Tokyo, the event was held every two years. Additionally, the IAAF decided to host an indoor world meet beginning in 1985 in Paris. The indoor meet is also held biennially. In 1983 the IAAF used the buccal smear test at the inaugural championship in order to determine female eligibility, and María passed hers.[2]

The Barr body test, like most other tests, can result in false negatives or false positives. These false readings in the buccal smear test can be explained by taking a closer look at the testing methodology. After the cells were obtained from the cheek swab, they were smeared on a slide, then stained and observed under a microscope. If the cells were properly stained, the Barr body would show up as a black region on the cell nucleus. Unfortunately, not every cell would stain correctly. In fact, of cells with two or more X chromosomes, only 30 percent or so had the characteristic appearance.[3] Depending on the staining procedure, the percentage of cells in which sex chromatin is visible can range from a low of 9 percent to a high of 53 percent.[4] Hence, in a sample of fifty cells out of the mouth of a female athlete, one would expect to find five to twenty-five cells in which the Barr body would show up well. This would constitute a positive test for sex chromatin. There are, however, other potential causes for black regions in the cell nucleus, so it was possible that someone without two X chromosomes would be read as having a positive test. Approximately 2 percent of male cells have a dense chromatin that resembles a Barr body.[5] If a female athlete failed the Barr body test, a more rigorous test was performed in order to verify the result. False positives faced no double-check, as the default outcome for female athletes was to register positive for sex chromatin. Just as we will never know how many women were excluded from sport by the Barr body test, we will never know how many athletes with a Y chromosome tested positive for sex chromatin and were allowed to compete. US swimmer Kirsten Wengler registered a false negative test for sex chromatin in 1985. Further testing revealed that her negative was caused by the presence of an unusual protein.[6] As it would turn out, Martínez-Patiño was allowed to compete in the 1983 world championships due to a false positive in her Barr body test. She wound up running 13.78, a time that would prove to be the best performance in her career.[7] María was twenty-two years old.

When Martínez-Patiño competed in the 1985 World Student Games in Kobe, Japan, she forgot her femininity card at home and had to be retested in Japan. This time she failed the buccal smear test. The day after she failed the Barr body test, María was taken to the local hospital for a "sophisticated karyotype analysis" and was told that the "results would take months to reach [her] sports federation in Spain." The Spanish team doctor told her to feign an injury and withdraw from the competition. María complied, spending most of the next week alone in her dorm room "feeling a sadness I could not share." That fall María received the news that she had a 46,XY karyotype. Almost any other person in the world would have quit athletics at this point, but Martínez-Patiño possessed a will far greater than the vast majority of humanity. She knew that she was a woman "with breasts and a vagina"[8] and saw no reason not to contest the Spanish indoor meet held a few months later. The Spanish team doctor felt differently and asked her not to compete. She refused the request and won the hurdle race. In return, he leaked her negative sex chromatin test to the world. The results were catastrophic for María. Her sports scholarship was revoked, she was expelled from the athletic dormitory, and her fiancée left her.

As bad as the fallout was for María, it proved to be a turning point in the battle to replace the Barr body test. Albert de la Chapelle and others reached out to Martínez-Patiño and offered her their assistance should she decide to protest the decision.[9] And protest she did. A Spanish professor helped María to put her thoughts and data into a compelling form, and she petitioned to be allowed to return to the sport she loved.

Although the IOC was initially not inclined to take María or her appeal seriously, the IAAF was another matter. At the time, the chairman of the IAAF's medical commission was a Swedish pathologist named Arne Ljungqvist, who was born in 1931, and grew up in Bromma, a suburb of Stockholm. Ljungqvist enjoyed early success in athletics and soon specialized in the high jump. At the time, the dominant technique in the event was the scissors—the lack of a suitable landing pit necessitated coming down on one's feet. Despite what would be considered inferior technique today, Ljungqvist cleared 2.00 meters in 1951 at the age of twenty, becoming only the fifth Swede over that barrier. The following year he was selected for the Swedish team that would compete in the 1952 Olympic Games in Helsinki, Finland. Ljungqvist had a poor outing in the games, but a few weeks later beat both the silver and bronze medalists in a competition in which he notched his all-time highest leap of 2.01 meters. Knee problems forced him from the sport the following year, and he threw his energy into a nascent medical career. In 1952 Ljungqvist won a place at the Karolinska Institute in Stockholm, one of the world's leading medical centers. He earned his MD and PhD at the Karolinska, specializing in pathology.[10] Ljungqvist would later become the head of the cancer program and the vice dean at the institute.

Ljungqvist had ceased to compete or train once he entered medical school, but he maintained an interest in athletics. In 1971 he was elected to the board of the Swedish Athletic Association[11] and before long became president of the organization. Ljungqvist's medical background, interest in sports administration, and prior sporting history led to his appointment to the IAAF board and later to the IOC medical commission. In 1986 Ljungqvist was a vice president of the IAAF and the chairman of its medical commission. He was also a member of the IOC medical commission but held much more clout with the IAAF than with the IOC. He had been opposed to the sole use of sex chromatin to determine the sex of athletes since the early 1980s.

In part due to the efforts of de la Chapelle and Ljungqvist, the IOC medical commission convened the first ever Working Group on Gender Verification in 1988.[12] This first meeting of the group would start a tradition; some form of the group would continue to meet as the need arose over the next thirty years to tackle various issues pertaining to gender-variant athletes and sport. The IOC also started the tradition of augmenting medical commission personnel with outside experts for these meetings. Joe Leigh Simpson and Kurt Götz Wurster joined de la Chapelle as invited outside experts. There was no support for the continued use of the buccal smear from the assembled experts, but the IOC, under the direction of Prince Albert, would not agree to any changes at this time. Frustrated with the IOC's response, Ljungqvist decided the IAAF could do better. Ljungqvist organized an IAAF workshop on femininity held in 1990 at the Monte Carlo home of the organization.[13] This workshop featured experts from around the globe, including Myron Genel, a Yale endocrinologist whom I would meet in 2015. Several recommendations came out of the meeting, but the most important was the abandonment of the Barr body test as the means to determine eligibility for women's sport. Instead, the IAAF suggested that by combining visual inspections as part of drug testing—in order to use urinalysis effectively in drug testing, the official must watch the urine leave the athlete's body and enter the testing cup—and mandatory health screening for all athletes, the goal of keeping masquerading men out of women's sport could be achieved.

This new policy was tested at the Tokyo World Championships in 1991 and quickly proved to be problematic. Canadian racewalker Ann Peel was not the only one who felt the visual component of the mandated health screen was a "step back in time for women,"[14] and many saw the new rules as a return of the nude parades. In 1992 the IAAF decided to abandon compulsory sex testing at any championship event. Instead the organization decided to test athletes on the basis of suspicion. An athlete who was deemed suspicious by virtue of phenotype or high T was given the choice of undergoing differential diagnostic testing for a DSD or retiring from the sport. The IAAF continued to use this approach until 2009, when it was undone by a young South African runner. There were many who touted this shift by the IAAF as the end of gender testing, but the reality was quite different. To be clear, the IAAF had merely ended the policy of compulsory testing for all women. With genital inspection being an implicit component of drug testing (at least for those women who were suspected of manifesting a DSD) and with the obvious physical manifestations of higher testosterone levels (such as a deeper voice, facial hair, etc.), there were still plenty of female athletes who underwent the modified form of gender testing.

What, then, was the fate of those athletes who were deemed not appropriate for women's sport? Although there are no public records from the time, it is not difficult to determine the probable course of action. Rather than ban women with XY DSDs from sport, the IAAF recommended that those women with Y chromosomes and whose bodies were sensitive to testosterone undergo gonadectomy This pattern was documented in a paper published twenty years later.[15] And what of the women who decided to have their testes removed and continued to compete? Again, there are no women who publicly acknowledged that they had gonadectomies, but it isn't difficult to guess a few cases from this period.

There was a middle-distance athlete from the 1990s whom I will call Marta. Marta ran some fast times and then she had a period of unexplained absence from the sport before regaining her old form. Marta continued to be successful in the sport for several years. I admit that the following is speculative, but it is based on careful research, analysis, and interviews. I believe that Marta was flagged as potentially being intersex and then tested, confirming the presence of a Y chromosome and testes, and the absence of complete androgen insensitivity syndrome. I also believe that Marta had her testes removed and that her surgery led to a prolonged absence and a slow recovery. Of course, there are many who might suggest Marta simply took a long time to recover from some unspecified injury, but I can find no record of any such injury. I remember that there was much discussion about Marta inside the running community in the 1990s. Although I knew far less about intersex conditions then than I know now, I remember telling my friends that it was important to understand that Marta had been born the way she was, and there shouldn't be any shame attached to the circumstances of one's birth. I have also had the opportunity over the past few years to speak to many women who competed against Marta. It was obvious to all of them that Marta was not like other women, but at the time Marta's competitors did not understand the implications of being intersex.

Let's examine the IAAF policy a little more closely. First off, prophylactic gonadectomy is often recommended for intersex women with undescended testes as they face a higher cancer risk than other women.[16] Second, gonadectomy was at the time the recommended standard of care for XY women with female gender identity. Hence, it is certainly understandable that the IAAF recommended the surgery to those women with XY DSDs. In addition to being the standard for the time, the surgery would reduce testosterone levels down into the female range and would create greater competitive balance in the women's category. Lastly, it should be noted that the IAAF never required anyone to have surgery. Seen, however, from twenty-five years later, there are problems with the 1990s era policy. A recommendation from a doctor is a powerful inducement especially for a young woman from a developing country. There are several drug regimens that can safely and effectively reduce testosterone and would be one option presented today. In their 2018 DSD policy, the IAAF would add an athlete ombudsperson into the mix and this would have been valuable in the nineties as well.

Unlike the IAAF, the IOC remained committed to the continued use of compulsory chromosome testing for female athletes, although it too abandoned the Barr body test as the preferred method of determining the chromosomal makeup of athletes. Instead the IOC switched to using a method called polymerase chain reaction testing or PCR.[17] The PCR test was a more sophisticated method of testing chromosome pattern than the Barr body test. The PCR test was designed to amplify the SRY gene on the Y chromosome so that a positive result would indicate the presence of the Y chromosome. The PCR test was, however, subject to false positives. It could be contaminated with Y chromosomes from the tester; as a result, all tests are performed by female lab technicians.[18] PCR testing was used in the winter and summer games in 1992 in Albertville, France, and Barcelona, Spain. One of the twelve positive PCR tests (out of 2,406 female athletes) at the Barcelona games was a false positive. Six other positives were found to result from the activation of a different gene than the SRY, leaving five athletes who actually possessed a Y chromosome. These five athletes were requested to undergo a gynecological exam. Four of the five submitted to the exam and were allowed to compete as XY women. Presumably, all four had some form of AIS and/or had already undergone gonadectomy prior to the games. The fifth intersex woman was a Bolivian athlete named Sandra Cortez, who chose to retire from the games rather than undergo further examination. There were some who suggested that Cortez's withdrawal indicated that she was a man masquerading as a woman;

others pointed out that Cortez was the biological mother of three children.[19]

Up until the 1990s, the summer and winter games were always held in the same year. It was decided that it would be best to separate the winter and summer games by two years, and so there was both a 1992 winter games in Albertville and a 1994 winter games in Lillehammer, Norway. The gender testing in Lillehammer was complicated by the refusal of the Norwegian government and scientists to cooperate. The testing was eventually performed by the same French group that had done the 1992 testing in Albertville.[20] There were no adverse findings from 1994, so the IOC continued testing in 1996 at the summer games in Atlanta.

In the summer of 1996, 3,387 female athletes were tested at the Atlanta games using the PCR method, there were eight positive results. Seven of the eight were determined to have either partial or complete AIS, and one athlete had 5-ARD. The athletes with AIS were all allowed to compete. The athlete with 5-ARD had already had a gonadectomy, so she too was allowed to compete.[21]

The final Olympic Games to use the PCR method were the winter games in 1998 in Nagano, Japan. No positive tests were reported. In 1999 the IOC finally gave up the notion that compulsory chromosome testing was an appropriate method to determine eligibility for women's sport, although, like the IAAF, the IOC reserved the right to test selected individuals.[22] As the twenty-first century dawned, there were no longer blanket rejections of intersex women from sports. Instead, organizations such as the IOC and the IAAF were looking a little more closely at the individual intersex condition possessed by each woman and determining if it was appropriate for each athlete to be allowed into women's sport.

The turn of the century also brought changing attitudes toward the presence of transgender athletes in women's competition. Renée Richards had been allowed to compete in women's sport in the 1970s because she had achieved legal recognition as female. There were fears among sporting officials—and among female athletes—that Richards would be the first of a wave of transgender athletes who would take over women's sport. There was also a growing recognition that the surgery and hormone therapy transgender women undertook caused them to lose many of their previous sporting advantages. Endocrinologists such as Louis Gooren of Amsterdam had observed significant changes in transgender patients, and this clinical experience would prove useful in the coming years. Gooren's clinic was one of the first to actively assist trans people in the quest to become more like others of their target sex.[23]

Although the flood of transgender athletes did not materialize, there was a trickle of trans athletes by the dawn of the twenty-first century, and I'd like to take a look at a few of these early pioneers now.

The first is American golfer Charlotte Wood, who enjoyed brief success at the amateur level of her chosen sport in 1987, six years after she underwent gender confirmation surgery. Wood placed third in the Senior Women's Amateur Championship before reaching the semifinals of the US Women's Mid-Amateur tournament. She would not compete again in women's golf.[24] First the United States Golf Association (USGA) and then the Ladies Professional Golf Association (LPGA) inserted female at birth clauses into their entry forms, and, unlike Renée Richards, Wood never challenged these policies in court.

Although Wood was only a minor blip on the radar, it was not long before a young Thai athlete would make a much larger impact on the world's consciousness. The sport of Muay Thai or Thai boxing, which combines Western-style boxing with liberal use of the elbows, knees, and shins, is one of the most popular sports in Thailand. The reverence for Muay Thai extends beyond mere sport, as the rigorous training required by aspirants to success has religious overtones as well. Thus, successful fighters are admired for both spiritual and athletic reasons. In 1981 a young boy named Parinya Charoenphol was born into a nomadic family in the Chiang Mai Province. He was delicate and feminine, and, like many effeminate boys, was the victim of much bullying when he was young. The bullying stopped after the child turned twelve and fought his first Muay Thai bout. He entered the ring hungry for the prize money, largely because he dreamed of saving enough for gender confirmation surgery. He easily won that first fight, and, with his abundant talent revealed, he entered a training camp for young boys aspiring to become famous fighters.[25] As a teenager, the young boxer started to visit with the local *kathoey*, learning about makeup and other ways to become more feminine. She took the feminine name of Nong Toom and started to wear makeup in the ring. Nong Toom fought her first bout in Bangkok in February 1998 at the major Muay Thai arena called the Lumipini Boxing Stadium, defeating her chagrined opponent.[26] This deeply outraged the traditional Muay Thai establishment, since women were not even allowed into the boxing ring, let alone to fight. To Thai men, Muay Thai is more than just a sport, it is a sacred tradition. But Nong Toom didn't just fight—she won. Often employing her trademark move called Crushing Medicine, which involved jumping high into the air and then brining her elbow down upon the head of her opponent, she continued to pile up victories—twenty out of twenty-two fights. She would often kiss her vanquished foe as he lay helpless before her.[27]

Although the stodgy old men may not have taken to Nong Toom, the Thai public was another matter. Despite the fact that many Thai have mixed feelings about the *kathoey*, the sight of one in the ring beating up on the men she faced was irresistible. Nong Toom soon developed a large following and established a pervasive media presence. She became a national celebrity of the highest order.[28] Nong Toom saved her money well, and by 1999 she had enough for surgery. She was becoming less effective in the ring as a result of her hormone therapy, and she retired from boxing after her surgery to become an actress and singer. In 2003 the film *Beautiful Boxer* was made about her life. She found success in her new life, but the allure of Muay Thai remained with her. She has since started up two schools to train young fighters and has occasionally stepped back into the ring. She has had both exhibition and more serious fights with women boxers and with one man since 2006.[29]

Another early pioneer was a Canadian transgender woman named Michelle Dumaresq who competed in the sport of downhill mountain biking. Dumaresq was cycling on the series of amazingly beautiful trails along the north shore of Vancouver, British Columbia, in 2001 when she encountered a group of top women mountain bikers who were making a film called *Dirt Divas*. Impressed by Dumaresq's ability, the other riders invited her to be part of their film and also suggested that she might want to try racing.[30] The other women had no inkling what would be the result of their encouragement. From the beginning, Dumaresq was open about the fact that she was transgender; she had undergone surgery in 1996 and had been on hormones even before her surgery. Dumaresq competed in a race called Bear Mountain in May 2001, winning the novice division in a time that was faster than the winner of the women's pro category. Naturally this caused something of an uproar. The initial reaction was to ask her to quit racing, but then Canadian cycling officials huddled with the world governing body, the International Cycling Union (UCI), and decided that she would be allowed to compete in the women's category; she was, after all, legally, hormonally, and anatomically female. In April 2002 she was granted a license to race in the women's professional category.[31]

Three weeks later, she entered her first pro race and finished third. She won her second race by ten seconds, and protest ensued. A petition was circulated asking for her disqualification. She has said, "I have found that as a trans person it's acceptable to compete but don't you dare win. Well I did just that."[32] Despite the protests, she was allowed to continue racing, and she went on to win the 2002 Canada Cup series, which qualified her for the national team. She managed to place 24th at the World Mountain Bike Championships in September despite some issues with her bike. She represented Canada at both the 2003 and 2004 World Championships with her highest placing of 17th coming in the 2004 race, which was held in France. In 2006 she was once again crowned Canadian champion, but the second-place finisher donned a shirt reading "100% pure woman champ" while on the podium, causing quite a stir. The woman was suspended, but only during the off-season, meaning her punishment was a token slap on the wrist. Michelle's last race was in 2006 when she won the UCI Masters World Championship.[33] She lives quietly today, eschewing the spotlight that she never sought.

In 2002 Arne Ljungqvist took over the reins of the IOC's medical commission, and one the earliest conundrums he faced was the question of how to deal with transgender athletes. In response to the questions he faced, Ljungqvist decided to convene a symposium in 2003 devoted to the transgender athlete question. Ljungqvist invited many of the same experts who had been present at the 1990 IAAF conference he chaired. The work and opinions of Louis Gooren were highly regarded by the group, which codified Gooren's suggestions into rules that became known as the Stockholm consensus,[34] after the meeting's location in Ljungvist's hometown. The Stockholm consensus, adopted by the IOC in 2004, required transgender women who wished to compete in the female category to undergo gonadectomy, two years of post-surgical hormones, and to obtain legal recognition as women by their home country. Although the IOC was not the first sporting organization to accept transgender athletes, its rule change was a groundbreaking event. Many other sporting organizations followed the IOC's footsteps in the forthcoming years, implementing rules that were essentially identical to the Stockholm consensus regulations.

There was also a substantial amount of backlash directed at the IOC and other organizations that opened the doors for transgender athletes. In a repeat of the dire prophecies that accompanied the advent of Renée Richards in the 1970s, there were many who said that the 2004 IOC decision would mark the end of women's sport. Despite these doomsday prophecies, no openly transgender athletes competed in the 2004 Olympic Games. Neither have there been any in subsequent Olympic Games all the way up to and including the 2018 winter games held in PyeongChang, South Korea.[35] There were, however, a small group of highly publicized, if not utterly dominant, transgender athletes who competed in their chosen sports in the years following the adoption of the Stockholm consensus. I was one of the new wave of transgender athletes who began to compete after 2004.

8

JOANNA'S STORY

Although many transgender athletes have been more successful on the playing fields, I have become well known for my analysis of transgender athletic performance. I would not, however, have turned my analytic gifts toward the performance of trans athletes had I not become one myself. Hence it is probably worthwhile for the reader to learn more about me. And if I am going to relate my personal story, I should probably start at the beginning, a beginning that was pretty much like everyone else's start in life: My parents had sex and I was conceived. I hope it was good for them, because it certainly was good for me. I was born in a small town in Ontario called Parry Sound, which sits on beautiful Georgian Bay, a tranquil portion of Lake Huron, one of the Great Lakes. The town is approximately one hundred miles north of Toronto; *Sports Illustrated* described the place as a lovely summer resort, but one of the last places on earth one would want to spend a winter, in a piece on the town's most famous native, hockey player Bobby Orr.[1]

My parents, John and Barbara, were both born in Sault Ste. Marie, three hundred miles to the northwest. Both of them were born into working-class families, but both of them managed to become educated beyond their families' norm, and they moved to Parry Sound for my father's teaching job at the local high school. Prior to my birth, my mother delivered a stillborn baby girl. She later told me that she was very much hoping that her second-born child would be another girl. Eventually, my mother would get her wish. I was the older of two children to survive and was named after my father; my fourteen-month-younger sister was named Kelly. It is difficult to recount one's early years very accurately; any memories of the time are, of course, dim and perhaps fundamentally altered by the passing years. What I can say with some certainty is that Kelly and I were very close as young children. We played together incessantly, and I have the distinct memory of us as equals at the time. I would like to say that these memories mean that I thought of myself as just as much a girl as she was, but who can really say for sure?

I can recount a couple of telling episodes from those years. Canadian children learn to skate shortly after they start walking. By the age of five or six almost all those children assigned male at birth are enrolled in youth hockey. And so it was with me. I was pretty enthusiastic about it . . . at first. I loved to get dressed up in my hockey outfit, with the sweater, pants, helmet, pads, stick, and skates. Our old family photo album contains a picture of me in the driveway; I'm wearing my hockey outfit and I radiate joyfulness. I was, however, in for a rude awakening when I got to the rink for my first practice. All the boys seemed more interested in body checking, slashing, high-sticking, elbowing, smashing each other into the boards, and generally inflicting violence upon one another, rather than engaging in the ostensible object of the game—advancing the puck to the other end of the rink and into the opponent's net. There was no way that I wanted any part of such mayhem. After a couple of practices, the coach seemed to sense my distaste with the on-ice violence and suggested that maybe I could be a goalie. The problem with playing in net is that the hockey puck is made of very firm rubber, and when it gets cold it becomes as a hard as a rock. The goalie is actually supposed to insert her body in front of this rocklike object as it hurtles towards the net and prevent the puck from entering the goal behind her. That wasn't going to work for me, either. I quickly grew disenchanted with practice and started to make up excuses to get out of it. My parents made me stick with it for one season before giving up. I never played organized hockey again. Apparently, I also went out for ballet at an early age, which would be very unusual for a boy in small town. I have absolutely no memory of the lessons, nor of anyone's reaction to my dance phase, but I did ask my mother about it. She stated that I only lasted three sessions before I came home and emphatically stated that I wouldn't be going back; clearly I wasn't any more successful in finding my niche in ballet than I had been in hockey.

I did, however, start running at a very young age. I would run the kilometer or so from school to home twice a day, at lunch and again after school was done. There wasn't any compelling reason I couldn't have walked it, but it seemed a way to celebrate the freedom of being released from school. Hence I discovered the sport that would become my passion, even though I never thought of it as a sport at the time. Running seemed a natural activity, a part of everyday life. I also discovered an early aptitude for, and love of, mathematics and science. My dad brought lesson books home from school for me, and I was completing fourth grade arithmetic work prior to starting grade one. Although this meant that my early school years were not very challenging, it did spur me on to further reading and learning.

I am often asked when I knew I was a girl. When does anyone know what gender she is? I certainly had a sense of femininity for as long as I can remember. I always had an affinity and preference for girl's clothing. I don't remember actually asking if I could wear girl clothes to school or around the house, a request that certainly would have been denied. I do know that I started wearing my sister's and mother's clothes secretly as early in life as I could manage it.

I think being transgender is like being left-handed. I imagine that most southpaws get an epiphany when they first understand that the world is engineered for right-handed people. My first realization that I was fundamentally different from others came at about age six or seven. I was leaving school with a friend and I asked him if he ever wished he could try life as a girl—maybe not forever, but just for a while, to see if he liked it. I've forgotten exactly what his response was—undoubtedly some 1960s version of "Whatever, dude"—but I do remember the look on his face. It was his nonverbal reaction to my question that told me, once and for all, that I was not like others. I never again asked anyone if they had a desire to live as the opposite gender, and it was then that I realized that I had better hide my gender identity if I was ever going to fit into the normal world.

Although my early memories are somewhat cloudy, my adolescent ones are much clearer, but not in a good way. On some level, I had always thought that when I went through puberty I would change into the woman I always knew I was. It therefore came as a shock and profound disappointment when the opposite happened. To my absolute horror, my body started getting more masculine in every way.

I spent most of seventh and eighth grades in a severe depression. And of course, it was made all the worse by the fact that I couldn't tell anyone about it. I remember sessions in the school counselor's office, and I simply had no words to tell her just what was wrong with me. The funny thing was that I wasn't even being honest with myself. I had managed to hide my feelings deep within, and I don't think I could have expressed them, even to a sympathetic listener. Of course, the odds of finding a trans-sympathetic small-town guidance counselor in the 1970s were remote indeed. Without any doubt, the two years of grades seven and eight were the worst two years of my life. While puberty might be difficult for everyone, it is much harder for transgender adolescents. According to one study, 41 percent of trans people attempt suicide, and I'm sure many of those attempts are made by teenagers. Perhaps because of my denial mechanisms, I never seriously contemplated suicide, and this, at least, was a very good thing.

Since I had no one to tell and no words to say, all I could do was endure and survive. This meant that I constantly felt alone and miserable. There was nothing I could do that could possibly bring me happiness in those years. It was my lot to endure the pain. I was not going to grow up to be a woman, and there was nothing I could do about it, so the less I thought about it, the better off I would be. The thing that really allowed me to move beyond my depression was sports, and I only really started to excel in them once I reached high school. I went out for the cross-country team at the start of my freshman year, and I was good enough to be a scorer on the Canadian equivalent of the JV team. By the time I graduated from high school I was the best runner in our district. Within the walls of our school, I was best known for my success in basketball, despite topping out at five feet, nine inches of skin and bones. I had a fantastic shooting touch and was very quick. The best team I played on was during what Americans would call my junior year. Our team featured two tall, athletic boys whom we called our twin towers, but my outside shooting was the key to opening up the middle, and I was the leading scorer on a balanced team that went undefeated within our district. I was also a gifted student who maintained high marks without too much effort. I was the best chess player in the school, regularly beating the teacher who ran the chess club. I was also a member of our high school team that competed successfully on a Canadian student TV quiz show called *Reach the Top*. We won the championship at the nearest television station three years in a row. When I graduated, I was named the school's valedictorian and athlete of the year. I was certainly a very big fish in a very small pond. My sex life in high school was not especially noteworthy, although I did lose my virginity.

Despite my academic and athletic success, I still felt very isolated throughout my high school years. At some subconscious level I was very aware that I was carrying around this horrible secret, that I was some freak who was different from everyone else. I was always very awkward in social situations because of this acute, if repressed, feeling of being fundamentally flawed. Somewhere in my mind I thought my life would be different when I got to university. I signed up for a coed residence not with the idea of meeting girls but, on some level, of joining them. I even made my parents buy me a powder blue trunk adorned with kittens to hold my belongings. I thought it was perfect, but my male roommate hated it. My school was the University of Western Ontario, located in the charming city of London, Ontario. The school had strong academics and athletics. I knew that my best chance of athletic success lay with running, and so I went out for the cross-country team as a freshman and found myself in over my head. The team won the Canadian collegiate championships that year, but I wasn't ready for that level of competition. It would take me until my senior year before I was good enough to be a factor for our team, and we narrowly missed being national champs that year. My freshman year at Western wasn't very challenging academically, but once I got into the upper realms of my undergraduate physics studies, I found myself in the unaccustomed role of a midlevel student within the very small group capable of mastering the difficult concepts inherent in the study of quantum physics. I decided that I would do graduate work in medical physics, a somewhat less rigorous subfield, where I found a home. Graduate school at Western might have been the best two years I lived in the male gender. My gender dysphoria was still haunting my life, but between my athletic and scholastic pursuits I was fulfilled, if not actually happy.

I did the best running of my life, finishing fifteenth in the Canadian university cross-country championships, and ran all of my lifetime personal bests, including a 2:23 marathon. My two most significant friends from my college years were actually a couple: Paul Roberts and Kathy Ricica, who had gone to college at the University of Windsor, a hundred miles or so southwest of London. Paul's event was the steeplechase, a 3000-meter race over barriers; he would run 8:54 for the distance. His career in the athletic gear business took him to London after graduation, and we lived together for two years. Like me, Kathy's best distance was the marathon, and she would become a star in the early 1980s, winning the Toronto Marathon among others. Kathy also competed on a few Canadian national teams, with her best placing being a silver at the World University Games in 1983. Kathy moved to London for graduate work in kinesiology and eventually became a high school teacher in the London area. In 1983 I would be the best "man" at Paul and Kathy's wedding, and later Paul would be the best man for both of my marriages. The three of us would maintain a lifelong friendship that endures to this day, and should I ever get married again I would ask Kathy to stand up for me.

I successfully defended my thesis in the fall of 1982 and accepted my first paying position in medical physics early in 1983. I moved to the United States, and seven years later relocated to Portland, Oregon, the city that I would grow to call home. In my first fifteen years in Portland, I become an established presence in the medical physics community; marry and divorce twice; lose my father and sister to cancer and suicide, respectively; and continue running at a relatively high level—but the most important milestone was my decision to transition at the age of forty-seven in February 2004. I started to see the psychologist who assisted me along the difficult path to my real self. One of the first things the psychologist asked me to do was make a list of things I would lose if I proceeded with my transition. I understood that my second marriage and my relationship with my mother were in jeopardy, but very close to the top of the list was the ability to continue distance racing. I can still remember how excited I was when I read in the paper in June 2004 that the IOC would allow transgender athletes into the Olympics. Although I was never good enough for the Olympics—and I was far too old at the time—I knew that the principles of the Stockholm consensus would trickle down and that I was going to be able to continue to compete in the sport I loved.

I started hormone therapy the day after running in the Hood to Coast Relay—a popular Portland-area race—in August 2004. I had expected that I would gradually get a little slower, but much to my surprise I was noticeably slower within three weeks. After nine months I had lost 12 percent of my speed. This latter number is significant because men run 10 to 12 percent faster than women. USA Track & Field (USATF), the governing body for track and field in the United States, decided to follow the lead of the IOC in February 2005, allowing transgender athletes to compete in women's sport after surgery and two years of hormones. Only months earlier I had been very excited by this prospect, but now I knew they had gotten the rule wrong. It seemed obvious to me that hormones and not surgery was the key, and it was equally clear that two years of hormone therapy was not required in order to drastically change the athletic capabilities of trans women. I wrote to Jill Pilgrim, the lawyer for USATF. Although she seemed sympathetic, there was no way that the organization was going to change a rule that it had just implemented, one that was undoubtedly controversial with many of the policy makers, let alone the athletes. USATF and I worked out a compromise where I was allowed to run in mixed-gender races as long as I declined any award. I could certainly live with that deal until after my surgery. I scheduled my surgery with Dr. Toby Meltzer in Scottsdale, Arizona, in January 2006. Paul Roberts came down from London to offer support, and we both stayed at the home of Eamonn Condon, a mutual friend. Both Paul and Eamonn were supportive, and the surgery went well.

It took me five months to return to racing, but once I did I found that I was running the same pace as I had run in 2005. The surgery didn't make me slower—and I was now able to wear the tightly fitted outfits favored by many women runners. I had been tracking my race results for more than a year, and I found an interesting relationship. Although I was now much slower, my age-graded scores were the same as they had been prior to transition. This requires a little explanation. The standard method used to compare masters runners of all ages and both sexes is called age grading. The method compares the times of the individual runners to the fastest time ever run by someone of their age and sex, then expresses the result as a percentage. For instance, in 2003 I had run 36:11 in a 10 kilometer road race. When my time was compared to the best time ever run by a forty-six-year-old man, I scored 80 percent on the tables. Two years later I ran the same race in 42:01, but now if my time was compared to the fastest ever by a forty-eight-year-old woman, I also scored 80 percent. Thirteen years later, in 2018, I still score roughly 80 percent on the age-graded tables, but now I am being compared to sixty-one-year-old women.[2]

Moreover, in 2006 I discovered that another trans woman runner had the same age-graded equivalency before and after her transition. The conformation of this pattern by another runner represented an epiphany for me, and it would change my life. I began to collect data from trans women runners I connected with. It took years of perseverance, but eventually I gathered enough data for a groundbreaking study. It was also in 2006 that I began to study the science and history of gender variance in sport, and in time I would learn enough to be considered an expert in the arena. I chose to end my racing year in 2006 with a half marathon in Los Vegas largely because Paul Roberts would be there. The race went well for me, and later that evening I joined Paul and the group he had traveled with for a night out that included a Cirque Du Soleil performance. The rest of the runners were sitting in the cheap seats, but I wanted to thank Paul for his support in Phoenix, so I bought us two of the best seats in the house. We were sitting in the third or fourth row and Paul was right on the center aisle.

Cirque performances often feature clowns who interact with the audience in a variety of ways. These interactions are usually funny at the expense of the audience member. That night, Paul and I became targets. Halfway through the show, a clown stepped into the aisle and began looking around with a gleam in his eye. He sauntered up to Paul and asked him to go up on stage. The two of them carried on a conversation while they were walking. Once Paul was on stage, a cage was elevated up to the stage from below. The clown motioned to Paul to step into the cage, and after Paul obliged, the clown locked him in. The cage then disappeared into the bowels of the performance hall, and who knew what would happen to Paul. At this point the clown pulled out a picnic basket and sauntered back to Paul's vacant seat. He made a big show of pulling a rose, a bottle of champagne, and two flutes out of the basket. He presented me with the rose using a great flourish and then proceeded to open the bottle and pour each of us a glass. He leaned over to me as if to propose a toast, and said, "I know all about you." At that point I was laughing almost uncontrollably, but I managed to respond, "I doubt that very much." After a few more clownish flourishes of flirting, he went back on stage, leaving me with my wine. Paul later told me that when he was walking up to the stage, the clown had asked him if I was his wife, and Paul had said no, we were just friends. Since this was Vegas, the clown would have assumed that we were having an affair; clearly that's what the clown meant when he said he knew all about me. Poor clown—he didn't understand that the joke was on him. Paul later told me that all of his friends from London, who really did know about me, were howling with laughter up in their seats. When Paul was taken below the stage, he got to meet some of the performers and see the intricate equipment that they use to make the Cirque shows so spectacular. So Paul, too, got a memorable experience. The clown released him a few minutes later, and Paul returned to his seat to watch the rest of the show.

One month after the Vegas trip, in January 2007, I turned fifty. I was accepted by USATF as a female runner in November 2007. My fist USATF race as Joanna was a memorable one as I captured first place in the 50–54 age group in the master's women's race at the National Club Cross Country Championships held in Ohio. This was a breakthrough for me, and I continued running successfully in UASTF masters events for the next few years. I also made a couple of important new female running friends. Suzanne Ray began running in her early twenties, and by the time she was in her forties she was one of the best masters women runners in the nation. Suzanne and her husband, Rick, moved to southern Oregon in 2006. I met Suzanne in the spring of 2007 when I was on a theater trip to the nearby town of Ashland, Oregon. A mutual friend named Becky had convinced me to run in a local race, and I wound up out-kicking Suzanne for second woman in the race, behind Becky. The next day Suzanne and I went for a run together and I told her I was transgender. Despite whatever misgivings she might have felt about me, Suzanne accepted me as a friend. In 2008 I asked another standout Oregon runner named Jeanette (Jeannie) Groesz to join Suzanne and me to form a team for that year's Club National Cross Country meet. Suzanne and Jeannie finished first and second in the 55–59 age group, I was fourth in the 50–54 division, and we placed third in the over-50 team division. This was the first time my running club, Team Red Lizard, garnered national attention, but we would soon become one of the best-known collection of masters women runners in the land.

In 2009 I became one of the organizers of the Portland Track Festival and in particular I brought a masters women's race to the event.

That 3000-meter race has attracted many top American masters women, and the meet itself has grown to be one of the best middle-distance meets in the United States. It has been very rewarding to offer other masters women an opportunity to shine, and I am grateful for the positive feedback I have received from many of them. Of course, I have received plenty of negative feedback over the years, too, from women all over the country who claim that I have an unfair advantage. Most of the women are too reticent to speak their minds to me, but I have heard plenty of secondhand reports of their comments. And there have been a few very unpleasant encounters with women who have voiced their displeasure directly to me. Despite the hatred, I have continued to race. I have the support of my friends and my teammates, and I am fairly thick-skinned.

The rest of my life during this period was a very mixed bag. I did indeed get divorced from my second wife, and my mother initially said that she never wanted to see me again. Although Mom eventually changed her mind, our relationship remained rocky for the rest of her life. On the other hand, my experience at work was as good as I could have hoped for. I was even elected president of the regional chapter of my professional organization; clearly, most of my colleagues were accepting of the new me. I refrained from dating until after my surgery, as I was quite uncomfortable with my body. Although I was uncomfortable, there were many others who thought my body was quite attractive. Instead of seeing me as transgender, most people perceive me as a tall, athletic-looking woman. After my surgery, I did date men, women, and a couple of trans people, too. I was in a two-year relationship with a woman, but most of my relationships were quite brief and none were entirely satisfactory.

Although my life failed to match up to my fantasies of a posttransition existence, I had work, running, and friends to keep me relatively satisfied. I am often asked if I am happy in my posttransition life. I always reply that I am much happier than I ever was before. My answer is slightly evasive, but true. Although I have a deep regret that I didn't transition when I was younger, I am fulfilled, respected, and engaged in my new life. It might not be everything I envisioned, but my life as Joanna is several magnitudes better than my life prior to transition. It is also good to know that I have made a difference in the world. I have always understood that my gifts as an athlete were not my strongest suit.

There were, however, a few transgender people at the time of my transition who earned some measure of fame for their athletic achievements, and now would be a good time to look at them.

9

TRANSGENDER AND INTERSEX ATHLETES, 2004–2009

There were many opponents to the IOC's 2004 decision to allow transgender women to compete against cisgender women athletes. Inevitably these foes would claim that the end of women's sports was nigh. Allowing trans women in would open up a floodgate, and women's sports would be overrun by "men pretending to be women." Guess what? It didn't happen! There was no plague of men willing to give up their male genitalia and privilege just so they could compete for the meager scraps of money and attention afforded women athletes. There were, however, a few transgender women who achieved some level of success in sports in the years after 2004, and I would like to look more closely at the two most prominent of these women. Consistent with twenty-first century transgender preferences, I will now start to use an athlete's preferred pronouns throughout any given story.

The most successful transgender athlete of the period was the golfer Mianne Bagger. Bagger was born on Christmas Day 1966 in Denmark and took up golf at the age of eight. Her family moved to Australia when she was thirteen, and she had her picture taken with Aussie golf legend Greg Norman the following year. As a young man she got her handicap down to 1. She started hormone therapy in 1992 and had vaginoplasty in 1995; during this period she discontinued golfing. She resumed her love affair with the game in 1998 and chose to be open about her history. In 1999 Bagger won the South Australian State Amateur women's title, and soon she was ranked among the top ten amateurs in the country. As her golf game improved, she also began to get negative feedback. Many other female golfers were concerned about competing against her. She said that others assumed, "If I happen to do well or win a tournament that it was because of an unfair advantage."[1]

At the dawn of the twenty-first century, no professional golf tour allowed trans women to play against other women. The Charlotte Wood episode in the late 1980s had prompted many women's golf organizations to implement a "born female" clause in their entrance requirements. Although the Australian amateur golf association had removed its female-at-birth clause in 1999, allowing Bagger to play, the pros had not followed suit. The 2004 IOC decision paved the way for the Ladies European Tour (LET) and the Australian Ladies Professional Golf (ALPG) tour to open their tours to trans athletes. As a result, Bagger was offered a spot in the 2004 Women's Australian Open tournament. Her entry into the event prompted a front-page story in the *Sydney Morning Herald*.[2] At this time Bagger also lobbied the LPGA to change its "woman at birth" rule, but this effort would not prove successful. It would be up to another transgender golfer to win that battle. Later in 2004 Bagger "sold up everything that I owned in Australia" in order to fund a year of European golf devoted to earning her LET tour card. In November 2004 Bagger took 292 strokes, or four-over-par, to finish the 72-hole qualifying tournament in Taranto, Italy, earning her LET card for 2005 and becoming the highest-profile transgender athlete since Renée Richards.[3]

In 2005 Bagger played in several tournaments in the LET, and the focus was always on the fact that she was playing in the women's game as an openly transgender golfer rather than on her golfing performance. Bagger's actual success was fairly modest; she was never a threat to the top golfers. Bagger played in the LET for seven years, from 2005 through 2011, earning just over €85,000 during that time. Her best year on the tour was in 2007 when she earned €39,000 and finished in 54th place on the money list. Her best-ever finish in an LET event came in 2006 when she tied for 6th place at the Nykredit Masters in Denmark.[4] During these years, she lived and golfed in Europe during the summers, then traveled to Australia to play in the ALPG events during summer Down Under. She earned a total of $35,000 on the ALPG tour from 2004 through 2011.[5] Given her career winnings, Bagger never managed to earn financial security from golf. In fact, after she sold her belongings in 2004, she never had a permanent address for the rest of her professional career. Instead, Bagger crashed at friends' places when she could, shared lodgings with other struggling golfers at tournaments, and lived a nomadic existence. Even after her retirement from professional golf, Bagger continued to live a life that was full of travel but short on stability. She spent a little time teaching golf in Spain, working in IT and web development in Australia, and performing odd jobs in exchange for lodging wherever she traveled. She remains outspoken in retirement, and she was recently named by Outsports as one of their Stonewall Spirit athletes.[6]

Another trans woman who received significant worldwide publicity at the time was Canadian cyclist Kristen Worley, who was born in 1967 and adopted into a sports-minded family in Mississauga, Ontario. Growing up, Kristen was an athletic child; both water skiing and cycling were important sports for her during her youth. She always suffered from gender dysphoria and attempted suicide a couple of times. She started on hormone therapy in the 1990s, and in 2001 she had surgery, including a vaginoplasty.[7] After the IOC adopted the Stockholm consensus in 2004, Kristen approached the cycling authorities and was allowed to compete in the women's category. Her chosen specialty was the individual pursuit, a 3000-meter cycling race contested on the cycling velodrome in which two competitors start on opposite sides of the track and attempt to overtake one another. Kristen trained hard for her return to cycling, but her results were always modest.

Worley was convinced that her lack of success stemmed from a lack of testosterone as opposed to a lack of talent, despite the fact that she was never very successful in men's sport prior to transition. Cisgender women get approximately half of their testosterone from their ovaries; the other half of their T is generated from their adrenal glands. Without gonads, postoperative transgender women must rely on their adrenal glands for all of their testosterone production, and their testosterone levels are only approximately two-thirds the amount cisgender women possess. The theoretical disadvantage to transgender women as a result of this testosterone deficit is extremely small, but Kristin was neither the first nor the last to suggest that trans women's low T levels were limiting. In 2006 Worley petitioned to be allowed to bring her testosterone up to the average of cisgender women. Her request was granted in 2007, but it made little difference in her cycling times; she still fell far short of her aspirations. By 2007 Kristen was competing in masters-level cycling events and was not approaching the 3:51 time[8] she needed to achieve in order to qualify for the Olympic Games, but that did not stop Worley from proclaiming her desire to be the first openly transgender Olympian. In the end, Worley did not make the time needed to qualify for the Canadian Olympic trials, let alone to make the team.

Kristen did succeed, however, in gaining recognition for the struggles transgender athletes have to overcome. She also captured the attention of the Canadian government, which funded studies on transgender issues in sport and gave her official recognition for her activism. One result of the support of the Canadian government was a review paper that described in substantial detail all the published research regarding the athletic capabilities of transgender individuals. The most important notion I gleamed from this review was that there was no published work comparing pre- and post-transition athletic performance of trans woman in any sport anywhere in the world. I was, however, in the very early stages of gathering data that could be used to eventually create such a study, and I was grateful for this review indicating that there was a need for such data.

Worley remains a vocal opponent of those who have tried to limit the opportunities of transgender and intersex athletes up to and including the present time. After the IAAF instituted a testosterone-based limit for female athletes in 2011 and the IOC followed suit in 2012, Worley decided in 2015 to sue for the right to compete with higher testosterone levels than those imposed by the governing bodies.[9] Her suit was settled in 2017, and although she did not receive the right to compete with enhanced levels of testosterone, she did get cycling authorities to "take some steps toward transgender inclusion"[10]

Although the IOC adopted the Stockholm consensus in 2004, there were still no openly transgender Olympic athletes by the close of 2008, a period that saw summer games contested in Athens and Beijing and winter games held in Torino, Italy. Far from taking over women's sport, transgender women were barely making a dent. In fact, if Mianne Bagger and Kristen Worley were the most competitive transgender athletes to emerge in that time period, then cisgender women athletes were in no danger whatsoever. Although Bagger and Worley were not overly successful in their sports, there was one transgender athlete of the period who was world-class by any standard. His name is Balian Buschbaum, and under his birth name Yvonne, he was one of the best women's pole vaulters in the opening years of the new century. The event requires athletes to use a long fiberglass pole to help them jump over a bar placed at ever increasing vertical heights. It was one of the last track events to be sanctioned for the "weaker sex," with the first women's Olympic pole vault completion taking place in Sydney, Australia, in 2000.

Buschbaum was born on July 14, 1980, in the small city of Ulm, situated along the Danube River in southern Germany. The city is approximately one hundred kilometers from the northern extent of the German Alps and sits at an altitude of approximately fifteen hundred feet. Balian was an athletic child and played football (soccer to North Americans) with the boys. Like many other transgender people, Balian found puberty to be very unsettling. He undertook very serious weight training in the hope that it would stop his menses and sculpt his breasts to look more like pecs.[11] The outside world was unaware of his struggles, however; all they saw was a rising young female athlete, albeit one whose closely cropped hair gave the appearance of masculinity. By the time he had reached eighteen years of age he was one of the best young vaulters in the world. He had already set a world junior mark while winning the 1997 European junior championships, and the next year he took his talents to the next level, placing fourth in the women's section of the 1998 world junior athletic championships held in Annecy, France.

Leading up to the 2000 Olympics in Sydney, Buschbaum continued to excel, winning gold at the 1999 European Athletics Junior Championships and bronze at the 1998 senior championships. Buscchbaum was just twenty years old at the Sydney games, but he had matured into one of the finest female vaulters in the world. Buschbaum placed 6th in the Sydney final with a height of 4.40 meters or 14′ 5″. He matched his sixth-place finish at both the 2001 and 2003 World Indoor Track Championships, and in 2003 he achieved a height of 4.70 meters, making him the second highest women's German vaulter at the time. His success combined with that of several other German vaulters to make the nation one the strongest in both the men's and women's pole vault.[12]

The women's pole vault quickly became one of the most popular events in track and field. Featuring a number of good-looking athletes and a compelling story of women conquering a new frontier, the women's vault quickly became a media favorite, and the world's top female vaulters became well-paid celebrities. Although American Stacey Dragilla was the biggest name during this period, there was plenty of love for other top vaulters. Buschbaum benefited from the attention given to the women's vault, both monetarily and in terms of publicity; however, all the money and fame could not make him content with his life. Like most transgender people, he knew that he had been assigned to the wrong gender at an early age. Even his success on the world stage could not make him happy.[13] Buschbaum was also dealing with a serious Achilles tendon issue that required four surgeries. He did not compete in the 2004 Olympic Games, and he never again matched his best vaulting of the early years of twenty-first century. Moreover, the best women in vaulting were continuing to raise the competition bar higher, and Buchbaum was falling behind. In 2007 he retired from competitive pole vaulting and began his transition. He had both top and bottom surgery, emerging as one of the world's most handsome trans men. He has worked as a pole vault coach and become a well-known celebrity in Germany; among other gigs, he bagged a spot in the German version of *Dancing with the Stars*. In many ways, Balian wound up with it all: looks, money, and fame.[14]

In addition to the transgender athletes who gained notoriety in the first decade of the twenty-first century, there were a few intersex athletes of note. Unlike the intersex athletes of the twentieth century, who were mostly European, this new crop of intersex athletes hailed from other parts of the world. The urbanization of Europe and North America during the twentieth century combined with an ever-increasing societal taboo against inbreeding had greatly reduced the incidence of intersex conditions in the Western world. Additionally, earlier medical intervention in the lives of intersex people meant that fewer intersex people reached adulthood without some sort of treatment. As the twenty-first century dawned, however, there were still many places in the world where consanguinity was the norm, and as a result there were still plenty of intersex athletes in the developing world, especially in rural locations.[15] Many of these athletes would not find out their conditions before they became international-caliber athletes.

Before talking about these early twenty-first-century intersex athletes, it would be appropriate to review the IAAF and IOC policies of the time. Officially, compulsory sex testing was no longer practiced by either of these organizations, but both of these governing bodies still maintained the right to test athletes as the need arose. Athletes tested for performance-enhancing drugs were required to urinate in the presence of testers, hence those women with atypical anatomy would often be spotted by officials. Moreover, there were also cases in which complaints would be lodged against women based on their appearance.[16] Although neither the IOC nor the IAAF acknowledged it at the time, documents published later confirmed that those XY female athletes without androgen insensitivity syndrome were consistently advised to have gonadectomy, an operation that would reduce both their testosterone levels and their athletic performance. Those athletes agreeing to surgery would have been allowed to continue in women's sport.[17] Although we will never know how often this happened, I would like to detail a case to illustrate how this process was designed to function. I will omit some details in the interest of the athlete's privacy.

In one year in the first decade of the twenty-first century, a young woman whom I will call Patricia had a stellar season in her middle-distance specialty. Patricia was rewarded with a large contract from one of the world's biggest shoe companies, which, when combined with her winnings from her glorious year, would have provided her with enough money to last a lifetime in her impoverished nation. Patricia's future seemed bright, but she missed the first several months of competition the following year, and when she did return to the track, she was markedly slower. In fact, Patricia was running more than 5 percent slower than she had the previous year, and she was no longer capable of beating the best women in the world in her event. Patricia competed for another few years before retiring from the sport at an age when most competitors were just reaching their peak. It is difficult to imagine that a teenage athlete could be so dominant in her event and then be so much slower for the rest of her career. In fact, the sequence of events in Patricia's career led to me to the conclusion that Patricia was one of an unknown number of athletes during this period who underwent gonadectomy after being flagged by the IAAF. After removal of their testes, these athletes would produce markedly less testosterone, and their athletic performance would suffer. This was, however, exactly as the IAAF and the IOC had imagined the process would function. Instead of possessing a large testosterone-based advantage, these intersex women would now be competing on a more or less level playing field with cisgender women. The IAAF policy was also designed to protect the privacy of individual athletes. The process did not always work, and the case of Indian athlete Santhi Soundarajan provides a telling example.

Soundarajan was born into the Dalit caste in southern India in 1981. The Dalit, formerly known as untouchables, are the lowest rung on India's caste system, and Soundarajan was raised in crushing poverty. Her family of seven lived in a one-hundred-square-foot cement hut with no running water, electricity, or even an outhouse. Her parents' combined weekly earnings totaled four dollars. Santhi was declared female at birth and raised as such. When Soundarajan was thirteen, her grandfather taught her to run and bought her a pair of shoes. Soon she was winning races by wide margins; she was recruited to a local high school, which paid all her expenses and provided her with a hot lunch, a luxury she had never before enjoyed.[18] With improved nutrition and coaching, Santhi began making large improvements, and she was soon sent seven hours away to a college where she could pursue running more intensely. The young Tamil runner failed to mature in the manner of other girls: Santhi never menstruated, nor did she have any discernable breast development, facts that were worrisome to her mother. The Indian railways provided jobs for athletes, and she applied for one of these positions in 2005, but the railways declined to take her on after a medical exam that was described as a gender test.[19] This failed medical test did not derail her rapidly ascending sports career. By 2005 Soundarajan was one of the brightest stars of Indian athletics, winning the 800, 1500, and 3000 meter races at the national championship meet. Later that year she boarded a plane for the first time, on her way to South Korea, where she won a silver medal in the 800 meters at the Asian Athletics Championships in Incheon, South Korea.

Soundarajan represented India in several international competitions in 2005 and 2006, competing in the 800, the 1500, and the 4x400 meter relay. One of her 4x400 teammates was another Indian athlete named Pinki Pramanik, who would later become enmeshed in her own gender controversy. In December 2006, at the Asian Games in Doha, Qatar, Soundarajan won the silver medal in the 800 meters, running 2:03.16 and finishing only behind Bahrain's Maryam Jamal, who would go on to earn an Olympic gold medal. Santhi said, "[I]t was the biggest dream of my athletic career." Her dream, however, was about to turn into a nightmare. Apparently, one of the chaperones at the doping control became suspicious while watching Soundarajan urinate.[20] The next day the Indian team physician summoned her for tests; blood samples were taken and four other doctors were brought in to examine her. The physicians explained the procedures in English, which is not Santhi's native tongue, and she claims that she didn't understand the purpose of these tests. Soundarajan claims she was asked to leave the games the very next day but received no explanation until she saw, on the evening news a few days later, that she had been stripped of her medal for failing the gender test. She says she got a call from a national Olympic official five days after the news report telling her she could no longer compete. The official claims he followed the IAAF instructions,[21] although the IAAF denies any involvement in the case.

At this point, the story begins to get puzzling. First, why didn't the gender test from the railroad company affect her sports career? Second, why didn't the results of her gender tests remain confidential? Why wasn't she given the opportunity to undergo gonadectomy and continue competing, like other intersex athletes of the time? She claimed she wasn't protected due to her caste, and this explanation seems plausible. Upon Soundarajan's return home, she was mocked and ridiculed for her gender irregularity. She fell into a deep depression and attempted suicide a few months later. She started a running academy with some of her prize money, but the business failed. She went to work as a day laborer, molding fire bricks by hand. Eventually, after many years without any acknowledgment that she had been wronged, she was offered a position as an athletics coach by the Athletics Federation of India (AFI).[22]

Pinki Pramanik, Santhi Soundarajan's teammate on the Indian national team, was born on April 10, 1986, in the West Bengal city of Purulia. Like many other intersex athletes, Pramanik achieved outstanding athletic success very early in life. In 2004, before her eighteenth birthday, she won two bronze medals in the Asian Indoor Athletics Championships. Her prodigious athletic talent was offset by her propensity to get into trouble away from the track; later in 2004 she faced a weapons charge as a result of a gun planted in her bag, the first in a long series of personal difficulties that eventually derailed her career.[23] By 2006 Pramanik had rebounded from her legal difficulties and had the most successful year of her athletic career. The 2006 Commonwealth Games were held in Melbourne, Australia, in March, near the end of the summer season in the Southern Hemisphere. Pramanik reached the semifinals of the 800 meters and served as the anchor for India's silver-medal-winning 4x400 relay team.[24] In the South Asian Games that August, Pramanik won both the 400 and 800 meter races while anchoring the 4x400 team to gold. At the same meet, Soundarajan won the 1500 and was second to Pramanik in the 800; the two teamed up to help India win the gold medal in the 4x400 relay.[25] Pramanik's success led to her being named the Asian representative for the 800 meters at the 2006 IAAF World Cup, a very large honor for a twenty-year-old athlete. She finished seventh out of eight runners in the all-finals format, and her future seemed bright. At the last meet of the year, the Asian Games, Pramanik was a member of gold-medal-winning 4x400 team and just missed a medal in the open 400. This was the same competition in which Santharjan placed second in the 800 before being outed as intersex. Instead of the shame heaped on of her teammate, Pramanik was feted by the Indian media and given a large parcel of precious land by the West Bengal government as a reward for her superlative performances.[26]

Unfortunately for Pramanik, injuries and accidents dogged her from 2007 onward, and she never again reached the heights she experienced in 2006. In 2012 her life took another turn for the worse when she was accused of rape by a female friend and neighbor.[27] The rape charge led to chromosome tests on the runner revealing, an XY DSD.[28] Pramanik was, however, judged incapable of penetrative sex, and the rape charges against her were dropped. It appears that the charges were fabricated in an attempt to grab the land that had been awarded to her in 2006.[29] The success of Parmanik, Soundarajan, and Patricia is indicative of the propensity for intersex women to succeed in those races from 400 to 1500 meters. This range of distances—it is here where power and aerobic capacity combine forces to create excellence—would eventually become definitive in a new IAAF policy. In these early years of the new millennium, however, the IAAF saw no reason to modify its existing policies. The relatively small controversy over the fates of Soundaran and Pramanik, and the whispering in the case of Patricia, was not enough to force the hand of the IAAF. However, there was potential for a public relations disaster. If an athlete possessing the talent of Patricia endured the public humiliation suffered by the two Indian athletes, the resulting furor could envelope the sport of athletics like no other case ever had. Such an athlete was on the horizon, and this athlete would come to define the problematic nature of the attempt to regulate women's sport.

10

CASTER SEMENYA

I mentioned in chapter 7 Eric Vilain's claim that the history of intersex athletes could be segmented using the lives of three intersex women. We now come to the second of these three athletes: Caster Semenya. The South African speedster might be the most talked-about intersex athlete in history. As David Epstein wrote in *Sports Illustrated*, "The saga became a global cause célèbre for anyone interested in voicing his or her opinion about gender, race, femininity, or the biology of sex."[1] Semenya's medical records have not been made public; however, the probability that she manifests a DSD is so close to 100 percent that I shall assume she is intersex from here on out. Semenya grew up in very modest circumstances in Limpopo, the northernmost and perhaps the poorest province in South Africa. In Limpopo, cars are few, and running water is not taken for granted. The average monthly income for the black majority in Limpopo is approximately $135.[2] Limpopo borders Mozambique, Botswana, and other countries that form a region known for its unusually high incidence of DSDs.[3]

Semenya was born on January 7, 1991, in Ga-Masehlong, a small village in Limpopo, pretty much in the middle of nowhere. She was declared female at birth and raised as a girl. She was a natural at sports from her earliest years; football and athletics were her favorites. Questions about her gender started early, too. Phineas Sako, her track coach in her early years, said that upon first spying his star athlete, opponents would say, "It looks like a boy," using the cruelest pronoun they could to describe her. Semenya would often take one female member of the opposing team into the lavatory with her and drop her shorts so the other girl could see her genitals. This gesture proved nothing of importance about her sports performance, but it would have certainly shut up the other girls. Semenya never menstruated (primary amenorrhea) and had no discernable breast growth. Her build and her voice were quite masculine as well.[4] In 2008, while still living and training in Limpopo, Semenya won the gold medal in the 800 meters at the 2008 Commonwealth Youth Games in India, running 2:04. The following year, after moving to Pretoria for college, she won the 800 meter gold medal at the African Junior Athletics Championships with the stunning time of 1:56.72. She had improved by almost eight seconds in the event, beating Zola Budd's national record in the process; it was also the leading time in the world for that season. She immediately became one of the favorites for the upcoming IAAF World Championships in Berlin.[5]

Given her time, her improvement, and her physique, Semenya soon became the object of intense scrutiny within the track community. Internet message boards were abuzz with rumors and very unkind comments. The IAAF took notice too, asking Athletics South Africa (ASA) to perform gender tests on her prior to the championship meet. In early August she was tested by a gynecologist in Pretoria. Semenya herself has said that she was not given a valid reason for her gender tests, stating that she believed that she would be undergoing drug testing. Almost a decade later, a former ASA member revealed that Semenya never signed an informed consent to undergo the testing procedure.[6] It is almost unthinkable that a government agency could submit one of its athletes to such testing without consent.

Harold Adams, the team doctor for ASA, told Leonard Chuene, the president of the organization, that the test results were "not good" and recommended withdrawing Semenya from the championships. Chuene, however, not only failed to heed Adams's advice, he would later become very belligerent over the topic of gender testing.[7] Semenya ran her 800 meter heat in Berlin on August 16 and the semifinals the next day. She was accosted by the media in Germany, and some very painful questions were asked of her. She refused to comment on any of the rumors but did undergo a second round of tests on August 18, the day before the 800 meter final.

With all of the fuss surrounding her, it seems incredible that her ability to race would remain intact, but the day after being tested she went out and dominated the world's best 800 meter runners. On the backstretch of the second lap, she went to the front and began to pull away. Around the final bend she upped her tempo noticeably but without any apparent increase in effort. She left her opponents more than two seconds in arrears, winning in 1:55.45. Semenya had just decimated the world's best runners in her event. To top it off, she raised her arms in victory in a boxer's salute, showing off her biceps, torso, and abs, none of which looked remotely feminine. Maria Savinova, who finished fifth, remarked, "Just look at her."[8]

And the world did, indeed, look at her and comment on her and ridicule her. On September 11 the Australian tabloid *Daily Telegraph* reported that Semenya's test results had been leaked and showed that she had no uterus or ovaries; instead she had undescended testes, which provided her with three times the normal female testosterone levels. Although the *Telegraph*'s statement was never confirmed, it seems very reasonable and could be explained by her having PAIS, 5-ARD, or some other XY DSD.[9]

Upon Semenya's return from Germany, she was met by thousands of her cheering countrymen. She had the opportunity to meet South African president Jacob Zuma and the legendary hero Nelson Mandela. Chuene thundered that he would not allow others to define African children and said that he would have no part of any gender testing, lying about his previous involvement. His behavior would eventually prove his undoing, as he was fired from his position in 2011.[10] The IAAF is supposed to keep gender testing confidential, but in the face of all of the noise, it did acknowledge that such tests had been performed on the South African runner. For most of that autumn, there was a great deal of uncertainty over her future, and it seemed that everyone—sports enthusiasts, ethicists, gender specialists, and feminists—had an opinion on her. In November 2009, ASA issued a statement that Semenya would be allowed by the IAAF to keep her medal and her prize money.[11] What remained unsaid, but undoubtedly agreed to, was that she would undergo some sort of feminizing procedure that would bring her testosterone levels in line with those of her competitors. It would become apparent later on that Semenya had chosen the chemical route.[12]

The IAAF did not clear Semenya to resume competition until July 6, 2010. She started with a couple of low-key meets in Finland, then won the ISTAF Berlin in 1:59 and change. She ran her season's best race in

Italy in September, winning in 1:58.16. She was still one of the top 800 meter runners in the world, but she was not nearly the dominant force she had been in 2009.[13] Additionally, she had experienced modest breast growth over the previous months and was also noticeably less muscular than she had been, although she still looked little like the women she raced against. Her breast development and reduced muscle mass were entirely consistent with lowered testosterone, as were her slower times. There were many who didn't see it that way, however; instead, they saw her still-impressive physique and her effortless running style and assumed that she was simply not trying to run her best. Many people suggested that she was running more slowly so she would not attract too much attention. Pundits claimed that she would once again dominate the 2011 worlds and the 2012 Olympics.

The IAAF realized that changes would be needed in its gender verification process after the Semenya debacle, and so it convened a working group of experts to determine new rules to regulate eligibility for women's competition. This group met several times between December 2009 and April 2011, eventually releasing two documents in May of 2011, one for women with hyperandrogenism (high testosterone levels) and one for transgender women.[14] Although the two documents and the supporting material total fifty-six pages, they can be summarized with a single sentence: Anyone who was legally female and had testosterone levels below the lower end of the male range would be allowed to compete in the women's section of IAAF events. The IAAF set a specific number of 10 nanomoles per liter (nmol/L) in serum as the limit, vastly larger than the upper female T range.

The new T limit was also of interest to dopers, since it would apply to all female athletes. Sophisticated doping coaches understood that beyond testing negative for drugs, they would also need to ensure that their athletes kept their serum testosterone below 10 nmol/L. At the time, I thought 10 was too high and that eventually the limit would be lowered. A limit of 10 would also mean that an intersex athlete (presumably like Semenya) who chose chemical means to lower her T would have a large advantage over one who chose surgery, since surgery would result in T levels of 1 nmol/L or less. If an intersex athlete given the choice between surgery or drugs to regulate T levels in 2011 could have seen four years into the future, she would have certainly chosen to take the drugs.[15] The IAAF also decided that it would make blood testing mandatory for every athlete, male and female, at the 2011 World Championships in Daegu, South Korea. All the samples would be analyzed for the usual list of illegal substances and would also be checked for testosterone levels.

Surprisingly, there was very little commentary about the new rules. Apparently the World Athletics Championships do not attract much attention outside of serious track fans. Within the track realm, however, Semenya was still big news. Her lead-up to the world championships was uneven, to say the least. She won the diamond league race in Paris, but recorded a time of only 2:00.18. At the Bislett Games in Oslo she ran 1:58.61, but finished third, as Halima Haclaf and Mariya Savinova both passed her in the final hundred meters. At the Prefontaine Classic in Eugene, Oregon, she finished second to Jamaican Kenya Sinclair, running 1:58.88. In Lausanne, she was much worse, finishing dead last in the 1500 with an unimpressive time of 4:16.[16]

Whenever Semenya won a race, her critics declared that it was unfair since she "was a man," and if she lost she was accused of sandbagging "so she wouldn't attract too much attention." There are a great many athletes who have good races and bad races, but Semenya was never judged in the same fashion as other athletes. Most track fans assumed that physically, she was still the same runner she had been in 2009, when she was head and shoulders better than anyone else in the world; these same fans assumed that she was going to win easily in Daegu, just as she had in Berlin. The field for the 800 final in Daegu was loaded with talent. The Jamaican Sinclair had enjoyed the best year of anyone coming into the final, but there was speculation that she had peaked too early. The Russian Savinova looked good coming in, and was joined by two of her countrywomen. Jeneth Jepkoskei, the 2007 world champ from Kenya, had shown good form, and the American Alysia Montano was also a medal favorite. But despite the talented field, all eyes were on Semenya. Tactically speaking, the 800 is one of the most interesting races on the track, because sometimes it is won from the front and sometimes it is won by a fast-closing finisher. The 800 in Daegu featured both types of tactics, and it is worth watching again—or for the first time, if you haven't seen it before.[17]

When the gun went off, Jepkoskei ran hard around the first bend out of lane one. She had won from the front in Osaka in 2007, and maybe she could again. At 300 meters she was leading Sinclair and Montano, while Semenya and Savinova were farther back in the pack. At the bell, Jepkoskei split 55.85 seconds, which was very fast—probably too fast. Down the second backstretch Semenya moved up, followed closely by Savinova. With 200 meters to go, Semenya moved to the shoulder of Jepkoskei, but the latter held her off through the turn, making the South African run the whole turn in lane two. Coming off the final turn, Jepkoskei ran out of gas and Semenya powered past. The race appeared to be over. But Savinova was still locked in behind Semenya, and she gradually closed over the final straight. It was one of those classic track finishes, with one runner trying to hold off another. Twenty meters from the finish, Savinova edged past and Semenya crumpled just a bit. Savinova won, and the times for the first three were Savinova, 1:55.87; Semenya, 1:56.35; and Jepkoskei, 1:57.42, just ahead of Montano in fourth.

It is notable that the first three embraced in a group hug a few seconds after the finish; Savinova and Semenya were smiling broadly. Two years earlier, the Russian had cast aspersions toward her South African rival, and now she was smiling and hugging her. After all she had been through in the last two years, Semenya had to be relieved at winning a medal, and her joy was evident. Almost everyone in the stands was cheering for anyone but Semenya, and they went wild with excitement at the finish. Savinova might have been the most popular Russian in the rest of the world on that day. Almost unbelievably, naysayers still claimed that Semenya threw the race. She was done in by the belief that she was unbeatable, and by her form, which didn't crack down the final straight. Some said she had already won a world championship, so why would she care about another? "Just wait until the Olympics," they said, "she will win there."

Although there was plenty of interest in the first two finishers in the Daegu 800 meter final, the last finisher in the race attracted almost no comments. Yuliya Rusanova was twenty-five years old at the time and should have been just coming into her prime as a middle-distance runner. Unfortunately for Rusanova, her career as an international competitor was nearing its close. She would compete in the 2012 indoor championships, once again finishing last in the finals. She never again competed internationally for Russia, but she would become one of the most important figures in athletics in 2014 under her married name, Stepanova. There will be more on her later.

After the close finish to the 800 meter race in the Daegu meet, it was assured that there would be more focus on gender during the lead-up to the 2012 Olympics. In the spring of 2012 the IOC released a document on eligibility for women's events and hyperandrogenism.[18] The IOC document was very similar to the one the IAAF had released in 2011, except that the IOC did not set a hard testosterone limit; the rule specified only that female T levels needed to be below the male threshold. The IOC also would enforce the rule differently. Unlike the IAAF, the IOC would not test every athlete at the games, as the cost would be substantial and some people have a religious objection to drawing blood. Instead, blood testing would be undertaken only upon suspicion. Unlike the public apathy that greeted the 2011 IAAF regulations, there was a flood of commentary in response to the IOC rule, much of it negative. The negative comments fell into two widely disparate categories. The first camp contained social scientists and activists of many stripes, many of whom suggested that anyone who claimed to be female should be allowed to compete. Others suggested that testosterone was like any other natural advantage, such as speed, height, strength, and so on. Why put a limit on hormones and not on other naturally occurring advantages? Others were upset that only women were to be subject to testosterone limits. Why not limit men too?[19] Although the social scientists felt the new rules were not inclusive enough, a second camp that contained much of the sporting world felt it was unfair to allow Semenya and other gender-diverse athletes to compete against "normal" women regardless of the current testosterone levels of the intersex women.

Semenya's build-up to the 2012 Olympics was even less impressive than her performance in 2011. Her season started late due to injury, and she did not excel in any of her tune-up races. In Rome in May, she was eighth in 800 meters in a time of 2:00.07, with both Savinova and Jepkoskei ahead of her. The first two places in the Rome race were captured by newcomer Fantu Magiso of Ethiopia and the resurgent 2008 Olympic champ Pamela Jelimo of Kenya. Semenya ran even worse in Monaco in July, where she was ninth in 2:01.67. Her poor results created an interesting dichotomy: Knowledgeable observers were suggesting that she would be lucky to make the final, while casual track fans were anointing her as the favorite based on her 2009 dominance and their belief that she held an unfair advantage. In the lead-up to the Olympics there was a nice article on her in the *London Telegraph* in which she assessed her chances by saying, "My head needs to be 100 per cent for me to compete. I can still win with only 70 per cent of my muscles,"[20] which, to me, implies that she was competing at lower testosterone levels but also demonstrates that she deals with the same mental issues as other inconsistent athletes. The South African delegation voted her to be the nation's flag bearer at the games, a huge honor for any athlete, indicating that she had the backing of her countrymen.[21]

Semenya responded well, winning her semifinal in 1:57.67 and hopefully setting herself up for a good race in the final. The first four runners from the 2011 world championships all made the final, as did Jelimo, two other Russians, and a teenage Burundian runner named Francine Niyonsaba (more on her later). The women's 800 final was once again shaping up to be a terrific race.[22]

Montano took the early pace in the final, with Jepkoskei right behind. Once again Savinova and Semenya trailed, but this time the South African was last at the bell, which the American reached in 56.31. Down the final backstretch Jelimo made a strong move to take the lead. Savinova was moving up behind her, and Semenya also started to move up a little but was still only seventh with 200 to go. Savinova really started to sprint with 200 to go and caught Jelimo coming into the home straightaway. On the final straightaway, Savinova powered away to a commanding victory. Semenya was sixth with a hundred to go, but on the verge of fourth and moving well. With 30 meters to go Semenya moved into third, passing the second Russian, Poistogova, and was bearing down on Jelimo. Semenya finished strongly to take second in 1:57.23, more than a second behind Savinova's 1:56.19. Poistogova caught Jelimo five meters from the line and finished third.

Semenya ran her season's best time and finished second on the biggest stage in the world, but still most of the talk after the race was that she wasn't trying to win. Certainly it might be possible to suggest, as her coach did, that she left her kick too late, but who would sandbag in the Olympic final? Noted South African exercise physiologist Ross Tucker analyzed her splits and concluded that she was giving an honest effort. Furthermore, he said, "The prevailing 'allegation,' ever since her return in 2010, is that she is running slowly to stay under the radar, avoiding winning and the questions this would undoubtedly bring. If that's the plan, then it sure isn't working."[23]

Although Semenya's Olympic silver medal seemed to bring her much joy, her career spiraled downward thereafter. More injuries in 2013 led to an even slower start than she ever had before. Semenya failed to gain a qualifying time for the 2013 World Championships and missed the meet entirely. She did manage to get her time down to 1:58.92 at a late-season meet in Rieti in Italy, but all in all it was a very disappointing year for her.[24] That year the World Championships were held in Moscow, and Savinova was a huge crowd favorite. Savinova did not have an ideal build-up to the race, and there were thoughts that she might be vulnerable. Once again Montano took the race out hard and enjoyed a large lead over Kenyan Eunice Sum at the bell. Sum had been primarily a 1500 meter runner until 2013, when she dropped down in distance and discovered she had the closing speed to excel in the shorter race. At 600 meters, Sum remained in second but had closed the gap slightly on Montano; at that point Savinova had moved up to third. Sum and Savinova closed on Montano around the final bend, and first Sum and then Savinova passed the American in the final straight. Sum held Savinova at bay, winning the gold. American Brenda Martinez caught Montano at the line for third. No one accused Savinova of deliberately losing the race.[25]

If 2013 had been disappointing for Semenya, 2014 was an even worse year. Her fastest race was only 2:02.66, which placed her tenth at the Golden Gala Diamond League meet in Rome in June. Semenya's abortive season included only a handful of international races, and she did little of note in any of them.[26] There was, however, off-track news of note for her. Many news outlets had previously reported that Semenya was not romantically interested in boys; same-sex attraction is very common in intersex women. Semenya was, however, very interested in a beautiful South African 1500 meter runner named Violet Raseboya, who was born on February 19, 1986, making her almost five years older than Semenya. The two athletes first met in the restroom at a track meet in 2007. Raseboya's first reaction was to ask, "What is a boy [Semenya] doing in here?"[27] Despite the somewhat difficult introduction and the fact that Raseboya had a heterosexual history, the two were soon dating. In 2014 Semenya's family paid an amount of R25,000 in lobola (it is traditional in South Africa for the family of the groom to pay a dowry for the right to marry a woman) to the family of Raseboya. On Sunday, December 6, 2015, the couple were married in a traditional

South African wedding ceremony in the Limpopo region where Semenya grew up.[28]

Semenya wore jeans and sneakers and a rather masculine mauve top trimmed in yellow and other bright colors. Raseboya was radiant in a fitted purple dress also trimmed in yellow and other colors very similar to Semenya's top. In pictures taken later on the wedding day, Raseboya had changed into a yellow top with a flouncy layered skirt of mauve and gold. The couple appeared to be very happy and were surrounded by a throng of well-wishers. Same-sex marriage has been legal in South Africa since 2006, but the Limpopo region is a conservative one and the decision to get married there might be seen as bold. But then again, it is Semenya's home and it also would cause less of a stir than getting married in a large city. There appears to be almost no negative backlash against the couple, and even the obvious fact that Semenya has taken the traditional male role in the relationship has drawn little comment. They have appeared together as a happy couple in a number of pictures over the years. Given all of the grief that Semenya has endured, she certainly deserves all the wedded bliss she can find. Semenya's life will, however, be forever defined by her exploits on the track. And in the early portion of 2015 it appeared that she was not going to be getting back to the upper echelons of the international track world. In the middle of July her fastest time of the year stood at 2:04, well outside the qualifying time for the world championships. But then there was a stunning turn of events in another part of the world that rejuvenated her career. We'll get to these events soon enough, but there are details to examine in order to set the stage for the 2015 drama.

11

TRANSGENDER AND INTERSEX ATHLETES, 2009–2014

Following Eric Vilain's nomenclature, everything dealing with intersex athletes after August 2009 could be characterized as the post-Semenya era. So let us start that era with the story of another intersex athlete who first surfaced in that tumultuous year. Her name is Sarah Gronert and she is a German tennis player. News reports from 2009 said that Gronert was born with both male and female genitalia and that she had chosen to have her male genitalia removed at the age of nineteen.[1] What this news probably meant was that Gronert has an XY DSD and that her external genitalia appeared female at birth although she also had internal testes. If her testes did not descend into her inguinal folds during puberty, she would be at an increased risk for cancer,[2] and she probably decided to undergo gonadectomy. There were some reports that Gronert has androgen insensitivity syndrome, and this is a reasonable, although unproven, assumption.

Gronert was born on July 6, 1986, in Linnich, a small town in the northwest corner of Germany, and grew up playing tennis. She has many of the phenotypical characteristics of women with AIS, including the height, but her shoulders are broader than one might expect for someone with CAIS. After her surgery, she had her medical records reviewed by the medical delegate for the Women's Tennis Association in order to be allowed to play in the women's game. The delegate wrote that there was "sufficient independent and verifiable evidence" to permit Gronert to compete against other women.[3] Gronert subsequently began to play tournaments in the developmental league called the International Tennis Federation (ITF). As with many other taller, stronger women, Gronert had a better serve and volley game than many of the smaller women, who tend to be baseline players. Despite her height and strength, Gronert did not see immediate success, and by the end of 2008 her world ranking stood at a modest 735.[4]

In 2009, when Gronert was twenty-two, she started to win some tournaments in the ITF, and just as other gender-nonconforming athletes discovered, she learned that winning comes with controversy. Despite her being ranked 619th in the world at the time, there were those who thought it was unfair that Gronert was allowed to compete. Some of her opponents and their coaches complained loudly about her supposed advantage. One coach claimed that "there is no girl who can hit serves like that, not even Venus Williams." The coach further claimed that Gronert would reach the top 50 within six months.[5]

Gronert did climb in the rankings, reaching 197th in June of 2010, but then her improvement began to stall. Gronert dropped to 289th in 2011, but rebounded to reach her all-time high of 164th in May 2012. Gronert never again played so well, and she retired from competitive tennis in 2013. She won a total of ten titles on the ITF tour, amassing lifetime earnings of just over $96,000. Her lifetime record was 143 wins and 86 losses, with all but four of those matches played in the developmental ITF tour. In the higher-level WTA, Gronert finished her career at 2 wins and 2 losses.[6]

Gronert never became the star that many predicted she would. It is also worth noting that the controversy that followed Gronert was much more subdued than that which followed Semenya in 2009 and beyond. Was this because Gronert never reached the pinnacle of her sport, or was it more to do with the fact that Gronert was white and middle class? Not only was controversy over her muted, but she has almost been forgotten in her post-professional life, although she has posted a few entries onto social media as of late. Notoriety can be a temporary phenomenon, and there were some transgender athletes in those first few post-Semenya years who have also become forgotten in a very short time. Another athlete I'd like to look at is the one who finally broke the LPGA door down.

Lana Lawless was a police officer for most of her adult life. She was also a 1 handicap golfer who once won the championship at her local club. A year after her 2005 gender confirmation surgery, she was watching the long drive competition on television and thought that she could be a factor in the contest. In 2007 Lawless laced up her spikes, entered the contest, and finished third. The following year she did even better, hitting a 254-yard drive into the teeth of a thirty-mile-per-hour headwind to win the contest.[7] Lawless won $12,500 and championship long driver title for her efforts—and, of course, the same condemnation that accompanies any successful trans woman athlete. There is little doubt that trans women golfers have advantages over cisgender women when it comes to driving distance, even after completing surgery and hormone therapy. On average, trans women will be taller, bigger, and stronger than other women,[8] and all of these advantages will contribute to extra length off the tee. Danish transgender golfer Mianne Bagger was not long off the tee when she played in the LET, averaging only approximately 240 yards per drive. She declined to compare this distance to her pre-transition driving distance, saying that there had been improvement in club design in the intervening time. Lawless also stated that her driving distance was reduced after transition but never gave exact figures.

In lieu of data on Lawless and Bagger, let me give you some of mine. In my high school days, golf was one of the sports I pursued regularly. I was good enough to play on my high school team for two years, and I once won the junior club championship at my local club. As an adult I played sporadically both before and after transition. I lost two or three club lengths of distance and maybe 30 yards off the tee after transition. I can say that I was relatively longer among women golfers than I had been among men golfers, but my driving distance was not phenomenal. I am, however, not nearly as sturdily built as Lana Lawless.

After the 2008 Lawless victory, the World Long Drive Association changed its rules to match those of the LPGA, which stated that in order to compete in the women's division, a golfer must "be born a woman."[9] When Lawless tried to enter the event in 2010, she was told she couldn't. Not content to simply lobby the organization, she lawyered up and sued the LPGA, charging that the ban violated California's civil rights policy preventing discrimination against transgender people. Her suit sought to prevent the LPGA from conducting any tournament in the state of California, a massive counterattack.[10] It took less than two months for the LPGA to capitulate. The LPGA members voted unanimously to adopt rules similar to those of the IOC and other organizations, which allowed transgender women to compete against cisgender ones.[11] This legal victory by Lawless was a signature moment for transgender athletes, although the exact dollar amount that Lawless won was never specified.[12] It isn't clear how much the victory changed her life, but Lawless never again competed in the long drive championships or any golf tournament of note. It is possible that one of the stipulations in the financial agreement was that Lawless had to stop competing in order to collect the money, although any such clause would seem to defeat the purpose of the suit. It is also possible that Lawless was uncomfortable with the amount of negative publicity she had generated and decided to keep a very low profile after her victory. Whatever the reason, Lawless never made golf headlines again.

The Lana Lawless story is not the only transgender athlete story of the time that featured a bittersweet ending. Two trans men gained a significant amount of publicity at the time for their exploits in women's sports prior to their medical transition. The first of these is a basketball player who was briefly very famous. Kye Allums, who was given the name Kay-Kay, grew up as an athletic tomboy in the small town of Hugo, Minnesota, just thirty minutes north of the Twin Cities. Kye always preferred dressing like the boys and often referred to himself as a boy while growing up. Once Kye reached high school, he found a home of sorts among the school's lesbian population, but as his high school years wore on, Kye realized he didn't really fit in that group either.[13] Where he did fit was on the basketball court. His height of 5 feet, 11 inches and his athleticism and basketball skills made Kye a standout on the court and earned him an athletic scholarship to George Washington University in Washington, DC. Like many other star high school athletes, Kye had to adjust to the higher level of play in Division I sports, and he spent much of his freshman year on the bench. In his sophomore year, however, he started twenty of the twenty-eight games his team played and put up very respectable averages of 7.4 points and 4.6 rebounds per game.[14]

As a freshman Kye took a course in human sexuality, and it was through this course that he realized his true identity: "I learned what trans meant and I realized that I was trans."[15] By the time basketball season started in his sophomore year, he was bothered by the fact that his teammates would "refer to me using female pronouns every second of the day,"[16] so he gradually came out to the other players on team. Allums asked his teammates to call him Kye and to use male pronouns. By the end of the season, he had told everyone on the team except Head Coach Mike Bozemen. When Allums told Bozeman about his gender identity in June 2010, it proved to be a difficult conversation. Bozmen asked Allums if he thought God had made a mistake. Although Allums didn't know what to say at the time, he later remarked that "I was meant to be like this for a reason."[17]

Allums decided he would delay any surgery or hormone therapy until after his college playing days were over. At the start of the 2010–2011 season his team and the university were both supportive of his decision, and the NCAA allowed trans men to compete in women's sport as long as they weren't taking testosterone. There was no reason why he couldn't continue playing college basketball.

Well, no reason other than the fact that Allums's public coming out in November 2010 was one of the biggest sports stories of the year. The headline in the *New York Times* read, "Transgender Man is on Women's Team," and every other major news outlet covered the story. In the *Times* piece, Allums claimed his transition had improved his game because "I'm just able to focus on basketball now. My outside life is not really a distraction to me."[18] Unfortunately, Kye's outside distractions were about to explode. Much was made of the fact that Allums would be playing his first two games of the season in a tournament in his home state of Minnesota. The team lost both of those games, setting the tone for the rest of the year.

Allums was the first openly transgender athlete to play in the high-stakes world of Division I sports, and the media hounded him at every game he played—at least during the early part of the season. Bozeman quickly tired of the distracting media presence and declared that the transgender subject was closed for all of his team for the remainder of the season.[19] Allums was demoted to the bench,[20] and his season was marred by two concussions in his first eight games. The second of the two concussions ended Allums's season. Although Allums was barred from talking to the media, his mother wasn't, and her interview with the *Washington Post* inflamed tensions at the school.[21] Allums was getting more attention while not playing than the rest of the team combined, and they *were* playing, albeit poorly. The team suffered through a dismal 8–21 season, during which they won only one game on the road.

Although Allums's teammates and coaches were initially supportive of his decision to come out, their support began to erode under the constant media bombardment. Other players began to question the wisdom of Allums's decision to come out. Allums said, "It was crazy to go from them all having my back to no one having my back."[22] In the world of Division I sports, the remedy for failure is to get rid of the coach, so it came as no surprise that Bozeman was fired at the end of the season. Allums had had enough, too. Distraught over the negative press, he attempted suicide during those dismal early months of 2011.[23] In May 2011 he announced that he would not return to the team the following season and that he would start his medical transition. Allums went on to graduate with a degree in fine arts. Although he no longer played for his school, his time as a transgender icon was far from finished. Allums became a tireless transgender advocate, and his efforts have been recognized in multiple arenas, including recognition by *Time* magazine in 2014 as one of twenty-five transgender people who influenced American culture and his 2015 induction into the National Gay and Lesbian Sports Hall of Fame.[24]

Despite all the media hype surrounding him, Kye Allums was not the first out transgender man to compete in women's college sports, nor was he the most successful. Keelin Godsey, a Division III All-American in four different throwing events during his time at Bates College,[25] was far more successful on the athletic fields and preceded Allums as a collegiate athlete by a few years. Godsey, however, competed in the lower-key atmosphere of Division III sports and hence created fewer headlines. Keelin Godsey was born on January 2, 1984, in Massachusetts, but had moved to Colorado by the time he started high school. As a high school athlete in Parker, Colorado, Godsey excelled in numerous sports, including the shot put and discus, but the 5-foot-9-inch athlete had planned on competing in basketball in college. Upon his arrival at Bates College in Maine, however, he quickly found his love for throwing heavy things long distances. Bates gave the young Godsey another gift: that of his gender. It was in a freshman seminar that Godsey learned about the term *transgender*. He quickly realized that his previous identification as a butch lesbian didn't fit his true feelings. By the summer of 2005, Godsey was referring to himself using male pronouns and looking for assistance in explaining himself to teammates and college officials. He found the help he needed in Bates professor Erica

Rand; Godsey says that Rand "was crucial to how smoothly everything went."[26]

Godsey also found support from track and field coach Jennifer "Jay" Hartshorn and his teammates at Bates. Although there were no NCAA guidelines in place at the time, it was clear to everyone at Bates that since Godsey was not taking testosterone, he could continue to compete in the women's division. And Godsey didn't just compete, he dominated. During his four years at Bates he earned sixteen All-American titles in the four throwing events: shot put, discus, weight throw, and hammer throw. It was in the latter discipline that Godsey truly shone. He still holds the Division III record in the hammer throw and he twice won the NCAA championship, defeating throwers from all the divisions.[27] The only drawback to Godsey's senior year at Bates was that he was banished to a separate locker room from his teammates as a result of his coming out as transgender. A few years later, Kye Allums would continue to change and shower with his teammates after he came out. Godsey said that he found the experience isolating. "I didn't like it," he understates. "I wasn't bonding with my team."[28] Godsey also faced taunting from opponents and their fans.

After graduation from Bates, Keelin went on to study physical therapy, earning a doctorate from Northeastern University in 2010. He also continued to throw the hammer at the national level, placing seventh in the 2008 Olympic trials. He packed on the muscle through diligent weight training, getting up to 186 pounds by 2012. He also continued to work on the technique that is so crucial to success in the hammer throw. In the 2011 United States Track and Field Championships, Godsey placed third, earning the right to throw for the United States at the Pan American Games in Guadalajara, Mexico, where he placed fifth. He was the first openly transgender athlete to compete for the red, white, and blue.[29]

Godsey entered 2012 with a very realistic chance of making the US Olympic team. He surpassed the Olympic standard for the hammer by throwing a personal best of 227′ 8″ at the Mt. SAC meet in April in Walnut, California. "All" that was left to do was to place in the top three of the Olympic trials, to be held in Oregon on June 21. The other Olympic qualifying track and field events were held at Hayward Field in Eugene, but Nike set up a throwing cage on its campus in the Portland suburb of Beaverton specifically for the men's and women's hammer throw qualification, staging an afternoon special dubbed Hammer Time. I took the afternoon off of work and drove the thirty minutes over to the Nike campus to cheer for Keelin. It was the biggest crowd I had ever seen for a field event, and the atmosphere was raucous. Godsey had some very vocal fans in attendance and got some of the loudest cheers of any of the throwers. Godsey came up with a big performance that day as he threw farther than he ever had before; 321′ 3″, to be precise. Unfortunately, it wasn't far enough, as others also had big days, and Godsey mustered only a fifth-place finish, eleven inches out of the all-important third place.[30]

I had the opportunity to meet with Godsey briefly after the competition, and he seemed relatively upbeat. He had a reputation for shyness, which was clearly well deserved. Godsey was dignified and polite, but not very interested in talking. He was also pretty buff; although we looked each other in the eye, he outweighed me by about fifty pounds, and it was all muscle. Later that summer he started to take testosterone injections, beginning his medical transition but ending his high-level athletic career. In the following years he competed in some low-key men's hammer throw competitions and did reasonably well, but by no means was he a threat to make the men's Olympic team. Godsey works as a physical therapist and has been officially recognized for his clinical excellence. He also serves as an assistant coach for the track team at Williams College in Massachusetts, specializing in the throws. In 2015 Godsey was inducted into the Bates Scholar-Athlete Society, and he was also named number four on the all-time list of the top ten Bates College athletes.[31]

I would like to look at one more transgender athlete who delayed transition in order to compete in sport. In an interesting twist, this athlete was competing in men's sport although her gender identity is female. Jaiyah Saelua was born on July 19, 1988, on the tiny island nation of American Samoa and was christened Johnny. In chapter 5 I wrote of the Samoan cultural acceptance of the *fa'afafine*, a third gender role assigned to those biological males who have a womanly nature, and Jaiyah is one of the *fa'afafine*. Jaiyah is also an athlete who was introduced to the world of football in school. She started playing at age eleven or twelve and was the MVP of the league in her first season.[32] By the time she was fifteen, she was a member of the national squad, a fact that speaks more to the exodus of young adults from the island due to a lack of financial opportunities than it does to her skill level. Don't get me wrong—Jaiyah can play. Standing 6 feet, 2 inches tall, she possesses fearsome tackling skills and a good nose for the ball; her fierce play belies her feminine nature. It is, however, also true that making the American Samoan national soccer team is not the most difficult task in sport. The island has only approximately sixty thousand inhabitants and does not have a strong tradition in the sport. The team had been consistently ranked 204th (or last) on the FIFA list of nations, and famously lost, 31–0, to Australia in 2001.[33]

Jaiyah embraced her feminine nature while in high school and was well accepted at home, as all *fa'afafine* are. She first experienced transphobia when she left the island after high school to study dance at the University of Hawaii in Hilo.[34] While there, she decided to try out for the university soccer team, only to be run off of the field within fifteen minutes by a coach who told her that he didn't "want to put the rest of the team into an uncomfortable position."[35] Jaiyah returned to American Samoa in 2010 and was given the opportunity to rejoin her country's soccer team as it prepared for the first round of qualifying for the 2014 World Cup. Jaiyah had been living full-time as female in Hawaii and had begun hormone therapy. Upon her return to men's soccer, she cut back on her hormones so that she could be strong. She said, "When I'm on estrogen, I love the way I look and feel, but I can't play soccer well."[36]

The American Samoan team would face Tonga, the Cook Islands, and Samoa in the four-nation tournament that was the first step in the World Cup qualifying process. Leading up to this tournament, the team had never won an international match of any type, let alone a World Cup qualifier; their record stood at an embarrassing 0–30, with a goal tally of 129–2 against them.[37] One indication that things might be different this time around was the fact that former Major League Soccer coach Thomas Rongen was recruited to coach the squad, bringing a higher level of commitment and toughness to the task than any previous coach. Another positive sign was that goalkeeper Nicky Salapu was convinced to come out of retirement to rejoin the team. Salapu was a talented keeper in spite of the fact that he had allowed the 31 goals to the Aussies in 2001. He was haunted by his history and hungered to make amends.

Rongen trained his charges hard and taught them skills they had never learned before. He also trained the team to "think as winners," a departure from the previous acceptance of defeat.[38] In their first game of the tournament, the American Samoan team would face Tonga, and Rongen surprised many when he inserted Jaiyah into the starting lineup for the first time in her career. Previously she had only played limited minutes, but the new coach liked her fierce attitude on the pitch. Jaiyah played the full ninety minutes of the Tonga game, getting the assist on the first goal, making a vital last-minute goal line clearance of a ball that had gotten behind Salapu, and delivering several bone-crushing tackles to cut off Tonga rushes.[39] Her play was no small part of the historic 2–1 victory the American Samoan team achieved that day. In the film *Next Goal Wins*, Rongen called her the "most valuable man, or perhaps woman" on the squad that day.[40]

The team went on to a 1–1 tie with the Cook Island team and tough 1–0 loss to the Samoan team. The latter match was scoreless up until the final minute—the American Samoan team had put a potentially game-winning shot off the goal post—and meant that Jaiyah's team just missed moving on to the second round of the tournament. The release of *Next Goal Wins* in 2014 gave Jaiyah the opportunity to travel the world, promoting the film and the acceptance of transgender people everywhere. Her "warm and engaging personality" made her well-suited for this role as a transgender spokesperson.[41] Jaiyah returned to Hawaii to finish her studies and currently plays on a club soccer team founded by Ramin Ott, the captain of the 2011 American Samoan team.[42] Jaiyah also played for the American Samoan team in the 2019 Pacific Games.[43]

Although Jaiyah Saelua is tall, she wasn't the tallest transgender athlete to emerge in those years. That honor goes to Gabrielle Ludwig, an American basketball player of German descent. And while Saelua's reception was mostly positive, Ludwig faced a much different fate because she gained notoriety competing against women. Born in Germany, Gabrielle Ludwig never knew her father. Her mother brought her to America after falling in love with a US serviceman. Growing up, Ludwig's cross-dressing brought her only temporary relief from the feeling that she didn't fit in. She attempted suicide when she was fifteen, swallowing as many pills as she could find in the house. Basketball was a savior for the young athlete. Ludwig grew to a height of 6 feet, 8 inches, and became a star in high school. She played for one year on the men's team at Nassau Community College in 1980. In 1984 Ludwig joined the navy and wound up serving eight years, including a hitch in the first Gulf War.[44]

Ludwig started taking female hormones in 2006, and the changes were a factor in her divorce from her second wife. In 2007 Ludwig transitioned on the job as a systems engineer at Roche Molecular Systems in Silicon Valley. In July 2012 her company paid for genital surgery. She was coaching a sixth grade girls' team when she met Corey Cafferata, the coach at Mission College, who was refereeing at a tournament. Coaches and referees often disagree during games, and Cafferata suggested that he could teach her the game if she came to one of his practices. Ludwig took Cafferata at his word, and in August 2012 she called him up and asked if she could join his team. He didn't remember her, and he had no interest in having some middle-aged coach join his team. Then Ludwig told Cafferata she was 6 feet, 6 inches tall.[45] There is an old basketball saying that you can teach a lot of things in the game, but you can't teach height. Cafferata was interested. Ludwig enrolled in online courses to obtain eligibility and started practicing with the team that fall. This was only a few months after her surgery, and there is no way she could be at full strength.

In her first game, Ludwig scored three points, all at the foul line, and grabbed four defensive rebounds in six minutes of playing time as her team lost, 69 62.[46] She also faced a slew of reporters who showed up to watch her play. The media attention was overwhelming at first. Two male talk show hosts at an ESPN-affiliated radio station referred to her as "it."[47] Ludwig offered to quit, but her teammates wouldn't hear of it. Not all of the attention heaped on Ludwig was bad. Christina Kharl at ESPN, inspired by Gabbi, wrote a wonderful piece, saying, among other things, that "[b]eyond just her willingness to play, her bravery in the face of some horrible reactions and even worse comments is every bit as inspiring."[48] Many others held Ludwig up as an inspirational figure.

Throughout that winter, Ludwig endured taunts from opponents and their fans, intense media scrutiny, and speculation that it wasn't fair to allow the taller, heavier player to suit up. Critics claimed that Ludwig would dominate the games, but it didn't happen; she averaged 5.9 points and 4.4 rebounds per game over the 2012–2013 season, hardly dominating stats. Part of the problem was that she had trouble, at age fifty-one, keeping up with the faster tempo played by the much younger players on the court. Ludwig averaged only 10.9 minutes per game. The team played well, however, winning their conference and making the playoffs in the competitive California Community College League. Ludwig was determined to play better in her second and last year playing for the college. She underwent a rigorous summer training program and returned in the fall of 2013 as a different player. Her playing time skyrocketed, and so did her stats. She became the team's starting center, logging almost thirty minutes a game. Ludwig finished the season as the second-highest scorer on her team and the second-leading rebounder in the entire league.[49]

Fan reaction had changed, too. On Veterans Day of 2013 the team played at Ohlone College, where Ludwig had faced intense heckling the year before. The PA announcer asked the fans to honor all of the veterans present, including Gabbi, and the crowd reacted with an extended round of applause. She commented, "After all the hate I saw last year in that gym and for me to see that, I'm human—I broke down and cried."[50] The media attention also waned considerably. Ludwig garnered so much negative attention during the 2012–2013 season, when she struggled on the court, yet she went almost unnoticed by the national press during the 2013–2014 season, when she averaged 14.0 points, 14.2 rebounds per game, and was named to the all-conference first team. Although I'm certain Ludwig was pleased with her improvement over her first season, basketball is, at its heart, a team sport. The 2013–2014 Mission College team was not as successful as the 2012–2013 one had been, and they failed to make the playoffs, disappointing Ludwig and her teammates. Although her college playing days are over, the game remains a large part of her life. Ludwig currently serves as an assistant coach with Mission College and as a mentor for several young basketball players. She also continues to play the sport recreationally.[51]

Keelin Godsey's failed attempt to make the 2012 Olympic team meant that no openly transgender athlete had ever competed in the games through the first thirty modern Olympiads. The controversy over the inclusion of both intersex and transgender athletes in women's sport was not about to go away any time soon, but there was a growing movement toward inclusivity that would shape the debate over the next few years. Some of the calls for more inclusion came from the media and some from academia, and it would be good to look at these voices next.

12

THE POST-SEMENYA LANDSCAPE

One sign of a changing attitude toward transgender athletes was a feature-length article that appeared in *Sports Illustrated* in May 2012.[1] The main focus of the article was Keelin Godsey's quest for an Olympic berth, but the article also contained shorter write-ups on Kye Allums, Lana Lawless, and other transgender athletes. The tone of the article was sympathetic to the struggles of trans athletes, and the fact that a major publication like *SI* was willing to publish the piece was groundbreaking. The article was cowritten by Pablo Torre and David Epstein, and the latter author would become an important person in the unfolding story.

David grew up in the Chicago suburb of Evanston, Illinois, where he was a track star and a standout student. He then matriculated at Columbia University, where he earned master's degrees in astronomy and journalism. David also ran track at Columbia, dipping down under 1:50 for the 800 meter distance. David spent several years at *Sports Illustrated*, where, among other things, he was one of the investigative journalists responsible for breaking stories on the doping habits of Alex Rodriguez and Lance Armstrong.[2] David's marvelous book *The Sports Gene* would become one of the most widely read and respected sports science books. I was pleasantly surprised when David took personal interest in my story. Here is how it happened.

In 2009 I had begun to write for a website called *Younger Legs for Older Runners*, which was hosted by USATF masters hall of fame athlete Pete Magill.[3] In addition to being a wonderful runner, Pete is also a very talented writer. He has published two books on running, and he previously worked as a Hollywood scriptwriter. At the time, Pete and I were merely acquaintances, but when he asked for additional writers to help with his website, I agreed. The Semenya saga began shortly after I started blogging for Pete, and I decided to write an article about gender-diverse athletes. Pete hosted my piece, called "Gender, Sport and Caster." One of Pete's readers said that my article was easily the best one that had been written on the subject. It was also that fall that I first contacted Ross Tucker. Ross had earned a PhD in exercise physiology at the University of Cape Town, studying under the widely known Tim Noakes. After earning his PhD, Ross spent four more years at UCT before becoming professor of exercise physiology with the School of Medicine of the University of the Free State. He is an adjunct professor at UCT and serves as a consultant to several international sporting organizations, including World Rugby, South Africa rugby sevens, SA Kayaking, SA Triathlon, USA Triathlon, and the UK Olympic Committee. Ross has written widely on many topics of sports performance and has been named one of the one hundred most influential South Africans.[4]

Ross has devoted quite a bit of space on his website *The Science of Sport* to the Semenya controversy over the years.[5] Back in 2009 I reached out to Ross, as he was someone whose opinion I valued. The most important point I raised during our subsequent discussion was a response to the uncertainty many of Ross's readers had concerning Semenya's gender. I commented at the time that although it was clear that Semenya's social gender was female, the IAAF had yet to determine her gender for the purpose of sport. I would later collapse the phrase "gender for the purpose of sport" to the term *athletic gender*. I don't claim that I was the first person in the world to suggest the concept of athletic gender, but I have found no other mention of an analogous term prior to 2011. I can say without hesitation that I came up with the concept of athletic gender independently of anyone else. I was familiar with the term *social gender*, and I merely extrapolated that idea to sport. In time, the notion of an athletic gender would become important, but in 2009 it was just an idea that I threw out to Ross and his readers.

I also continued to gather data on transgender distance runners. The work was very slow, as most transgender athletes of the time were very secretive. However, perseverance is one of my strongest qualities, and by 2012 I had amassed data on six trans runners including myself. While researching his *SI* story, David Epstein found my name as a result of my blogging, but it was the data I had gathered that would prove to be my eventual contribution to the article. David said that he had been scouring the internet for performance-based studies on trans athletes, and that there weren't any. David was the first cisgender person who understood the importance of the data I had been patiently gathering. David was strongly supportive of the need to get my data published, but I had reservations. I understood how unique and valuable the data were, but I also knew that trying to get the study published would be an uphill battle. I had only six subjects at the time, I had no academic credentials, and I was transgender—all strikes against me. David, however, was persistent, and he lit a fire under me. He gave me some contact information that ultimately proved to be a dead end, but the most important thing he gave me was hope. I promised David I wouldn't give up and that I would eventually find a way to get the paper published.

My connection with David would prove to be a very important one in my life. David's 2013 book *The Sports Gene* would also include my data,[6] widening the circle of people who knew about my work. After countless e-mails, I had the opportunity to meet David for the first time in 2013, and I came away from that night convinced that I needed to devote more of my life to the study of gender variance in sports.

Another important development in the lives of transgender athletes was the adoption of hormone-based rules by the NCAA in August 2011. Pat Griffin and Helen Carroll were the two main authors of the policy but they also leaned on Eric Vilain and others for medical wisdom. The policy was initially drafted in 2010 and was the first time that rule makers determined that hormones rather than surgery were the key requirement. Trans women were required to undergo one year of hormone therapy prior to competing in women's sport while trans men were prohibited from competing in women's sport after starting on T.

The period between 2012 and 2014 was important in terms of shifting attitudes toward intersex athletes. The general public becomes much more aware of sports-related topics during an Olympic year, and 2012 was no exception; the Caster Semenya saga reached a wider audience that year than it had when she was competing in IAAF events. Likewise, the IAAF's adoption in of hyperandrogenism (HA) regulations for intersex and transgender athletes[7] was similarly underreported in the mainstream press. On the other hand, the 2012 adoption of similar rules by the IOC[8] ignited a firestorm of protest. Two American-based academics, Rebecca Jordan-Young and Katrina Karkazis, were at the forefront of the movement opposing the IOC and IAAF rules. Rebecca Jordan-Young is an associate professor in the Women's, Gender and Sexuality Studies Department at Barnard College, a liberal arts institute affiliated with Columbia University. She earned her PhD degree in sociomedical sciences (a sociological degree) from Columbia University. Her teaching and research interests are diverse, mostly involving science, gender, and sexuality.[9] She has written the book *Brain Storm*, which is a critical analysis of the science behind gender-based brain differentiation.[10]

In the first couple of years after the implementation of the IOC's version of hyperandrogenism rules, Jordan-Young was probably the most important voice opposing these rules, but beginning in 2014 she was replaced at the forefront of the movement by her younger colleague Katrina Karkazis. Karkazis earned a PhD from Columbia University in medical and cultural anthropology. She currently holds academic positions with City University of New York and Yale University,[11] although she was at Stanford University during the time period in question. Like Jordan-Young, Karkazis spends much of her efforts in critical analysis. Her book *Fixing Sex* deals with controversies in the medical management of intersex issues.[12]

Together Jordan-Young and Karkazis coauthored several well-written and thoughtful critiques of the endocrine-based rules for eligibility for women's sport. Probably the most often cited of their scientific articles is the paper "Out of Bounds," which was published in the *American Journal of Bioethics* in 2012.[13] The pair also cowrote a number of op-eds for the mainstream press during the time between 2012 and 2104. One of the most prominent of these pieces, entitled "You Say You're a Woman? That Should Be Enough," was published by the *New York Times*.[14] The title of the *Times* article implies that the pair believed gender identity should be the foundation for the division of sports into male and female categories, although it would later appear that Karkazis abandoned this position. Karkazis and Jordan-Young were fundamentally opposed to the use of testosterone as the marker to split athletes into male and female categories. They felt that the effects of higher endogenous testosterone levels (as opposed to exogenous forms, such as doping) are poorly understood, and their potential advantages are unproven. The pair stated many times that it is unfair to single out intersex women, whose bodies make more testosterone (i.e., male levels), when no other natural advantage is prohibited and given that elite athletes have many advantages over less elite competitors. As an example, no one would try to limit the height of female high jumpers, even though extra height is clearly an advantage in the sport.

Karkazis and Jordan-Young also took considerable umbrage over the fallout experienced by intersex athletes as a result of policing gender in sport. They decried the medical interventions required to bring intersex athletes into adherence of this policy, and furthermore, they believed it is unfair to stigmatize women as being unnaturally masculine when there is considerable overlap between those qualities seen as manly and those needed to succeed in sports. In the article "Out of Bounds," Karkazis and Jordan-Young state that "female athletes have always been under suspicion, and women with intersex traits have often been scapegoats for broad anxiety about the gender contradiction inherent in the very concept of an elite female athlete."[15] Although the positions of Jordan-Young and Karkazis are thoughtful, their writing is excellent, and their empathy for intersex women is admirable, it is also true that their take on testosterone is a minority one. The overwhelming majority of biologists accept that testosterone is the most important difference between male and female athletes. Furthermore, the suggestion that endogenous and exogenous testosterone should be regarded as fundamentally different has gathered little support among scientists.[16]

The suggestion that all naturally held advantages should be allowed, however, has gathered wider support, including from Bruce Kidd. As a young athlete in the sixties, Kidd had won two distance medals in the Commonwealth Games and was a member of Canada's 1964 Olympic team, running the 5000 and 10,000 meter races in Tokyo. Kidd went on to earn his PhD in history from York University and became a professor at the University of Toronto, where he at one time was the head of the School of Physical and Health Education. Kidd was subsequently inducted into the Canadian Sports Hall of Fame, both as an athlete and as a builder of sport.[17] Over the years, Kidd has consistently been a vocal advocate for social justice within the realm of athletics. Kidd is also a champion for gender self-identification. With regard to the hyperandrogenism rules, he has stated more than once that any attempt to use endocrine-based criteria for eligibility for women's sport is simply another method of "policing femininity" and is, in his opinion, unacceptable.[18] I had the opportunity to speak with Kidd in 2014, and I asked him about the importance of testosterone in sport. He replied that although the effect of testosterone on athletic performance was debatable, "the main point is that if it's naturally occurring, it should be treated just like any other favorable genetic characteristic, and allowed without qualification."[19]

The reason I was able to speak with Bruce Kidd arose indirectly from my connection with David Epstein. David coauthored a response to the Karkazis/Jordan-Young position with Alice Dreger,[20] with whom he had become friends. In 2014 David connected me to Alice, and in turn Alice connected me to a number of people involved with the intersex athlete controversies. Alice Dreger is a complicated person, and I'm not certain that I can do her justice in two hundred words, but let me try. She earned her PhD in history and philosophy of science from Indiana University in 1995.[21] She had been studying topics that would become important for her book *Hermaphrodites and the Medical Invention of Sex* when she met the intersex activist most of us know by the name of Cheryl Chase. Cheryl and Alice worked hand-in-hand to run the Intersex Society of North America for the next ten years.[22] Cheryl was invited to the 2005 meeting that resulted in many revised standards of care for intersex patients, and Alice was invited to the meetings held by the IAAF and the IOC in 2009 through 2011 to help determine precisely how to separate male athletes from female athletes. It was through her intersex activism that she knew many of the same people from whom I needed to learn in 2014. At the time when I was just beginning to get involved in these controversies, Alice was moving on to other topics. You see, Alice Dreger is much more than an intersex activist—she is an amazingly gifted writer and author of several books and articles—but it is not the purview of this book to explore her life. Although Alice also supports the unqualified inclusion of intersex athletes in sport, she is far more sanguine on the role of testosterone than Jordan-Young or Karkazis. I will be forever indebted to Alice for the assistance she offered me in 2014, and I remain appreciative of her commitment to the scientific method.

Alice also suggested that I speak to Dr. Sari van Anders, a scientist who was often cited by Karkazis and Jordan-Young as a source for their views on testosterone. I spent much of one week in June 2014 emailing back and forth with van Anders and found the exchanges to be enlightening. Sari van Anders grew up in Toronto and, like me, earned undergraduate and master's degrees from the University of Western Ontario. She then earned her PhD in biological and cognitive psychology from Simon Fraser University. At the time of our correspondence, she was an assistant professor in the departments of Psychology and Women's Studies at the University of Michigan and was later promoted to associate professor. In July 2018 she moved to Queens University in Kingston, Ontario.[23] Dr. van Anders has performed a great deal of research on the effects of testosterone, including papers about the difficulty in accurately measuring testosterone levels and misconceptions about the role of T in social and sexual behavior. She is dubious about attributing the majority of the difference between male and female athletic performance to differences in T levels.

Although my conversations with van Anders did not change my opinion on the use of testosterone in the determination of athletic gender, she did have more luck on a related subject. One of the arguments of Jordan-Young and Karkaizs was that it is inherently discriminatory to set an upper T limit for women but not for men. I admit I found van Anders's arguments in favor of this position to be persuasive (I would later find counter arguments to be even more persuasive). I asked van Anders if she would be willing to give me a position statement concerning eligibility for women's sports. She replied, "My position is that all people have the right to compete in their legally recognized gender/sex category. People cannot be excluded for endogenous bodily difference, and women cannot be selectively policed."[24]

Although it was interesting to speak to Kidd and van Anders, the most important connection provided to me by Alice Dreger was to Arne Ljungqvist, who had been perhaps the most important person in the extremely contentious world of gender variance and sport since the time of the María José Martínez-Patiño situation in 1985. Once Ljungqvist learned about the science behind CAIS, he became one of the leading voices calling for the cessation of universal chromosome testing on athletes. At the time, he was a vice president of the IAAF and a member of the IOC medical commission, and thus held more clout in the former organization. Ljungqvist's influence was one of the reasons the IAAF stopped using universal testing in 1990, while it took the IOC until 1998 to adopt a similar stance. It is not a coincidence that the IOC also stopped universal chromosome testing once Ljungqvist became chairman of its medical commission.[25] One of the more interesting human aspects of Ljungqvist's life is that his support of Martínez–Patiño led to a long-term friendship between the two that continues today.

María José Martínez-Patiño has an interesting story after her brush with fame in the 1980s. She did not let all the personal strife that she was subjected to at the time ruin in her life. Instead, after her athletic career was over, she went back to school and earned her PhD in physical education; today she is a professor today at the University of Vigo in the Galicia region of Spain. In addition to her friendship with Ljungqvist, she also coauthored a scientific paper with him in 2003.[26] Martínez-Patiño also has had an interesting relationship with the rules governing intersex athletes. As could be expected, she was initially opposed to any attempt to regulate the participation of intersex athletes, but she later changed her mind. The IAAF invited her to the table as part of its process in developing hyperandrogenism rules. At one of the meetings, Martínez-Patiño met the British runner Paula Radcliffe. The two athletes had some fruitful discussions, and Martínez-Patiño came away from the meeting with a greater appreciation of the position of elite female athletes. Martínez-Patiño is now a powerful speaker in favor of the position of some kind of limitations on intersex athletes.[27]

Ljungqvist was generous enough to speak to me when I first contacted him and was also kind enough to make introductions to other members of the IOC and IAAF medical commissions. One of the most important of Ljungqvist's introductions was to Dr. Stéphane Bermon. Bermon was born in Nice, France, and earned MD and PhD degrees in 1992 and 1998, respectively. For three years in the late 1980s he was a professional snowboarder, and he is still active in the sport. In the summer he does triathlons and surfs.[28] Bermon has his own private sports medicine practice in Monaco, and he heads up the IAAF Science and Health Division.[29] In the latter role he has gained significant expertise in dealing in issues regarding athletes with DSDs. Bermon has published widely on issues regarding intersex athletes and sports. He consistently advocates for fair and meaningful competition for all female athletes and feels that restrictions on intersex athletes are justified in the larger context of the attempt to create a level playing field for all women.

As of 2014, the IAAF had little published research on the advantages held by intersex athletes, but cited research showing advantages resulting from the modest testosterone increase inherent in a condition called polycystic ovary syndrome (PCOS). PCOS is a condition in which the ovaries are enlarged and contain multiple small cysts along the edges. The most common symptoms of PCOS are irregular or prolonged menstrual periods and elevated androgen levels. In most cases the elevation in T is fairly mild and usually within female norms. Even so, "endurance athletes with PCOS demonstrated the most anabolic body composition, highest VO2 max, and highest performance values."[30] Beyond the studies on PCOS, there was more evidence in support of the advantages of higher T. Bermon also cited the significant overrepresentation—by a factor of 140—of athletes with DSDs at the Daegu world championships in 2011 as a powerful, if indirect, indication of advantage.

One important matter Bermon emphasized in our conversations in 2014 was that athletes were not prevented from competing simply on the basis of a single testosterone reading. Instead, the high T result triggers an investigation into the cause. The athlete is summoned to one of the four IAAF-affiliated medical centers worldwide, where extensive testing is performed on the athlete. These tests include a second blood test, a determination of karyotype (chromosome pattern), an assay of steroid and polypeptide hormones, a pelvic MRI, and bone density measurements. If the IAAF scientists suspect a DSD, molecular analysis of the pertinent gene is performed in order to determine any mutations that might exist. Only when the specialists at the center have determined the source of the hyperandrogenism do they make a decision about the athlete's future.[31]

One of the most important publications to come out of the IAAF camp at this time became known as the Fénichel paper, after its lead author Patrick Fénichel, a French physician working with the IAAF. The paper, which reported findings from the medical study of four young athletes with 5-ARD, was published in the *Journal of Clinical Endocrinology & Metabolism* in 2013. The four athletes from developing countries were studied at two hospitals in France. The athletes all had T levels between 15 and 18 nmol/L, well above the 10 nom/L cutoff, and only slightly below the mean T level for men. All four had testes, located in either their labia or their inguinal regions. All four were from remote areas, and three of the four reported consanguinity (their parents were either siblings or cousins), while the fourth suspected it. The four athletes all had larger than typical clitorises, and they also decided to continue living as female. The IAAF doctors recommended the four athletes undergo bilateral gonadectomy—an operation they were told "would most likely decrease their performance level, but allow them to continue in elite sport in the female category." It was also proposed that the athletes should undergo clitoral reduction surgery and vaginoplasty (not required by IAAF eligibility regulations, but desired by those gender diverse people who long for female-typical bodies), and start estrogen replacement therapy. All four athletes agreed to these surgeries "after informed consent."[32] Although it is admirable that the IAAF allowed these data to be published, there were some troubling aspects to the paper.

A 2014 paper whose coauthors included Eric Vilain and María José Martínez-Patiño took issue with many of the details of the Fénichel paper. The authors criticized the consent process outlined in the Fenichel paper, suggesting that "informed consent should be obtained following a process that provides the athlete with clear, intelligible information in a context that will maximize her autonomy and choices to pursue or not to pursue medical interventions."[33] Further, the authors suggested that the addition of a neutral third party or ombudsperson to the process would allow the athlete to obtain truly informed consent.

The UCLA group was not the only one to comment on the Fénichel paper. Rebecca Jordan-Young, Peter Sonksen, and Katrina Karkazis published a paper in the April 2014 edition of the *British Medical Journal* objecting to the details of the Fénichel paper. The Jordan-Young paper took issue with the partial clitoridectomies of the four athletes in the Fénichel paper, stating that "clitoral surgery should have no role in interventions undertaken for athletes' eligibility or health."[34] Perhaps the most important difference between the Jordan-Young paper and the UCLA one was that the former called for an end to the testosterone-based rules, while the latter did not.

The Fénichel paper and the responses to it had a significant effect on my views at the time. Since 2009 I had believed that testosterone levels were the best method to differentiate between male and female athletes, but I was troubled by some of implications of the Fénichel study. I also suspected that the IAAF had probably not told the four young women just how much slower they would become after gonadectomy. A later Bermon paper would detail a 5 to 6 percent performance reduction.[35] Although Jordan-Young and Karkazis were eloquent in their dissent, their alternative—allowing intersex athletes to compete without restriction—was not appealing, as it would not allow meaningful competition for all women. I was more taken with the constructive criticism of the Ha response. Not that anyone cared what I thought. Without any published works, I had little clout, so getting my data published in a peer-reviewed journal was paramount. By 2014 I had amassed data from eight transgender distance runners, and in December of that year my paper was accepted for publication in the *Journal of Sporting Cultures and Identities*.[36] Although it is a minor journal, this publication would be a turning point for me. And it came just in time. It had become clear to me that a showdown was certain to happen in the not-too-distant future. In June 2014 I wrote in my journal that it was only matter of time before an intersex athlete sued for the right to compete in sports as she had been born. My prophecy was about to become true, and far sooner than I would have imagined.

13

DUTEE CHAND

We now come to the third of Eric Vilain's three history-defining intersex woman athletes, an Indian sprinter named Dutee Chand. Caster Semenya may be the most talked-about intersex athlete of all time, and María José Martínez-Patiño the most respected, but Dutee Chand's effect on history might be as large as either of the other two giants. Chand was born in 1996 to an impoverished weaver couple in the small remote village of Gopalpur in the state of Odisha, one of the poorest regions in India. She was the third-born child in her family; in all she has six sisters and one brother.[1] Chand got involved with sports early in life; at the age of four she began to accompany an elder sister on her track workouts. By the age of ten, Chand was living three hours from home as part of a government-run sports group in her district.[2] Early on she competed in multiple sports, but it did not take long to discover that her real talent lay in sprinting. By the age of fifteen Chand was an Odisha state champion in the 100 and 200 meter races in the under-eighteen division, defeating girls more than two years her senior.[3] Chand's meteoric rise continued in 2012, when, at the age of sixteen, she became the national under-eighteen champion in the 100 meters. In 2013, at age seventeen, Chand became the first Indian athlete to ever make a global 100 meter final at the World Youth Championships in Donetsk, Ukraine, placing sixth overall. She had now also become the best sprinter of any age in her country, winning the 100 and the 200 at the national championships.[4]

The money Chand has earned as an athlete has been invaluable to her family, enabling them to move out of the two-room mud hut she grew up in and into a four-room house with running water.[5] Chand's prowess as a sprinter also opened doors for her that would otherwise have remained closed. She was accepted as a student at KIIT University in Bhubaneswar and was in her second year there when her world was turned upside down in 2014.[6] In June of that year the now-eighteen-year-old Chand won two gold medals at the Asian Junior Championships—but these victories came at a high cost, as a complaint was lodged against her.[7] Sensing that Chand was too masculine, this unnamed source requested that a hyperandrogenism test be performed on the Indian sprinter. Upon Chand's return home, the Athletics Federation of India requested that medical tests be performed on her. The governing body for all Indian sport, known as the Sports Authority of India (SAI), investigated, conducting blood tests and an MRI scan to determine her internal anatomy.[8] Chand's testosterone level was deemed by the AFI to be too high to allow her to continue competing in the women's division. She had already been selected to run in the Commonwealth Games but was dropped from the team.[9] And then a most unexpected thing happened. The national media, which had been very unkind to Santhi Soundarajan and Pinki Pramanik, rallied to Chand's support. The *Hindustan Times* compared Chand's androgen advantage to the many advantages of her competitors from "affluent nations, who ate foods as children that she had never seen, received healthcare that she was not fortunate to receive, and were trained in ways that were beyond her means until late in her life. Her competitors, by the virtue of their birth in places that are very different from Odisha, enjoyed unfair advantages. Her androgenic hormones, in contrast, are her being."[10]

Perhaps the most important thing the press did for Chand was to alert Dr. Payoshni Mitra about the case. Mitra had been interested in gender and sport since her days as a PhD student. In 2010 Mitra began to research intersex issues, and her PhD dissertation was entitled "Ungendering Sports: Towards a Re-evaluation of the Female Athlete in India."[11] She had the opportunity to meet both Santhi Soundarajan and Pinki Pramanik in 2011 and had become one of the most influential Indian voices with respect to intersex athletes. Among other things, she had this to say: "There is an overall insensitivity towards difference. We laugh at someone who is taller than usual, bigger than the average and we laugh at those who are gender variant."[12]

Like many other intersex activists, Mitra has a strong distaste for "normalization" surgery. She says that "[s]urgery is required only when one has a disease or life-threatening medical condition. Not when one is different." Mitra also says that not just surgery but also medical intervention in those with DSDs is wrong, except in cases where it is needed to preserve life. She says, "The most ideal course of action I can think of is to have no course of action at all."[13] Once Mtira heard about Chand, she contacted the athlete, and after their phone call Mitra took an eight-hour train ride to meet the sprinter.[14] Given Mitra's views on intervention, it is not surprising that she advised Chand against consenting to either surgery or drugs but instead suggested mounting a challenge to the current rules.

Shortly after Chand was outed, I contacted Katrina Karkazis, who confirmed that she was in touch with an unnamed person (presumably Mitra) in India. By August 2014 it was apparent that Karkazis had joined forces with Mitra in a battle to allow Chand to compete without submitting to any medical procedures. Bruce Kidd became a third member of their crusade, and they spearheaded an impressive attack on the androgen-based rules of the IAAF and the IOC. There were multiple media articles sympathetic to Chand's plight, a website, and an online petition to "let Dutee run!"[15] Karkazis, Mitra, and Kidd argued that Chand had been born and raised female and should be allowed to compete with other women. This statement and others that would follow marked a shift for Karkazis and company. Rather than suggest that gender identity should be the most important factor determining eligibility for women's sport, they were suggesting that intersex athletes should be allowed to compete with "the body they were born with."[16] This notion that one is "born female" relies on a superficial examination of external genitalia at birth. In Karkazis's book *Fixing Sex* she had consistently belittled the notion that sex was easily determined at birth,[17] but now she was championing the idea.

In addition to all the press Karkazis and her colleagues generated, they also secured some impressive legal representation: On September 26, 2014, Jim Bunting, a Canadian lawyer with experience in sports-related cases, filed an appeal with the Court of Arbitration for Sport (CAS) challenging the IAAF's androgen-based rules on Chand's behalf.[18] Only the hardest-hearted person could fail to find sympathy for the distraught Indian athlete, as Chand went through a very difficult period. She says that she "cried for three straight days" after people began to question her gender.[19] At first she was more than willing to be "cured" so she could return to sports, but once Mitra more fully explained Chand's predicament, her tone changed. Chand was later quoted as saying, "I am what I am" and that she feels "it is wrong to have to change your body for sports participation." More defiantly, she has also stated that she is "not changing for anyone."[20]

Amazingly, within ten days of the Chand story breaking, word of another probable intersex runner reached the public. The World Junior Track and Field Championships were held in Eugene, Oregon, in July 2014, and once again there was controversy in the women's 800. The winner of the race was a tall, masculine-appearing Kenyan woman named Margaret Wambui. Like many young athletes, Wambui had participated in several different sports. She was a standout volleyball player and sprinter, and also decided to try the heptathlon. It was in the seven-event competition that her talent for the 800 became apparent. In 2014 she finished second to Maximilla Imali (Imali would later be revealed to be intersex)[21] in the finals of the Kenyan junior championships, in 2:04, earning a spot on the Kenyan team for Eugene.[22] In Eugene, Wambui ran personal bests in her heats and semifinals. In the final, Iceland's Aníta Hinriksdóttir took the field out in a much-too-fast time of 56.3 seconds. Only Wambui and Cuban favorite Sahily Diago dared to follow the frenetic pace set by the Icelandic athlete. The fast pace took its toll on the three leaders, with Hinriksdóttir failing to finish the race and Diago fading to a 2:02 time. Although Wambui slowed, she still ran powerfully through the finish line, stopping the clock at 2:00.49 for a massive win.[23] It is almost unfathomable that an athlete with no international experience should become so successful in such short order. Not only was Wambui now the best junior 800 runner in the world, she was certainly among the top ten in the world of any age. Wambui would undoubtedly be offered a lane in any of the Diamond League track meets, which admit only the crème de la crème of all of the world's track athletes. How could this be possible?

The running website *LetsRun* has a very active message board, and it didn't take long for the accusations against Wambui to start. Many of the anonymous people posting on the message board described her as a man, and others took to calling her Semenya version 2.0.[24] I e-mailed Robert Johnson, one of the two brothers in charge of the website, telling him that Wambui was probably only one of a long string of intersex athletes (I gave Robert the names of some other probable intersex runners, including Francine Niyonsaba) and that it was not a good idea to make too much of a fuss over her. I outlined the procedures the IAAF followed in its examinations of intersex athletes and provided some of the recent scientific papers on the subject. Robert and I decided that it would be beneficial for me to write an article for his website, and the article was published in September.[25] Wambui did not compete again until June 2015 at the Prefontaine Classic, and her time at Pre was more than a second slower than the time she recorded in July 2014.[26] It would be reasonable to assume that in the time between the two meets she had undergone some sort of testosterone-reducing procedure. The Pre meet is also held in Eugene, and I was in attendance when Wambui stepped onto the track in the spring of 2015. In fact, I was close enough to the track to overhear an announcer ask one of Wambui's competitors if she had heard of the Kenyan. The athlete declined knowledge of Wambui, but would surely hear about her in the not-too-distant future.

Prior to the Chand and Wambui incidents I had been in contact with both Karkazis and Stéphane Bermon. I had told each of them that I was trying to be a neutral observer of their differences rather than take either side. And so I did observe what transpired in the fall of 2014. I saw the press barrage by the Karkazis faction around their very sympathetic athlete. These articles alleged that testosterone was only one of several factors that determine excellence in sport, often mentioning height, hand size, and other physical attributes that also contribute to sporting success.[27] There is no limit placed on the height of female athletes, for example, and very tall women will excel at sports such as basketball. The articles said that if allowing very tall women to play is considered fair, then why should a limit be placed on how much testosterone a woman's body makes? Couldn't those who govern sport understand that Chand and others like her had simply won the genetic lottery with regard to testosterone? The articles often challenged the scientific validity of using testosterone as the sole determinant of eligibility for women's sport. Karkaizs and company argued that research showing the massive advantages of exogenously administered testosterone—that is, doping—did not apply to those women with higher levels of endogenously produced testosterone.[28] A further argument put forward by the Chand team was that placing an upper limit on women's T levels without a corresponding limit on men's T levels was inherently discriminatory.[29] The same articles bemoaned the horrors of surgical intervention for intersex athletes. Often, the Chand team also painted a very grim picture of the potential side effects of hormone therapy.[30]

Although I was certainly impressed with the level of organization and commitment of Karkazis and her colleagues, I became disenchanted with much of the content of the arguments. First, there was no acknowledgment that some intersex women have a huge advantage over other women. Comparing the testosterone advantage of intersex women to the advantages held by those who are taller or who have bigger hands was, I felt, disingenuous. The point in dividing sport into specific categories is to ensure equitable and meaningful competition within any given category. In his book *Good Sport*, Thomas Murray puts it this way: "Every sport that creates eligibility categories . . . [stages] separate events so that raw biological differences don't overwhelm talent, dedication and courage."[31] In particular, we divide men and women into different categories because, at the elite level, women cannot compete equitably with men in the vast majority of sports. If we care about the success of female athletes, this sporting division between men and women—athletic gender—should be determined using a sexually dimorphic biomarker that is an important differentiating factor between male and female athletes. Testosterone is such a factor. Hand size is not.

I especially took issue with the fact that Karkazis often used selective quotes from the papers of scientists working with the IAAF, such as Bermon, to support her positions on endogenous testosterone.[32] I was disturbed by the fact that many of the selective quotes from the papers would lead one to believe that Bermon opposed the IAAF rules, when in fact he was an ardent supporter—and one of the coauthors—of the rules. Additionally, I thought she was exaggerating the negative effects of hormone therapy. I took the testosterone-suppressing drug spironolactone for a year and a half, and the side effects were relatively minor. Of course, I acknowledge that I took the drug by choice and that one's view of the side effects might be different if one was required to undergo antiandrogen therapy. In response to all the articles published by the

Chand supporters and the many deficiencies I found in them, I decided the time had come for me to abandon my neutral posture. I wrote to Bermon suggesting that I would be willing to offer my assistance to the IAAF in the Chand case, and a few weeks later Bermon invited me to join the IAAF team for the trial that would be held in Lausanne, Switzerland, in March 2015. Bermon also sent me the witness statements from the Chand team and told me that I would be required to write a statement of my own.

Three days after I received the e-mail from Bermon, the Russian doping scandal hit the IAAF.[33] The German television station ARD had already broken the news of a widespread doping conspiracy in Russia,[34] and now IAAF officials were being implicated. Among other violations, it was alleged that Liliya Shobukhova, the world's best female marathoner three years running, had paid a bribe of €450,000 to Russian authorities to cover up an adverse biological passport finding. The payment was facilitated by the treasurer of the IAAF, Valentin Balakhnichev. Shobukhova had received a doping ban despite her bribe, and under pressure from the marathon champion, Balakhnichev had sent her a refund amounting to €300,000. Balaknichev and three others, including Gabriel Dollé, Bermon's boss in the IAAF medical commission, wound up resigning. In chapter 10 I mentioned one important figure in the scandal: Yuliya Rusanova was a middle-distance runner who competed for Russia in the 2011 World Championships and the 2012 Indoor World Championships, finishing last in the finals at both meets. She met and married Vitaly Stepanov, who worked for the (so-called) Russian Anti-Doping Agency (RUSADA). Vitaly was horrified by the level of corruption he saw at RUSADA and longed to make changes. Yuliya was one the protected athletes who was never going to fail a drug test in Russia as long as she kept winning.[35] Understandably, there was a lot of tension in their household.

Their lives changed in 2013 when Yuliya's protected position was usurped by younger rivals and she failed a drug test.[36] Yuliya Stepanova was suspended for two years retroactive to 2011, with the suspension wiping out her World Championships results. It was at this point that the pair decided to team up to expose the Russian system. Yuliya secretly recorded conversations and saved e-mails and texts from many prominent Russian coaches and athletes, including 2012 Olympic 800 meter champion Maria Savinova. The evidence gathered by Vitaly and Yuliya formed the basis of the ARD program and the investigation that led to the resignation of Dollé and the others.[37] Vitaly and Yuliya left Russia for Germany in 2014 and later moved to the United States, where they became two of the many participants in the witness protection program operated by the US Department of Justice.

The Stepanovs were not the only important witnesses against the Russian doping system. Grigory Rodchenkov was the head of Russia's national anti-doping laboratory in 2014. It was in this role that he participated in one of the most audacious schemes to thwart anti-doping efforts.[38] When athletes are tested for drugs via urinalysis, their urine samples are saved in two bottles labeled the A and B samples. The A sample is tested immediately, and the B sample is saved for later, for use in case the A sample comes back positive. In order to convict an athlete of a doping offense, it is necessary for both the A and the B samples to test positive. Rodchenkov ran the anti-doping lab for the IOC at the Sochi Winter Olympics, and it was there that that the Russians found a way to break into the supposedly tamper-proof bottles that held the B samples. Every night Rodchnkov and the Federal Security Service of the Russian Federation (FSB) would switch out the dirty urine of Russian athletes, replacing it with clean urine that had been saved up from months earlier. In this way, the Russian athletes could keep doping right through the games without fear of being caught.

The Russians were very successful in Sochi, leading the medal parade with thirteen gold and thirty-three total medals, and Rodchenkov was awarded the Order of Friendship by Vladimir Putin.[39] This was the high point of Rodchenkov's career, but things spiraled downward quickly. Vitaly Stepanov recorded fifteen hours of conversation with Rodchenkov, discussing Sochi and other misdeeds by the laboratory chief.[40] In 2015 Rodchenkov admitted to destroying 1,417 samples before a WADA audit, and later that year two former heads of RUSADA died under mysterious circumstances.[41] Rodchenkov knew it was time to get out, so he too fled the country, turned whistleblower, and wound up in the witness protection program.

The trail of guilt within the IAAF reached all the way to the head of the organization. Papa Massata Diack, the son of IAAF president Lamine Diack, was among those who resigned in December 2014.[42] The younger Diack had held several roles within the IAAF, and there were widespread allegations of bribery against him, especially surrounding the awarding of world championship meets. These allegations and the nepotistic nature of the younger Diack's appointment were bad signs for the trustworthiness of the regime of the elder Diack.

I understood that the whole scandal, and especially the resignation of Dollé, meant that Bermon and his cohorts within the IAAF medical commission would have their hands very full with other obligations, so I was not surprised that I didn't hear from him over the following month. In mid-January Elizabeth Riley, one of the IAAF lawyers with the Chand case, contacted me from her office in London, and I sent her my witness statement. Even from several thousand miles away I could sense that something didn't seem right. Riley was not very communicative, and lead attorney Jonathan Taylor was even less so. No one from the IAAF, nor their lawyers, contacted me to talk about any of the details of my trip to Lausanne. Undeterred, I purchased airline tickets and reserved a hotel room in Lausanne. I did this despite the fact that Bermon had offered, on behalf of the IAAF, to cover my expenses. Perhaps the IAAF would reimburse me and perhaps they wouldn't. Either way, I had been invited and I intended to go.

As the time for trial drew close, I got the sense that the IAAF, as represented by their lawyers, didn't really want me to be part of the trial. At one point, I asked if I could see the statements from the other IAAF witnesses; Riley denied my request. I imagine that I was the only witness on either side who didn't have access to all of the other witness statements. And then, two weeks before the trial, Riley suggested that I should testify via Skype. I pointed out to her that I already had my itinerary set and that I would be in Lausanne the day before the start of the trial. I hoped that whatever was going on would become clear to me once I got there.

If my involvement in the Chand trial was uncertain at best, I was heartened that winter by the publication of my study.[43] The paper appeared as the lead article in the March 2015 issue of the journal, and a wonderful opportunity resulted from its publication: The *Washington Post* invited me to submit an op-ed story based on my experience in a recent race and the science behind my study. I spent a fair amount of time working with the editors at the *Post* to make certain that the tone and content of the article were appropriate, and the final version of the article was written just before I hopped on the plane. That time was well spent, as the article would remain relevant and much read over the next few years.

It had been ten years since I was last in Europe and I decided to spend a few days prior to the trial sightseeing and getting used to the time difference. I flew into Frankfurt and then spent a couple of days each in Heidelberg and Zürich. I enjoyed my mini-holiday and was as relaxed as possible as I arrived in Lausanne. The small city is fifty kilometers outside Geneva and is located on Lake Geneva (the French say *le lac Léman*). The French Alps looming on the other side of *le lac Léman* make an amazing backdrop. My hotel room looked out over the lake, and the view was very easy on the eyes. The beauty of the city and the famed Swiss neutrality combine to make Lausanne a favorite of diplomats worldwide. John Kerry, then US secretary of state, arrived in town to meet with the Iranians over nuclear concerns a few days after my Sunday arrival.[44]

I had been in touch with Liz Riley after I arrived in Europe, and she suggested that I should come over to the hotel where she and Jonathan Taylor were staying. I met Liz in the meeting room the IAAF was using as its strategy headquarters, and we had a very pleasant discussion. Approximately an hour later Jonathan arrived, and it didn't take long to determine one major problem he had with me. He said it made him very nervous that I was writing a book that would, in part, cover the trial. I promised him that I would share everything I wrote about the trial with the IAAF prior to publication and allow the organization to redact any portion that it felt betrayed confidentiality. That seemed to help somewhat, but I made a point to excuse myself when Thomas Capdevielle, the new head of the IAAF' medical division, showed up to discuss the week's strategy with Jonathon and Liz.

At last I understood the behavior of the two lawyers. Jon Taylor, especially, was worried that I couldn't be trusted to maintain confidentiality, and so he didn't want me in the courtroom. With four years of hindsight, I can appreciate Taylor's point of view. The events that would transpire over the next week were but the first in a series of high-level, confidential arenas I was privileged to attend. No one invited me to any of these meetings because they wanted to enhance my book. I was invited because people thought that I could contribute something useful. It was expected that I would keep to the same standards of confidentiality as the other participants. In reporting what happened from 2015 onwards, I have tried to find some balance between being factual and not betraying confidentiality. It hasn't always been easy, but I hope that the following chapters manage to achieve this balance.

If the IAAF and their lawyers had qualms about my presence at the trial, they did at least want to dine with me. We met later that evening for a wonderful dinner at the swanky Chateau D'ouchy. I had the opportunity to meet María José Martínez-Patiño, Stéphane Bermon, Arne Ljungqvist, and others that I had only read about. I thought that Arne was in incredible shape for a man in his mid-eighties, and the meal was very pleasant. After the dinner, I walked back to my hotel and considered what was in store for me that week. It would prove to be an exciting few days and an important step in a journey that was about to change my life.

14

DUTEE CHAND VERSUS THE IAAF IN THE CAS

The Dutee Chand trial, which started on March 23, 2015, featured an international cast of characters. The appellant, Chand, and her adviser Payoshni Mitra are Indian; her legal team, led by Jim Bunting, are all Canadian; her scientific advisers Richard Holt and Sari van Anders are English and Canadian/American, respectively; and the mastermind of her operation, Katrina Karkazis, is American. The team representing the respondent, the IAAF, included the legal team of Jonathan Taylor and Elizabeth Riley, who are British; scientific advisers Martin Ritzen and Angelica Hirschberg, who are Swedish, as is the grand old man of gender issues, Arne Ljungqvist; the physician who runs the hyperandrogenism program for the IAAF, Stéphane Bermon, who is French, as is Thomas Capdevielle, the head of the IAAF medical commission; María José Martínez-Patiño, who is Spanish; and me, a Canadian/American. The three-person panel of judges was headed by Justice Annabelle Bennett from Australia and also included Justice Richard McLaren of Canada and Justice Hans Nater of Switzerland.[1]

The trial was held at the headquarters of the Court of Arbitration for Sport, which is located in a wonderful building known as the Château de Béthusy. The CAS hears cases from sports disputes from all over the world and is the highest-level tribunal to determine such cases. I was honored that I had been invited to be a witness, even if my role for the week was somewhat undefined. The trial began on a Monday and was to conclude on Thursday, although the verdict of the judges would come much later. Originally the case had been brought against the Athletics Federation of India, and the IAAF was technically only the second respondent.[2] The AFI and the larger Sports Authority of India had, however, ceased to oppose the appellant and had actually withdrawn their own hyperandrogenism regulations before the trial opened. Neither Indian organization was represented in Lausanne, although there were a couple of witnesses who testified via Skype from India.

The case had begun in India in late June of 2014, when the AFI decided to test Chand to see if her T levels were high.[3] By mid-July the news of her tests and subsequent high T reading was leaked to the press in India.[4] It was clear that the IAAF protocols for such cases had not been followed in the Chand case, and it was equally clear that someone from India should be held accountable for the whole mess. It had become obvious, however, from press releases over the preceding months that determining exactly what had gone on in India would be challenging in the extreme. Chand's lead attorney, Jim Bunting, described all his interactions with anyone in India as a black hole. Most of Monday was taken up with testimony about exactly what had gone down in India in 2014. Chand herself opened up the proceedings, followed by Mitra, and there was also testimony given via Skype from India. Nothing that transpired Monday would be very helpful in determining exactly what had happened in India during the summer of 2014. Although it is abundantly obvious that Dutee Chand had been grievously wronged by authorities in her native land, it did not appear that anyone in particular would be stepping up to take responsibility.

Arne Ljundqvist also testified on Monday,[5] and while his testimony was interesting from a historical perspective, it did little to shine light on the current case. Perhaps the most interesting aspect I gleaned from my time with Arne was the obvious affection that he and María José Martínez-Patiño have for one another. Arne had to leave at the end of the day, as he had royal obligations Tuesday in Sweden, but before he left, María and Arne posed for pictures and embraced warmly. María turned to me after he left and said, "There goes my second father."

If Monday was a somewhat disappointing day in terms of illumination or drama, Tuesday would be drastically different. Katrina Karkazis gave testimony regarding her role in the case.[6] Jon Taylor grilled her rather intensively over the speculation that she had engineered the whole trial more to satisfy her personal goals of overturning the IAAF regulations than in the interest of helping out Dutee Chand. Karkazis remained unflustered and withstood the strong cross-examination well.

Karkazis, however, was not nearly the most interesting witness of the day. María José Martínez-Patiño's testimony was not only powerful, it would be the emotional highlight of the week. Over the past several years she has been a coauthor of scientific papers, both opposed to and supporting the concept of regulating intersex women in sport. She also made contradictory public statements during this time period, and people on both sides of the divide have claimed María's support, but by the time her very emotional testimony concluded, there was very little doubt where she stood in 2015. One possible cause of confusion over her stance was the fact that Spanish is her first language, and while her English is passable, it is, in her words "not perfecto." Here in Lausanne she had an interpreter, and her eloquence in her native tongue was obvious. She detailed all the pain that she had suffered as a result of her leaked test. She reached an emotional peak when she forcefully declared that no intersex athlete should ever again have to suffer over a leaked test, as she and Chand had. Additionally, she lamented her lost opportunity to compete in the Olympic Games—the pinnacle of sports.

María also spoke of the need to establish rules to govern participation in women's sport. She acknowledged that previously she believed that there was no place for regulations concerning intersex women in sports, but noted her reverence for Paula Radcliffe and how crucial her meeting with Paula in 2013 had been in reshaping her point of view. María's opinion is that the current hyperandrogenism regulations need to be modified but not abandoned.[7]

Although there might have been some dry eyes at the end of Martínez-Patiño's testimony, mine weren't among them. And to top off the emotional impact of the morning, Paula Radcliffe herself joined the trial via Skype to testify how important the current rules were in safeguarding the integrity of women's sport.[8] Although María's emotional testimony ruled the morning, science would take center stage that afternoon. As is standard at science-heavy cases before the CAS, the opposing scientists were placed in a witness hot tub—a session in which the opposing teams of experts try to make sense of important scientific questions—and subject to questions from attorneys as well as the panel of judges.[9]

The scientists on the side of the IAAF were eminent indeed. Ritzen is a distinguished pediatric endocrinologist who sat on the board to advise the choice on the Nobel Prize in Medicine, and his work has been cited more than eleven thousand times.[10] Bermon described Ritzen as the world's leading authority on DSDs and sport. Hirschberg is on the faculty at the Karolinska Institute in Stockholm, one of the leading research and treatment hospitals in the world.[11] The IAAF could have its pick of the many scientists who support its position, but the appellant had to choose from the smaller pool who think testosterone is not so important in determining athletic success. Although both Holt[12] and van Anders are faculty members at well-respected institutions, they are not as eminent as the IAAF scientists. Dr. van Anders was further hampered by the fact that she was testifying via Skype since her pregnancy prevented her from traveling from Michigan to Lausanne.

Despite a deficit in the eminence department, Holt displayed his scientific knowledge and his ability to effectively engage in the back-and-forth discourse that is vital in trying a case such as this one. Perhaps the highlight of the hot tub interactions occurred when Ritzen drew a testosterone dose response curve on the whiteboard in the room. The sigmoid-shaped curve Ritzen drew was relatively flat in the "normal" female range (below 3 nmol/L), but between 3 and 10 nmol/L, the curve rose sharply. Ritzen used this curve to demonstrate the large advantage that would result if T levels were increased above female norms. Holt countered that the dose response curve would look very different for those with complete or partial androgen insensitivity syndrome, and when Holt and Rtizen were finished drawing curves that represented testosterone responses for those of varying T-sensitivity, the whiteboard probably looked indecipherable to anyone who hadn't witnessed the display. And that may have been Holt's primary goal all along.

Although Holt fought bravely, one thing was clear at the end of the day: The appellant's team had lost one major cornerstone of their argument. The suggestion that endogenous and exogenous T would provide different levels of sports enhancement[13] had been rejected by the president of the panel, Justice Annabelle Bennett.[14] All the people on the IAAF side were impressed by the fact that Bennett had a background in biology, and it showed on Tuesday afternoon. Bennett was able to follow the back-and-forth argument of the four scientists, and she came up with cogent questions to ask all four. Bennett clearly was not going to buy the arguments of Holt and van Anders regarding exogenous testosterone acting differently than endogenous T. It was an enormous victory for the IAAF.

Tuesday was a big day for the IAAF, but Wednesday would see the tables turn. The scientific argument du jour concerned all the testosterone-based data that had been gathered on athletes and the meaning of the different studies. One of the most contentious issues was the issue of the potential overlap of male and female T ranges. It is generally accepted that the "normal" male range in adults is approximately 10–30 nmol/L and that the "normal" female range is approximately 1–3 nmol/L.[15] However, both intersex women and those with polycystic ovary syndrome often have higher T levels than the standard 1–3 nmol/L, and many intersex women exceed 10 nmol/L. The IAAF argued that women over 10 should be excluded from studies as outliers, but the appellant disagreed. Another area of contention concerned T levels for elite athletes as measured at major championships. One paper, published by M. L. Healy and colleagues, took data from a study of Olympic athletes at the 2000 summer games to show that there were many male athletes whose T measurements were below 10 nmol/L, and a few whose T values were as low as 3 or 4 nmol/L.[16] The study had been criticized in many quarters, but if these numbers were valid, the study would cast doubt on the notion of using T levels to distinguish between men and women for athletic purposes.

One of the most important moments of the week occurred prior to the start of testimony on Wednesday. Justice Bennett asked both attorneys if they would be willing to accept a verdict that was somewhere in between the two positions. Both lawyers had answered that of course the judges could issue a verdict that fell somewhere between a simple yes or no answer. In fact, both attorneys had undoubtedly anticipated such a result and had designed their cases accordingly. Throughout the week, Taylor had constantly referred to the IAAF regulations as a living document, one that the IAAF would improve with time. On the other side of the aisle, Bunting suggested several times that the science did not yet support the IAAF regulations but that it might be possible in the future to say that it did. Clearly both men understood that a partial victory was probably the best that either side could hope for.

Bermon took the stand after Bennett was finished with her opening question. He presented data the IAAF had gathered on elite athlete T levels and also presented data from hyperandrogenistic athletes. His testimony began at 9 o'clock in morning and was interrupted twice for Skype-based witnesses and twice for procedural motions. He did not leave the witness stand until 2 o'clock that afternoon. Perhaps the most telling information Bermon shared with the court were data from the 2011 and 2013 World Championships that confirmed some of the Healy study data. In particular, there were plenty of men at major championships whose T levels measured below 10 nmol/L.

Although it might seem contradictory that elite male athletes would have lower T than the general population, there are reasons why this can happen.[17] It is widely acknowledged that many elite athletes dope. When athletes were given the opportunity to confess anonymously at two international championship venues, approximately 50 percent of them admitted to using PEDs,[18] but the actual numbers are probably higher. It has long been known that taking exogenous T suppresses the body's production of testosterone. Athletes who dope and then stop using steroids before a major meet hope that the drugs will not be detected by the doping tests. Male athletes whose T levels are measured after they cease doping often score well below average. The reduction of endogenous T production in the face of steroid withdrawal is the major reason that some of the men's T levels would be low, although overtraining might also be a cause.

Bermon did his best to convince the panel that these low T numbers weren't a problem for the IAAF case, but he was not convincing. Bennett, who had been very comfortable with the endocrine issues raised on Tuesday, was less comfortable with the statistical issues raised on Wednesday. It was clear that she had a problem with using T as the basis to separate male and female athletes given the overlap issue. The IAAF had done itself no favor in its hyperandrogenism policy when it stated that athletes were eligible for the women's category if their T levels were less than 10 nmol/L or "below the normal men's range"[19] (the scientific meaning of the word *range* is synonymous with the 95 percent confidence level, meaning that by definition 2.5 percent of men would be below the bottom of the range). All the IAAF scientists had gone to great pains to demonstrate that, in fact, the origin of the hyperandrogenism rules had little or nothing to do with men's T levels. In painstaking detail they told of the research on female T levels and what upper limit they thought was best. It simply happened that all of their work on women pointed to an appropriate T level that was close to the low end of the "normal" male T range. They decided it would be easier for the public to understand the T limit by referencing the bottom of the men's range rather than by detailing all of the work that had gone into coming up with the value. In hindsight, I'm certain the IAAF regretted this decision.

Despite all of the focus on science, perhaps the most important moment on Wednesday was one that concerned human rights. Bunting managed to get Bermon to admit that the existing hypoandrogenism rules were discriminatory in nature.[20] I remember wincing when Stéphane made this admission, but overall I thought there were more important issues to be decided. I might have been wrong. It was at that point that the burden of proof shifted from the Chand team to the IAAF. One other item from Wednesday would prove to be historically significant: Justice McLaren asked Bermon on two or three occasions if he could use the data from the Daegu and Moscow studies to create an exploratory study to see if there was a correlation between testosterone levels and performance in women. At the time, Bermon was reluctant to commit to such a study, but he would later change his mind.[21] As the day wore on, Bunting proved to be effective in his cross examination of Bermon. Although Bunting was detailed, he had not been a bully in previous cross-examinations, but he really went to town on Bermon, subjecting him to a barrage of lawyerly tactics. By the end of the day, Stéphane looked ten years older than he had in the morning. Taylor privately acknowledged that his aggressive tactics on Karkazis the day before might well have been a factor in the return treatment Bunting inflicted on Bermon.

Each of the two legal teams had private rooms that we could use to discuss strategy. After the conclusion of Wednesday's events, those of us on the IAAF team had much to discuss in our room. We were all aware that it was important to make the judges understand that testosterone was still the key parameter to use to define participation in women's sport, despite what had transpired earlier in the day. Taylor was clearly worried about the overlap issue and how it would affect the outcome of the case. Although everyone in the room understood that despite any overlap, T was still the best quantity to use to separate men and women, the judges might not see it that way. Taylor asked the rest of us if he should he use a graph, statistics, or some other tactic to make the panel understand that T was the quantity to use for the regulations. It was at this moment that I provided my most important input of the week. I took out a piece of paper and drew two sharply peaked normal distributions, with clearly separated maximum values, but with a small area of overlap between the two peaks. I labeled one *M* and one *F*. I showed the graph to Taylor and everyone else in the room, commenting that any reasonably intelligent person would understand that these were two different distributions despite the overlap. I saw a gleam in Taylor's eye, and he announced that this was the strategy to pursue.

Thursday had been reserved for the two lawyers' closing arguments. In fictionalized courtroom dramas the closing arguments are always the climax of the plot. I had always imagined that this treatment of a trial was rather simplistic, but that was before I got to witness two such outstanding litigators as Bunting and Taylor in action. Bunting was up first, and although I had heard all of the appellant's arguments before, they seemed fresh out of Bunting's mouth. He covered the great harm that had been done to Chand, the notion that the effects of exogenous T should not be used to determine the effects of endogenous T, the evils of forcing intersex women to have surgery or hormone manipulation in order to compete, and, of course, the overlap issue. He also mixed in salient points from the trial to illustrate the appellant's view that the science wasn't settled, that the harm the regulations inflicted on intersex women was great, and the benefit to other female athletes was sketchy at best. All of his rhetoric should have seemed stale to me, since I had read it all many times prior to the trial, but Bunting wove a compelling story, and surely his arguments would be very effective with the judges.

After a short break, Taylor was up. Unlike Bunting, he didn't mention the human aspect of the trial very much at all. He knew that the money was in the science, and he stuck to it. Soon Taylor was rolling, and it was hard not get caught up in his wake. By the time he got to the overlap issue, he was very much in command. He said that the IAAF had made a mistake in even mentioning male levels of T when determining appropriate female T levels. He brought out graphs of male and female T levels and made it abundantly clear to everyone in the room just how different those graphs were, despite the small overlap. He concluded by saying that the overlap issue was a red herring and had no bearing on the case at all.[22] At this point Bermon looked over at me at gave a nod of appreciation.

To all of us on the IAAF side, it seemed clear that the case had been won by the close of the trial. It would turn out that the IAAF had indeed won the testosterone battle but, in focusing so much effort on that battle, had neglected the human rights issues raised by the appellant. Those issues would turn out to be crucial. The appellant would also win a temporary victory that week. Prior to the trial, the CAS had given Chand the right to compete in India while the case was in progress.[23] On Thursday Chand asked for more: permission to compete in the Asian Athletics Championships to be held in China in June of 2015. The IAAF would not hear of deviating from its normal rules prohibiting athletes under investigation for hyperandrogenism from competition, but the judges saw it differently, ruling that Chand was free to compete in any meet anywhere in the world until the case was decided.

Although that decision was certainly a welcome one for the athlete, the preceding months of turmoil had taken a toll on her fitness, and she couldn't recapture her 2014 form by the time of the Indian trials for the Asian Championships. Moreover, her times in the 100 and 200 meter sprints were well off the standards the AFI used to select the national team. She wound up running the anchor leg of the Indian 4x100 meter team that placed fourth in the Asian meet in Wujang.[24] Chand was also not named to the Indian team for the World Championships that were held in Beijing later in the summer. The AFI sent no short sprinters to that meet, although India did field a team for the 4x400 relay.

During the trial I learned that the IOC would be sponsoring a conference with the purpose of revising its rules on transgender athletes in November.[25] Although I hadn't been invited to the conference prior to the trial, Arne Ljungqvist said he would see what he could do about getting me in. Apparently his intervention worked, as I received an invitation in early April. Although I had made some rookie mistakes during the trial—twice speaking out of turn were my worst offenses—I had also earned enough respect that the IOC was interested in working with me. Another important event happened while I was in Lausanne: The *Washington Post* informed me that my op-ed would be published that Sunday,[26] and the paper wanted to take some pictures of me for the story. Due to time constraints, that meant that I rushed out of the trial at the close of the last day to meet with the photographer. I then got to pretend that I was a model as we spent two hours on a photo shoot that had me switching from professional dress to athletic wear halfway through the shoot. It was the most fun I have ever had getting my picture taken.

It is customary for the verdict in CAS cases to be delivered well after the case is heard. The judges have much to consider and need time carefully weigh all of the scientific and social principles. The Chand case was more complicated than most, so the usual two-month delay in the verdict stretched out to almost four months before anyone heard from the judges.

And when we did hear back, the verdict was stunning. The judges had decided that the IAAF had won the science battle over testosterone, stating that "there is a scientific basis in the use of testosterone as a marker for the purposes of the HA Regulations," and that "testosterone is the best indicator of performance differences between male and female athletes." Furthermore, the CAS panel did not accept that the argument that endogenous and exogenous testosterone acted differently.[27] Unfortunately for the IAAF, the good news did not last. The CAS panel had given great weight to the discriminatory nature of the regulations. (The IAAF had agreed that the regulations were discriminatory but felt that this discrimination was necessary.) The CAS panel used the discriminatory nature of the hypoandrogenism regulations to turn the tables on the IAAF. At the beginning of the trial, the burden of proof had been on the Chand team to prove that testosterone was not a valid method to separate male and female athletes. The Chand team had clearly failed to prove that point; however, the fact that the hypoandrogenism regulations were universally acknowledged to be discriminatory now meant that the CAS panel was placing the burden of proof on the IAAF to justify the hypoandrogenism rules.[28] The CAS panel did not accept that the regulations were a proportionate method to maintain a level playing field, suggesting that the regulations were problematic because they were excluding women from women's sport—that is, "the Regulations do not police the male/female divide but establish a female/female divide within the female category."[29]

The CAS panel went on to state that

> in order to justify excluding an individual from competing in a particular category on the basis of a naturally occurring characteristic such as endogenous testosterone, it is not enough simply to establish that the characteristic has some performance enhancing effect. Instead, the IAAF needs to establish that the characteristic in question confers *such a significant performance advantage* over other members of the category that allowing individuals with that characteristic to compete would subvert the very basis for having the separate category and thereby prevent a level playing field. The degree or magnitude of the advantage is therefore critical.[30]

The CAS panel accepted that a performance difference of 10 percent—roughly the difference between male and female results—would be enough to justify discriminatory regulations, but that 1 percent was not enough. Bermon had suggested that on average, those women excluded by the current rules had approximately a 3 percent advantage. Although it wasn't explicitly stated that this 3 percent advantage was too small to justify the current rules, the CAS panel was clearly not impressed by the 3 percent figure given by the IAAF.[31]

The CAS panel gave the IAAF two years from the July 27, 2015, verdict to come up with better justification for the hypoandrogenism regulations or they would be terminated.[32] The mood among the IAAF people and the lawyers was very subdued after the verdict. Although it would be easy for the IAAF to allow women with high T to compete in men's competitions, thereby eliminating the ineligible female component of the regulations, the "female/female divide" would be much harder to overcome. Either the IAAF needed to show enough data to indicate that the T advantage possessed by those intersex women excluded by the regulations was large enough to destroy the notion of the level playing field or it needed to show that excluding some women from women's sport was not discriminatory. The prospects for completing either of these tasks in two years seemed dismal indeed. However, Bermon suggested that those of us involved in the case should get together in Lausanne in November, since we were all going to be there as part of the IOC meeting on transgender athletes. That November meeting would prove to be an important milestone, but before I talk about it I would like to explore the details of what transpired in the realm of transgender athletes starting in 2013. It is probably appropriate to start with perhaps the most-hated transgender athlete of all time.

15

TRANSGENDER ATHLETES, 2013–2017

If one were to pick the sport least likely to be accepting of a transgender athlete, it might well be the testosterone-soaked world of mixed martial arts (MMA), also known as cage fighting. The sport is an amalgam of boxing, wrestling, Muay Thai, and other striking arts, in which no quarter is asked or given. It should probably come as no surprise that transgender MMA fighter Fallon Fox was never going to be accepted in this sport. Fox was born on November 29, 1975, and grew up in an extremely religious, ethnically mixed household in East Toledo, Ohio. Fox and her siblings were taken four times a week to a church where it was considered normal to speak in tongues. Like many trans women, Fox started dressing in women's clothes at an early age. Fox wrestled in high school, found herself attracted to girls, and got one pregnant when she was nineteen. The two got married, and Fox joined the navy to support her family.[1] By the time Fox finished her hitch, her marriage was over, but she was still close to her daughter.

After Fox got out of the navy, she studied graphic arts at the University of Toledo with the support of Uncle Sam. When Fox told her parents about her desire to live as a woman, they sent her to a Christian reparative counseling group. It didn't work. Fox dropped out of college, took a job as a long-haul trucker, and started taking hormones. Fox had surgery in Thailand in 2006, at the age of thirty, moved to the Chicago area, and lived in stealth mode for the next few years. She worked as a bus driver and a clerk at a Blockbuster store in a working-class suburb of Chicago.[2] Fox stayed active and athletic, flirting with jiu-jitsu before deciding that MMA was more for her. In 2010 she joined the Midwest Training Center, a gym run by trainer Joe Smith. Women are a rare sight in an MMA gym, and the men who trained at Smith's gym were skeptical of the feminine newcomer, but Fox trained hard and showed talent. Smith convinced Fox that she should go pro, and at the close of 2012 she did so. Fox won her first two fights in 2013 with ease, earning a first-round TKO over Elisha Helsper and then knocking out Erika Newsome a mere thirty-nine seconds into her second bout. Neither Helsper nor Newsome has ever won a professional bout, either before or after fighting Fox.[3]

Fox's victories were the catalyst for a more detailed look into her background. Smith started to hear rumors about Fox's past and suggested that she take a test to disprove them. It was only then that she told him she was transgender. An MMA blogger threatened to out Fox after the fight with Newsome; when Fox's manager suggested that they preempt him, Fox took her story to *Sports Illustrated*.[4] And then things got nasty in a hurry. The *Sports Illustrated* piece was well balanced, and some other media coverage was positive, but reaction within the MMA world was almost unrelentingly negative. Matt Mitrione, a UFC fighter and former NFL player, called Fox a "lying, sick, sociopathic, disgusting freak."[5] And this is just the printable stuff. Others used words that had to be redacted from the press releases quoting them. There were also questions about Fox's license, as she hadn't revealed her history in her application—not that there was any place to do so. In 2012 the Association of Boxing Commissions had adopted rules similar to the 2004 IOC rules allowing transgender participation, and there was no cause to suspend Fox's license or prohibit her from fighting other women.[6] The fight-loving public, however, saw it in a much different light. To them, she was a man who had cut off his dick so he could beat up girls. Her next fight, with Alana Jones in May of 2013, generated huge publicity—and plenty of controversy. Jones chose to enter the ring using Aerosmith's "Dude Looks like a Lady" as her entrance music, and this got the crowd into a fevered pitch.[7] The fight itself was pretty even. Jones used her superior boxing skills and excellent footwork to keep Fox at bay, but Fox hit harder, using her strength and superior grappling skills well once she managed to wrestle Jones to the canvas. Fox forced Jones to submit with a shin-to-throat choke move toward the end of the third round. Fox was probably ahead on points on the scorecard, but Jones's submission made the outcome more certain. Fox exhibited a lack of stamina that hampered her ability to fight effectively beyond the first round, but the fact that she was clearly the stronger of the two fighters helped fuel the continuing controversy.[8]

Her victory in the Jones fight qualified Fox to fight Ashley Evans-Smith for $20,000 in October of 2013, as part of an eight-woman tournament. Her fights against Newsome and Jones had been the first two rounds of the tourney. Fox went into the fight as the overwhelming favorite in Las Vegas; the bettors clearly believed that a "former man" would never lose to a girl. Fox clearly won the first round but couldn't finish the fight. Evans-Smith dominated the second round. When they went to the mat, Evans-Smith managed to trap Fox with her legs and landed a series of blows that would have ended the fight if the bell hadn't saved Fox. The crowd, smelling blood, went crazy between rounds. Evans-Smith again was dominant in the third round, got on top of Fox, and was pounding the defenseless trans woman on the canvas when the ref stopped the fight.[9] Evans-Smith was gracious immediately after the fight, but within a week she went on record as saying that transgender fighters shouldn't be allowed in women's events. Evans-Smith claimed that Fox "hit hard," too hard, apparently, and said Fox "did have an advantage—she definitely did."[10] And this is after Evans-Smith won the fight! Obviously, Evans-Smith had advantages too, or she wouldn't have won. Fox was undeterred by the loss, continuing to train and fight. She defeated Heather Bassett in March of 2014, causing her opponent to submit forty-four seconds into the second round in a fight that garnered significantly less publicity than her previous bout.[11]

Fox's last fight was against the woefully overmatched Tamikka Brents on September 16, 2014. Brents put up little opposition, and the fight ended two minutes after it started, with Fox sitting on top of Brents and pummeling her in the face. Brents suffered a concussion and a broken orbital bone.[12] No other fighter was willing to fight Fox, and Fox's fighting career was over. Brents also never fought again professionally, and that was just as well; she did not belong in the ring with a professional MMA fighter.

Although Fox finished her career at 5–1, she never got to fight in the Ultimate Fighting Championship (UFC), which is the big leagues of MMA fighting.[13] Ashley Evans-Smith did get called up to the UFC, and as of December 2018, Evans-Smith has a 3–3 record in the UFC.[14]

Since Fox is more than decade older than Evans-Smith and well past her prime fighting years, it is doubtful that Fox would have outperformed Evans-Smith in the UFC. Back in 2014 Jonathan Snowden said, "Fallon Fox is not ready for high-level MMA,"[15] and I am certain that his assessment was correct. To this day Fox remains one of the most divisive transgender athletes to ever compete, a heroine to those looking for a transgender role model but a villain to all those who saw her as a dude willing to beat up on women.

If the end to Fox's career was sad, it was nothing compared to the end of Lauren Jeska's racing days. Jeska's fate was downright tragic. Lauren Jeska was born in 1974 in Lancaster, England, to a mathematician father and a stay-at-home mother. She was a stellar student and a successful cross-country runner in school. It was while she was a doctoral physics candidate at Oxford University in 1998 that she told her parents she was going to transition. She dropped out of Oxford, had gender confirmation surgery in 2000 at Brighton, and later earned a master's degree in gender studies at Leeds University. She also took up running again and "trained like a demon."[16] It was in the very demanding world of fell running—the British version of mountain racing—that Lauren found her niche. Lauren came out to some of her clubmates at the Todmorden Harriers but was not out to the general public. Lauren's first national championship came on July 18, 2010, when she won the English Fell Running Championships that were held in conjunction with the Holme Moss Fell Race. The course is 25.5 kilometers of steep climbs and brutal descents—at one point the course drops 1,000 feet in less than 2 miles—which Lauren ran in 2:49:31, defeating the second-place woman by a minute and a half.[17] Farther back in field, at 3:05:57, was another trans runner named Paula Payne, who had yet to transition. A few months ather the fell race, Payne would run a 2:38 marathon. Payne acknowledges that she was never a fell runner but is awestruck that Jeska could have beaten her by more than sixteen minutes.[18]

Jeska went on to win English Fell Running Championships in 2011 and 2012, and she was the UK champion the latter year. In 2012 she also earned a fifth-place showing in the Pike's Peak Marathon, one of the world's most famous mountain races. She was truly world class in her discipline. She also ran decent times on the road, as evidenced by her 35:25 10K time from 2011,[19] but she was not nearly as proficient on the flats as on the hills. Lauren was open about her trans status with officials, if not to the public. When I first met Stéphane Bermon in March 2015, I asked him if there had ever been a trans athlete in the IAAF World Championships. Stéphane replied no, but said he had dealt with the case of an elite mountain racer. Stéphane did not mention a name, and I had no idea who he was referring to at the time,[20] but I would soon learn about Lauren.

Apparently Lauren had requested that she be allowed to run in the elite women's section of the 2015 London Marathon, and this was the start of her troubles. UK Athletics (UKA) requested that she submit to a blood sample to prove that her testosterone levels were low enough to permit her to compete in women's races.[21] Such a request was within UKA's rights, as the IAAF had established its endocrine-based rules in 2011, but UKA also claimed that because it had no documentation of her 2000 surgery, it did not know if she was compliant. The latter statement is clearly misguided, as Lauren raced in the same style of shorts as most elite women—shorts that left little doubt as to her anatomy. UKA also threatened to expunge all of her previous race results unless they got blood values, a threat Jeska took as a personal attack.[22]

In retaliation, on March 22, 2016, Jeska showed up to the UKA office in Birmingham armed with two large kitchen knives hidden in a backpack. Upon admittance to the office, Jeska took out the knives and proceeded to repeatedly stab at UKA official Ralph Knibbs—who had met with her just a week earlier to discuss her case—and admits that she was attempting to kill Knibbs. Although Jeska did not succeed, she did inflict serious, lasting nerve damage upon Knibbs, who also suffered a stroke as a result of the attack. Knibbs fought back, and with the assistance of two other UKA officials managed to restrain her. The other two officials suffered minor injuries. At Jeska's 2017 trial it was revealed that she suffered from mental issues along the autism spectrum and had asked for psychiatric assistance prior to the attack. Jeska was sentenced to eighteen years in jail but was allowed to serve her time in a women's prison, unlike many other English transgender prisoners. Her records remain intact and she was allowed to keep her national championships.[23] Although it is clear that Jeska is culpable for the attack, it is not difficult to feel sympathy for her plight. Surely, this tragedy could have been avoided.

Next I would like to move from an athlete born in Lancaster to one whose name is Lancaster: Dr. Bobbi Lancaster, a family physician and ace golfer. Like me, Bobbi was born in the Canadian province of Ontario and immigrated to the United States. One of the pivotal occurrences in Bobbi's early life was her first time on a golf course at age ten. Her father brought her along, ostensibly to caddy for him. On the second hole her dad scored his very first hole-in-one, and this served as an auspicious beginning for Bobbi's love of the game. Before long Bobbi was playing regularly, and at age eleven she had won the caddy championship at the Hamilton Golf and Country Club, beating several much older caddies.[24] In high school she captained her team to the city championships and was regularly winning junior tournaments in the southwestern Ontario. Golf was not her only athletic love—she also, for instance, high jumped 6 feet for her track team—but it was certainly the sport at which she exhibited the most potential for success. Bobbi was also a successful student and was involved in other activities such as the chess club.[25]

After Bobbi graduated from high school, she won an academic scholarship at McMaster University in Hamilton, where she earned a spot on the golf team during her freshman year. Her golf game improved enough that by her sophomore year, she was the captain of the team that won the first of two Ontario University Athletics Association championships.[26] She was also a first-rate student whose grades were good enough to get her into the medical school at McMaster.

During this time Bobbi also began her first serious relationship, with a young woman named Mary Jo, who accepted Bobbi's feminine side to the point that she made women's clothes that would fit Bobbi's adult height of 6-foot-2. Bobbi dressed as a girl alone in her apartment and only very occasionally ventured outside in female attire. Despite whatever misgivings Bobbi had about her gender role, she and Mary Jo were married in a large wedding befitting the social status of Bobbi's wealthy new in-laws. The couple had three children and moved to Arizona in 1991; the two became increasingly estranged as time wore on. Shortly after the move to Arizona, their relationship fell apart.[27] Bobbi eventually got over the split with Mary Jo and by the end of the decade was married to Lucy, a nurse she had met through work. Although no relationship is perfect, Lucy and Bobbi would stay together through some very challenging times to come. Bobbi also resumed golfing and was playing at the senior level on the Western States Professional Golf Tour. With a successful medical career, a wonderful marriage, and a high level of athletic success, it would seem that Bobbi had it all—but gender dysphoria is a very stubborn opponent. After a failed suicide attempt and a stroke, Bobbi knew she needed to live as her true self. She started hormone therapy and had surgery in 2010 with Toby Meltzer,[28] the same surgeon who had operated on me four years earlier. Although Lucy was reluctant to surrender her husband, she eventually came to understand that Bobbi's essence hadn't changed, merely her physical form.

Bobbi's employers were not so understanding of her changes. She eventually lost two of her three medical positions, keeping only a small private practice in the Phoenix-area suburb of Gold Canyon. Finding herself with plenty of extra time on her hands, Bobbi decided to dedicate herself to becoming the best golfer she could. She started out playing at an amateur level against young women, but soon decided that she would try to become a touring pro on the LPGA.[29] By this time the LPGA opened its doors to trans women as a result of the Lana Lawless suit, and Bobbi was given the green light by tour officials. Bobbi has repeatedly stated that she does not believe that it would be fair for her to play against cisgender women her own age, so she set out to compete against the best young golfers she could find. Bobbi started out by playing on the Cactus Tour in 2013 and was quickly discovered by the media. It wasn't long before she was a national celebrity: a sexagenarian transgender golfer trying to play against the best women golfers forty years her junior. Among many other honors, the Golf Channel did a half-hour documentary on her in 2014.[30]

Like many other trans athletes, Bobbi discovered that women's sports aren't so easy if you have to compete with women's testosterone levels. In 2003 her swing speed was measured at 109 mph at a Hot Stix club fitting in Scottsdale, and by 2013 it had dropped to 96 mph, a substantial decrease.[31] Part of that decrease was due to aging, but most of it was probably a result of her altered hormonal milieu. Bobbi was still longer off the tee than most women when she played in the LPGA qualifying event in Rancho Mirage, California, in August 2013, but that advantage was not enough. Bobbi started each round strong, but she faded in the last four or five holes every day; she failed to make the cut for the next round.[32] Bobbi sought out a sports psychologist, worked on her game, and tried out for the LPGA tour again in 2014, but she still failed to make the cut. In the end, she gave up her dream of becoming a touring professional and regained her amateur card. Bobbi still plays in golf tournaments, although her advocacy—she was elected to the board of directors of the Human Rights Campaign in 2015[33]—and other interests have cut into her practice time.

Bobbi and I were both invited to the 2017 Stanford University Law Review.[34] There, two Stanford-trained lawyers argued that transgender women should be allowed to compete against cisgender women without hormone therapy. Bobbi and I both disagreed with our hosts. I spoke of the tremendous changes that hormone therapy makes in the athletic performance of transgender women and argued that only after such therapy should we be allowed to compete against cisgender women. Bobbi went farther, suggesting that some of the inevitable remaining advantages were great enough that trans women should also be handicapped in some way in many sports, just as she had handicapped herself by competing against much younger women. It was an honor to meet Bobbi, and I wish her all the best in the years to come.

Just as there is an assumption of the unassailable superiority of trans women, it is also assumed by many that trans men will never be competitive against cisgender men. The first trans man to disprove this myth was Chris Mosier, who competes in the duathlon, a sport combining running and cycling. Chris Mosier was born in Chicago in 1980, and at the age of eight he started taking karate classes; by age ten he had his black belt. Mosier was extremely tomboyish and was often asked if he was a boy or a girl. Mosier enjoyed his androgynous status, and he always envisioned himself growing up to be a man. Of course, it didn't happen quite that way.[35] In 2008 Mosier ran his first marathon in Chicago, then he bought a bike and also took up swimming. A year later he had won his first triathlon in the women's category. By 2011 he was competing in the men's category, despite his concern over whether he could continue to be competitive and whether he would be accepted. Acceptance turned out to be no problem, largely because he wasn't seen as a threat. As Chris said, "[M]ost people . . . have no fears of a trans guy switching over because he isn't seen as competition."[36] Becoming competitive in the men's division took a lot of hard work, but Chris was determined to succeed. Chris trained hard over the next few years, and his testosterone injections helped, of course. Soon Chris routinely placed well in his age group in his races, and even won a couple of low-key events.[37] Chris aspired to become a member of the

US men's team, and he decided to focus on the duathlon rather than the triathlon. Athletes naturally tend to gravitate to sports at which they are more successful, and Chris is no exception.

Trans men have a large deficit in strength with respect to cisgender men at the start of transition. With testosterone and training, trans men can make up a large portion of that deficit, but not necessarily all of it. Janae Kroc, who serves as a trainer for trans men and whose story I will relate next, told me that trans men have more difficulty matching cisgender men in upper body strength than in lower body strength, meaning that swimming is likely to be the weakest of the three triathlon sports.[38] Chris switched his primary focus to the duathlon in 2015, and it paid off. Chris placed 37th among all men and seventh in the 35–39 age group in the sprint duathlon event at the USA Triathlon (USAT) Duathlon National Championships in St. Paul, Minnesota, punching his ticket for the world championships to be held in Spain in June of 2016.[39] On June 5, 2016, in Avilla, Mosier placed 142nd among 432 men of all ages and 28th among the 47 men in the 35–39 age group in the sprint duathlon at the World Duathlon Championships.[40] Mosier was the second American in his age group to finish the event. It was the highest level of success ever for a trans man in men's sport. Chris thus became an important role model for aspiring trans male athletes everywhere in the world.[41] Subsequently, Chris has qualified for other multisport national age group teams and has appeared in a Nike ad and in the *ESPN The Magazine* Body Issue.[42]

Chris has also been very involved in activism for transgender athletes. His website *transathlete* has provided a wealth of information and support for many. In 2016 Chris teamed up with Nike's You Can Play program, designed to assist LGBT athletes with opportunities to be who they are and still compete.[43] The actions of Chris and other like-minded activists have positively impacted the lives of transgender athletes everywhere.

The acceptance of transgender athletes has also been greatly helped by the mostly positive publicity accorded to three former world-class athletes who transitioned in the middle of decade. As promised, I'll start with Janae Kroc. Janae was born as Matt Kroczaleski on December 8, 1972; both before and after transition she used the nickname Kroc, and she has described her life with a mixture of pronouns, so I will follow her lead. Kroc grew up in a run-down mobile home in the woods outside of Sterling, Michigan.[44] From a young age, Kroc was torn between two desires that would shape her life. Kroc longed to be big and strong so that no one else would ever be able to bully him. Kroc also longed to be a woman. Clearly, there was bound to be plenty of conflict between these two yearnings.

For most of the first forty years of Krocs's life, the macho side of his personality won out. Kroc served as a Marine from 1991 until 1995, including some time providing presidential security for Bill Clinton.[45] Kroc's stint in the Marine Corps also introduced him to the world of powerlifting. Kroc had been lifting since he was six years old, but winning his first contest "fresh out of high school" was a huge motivator for the young Marine.[46] Kroc would eventually set the world record for men in the 220-pound class by benching 738 pounds, deadlifting 810 pounds, and squatting 1003 pounds in 2009.[47] Kroc was known for his incredibly hard training, including his famous Kroc rows, dumbbells that could hold as many as 300 pounds in long rows of small plates.[48] Shortly after setting the world record, Kroc turned his attention to bodybuilding. Although there is clearly some carryover between the two sports, there are important differences. Powerlifting is about strength, while bodybuilding is about physique. The dieting and weight cuts that are necessary to obtain the sculpted appearance sought by bodybuilders have a negative impact on strength. Despite trying to excel at both sports, Kroc was still able to compete successfully as a bodybuilder.[49]

Kroc's whole life has existed between the pull of two opposites. Despite the hypermasculine world in which Kroc spent most of her time, she also spent time dressing as a woman. In this mode Kroc was very interested in makeup, hair, and clothes.[50] Kroc was open about her gender dysphoria with those who were close to her. Kroc's first wife, Patty Stoll, with whom she had three sons, was aware that Kroc was transgender and tried to convince Kroc to undergo Christian reparative therapy. Kroc refused, and the couple divorced in 2006; they now have a relatively amicable relationship in which they share custody of their boys. Kroc let the boys know she was trans by wearing women's clothes around them starting when the youngest son was two years old. The youngest two sons were nonplussed, but the six-year-old said, "Daddy you look like a girl . . . a really big girl."[51] Kroc also told her parents and brothers. Although her sons are Kroc's biggest defenders, there has been plenty of tension with the rest of her family. Kroc married again in 2010 to Lauren Starky. Although Kroc says that Lauren was the love of her life, the two split up in 2012 because Lauren, too, could not deal with a transgender spouse.[52] Kroc also survived a bout with testicular cancer in 2004 that required surgical removal of one testicle and radiation therapy. It helps to understand Kroc's mindset at the time that she was hoping the cancer would spread to the other testicle and her penis so she could have them all removed. The cancer remained confined, and Kroc survived and thrived after recovery, going on to set her world record.[53]

Kroc did not, however, come out to the public until 2015, when a leaked video exposed her secret. She quickly took control of the situation with a legal name change and many media efforts at describing her life accurately and in an unsensational manner. Describing herself as both hypermasculine and hyperfeminine, she spoke openly about the challenges this duality has caused for her. She has described herself as both nonbinary and genderfluid. She has frequently posted side-by-side before-and-after pictures of herself. Her candor earned her great respect in much of the world, although she lost both employment and sponsorship as a result of her transition.[54]

Janae and I had the opportunity to Skype and e-mail each other in 2017 and 2018. It was during this period that Janae told me that she has given training advice to many trans men trying to gain strength and muscle mass after their transition. Janae has also been candid about her use of anabolic agents prior to and even occasionally after her transition. She is still torn between her desire to be feminine and her desire to be strong, going through periods where she attempts to drop weight so she can look more feminine and then periods where she uses anabolic drugs as she feels the old pull to be bigger and stronger.[55] Janae allowed a video crew to film her for two years after her transition, and the resulting documentary, *Transformer*, was released in the spring of 2018. Janae still lives in suburban Detroit, works as a pharmacist, tries to fit in advocacy time, and struggles with the duality of her nature.[56]

Although Kroc's transition story was a very big news item in 2015, the publicity that she received paled in comparison to the media frenzy caused when the former Olympic decathlon champion asked the world to call her Caitlyn. Caitlyn Jenner had tried to transition in the 1980s: She had her beard removed via electrolysis, saw a counselor, and started hormone therapy. Eventually, she desisted, largely because she met the woman who would become her wife and the mother of two of her children. That woman was Kris Kardashian, who was in the middle of a divorce from lawyer and businessman Robert Kardashian.[57] Robert and Kris Kardashian were married for twelve years and their union had produced four children. Bruce (as Caitlyn was known at the time) and Kris fell in love, got married in 1991, and had two girls together. The couple became even bigger celebrities when the reality TV show *Keeping Up with the Kardashians* became a megahit after it debuted in 2007. Despite the fame and fortune, Jenner was deeply unhappy and began to reexamine the idea of transition. Jenner had maintained a female wardrobe and wore it when Kris was not around. Kris, of course, knew about the wardrobe, but the Kardashian matriarch didn't want to deal with her husband in female mode. Caitlyn went back on hormones, grew her hair long, and had a few minor surgical procedures to make her look more feminine. By this time, the tabloids had gotten wind of the story and often featured pictures of Jenner around town looking very androgynous.[58]

In April 2015 Jenner came out to the world in a *20/20* interview with Barbara Walters, but didn't debut her new name until it was splashed across the cover of *Vanity Fair* in June 2015.[59] Caitlyn Jenner was now one of the world's biggest stories. Jenner's timing was perfect, as society was reaching the transgender tipping point,[60] a point when the world began to see trans folks not as delusional freaks, but rather as human beings with a unique set of challenges. Caitlyn became the poster girl for all that was transgender, despite the fact that her wealth, fame, and race gave her more privilege than any other transgender person had ever known. She was a finalist for *Time* magazine's Person of the Year in 2015,[61] and won the Arthur Ashe Courage Award from ESPN at the ESPY Awards in July 2015, among many other honors. At the ESPY Awards Jenner gave the most meaningful speech of her life, ending with these words: "This transition has been harder on me than anything I could imagine. And that's the case for so many others, besides me. For that reason alone, trans people deserve something vital. They deserve your respect. And from that respect comes a more compassionate community, a more empathetic society, and a better world for all of us."[62]

Caitlyn also has received backlash from many sources. There are still many who hold animus towards trans folks, and she became a lightning rod for those who still wish to mock transgender people. On the other hand, many in the transgender community have disavowed Jenner for her extreme privilege and her conservative political views. Caitlyn has joked that it was harder to come out as a Republican than as a trans person.[63] I could go on about Jenner's social impact, but when I had the chance to interview her, I wanted to know more about her golf game. In her sixties, golf has become her sport of choice; she belongs to a fancy club and carries a 7 handicap. She has also played in pro-am events on the LPGA circuit and has even been part of a winning team at one such event.[64] I asked her about her length off of the tee and which tees she plays from. Caitlyn replied that when she plays with her women friends she hits from the women's tees, but if she plays with men, she hits with them as well. Caitlyn hits the ball a long way, although she didn't commit to an actual average driving distance. All golfers lose distance off the tee as they get older, but Caitlyn said that she didn't notice an obvious reduction in length with her transition. Caitlyn also said that she was considering playing in the women's division in her club championships, and I encouraged her to do so.[65]

Caitlyn is considering a political future; is still close with most of her many children, including the Kardashians; continues to be a media presence; and engages in plenty of transgender activism. Although there are many on both ends of the political spectrum who hold her in contempt, I think she has been a positive force for transgender acceptance, and I wish her well.

Although Caitlyn is still the most famous athlete to transition, the UK would have its own equivalent of the Caitlyn moment in 2017, when Robert Millar emerged from seclusion and announced that she was now Philippa York. Around the turn of the century York had faded from public life, moved to the southeast portion of England, and started her gender transition. Since she was very private about her life, there are few details from this period. She has stated that she took a very gradual approach to her transition and that it took more than three years to complete. At first she simply dressed as a girl on weekends, but she took additional "little steps" and after each step she would think, "No, I don't want to stop."[66] York's privacy during this period was paramount to her, but there were multiple newspaper articles about her disappearance in the early 2000s.[67] York's transition took a toll on her relationship with her partner, Linda, and daughter Liddy, but the family unit has remained intact through all of the struggle.

Up until 2017 York continued to do a little journalism under the name of Robert Millar, but privately she was living as a female. All that changed in 2017 when ITV asked her to commentate for the Tour de France. Liddy convinced Philippa to take the job, and in July 2017 *Cycling News* introduced York to the world.[68] York's insight and humor won her praise in her commentating job and facilitated her reintroduction to public life. At the 2018 British Cycling Awards dinner she was received warmly by fans and colleagues. York has said of the love shown her by the public: "I never knew that I was held in high esteem," a statement that might seem hard to believe unless one has known the tremendous self-doubt that often accompanies gender dysphoria. York plans to continue journalism and commentary and also is starting to do advocacy work for transgender causes. She also still gets on a bike frequently, although she seldom rides very hard. She says that "given the choice, I would have transitioned at 16 and not been a bike rider," noting that happiness is more important than fame. Although York admits that her current life isn't perfect, she is much happier now than when "most days were crap and the occasional day was fine."[69] I wish her happiness as she embarks on this new phase of her life at age fifty-nine.

16

THE 2016 IOC TRANSGENDER GUIDELINES

The 2015 CAS ruling was a bitter blow to everyone on the IAAF side, as we hadn't expected to lose over the human rights issues. Fortunately, the ruling was not final, and the IAAF had two years to develop a remedial strategy. The problem was how to do it. Stéphane Bermon, Martin Ritzen, and Angelica Hirschberg started almost immediately to reevaluate the data they possessed in order to demonstrate more effectively the huge advantage athletes with hyperandrogenism held, especially in middle-distance races. It was also clear to us that the rules had to be changed in order to allow intersex women to compete as men if they refused to lower their T levels. Not only would it help the rules be less discriminatory, it was also the right thing to do for the athletes. As I saw it, the bigger question was how to handle the seemingly obvious discrimination inherent in fact that many intersex women could not be allowed in women's competition with their natural T levels. The timing of the CAS ruling in the Dutee Chand case was also difficult for the IAAF, as the World Track and Field Championships would be held in August 2015 in Beijing. Those intersex women who had been taking testosterone-suppressing medication could now get off it. I was asked several times by various media outlets whether these intersex women could regain their previous form in time for Beijing. I always responded that I didn't know.

Margaret Wambui, who had returned to competition in June slower than she had been in 2014, was named to the Kenyan 800 team in early

August 2015, even though she hadn't run in the Kenyan championship race in mid-July. This suggested that Wambui had gone onto suppressive treatment after the world junior race in 2014 and then come back off of it once the CAS ruling was released. If the Kenyans were expecting big things from her in Beijing they had to be disappointed, as she ran only 2:03 and didn't make it out of the heats. But this was only a temporary setback for the young runner.

Caster Semenya, who had been having a dismal season in 2015, seemed to find a new spring in her step after the CAS ruling, and she managed to qualify for the Beijing championship even though it appeared that she stood no chance to make it to the meet as late as early July. Semenya too found no joy in Bejing; she qualified for the semifinals but was the slowest of the twenty-four women in the semis at 2:03 and did not advance to the finals.[1]

One runner who would appear to have benefitted from the ruling in the Chand case was Francine Niyonsaba from Burundi. Niyonsaba had made the final of the 2012 London Olympic 800 meter race at age eighteen, and later in the season brought her personal best down to a very impressive 1:56.59. Niyonsaba ran almost as fast in June 2013 at the Prefontaine Classic meet in Eugene, Oregon, where she beat the world's best runners with her 1:56.72. Shortly thereafter, she disappeared from the sport until 2015. Her return was inauspicious at first, as she didn't manage to run faster than 2:05 before the CAS ruling. By September, however, she had almost returned to peak form, winning in Rieti, Italy, in 1:57.62.[2] The world had only begun to hear from the Burundian.

The CAS ruling was not the only problem for the IAAF. There were fresh allegations of doping-related misconduct in August, when German television's ARD follow-up program on doping was released, including the allegation that suspicious blood results had been ignored by the IAAF. Longtime IAAF president Lamine Diack stepped down in August when Sebastian Coe was elected to replace him.[3] It would soon become apparent just how corrupt Diack's rule had been.

Meanwhile, I had been allowing the details of the CAS ruling to percolate in my brain, particularly the question of what to do about the "female/female divide" in the hyperandrogenism policy. Then, in September, I had an epiphany of sorts. In order to understand my thought process, it is necessary to look at other aspects of the verdict. The CAS panel had stated that being female was a matter of the law and that, with very few exceptions, laws surrounding legal gender did not vary from country to country. Both of these statements are certainly not true, and I was bothered by the fact that these misconceptions may have played a part in the unfavorable ruling. My solution was that the IAAF should challenge the suggestion that gender was a matter of law. I suggested that the IAAF should recognize that there exist at least three types of gender: social gender, legal gender, and athletic gender. Social gender is governed by the gender expression of any given individual. One would hope that in the twenty-first century, the world is ready to allow gender-diverse people to live in their authentic gender as long as they aren't hurting anyone else. Legal gender is governed by the rules of the nation in which the individual resides. Contrary to the opinion of the CAS panel, these rules vary widely from country to country. As of this writing, there are at least twenty nations that recognize a third legal gender.[4] The existence of a third legal gender makes it impossible to match legal gender to athletic gender, as there are only two sex-based sporting categories. There are also at least fifteen nations that allow anyone to change their legal gender at will, another problem for the CAS ruling.[5] I thus proposed that the IAAF should state that the hyperandrogenism rules constitute a de facto athletic gender. And that for the purposes of sport, anyone whose functional testosterone is not below 10 nmol/L would be considered male. Although the rules would not change because of this shift in verbiage, the regulations would no longer be imposing a female/female divide. I e-mailed a brief version of my athletic gender proposal to Jon Taylor and got no reply. I also emailed it to Stéphane, who seemed unimpressed. Fortunately, I am not easily deterred, and I decided to work these ideas into my presentation to the IOC in November.

Prior to the IOC meeting, I stopped in Spain to spend a few days with María José Martínez-Patiño and her family and friends. I had a wonderful time in Spain, and then María and I flew to the conference together. We were quickly whisked to a waiting car and driven to the Hôtel de la Paix in Lausanne. No sooner had we entered the hotel lobby than María was greeting Eric Vilain and his partner. Although I have mentioned Eric several times in the book, this was the first time I met him in person. Eric was born in Paris, and earned undergraduate, PhD, and MD degrees from various institutions in France. His first clinical rotation as a medical student involved taking care of intersex infants, setting the course for his future career. After finishing his dual doctoral degrees, Eric completed a postdoctoral fellowship at the University of California, Los Angeles. Eric liked the school, the weather, and the Southern California lifestyle enough to stick around, eventually becoming the chief of medical genetics and a full professor.[6] Shortly after I met him, Eric was lured to George Washington University to become the chair of the Department of Genomics and the director of the Center for Genetic Medicine Research at Children's National Health System in the nation's capital.[7]

That night we had a wonderful dinner at the Lausanne Palace, the site of the annual IOC meeting. The medical commission meetings were but a small part of the overall meeting, and the dinner was open to anyone attending. At dinner I sat beside Myron (Mike) Genel and his wife, Phyllis. Mike had been a part of the working group on gender and sports for thirty years,[8] and he is one of the few current members of the IOC working group who believes that it is wrong to regulate intersex women in sports. I wound up spending most the evening talking to Mike and Phyllis; they turned out to be terrific company.

Our meeting started the next morning at the Palace. I recognized approximately half of the twenty-five people in the room,[9] either from the Chand trial or from dinner the previous evening. Attendees included members of the IOC medical commission and twelve invited experts; I was one of the latter group. The chairman of the meeting was Arne Ljunqvist, who did a masterful job keeping all of us on task and on time. Given his high level of competence and his obvious vitality, one would assume that Arne was in his sixties rather than his eighties.

During the morning session, Jon Taylor summarized the IAAF's legal position in the wake of the Chand decision, while Stéphane Bermon and Martin Ritzen went over the scientific options available to challenge the Chand ruling. Eric Vilain thought the only chance to overturn the ruling lay not in science but in crafting regulations the CAS panel thought were nondiscriminatory. Stéphane disagreed with Eric, and the two men had an interesting discussion about the relative merits of the scientific versus the human rights issues involved. It was decided fairly quickly that the IOC, as represented in that room, saw no point in trying to enforce the hyperandrogenism rules that had been used in 2012. Given the interim Chand ruling, a challenge to any IOC rules would certainly be upheld, and it was pointless to adopt a policy that couldn't be enforced. As the morning wore on it became obvious that consensus on the intersex issues would elude us. The best we could do was to put all of the options on the table and let the IAAF and the legal team of Jon Taylor and Liz Riley proceed as they saw fit. It did, however, seem likely that we would be able to reach agreement on updating the transgender regulations. Almost everyone agreed that the Stockholm consensus needed to be updated; however, it was clear that some of the details would be contentious.

I was thrilled by Liz's presentation during the morning session. She spoke of the worldwide variations in legal gender, noting that some countries had adopted a third gender and others allowed gender self-identification. She also stated that many countries do not allow trans people to change their legal gender at all.[10] She argued that all the muddiness of legal gender rules suggested that moving to gender self-identification would be an optimal starting place for IOC regulations. Was it possible that my e-mail to Jon had informed Liz's presentation, or had Jon and Liz reached their conclusions independent of my suggestions? Either way, I was delighted by the turn of events. During lunch, I could only pick at my food despite the fact that we were served salmon and bok choy, both favorites of mine. I was fairly certain that I was going to be the first openly transgender person to address the IOC, and I was extremely nervous about my reception. It seemed to me as though I would be representing all trans people, and I felt an enormous responsibility. María spoke first after lunch, and I was surprised that she didn't tell her famous life story. All of us in the expert group were very familiar with her saga; Eric and Mike referred to it during the meeting. Others in the room had no idea of María's significance in the history of gender and sport, and it would have enhanced María's presentation had she referred to her amazing role.

After María finished, it was my turn. I started with a brief introduction, sharing my history and my published study on transgender athletes, then I outlined my proposals for rules governing transgender athletes. There were three aspects I thought needed to be altered: the need for surgery, the waiting period for trans women, and the requirement for legal gender change. I spoke about the irrelevance of surgery to the performance of trans athletes, using my own experience as an example. I also suggested that the two-year waiting period imposed on trans women was too long. Louis Gooren's paper (discussed in chapter 7) and the experience of many trans women argue for a shorter period. I then shifted to the Chand case, introducing the idea of athletic gender as separate from social gender or legal gender. I argued that framing the hyperandrogenism rules as enforcing athletic gender might lead the CAS panel to see them as nondiscriminatory. I then took questions.

Some people in the room clearly doubted the fairness of allowing trans women to compete. Yannis Pitsiladis, one of the world's leading researchers on elite runners, raised the issue of muscle memory and transgender athletes. Eric Vilain mentioned the role of Q angle in performance. The Q angle refers to the angle formed by drawing a line from the knee to the iliac crest. Those people with narrower hips have a smaller Q angle which is more optimal for sustained running. I responded, as I have before, that of course trans women have athletic advantages over cisgender women, but that trans women also have disadvantages. I noted that trans women were underrepresented in high-level sports, using the example that not one trans woman played in the WNBA, despite the fact that basketball might be the sport with the most obvious advantages for trans women. There was one more speaker after me, and then a break was scheduled. At the break, Yannis and two or three others came over to talk to me; clearly I had made a good impression.[11] Like me, Yannis was a science and sports geek, and we spent a lot of time together over the next day and half.

After the break, Stéphane and Martin spoke further on some of the scientific issues for both transgender and intersex athletes, and then Eric spoke on both sociological and scientific issues. Eric went farther than I did on the question of legal recognition for trans athletes, claiming that it was an unfair burden to expect transgender people to be able to obtain legal recognition of their social gender in order to play sports. Eric also reiterated the fact that genital surgery was not important to athletic performance. After Eric's talk, we adjourned until dinner. Yannis and I walked back to our hotel together. Yannis had previously known little about the scientific issues surrounding transgender and intersex athletes but was clearly captivated by them. Yannis expressed a great deal of interest in doing research on transgender athletes. A couple hours later, I walked back to the Palace for a dinner that was being held in the grand ballroom. As I was walking from the entrance of the Palace toward the dining area, I met a small woman balancing on enormous heels. We engaged in a couple minutes of idle conversation as we made our way to the dining hall. She then turned to me nonchalantly and introduced herself as Nadia Comaneci. I replied that I was no one famous but I was pleased to meet her. I enjoyed some wonderful dinner conversation that night. In particular, Eric and I spent a good deal of time rehashing the day's events. I remember telling him that I wasn't opposed to abolishing the legal requirement for trans athletes but I didn't think the idea would fly. Eric accused me of engaging in realpolitik instead of advocating from my heart. Eric's words struck home, but I still didn't believe his proposal would be adopted the next day. I would be proven wrong.

Tuesday morning began with a phone conversation with Louis Gooren. His health had prevented him from traveling to the meeting, but his opinion was highly valued by the group. We spent the next forty minutes asking questions of the man who had been the primary driver of the Stockholm consensus. Gooren clearly felt that it was appropriate to update the regulations. And twice, in passing, Gooren said that he "really liked the ideas of Dr. Harper."[12] My heart soared. Once Gooren got off the phone, events moved very quickly. Much to my surprise, there was no opposition to dropping the legal requirement for trans athletes. We agreed to substitute a declaration of gender for legal status. Since there was still some concern that male athletes would opt to compete in the women's division, we stipulated that this declaration of gender was binding for four years, at least in terms of gender for the purpose of sport. Not only was I thrilled to see the legal requirement go away, I was also excited to see language reflecting the notion of athletic gender. As I had expected, everyone was willing to drop the surgical requirement.

The length of the waiting period for trans woman after commencement of hormone therapy was more contentious. Arne asked for suggested time frames, and I raised my hand immediately. I said "six months," knowing full well that others would suggest a longer time frame. Yannis offered four years (he later claimed that I shot a dagger look his way), and suggested muscle memory as the primary reason for the longer waiting period. Once again I reiterated that while trans woman have advantages—some of which never go away—it is still reasonable to allow them to compete with cisgender women. I was also forceful in stating that the existing two-year period was too long. The group gave much weight to the fact that Gooren's work suggested one year, and that became the consensus time frame.

While we were debating the length of the waiting period, Arne asked the four lawyers in the room to go outside and draft regulations—in fifteen minutes! They returned with a draft proposal and we spent the next hour or so refining it. One further point of contention was the maximum testosterone level a trans woman could carry and still be eligible. Since we were not requiring surgery, it would be possible for a trans woman to skimp on her suppressive treatments and maintain a higher T level than would be possible for a cisgender woman without doping. We debated the merits of using 3 nmol/L, the 99 percent level for "normal" women, but in the end settled on keeping the 10 nmol/L that is used for intersex women. Amazingly enough, we got all of this accomplished by our noon deadline. Arne did a wonderful job of chairing the meeting, and the willingness of the attendees to reach consensus was impressive.

Although the IOC medical commission had other matters to attend to that afternoon, the gender experts were finished with our required tasks, and we settled in for a lengthy lunch. We were all impressed that it had been relatively painless to reach consensus on new transgender guidelines. Before too long, the discussion turned to the Chand case. It was unclear at this point exactly how the IAAF would proceed, but most of us were hopeful that the organization would find a way to preserve some form of regulation over intersex athletes. We also discussed the ongoing scandal at the IAAF. Just a few days before our meeting, Lamine Diack was placed under investigation by French police on suspicion of taking drug-related bribes totaling more than €1 million. It was quite a fall for the man who had run the IAAF for eighteen years. Also placed under investigation were Gabriel Dollé and Habib Cisse, Diack's lawyer. The three were released on bail but had their passports confiscated.[13] Papa Massata Diack would also have been arrested, but he was holed up in his native Senegal. Stéphane said that he had become aware of problems in the handling of positive doping tests a few years earlier, in effect confirming the ARD report from a few months earlier. Stéphane had noticed that some athletes were not being convicted of doping offenses despite clearly failing their tests. At the time Dollé was his boss, so Stéphane went to him with the news that there must be some sort of cover-up. Stéphane said that Dollé told him not to worry about it and just concentrate on doing his job. At that point Stéphane knew that Dollé was involved. Stéphane's next step was to go to Diack, who was Dollé's boss. Again Stéphane was rebuffed, and at this point he understood just how deeply corrupt the Diack regime was. Stef resigned his position within the IAAF at this point. Some months later, he was convinced to return to the IAAF by others who knew of the corruption but insisted that he could still do good work even within a corrupt system. As a way of summing up all of the bad news, Stéphane shrugged sadly and said, "We will survive." Arne was a little more upbeat, suggesting that the arrival of Sebastian Coe as president was promising and that Arne had "high hopes" for the new regime.

In the weeks after the meeting, we engaged in some additional fine-tuning of the language in the proposed transgender guidelines via e-mail. We didn't sign off on all the verbiage until almost Christmas. In the interim, there was more bad news for the IAAF. In mid-November WADA's independent commission report, which suggested that the doping in Russia was state-sponsored and systematic, resulted in Russia being suspended from all IAAF-sponsored competitions.[14] Then, in December, Nick Davies, who had been promoted to chief of staff for Sebastian Coe, stepped down over allegations of unethical behavior regarding handling the news of Russian drug cheats in 2013.[15] In January, Papa Massata Diack and former treasurer Valentin Balakhnichev were banned for life, while Gabriel Dollé received a five-year ban.[16] In response, Sebastian Coe set out a ten-point road map to rebuild trust in the IAAF and the sport in general.

The IOC released its new transgender guidelines in January 2016, and sent everyone in the working group a link to the posting on the IOC website.[17] The organization did not, however, send out a press release, despite the fact that the policy was now publicly available. The IOC told me I could contact the press, but my housemate Steve beat me to it. Steve, who is gay, read a story on the website *Outsports* about the difficulties Chris Mosier was facing with the lack of a coherent transgender policy within the International Triathlon Union (ITU).[18] Steve sent a Facebook message to Cyd Zeigler, the man who runs the website, and that is how *Outsports* got the global scoop on the new IOC guidelines.[19] Within days, every news outlet in the world had picked up the story.

The reaction to the new IOC guidelines was wildly mixed. Many hailed the fact that surgical requirements were dropped as a major breakthrough, while others claimed it meant that men pretending to be women could now take over women's sport more easily. The apocalypse was nigh for women's sport, according to these doomsday prophets.[20] Of course, the same thing had been proclaimed in 2004 when the IOC enacted the Stockholm consensus.

There were many people involved in the running of international sporting federations among those troubled by the new guidelines. These sporting federations were so troubled that they asked the IOC to hold another meeting to address their concerns. And so in May of 2016, I was once again one of twelve experts invited by the IOC to the lovely city of Lausanne. I was pleased that Dr. Joshua Safer, an endocrinologist specializing in transgender care, was part of the expert group. After reading a couple of articles about him, I felt he would be a valuable addition to the group. On the other hand, I was disappointed that Eric Vilain was not at the meeting. Eric had been invited but was unable to attend, and his absence would prove to be an important factor in the outcome of the meeting.

Our first official function was a welcome dinner the night before the meeting at the Mövenpick hotel. I wound up sitting at the same table as Alan Vernec from WADA and noted Australian endocrine expert David Handelsman. At one point Handelsman introduced the notion of trans regret, suggesting that the fact that some trans people de-transitioned after their initial gender shift, could be used by those wishing to game the sports system. There are many others who have expressed sentiments similar to those expressed by Handelsman, despite the fact that there are not any known cases of it ever happening. I was glad that Josh was also seated at the table; he assured Handelsman that trans regret was actually extremely rare,[21] and that it was unlikely that anyone not really transgender would pretend to be so.

At the meeting the following morning, Vernec and Handelsman spoke first, talking a lot about testosterone levels and the resulting performance implications. They also pointed out that the accepted lower men's T limit of 10 nmol/L was flawed since it wasn't based on mass spectrometry, the best method of measuring T. If one used liquid chromatography and mass spectrometry (LC-MS) methods to measure T, the actual lower limit was approximately 7.7 nmol/L. Hence, even if the committee decided to keep the upper T level for transgender athletes at the lower limit for men, the number would need to come down. The Chand case had already shown the weakness of using the lower end of the men's T range as an upper limit for female athletes, but the presentation from Vernec and Handelsman cemented the need for change.

Vernec and Handelsman were not the only ones at the meeting who were unhappy with the T limit in the new IOC guidelines. Mike Genel had previously made it clear that he thought the limit should be much less than 10 nmol/L, and Angelica Hirschberg told me at breakfast that she thought we needed to have a lower T limit. Without much doubt, all of the representatives of the sporting federations also preferred to see the T limit for trans women be as low as possible. It would be a major athletic advantage for any female competitor to carry a testosterone level just under 10 nmol/L, since the upper end of the female range (using LC-MS measurements) was less than 2 nmol/L. It would a simple matter for trans women athletes to take less of their antiandrogen medicine in order to maintain a higher T level, and it was clear that many in the room were concerned this would happen. What the people around the table failed to realize is that most trans women athletes will self-regulate their T levels at a much lower level than 3 nmol/L primarily because of our desire to become more feminine. It is, however, true that there are trans women who would be willing to compete against cisgender women with as much T as they were allowed to carry.

After Verenc and Handelsman spoke, Eric Vilain gave a presentation via Skype and then Josh Safer had his turn. Perhaps the most relevant data Josh shared was the testosterone levels of his patients. Although most of the trans women under Josh's care achieved typical female T levels while on hormone therapy, many also did not. Josh explained that some trans women are worried about libido and/or sexual performance, leading them to skimp on their meds, but he also expressed concern that the prescribed doses might not allow all trans women to stay consistently at female-typical testosterone levels. In fact, Josh showed that as many as 25 percent of his trans patients had T levels greater than 5 nmol/L at some point during their therapy. His data had important implications for trans women and sport.

I was up after Josh. It seemed clear that WADA and the federations were not on board with allowing trans women to compete without surgery. It was also clear that the bulk of the heavy lifting in convincing these people to be more open-minded had been placed on my shoulders. I was given the last and longest time allotment of the three speakers supporting the new IOC guidelines. I had no intention of letting the IOC or Arne Ljungqvist down. And I didn't. I started by reminding my audience that there had been a great deal of skepticism about the Stockholm consensus in 2004. Many feared that letting trans women compete under any circumstances would mean the end of women's sport. Clearly that hadn't happened. I then spoke of the deficiencies of the Stockholm consensus in terms of the human rights of trans people, and how the new guidelines rectified those human rights issues. I talked about the advantages and disadvantages trans women face when compared to cisgender women, and the rabid, unreasonable opposition faced by many trans women athletes. I summarized the science in Gooren's research and mine, and then made the comparison with left-handed athletes. I spoke about how underrepresented trans women were in sports, using as an example the lack of trans women in the National Collegiate Athletic Association (NCAA) five years after it adopted a no-surgery rule.[22] When I sat down, Stéphane reached over, patted my arm, and told me that I had been outstanding.

At lunch Alys Lewis and Mike England, who were representing women's rugby, came over to speak with me. Alys said she thought my presentation had been riveting. Mike told me that they had six trans women competing out of a total of five hundred thousand athletes. Mike said that he hadn't realized how underrepresented trans women were in rugby, but that he did the math while listening to me speak. Alan Vernec also approached me over lunch and said that he was impressed with my talk. Alan is Canadian, so we also spoke about our shared heritage and also about Kristen Worley.

After lunch, Liz and Jon led the group in discussion of a draft template that individual federations could use as model rules for transgender athletes. We spent the afternoon trying to reach consensus on all the details of this template. Without much doubt, the most contentious detail was the upper testosterone limit for trans women. It was clear that the consensus in the room was to make this limit as close to 2 nmol/L as was reasonable. We never reached a formal consensus on a modified T level, but it was clear that this consensus limit would be far less than 10 nmol/L.

Just when it seemed that the afternoon was winding down, Mike Imani from weightlifting dropped a bomb on the rest of us. Several times that day the point had been made that no trans athlete had yet competed in the Olympics and none were on the horizon. However, at the end of the day, Imani stood up to say that two trans women, one of whom was a medal contender, were interested in competing in that year's Olympic weightlifting competition.[23] After Imani dropped his bombshell, he asked Jon and Liz if they could have the template for the federations finished by early June so the weightlifting federation could use it for the Rio Olympic Games. I pointed out that June 1 was only one week away; Jon and Liz just smiled weakly. There was no way the document would be finished as early as Mike Imani requested. In fact, the template would not be released as this book goes to press.

Over the next few days, the IOC working group passed some e-mails back and forth. Eric Vilain, who had not been part of the discussion about T levels, was incensed that we would change from the 10 nmol/L we had agreed upon in November. I was more sanguine, but I agreed with Eric that the testosterone limit should be the same for trans woman and for intersex women. Mike Genel had suggested that whatever limit we decided upon should be reviewed in the future, and I suggested that it would be wise to do so prior to every summer Olympics for the foreseeable future. A subcommittee consisting of Stéphane, Angelica, Josh, and David Handelsman was formed[24] that wound up suggesting a limit of 5 nmol/L. Our group reconvened via e-mail in the summer of 2017 and we agreed on the new limit, although Eric was still adamant in his opposition to any reduction. Both Eric and I pointed out that there would be substantial opposition to the reduction from trans rights organizations and there needed to be appropriate scientific justification of this new limit. We were then informed that David Handelsman was publishing a paper that would give justification for the choice of 5 nmol/L. At this point there was nothing to do but wait for the publication of the paper. Yannis Pitsiladis has said that international sports federations move at two speeds: slow and stop. We were now in the stop phase.

17

AFTERMATH OF THE CAS DECISION IN THE CHAND CASE

The first indication that the sport of track and field would be drastically different as a result of the CAS decision in the Chand case came at the 2016 World Indoor Championships. These championships had been awarded to my adopted hometown of Portland, despite the fact that the city did not possess an indoor track at the time of the bidding. The track deficiency was rectified when Nike commissioned a 200-meter banked indoor track that was built in a warehouse in the industrial part of town. The temporary home of the championship track became known as the House of Track, and Portland hosted four low-key but high-quality indoor meets there in January and early February before the track was moved to the Oregon Convention Center for worlds.[1] The World Indoor Championships took place from March 17–20, 2016. Naturally enough, I purchased seats for every session and so did other friends of mine.

Both Francine Niyonsaba and Margaret Wambui were entered in the 800 meter race. The heats were held on Saturday, March 19, with the finals the following day. There were three heats, with only the winner of each heat guaranteed a spot in the final. The other three spots in the final would be awarded based on time.

Wambui was in heat one along with pre-meet favorite Ajeé Wilson of the United States. Wilson took the race out hard, passing 200 meters in 28.7. The shorter straightaways and tighter turns of indoor tracks means that leading is often a very good strategy in the 800 meters. Wilson led the whole race but was challenged hard by Wambui at the end, and they ran 2:00.6 and 2:00.7, respectively—terrific times for a preliminary race indoors. Wambui would certainly make the final based on her time, and in fact all three time qualifiers would come out of this heat.

Niyonsaba was in the second heat, and she too took the early lead in her race. Niyonsaba, however, went out much slower, splitting 30.6 at 200 meters, meaning the other runners in the race were bunched up behind her. Every time one of Niyonsaba's competitors challenged for the lead, she would surge away from them, seemingly with ease. On the backstretch on the last lap, Britain's Lynsey Sharp made a strong move to try to take the lead, but Niyonsaba powered away from her rival through the final curve and into the homestretch. Niyonsaba ran 2:02.4, a Burundian national indoor record, off of what appeared to be a fartlek workout, while Sharp's 2:02.7 would miss the final by less than half a second. The third heat was the slowest of all, with the former University of Oregon Duck collegiate champion Laura Roesler winning in 2:04.[2]

After watching the heats it would appear that Niyonsaba, Wilson, Wambui, and Roesler would battle for the medals in the next day's final. Roesler spent much of the rest of the day sitting right in front of the group I was with, and one of the guys in our group got his picture taken with her. During the postrace interviews, Sharp—a medal contender with a proven international record—was asked if she was disappointed not to make the final. It was a loaded question, since there were plenty of rumors about Niyonsaba being intersex floating around the internet. Sharp did not rise to the bait, instead claiming she was happy with her indoor season.

Later that evening I got an e-mail from Weldon Johnson, one of the two brothers who founded the website *LetsRun*, asking me how I thought they should handle the intersex angle to the 800 final. I said that it was a difficult call, since the last thing anyone wanted was a replay of the Semenya fiasco. On the other hand, the CAS decision was probably going to play a huge factor in a global athletic contest, and it didn't seem right to ignore the probable intersex status of two of the medal favorites. The women's 800 final was part of an outstanding concluding day of competition, with American athletes vying for medals in most of the events, a fact that was bound to have the audience at a fever pitch. My seat was immediately adjacent to the high jump bar and parallel to the finish line. I was close enough to the action that Kathy

Roberts said she saw me on TV. As the gun sounded to start the 800 final, Wilson once again shot to the front, but not quite as quickly as she had the day before; she hit the 200 meter mark in 29.2 seconds. On the second lap, Wambui and then Niyonsaba moved past Wilson, with the Kenyan in the lead at 400 meters in 1:00.6. Niyonsaba put in a cruel burst of speed on the third lap to take the lead, passing the 600 meter mark in 1:29.8, with Wambui close behind. At this point it appeared likely that the pair would finish first and second, but Wilson closed well over the final lap, edging past Wambui on the final straight, but never threatening Niyonsaba. The times for the first three were 2:00.01, 2:00.27, and 2:00.44, with Roesler moving up well to take fourth in 2:00.80.[3] Although Niyonsaba was neither as dominant nor as masculine appearing as Semenya had been in Berlin, she won with relative ease, and her build was noticeably more powerful than most of her competitors. Wambui's appearance was even more masculine—a casual observer of the race would probably assume she was a man—and she had given the pre-race favorite all she could handle twice on successive days. It was not unreasonable to expect that there might be a media flurry not unlike that which had occurred after Semenya's 2009 Berlin victory. Amazingly enough, it didn't happen. I heard through my contacts that the female competitors were furious that Niyonsaba and Wambui were now dominant,[4] but nothing was made of it in the press. It would take something more to break this story open.

And not surprisingly, that something was the resurgence of Caster Semenya. After some low-key but fast races, she stunned the world with her performance at the South African National Track & Field Championships in Stellenbosch on April 16. Semenya ran the 400, 800, and 1500 in the meet, and all the finals were held on Saturday. She first won the 400 meters in 50.74, the fastest time by a South African woman in fifteen years. Then, a mere fifty minutes later, she ran the 800 in 1:58.45, a stadium record and her fastest time in four years. Three hours later she lined up for the 1500 final. She was content to follow Dominque Scott, the NCAA champion for Arkansas, for three and half laps before blowing past her to win in 4:10.95.[5] Not only was Semenya running faster than she had in years, but her body looked more chiseled than it had recently. It was clear that something was different in 2016, and one could only conclude that she had ceased taking testosterone-suppressing medications once the CAS verdict was rendered. Semenya soon showed the world that her results in Stellenbosch were not an aberration. The first Diamond League meet of the year was held in Doha, Qatar, on May 6. Semenya ran the 800 content to run in the middle of the pack in lane 2 for most of the race, but her last 100 meters were awe inspiring as she flew past her overmatched opponents to win in 1:58.26.[6] British commentator Steve Cram said that Semanya's run looked "sooooo easy." Semenya's next race would be a little bit more challenging as she would face Niyonsaba in Rabat, Morocco, on Sunday, May 22. The rabbit took the field through the 400 in 56.7 seconds with Niyonsaba close behind. Once on her own, the Burundian led by default, passing 600 in 1:27.9, and dropped everyone but Semenya. The South African powered past Niyonsaba to finish in 1:56.64, just missing Niyonsaba's Diamond League record by 0.05 seconds. Niyonsaba ran 1:57.7 for second, with everyone else more than another second back.[7] After watching the race, one couldn't help but think that Semenya and Niyonsaba were huge favorites for gold and silver medals in Rio.

After Semenya ran her eye-popping triple at the South African national championships, Ross Tucker reentered in the conversation surrounding intersex athletes and sports. He blasted the 2015 CAS decision in the Chand case as "one of the stupidest, most bemusing legal/scientific decisions ever made."[8] After Ross reengaged on the Semenya subject, I contacted him to express my appreciation for his return to the sports-and-gender arena.

Ross's response stunned me and had a profound impact on the next several months of my life: He proposed that we jointly put together an article for his website. We settled on a format that would see Ross e-mailing me questions over the three-week period from the middle of April until early May. The resulting question-and-answer piece topped seven thousand words and was published on May 23, one day after Semenya's Rabat victory.[9]

The article was widely read and thrust both Ross and me into the ensuing debate that rocked the world of sports at the 2016 Olympics in Rio de Janeiro in August. As the start of games loomed, I was fielding questions from journalists on an almost daily basis over the intersex athlete question. In addition, I spent much of my summer dealing with rumors about transgender athletes in the games. In early July there were reports in the British press two British trans women had competed internationally for their country and were on the cusp of being selected for Rio.[10]

Despite the rumors, no openly trans athletes competed in Rio. Given that there were ten thousand athletes at the games, there must have been several trans athletes competing in their birth gender. There might have been a few stealthy trans athletes competing in their true gender, but the dire predictions made by pundits back in January of a trans takeover of women's sport in Rio failed to materialize.

There was, however, a substantial impact made by probable intersex women in Rio. Approximately one month prior to the games, Semenya, Niyonsaba, and Wambui all ran the same race for the first time at the Herculis meet in Monaco on July 15. The race had been billed as a world record attempt, and expectations were high. Semenya won in a new Diamond League record of 1:55.34, with Niyonsaba and Wambui finishing in 1:56 and change, while no one else could break 1:57.[11] Wambui was eventually disqualified for a lane violation, but the race left little doubt who the medal favorites for Rio would be.

The heats for the women's 800 in Rio were held on Wednesday, August 17, and there were sixty-four women in eight heats of eight runners. The field would be reduced to twenty-four runners for three semifinals to be held the following day, and all of the favorites qualified. The semifinalists could qualify for the final either as one of the two top finishers in each semi, or as one of only two time qualifiers.

Ajeé Wilson was one American running in the semifinals, and she had the misfortune to draw the first section, containing both Francine Niyonsaba and Margaret Wambui. Just as she had in the semifinal in the indoor world meet, Niyonsaba controlled the race from the front while keeping the pace relatively modest. Wambui sprinted past the short but powerfully built Burundian in the final meters of the race. Niyonsaba eased off at the tape, as she was concerned only with securing one of the two auto-qualifiers. Wilson finished third in the semi with a time of 1:59.75, meaning she was unlikely to advance. In the second semifinal, Poland's Joanna Jozwik outkicked Canadian Melissa Bishop for the win, while Eunice Sum faded badly, ending her Olympics prior to the final.[12] The other American, Kate Grace, had good and bad news with her semifinal draw. By virtue of being in the third heat, she knew the time she had to beat. Unfortunately, she also had the deepest semifinal, with Semenya, 2015 world champ Maryna Arzamasova of Belarus, and Britain's Lynsey Sharp. Arzamasova was determined to make the race fast, and she led from the gun until the 700 meter mark, when Semenya strode past, winning with ease. Down the final straight, Grace battled with Sharp and Arzamasova, eventually finishing third behind the Briton.[13] Thanks to the front-running Belarusian, all four of the women qualified for the final.

Since neither Wilson nor Sum made the final, it meant that five Caucasian women would be lining up with three presumably intersex African women, a lineup that was certain to increase the already high level of tension. If, as expected, the three African women took the medals, and there was an ensuing cry of unfairness, many viewers would see the obvious racial overtones of the situation.

When the women lined up for the final, the three African women were in lanes 3, 4, and 5. No one burst to the front after the gun, but by the middle of the backstretch, Semenya had taken the lead. After a fast but not outrageous first 400 of 57.7, Niyonsaba moved to the front, picked up the pace, and strung the race out, splitting 1:26.8 at 600 meters. Semenya moved up to Niyonsaba's shoulder coming into the final straightaway and blasted the final 100 in 14.0, for a final time of 1:55.28. Semenya's splits clearly indicated that there was more in the tank. Although Niyonsaba lost a second to Semenya in the final 100 meters, her silver medal wasn't threatened and she finished in 1:56.49.

The closest and most interesting race was the one for the final medal. Coming into the last 100, Bishop held a slight lead over Wambui. Down the final straightway, the Kenyan slowly began to reel the Canadian in. Wambui edged ahead with 20 meters to go, running 1:56.89 to Bishop's Canadian record of 1:57.02. Jozwik finished with a flourish to nab fifth place, with Sharp holding on to sixth. Grace was in seventh place at 600, but couldn't muster her usual strong finish as she wound up eighth and last.[14] Although disappointed with her race, Grace reached out her hand when approached by Semenya after the race. The other non-medaling finalists were not as gracious as Grace. Sharp was obvious in her rebuff of Semenya. Engaged in a group hug with Bishop and Jozwik when Semenya tapped her on the shoulder, Sharp continued to hug the other two white women and refused to even glance in Semenya's direction. It made for a bad show. Bishop was unable to speak to reporters after the race as she walked through the media zone in tears. She later said that she was not in control of her emotions.

Bishop undoubtedly knew that she might well have won the Olympic gold medal without the CAS decision, but wound up without a medal in the actual race.

There was one more women's 800 of note before the end of the season. The Weltklasse meet in Zurich is generally considered the world's best one-day meeting, and all eight of the Rio 800 finalists plus a few others would take to the track. This would be the last chance for Semenya to set a world record in 2016, and the rabbit was tasked at going through 400 meters in 55 seconds. Unfortunately, she blasted the first 200 meters and no one went with her. The rabbit slowed in her second 200 and did pass the 400 split in 55 point, but Semenya was over 56 seconds and leading the race proper. There would be no world record on this day. Semenya even failed to produce her usual blistering finish and settled for the win in 1:56.45.[15] The last 100 meters provided a snapshot of the entire year, with the three presumably intersex runners together, 20 meters up on the rest of the field. It certainly looked like two different races.

The post-race reactions in Zürich, however, were noticeably different than in Rio. Semenya first greeted Wambui and Niyonsaba and then sought out Grace. It was what happened next that made the moment special: The rest of the field reached out to the three Rio medalists and there were hugs all around. Even after everything that had happened to these women over the season, their essential humanity showed up in the end. It was a touching sight to see. Surely the 800 meter runners knew that it was senseless to blame the probable intersex athletes for doing nothing more than racing with their natural gifts.

Although most of the world was focused on the women's 800 meter race in Rio, I was looking at other races too, and I believe that the number of intersex women in Rio matched up well with the 8 intersex athletes who competed in the Atlanta Olympic Games in 1996[16] and the 7 in the 2011 World Championships in Daegu.[17] Moreover, intersex athletes were hugely over-represented on the podium in Rio.

It might be reasonable to ask at this point what the IAAF was doing to reverse the CAS decision. The IAAF had been given two years to publish more data to support its hyperandrogenism rules, but that is a fairly short time in which to both gather and publish data on a small, secretive segment of the population. It was not until the beginning of the spring of 2017 that Stéphane Berman published the first of two papers that would be important for the IAAF in its battle to regain control over the participation of intersex women in the sport of athletics. The paper, entitled "Androgens and Athletic Performance of Elite Female Athletes," was mostly a review of existing data, but toward the end of the paper Bermon noted that "performances obtained from hyperandrogenic DSD athletes before and after they had their T levels lowered" indicated that the three athletes in question were 5.7 percent slower after two years of testosterone suppression.[18]

I thought these data were of enormous importance, as they demonstrated that intersex athletes had a larger advantage than the 3 percent figure Stéphane had quoted in the Chand trial. There were many who would bemoan the study's small sample size, but the number of world-class intersex athletes who continued to compete for two years after testosterone reduction is also very small. I had previously estimated that intersex athletes held approximately half of the advantage of male runners (10–12 percent) when compared to the majority of the female population. I was pleased to see that Bermon's data backed up my estimate.

The second paper from the IAAF, coauthored by Bermon and Pierre-Yves Garnier, was published in the *British Journal of Sports Medicine* in July 2017. The paper reviewed data from women and men competing in the 2011 and 2013 World Athletics Championships. The women were divided into tertiles (three groups) based on their testosterone levels. The women in the high-T tertile outperformed the low-T tertile women by a statistically significant margin in five events: the 400 meters, 400 hurdles, 800 meters, hammer throw, and pole vault. The pattern was not repeated in the men's data. This somewhat contrived study was important because there were plenty of data showing that testosterone made a world of difference between male and female athletes, but there was, up until this point, no data indicating a difference between women with high T and women with low T.[19]

The CAS deadline for the IAAF to respond to the interim decision in the Chand case was the end of July 2017, but the IAAF asked for an extension of two months.[20] The CAS granted the extension, which meant that intersex athletes could continue to compete with their natural testosterone levels in the 2017 World Championships to be held in London in August. I had been planning a trip to watch this championship meet for years. I was part of a group that included Paul and Kathy

Roberts and Andy and Elaine Buckstein. Andy was a college teammate of Paul and Kathy, and the three of them had stayed friends for years. The five of us went as part of the *Track and Field News* tour. There were others in the tour whom I knew, including an old running friend named Jerry Yunker who was doing his best to cope with the new me.

The meet was wonderful and we had a great time in London, but the specter of domination by the intersex athletes was ever present. On multiple occasions I heard talk from different spectators in our vicinity about masculine-appearing African women who were doing well. These knowledgeable fans of the sport understood that at least some of these women were intersex, and the fans were clearly unhappy about it.

Prior to the London world meet there had been some notable action in the women's 800 that season. Semenya was clearly better than anyone else in the world, although Wambui had given her a very close race in May in Eugene at Pre.[21] Unfortunately for the tall Kenyan, she had picked up an injury shortly thereafter and was no longer a threat to the South African speedster. Niyonsaba was clearly the second-best 800 woman on the planet, but Ajeé Wilson was having a superb year. She broke the American record in Monaco in July with her 1:55.61 but could still only finish third to Semenya and Niyonsaba in the race.[22]

The final in London got off to a brisk start as Niyonsaba took the early lead and went through 200 meters in 27.11 which was way too fast. The second 200 was much slower, and at the bell Niyonsaba led from Wilson and Wambui with Semenya lurking. With 250 meters to go Wilson kicked hard, making a long charge for gold. Niyonsaba followed the American closely, and the two established a clear lead on the rest of the field. And then the inevitable happened: Semenya switched on her closing speed and blew past the leaders to finish in a world-leading time of 1:55.16. Niyonsaba pulled away from Wilson to finish second in 1:55.92, and Wilson claimed the bronze in 1:56.65. Although Wambui was well beaten, she still finished fourth in 1:57.54. Melissa Bishop had promised before the race that she wasn't going to place fourth this year, and she was as good as her word, finishing fifth in 1:57.68.[23] Semenya's time in London was the fastest of her career, and she would run no faster for the rest of the season. The world record was safe for another year.

The astute reader might ask about the racing times of Dutee Chand after the 2015 verdict in the case named after her. Since Chand was never affected by the hyperandrogenism policy, her times weren't going to get markedly faster after the 2015 CAS decision. On the other hand, she was now free to train without the trial hanging over her head. She set a national record of 11.24 for 100 meters in 2016 and won bronze in the 2017 Asian Championships in the 100 meters, but she has been less-than-impressive in global athletics meets. She did make the semifinal in the 60 meters in the indoor world meet in Portland in 2016,[24] but otherwise she has been eliminated in the first round in all of her other global meets, including the Olympic Games in Rio.

I have engaged endocrine experts on the question of Chand's probable DSD, and the consensus opinion is that she likely has PAIS.[25] One cannot be certain what the IAAF would have done had it been allowed to examine her back in 2014, but the overwhelming consensus is that the IAAF probably would have allowed her to compete without modifying her body in any way. Her subsequent results have clearly indicated that she is not any threat to the playing field at the global level of women's athletics. And this raises a serious issue. Surely Katrina Karkazis and her team ran tests on Chand back in 2014. If Chand really has androgen insensitivity, then why proceed to trial? There was probably no need to do it on Chand's behalf. Why subject the Indian athlete to all the rigors of a trial, when she could have been back competing by late 2014? Did Karkazis and her team callously use Chand as a test case? We will probably never know the answer to these questions, but what was hyped as a holy crusade certainly has some very dark clouds hanging over it.

After the 2017 world meet was over, the IAAF finished its response to the CAS, submitting a proposal in late September that had included modifications to the 2011 hyperandrogenism rules, as well as data supporting these proposed new rules. Although I never saw the proposal, the IAAF certainly used Bermon's two 2017 papers as part of its submission. I assume the IAAF would also use the work Liz Riley had done on the legal gender aspect of the CAS verdict. Liz had published a paper called "The Participation of Trans Athletes in Sport—A Transformation in Approach?"[26] that spoke of the need to look beyond the legal gender of transgender athletes. Liz's paper made it clear that legal gender cannot be used to separate male athletes from female athletes in a world where nonbinary legal gender is a reality.

On January 19, 2018, the CAS issued a media release detailing some aspects of the IAAF proposal and the response of the Chand team. The most important aspect of the IAAF submission was that the modified regulations "would only apply to female track events over distances of between 400 metres and one mile."[27] Without doubt this subset of events encompassed most of the intersex athletes of the last twenty five years. The list of restricted events also had important consequences for the Chand case. A mere week after the IAAF submission, Chand's lawyers responded that since the Indian sprinter had no desire to compete in any race as long as 400 meters, the modified regulations were never going to apply to her. As long as the IAAF came up with regulations using the proposed model, the Chand case was over. Until that time, however, the CAS maintained the suspension of the old hyperandrogenism rules.

In response, the IAAF stated new regulations for intersex athletes would take effect on November 1, 2018, and that these new regulations would indeed follow the proposed model.[28] The new regulations were announced during the 2018 World Indoor Athletics Championships in Birmingham, England. I think the following quote from IAAF president Sebastian Coe is especially relevant: "We choose to have two classifications for our competition—men's events and women's events. This means we need to be clear about the competition criteria for these two categories. We have always believed that testosterone, either naturally produced or artificially inserted into the body, provides significant performance advantages."[29]

I was pleased to see that the IAAF called these new rules the DSD rules and specified that the first *D* was to stand for *differences*, since I had made both of those suggestions earlier. I was also pleased to see that the IAAF accepted the suggestion of Eric Vilain and María José Martínez-Patiño[30] to allow any affected intersex athlete an ombudsman to assist in her case. It was also good that the IAAF explicitly noted in the policy that surgery was not required for any intersex athlete.

I might have been pleased by the new rules, but others were not. There were many who claimed that these new regulations were aimed squarely at Caster Semenya, but that clearly wasn't true, as the 800 meter final in the Birmingham meet demonstrated. Semenya was not present at the meet, and yet a probable intersex athlete (Francine Niyonsaba) won the 800 meter race. Caster Semenya is neither the first nor the last intersex athlete to dominate at middle-distance running,[31] and I think these modified regulations will help to restore the more or less level playing that existed before the 2015 CAS decision. And, of course, anyone who has read this book will understand that the issue of intersex runners in the sport of athletics has been ongoing for more than eighty years. These new rules were hardly about Semenya.

Within two months of the announcement of the IAAF's new DSD regulations, the legal firm of Norton Rose Fulbright announced that it would be taking the IAAF to the CAS on behalf of Caster Semenya.[32] The Semenya versys IAAF trial would be the culmination of ten years of turmoil since Caster first burst onto the scene in 2009. I will get back to the Semenya trial soon enough, but I have been remiss in not updating the reader on the ongoing drug issues that were very important within the international sporting world. Allow me to rectify the omission.

In May 2016, WADA commissioned an independent investigation into the allegations of state-sponsored doping led by Richard McLaren, one of the judges in the Chand case. The resulting McLaren report was released in two parts, with the first part released just one month before the Rio Olympic Games in July 2016. The first part of the McLaren report claimed that state-sponsored doping in Russia existed "beyond a reasonable doubt" and that several state agencies had joined forces to operate "for the protection of doped Russian athletes";[33] the report then called for a total ban of Russian athletes from the summer Olympics. It didn't happen.

Despite this damning report by an expert with a stellar reputation, the IOC instead decided to leave the matter up to the individual sporting federations. The IAAF was the only governing body to enact a blanket ban on all Russian athletes within its sport for Rio. All but one of the sixty-eight-person Russian athletics squad were prohibited from competing, as were forty-four other athletes from all remaining sports. The IAAF did allow long jumper Darya Klishina to compete in Rio, as she had been living in the United Sates for three years and had been tested several times outside of Russia.[34] A total of 278 Russian athletes competed in other sports at the games, wining enough medals to place the nation fourth in the medal count. All Russian athletes were banned from the subsequent Paralympic Games.

Part 2 of the McLaren report, released on December 9, 2016, was even more damning than part 1, claiming that more than one thousand

Russian athletes in all sports benefited from the cover-up between 2011 and 2015.[35] In particular the McLaren report backed up Grigory Rodchenkov's allegations of a widespread government-coordinated effort in Russia to subvert the anti-doping process. The investigators found telltale scratches on the inside of the bottles used to store the B samples of Russian urine from the Sochi games. These scratches were evidence that the bottles had indeed been opened with a specially designed tool. As a result of the McLaren report, several international winter sporting events were relocated from Russia, and several Russian skiers and biathletes were banned from competing.

The IAAF extended the ban on the Russian team through the 2017 World Championships but allowed nineteen select individuals—athletes who had been tested numerous times outside of Russia—to compete. These select Russian athletes were given the moniker Authorized Neutral Athletes (ANA)[36] and were outfitted in a generic Nike kit. The London World Championships were the first time the ANA athletes competed as a group, and Jerry Yunker started calling these competitors "Authorized Nike Athletes." Soon everyone in our spectator group was doing the same thing. The ANA athletes won six medals, including the gold medal in the women's high jump won by Mariya Lasitskene.

The Russians had done little to clean up their act by the end of 2017, and so the IOC suspended the Russian Olympic Committee from the 2018 Winter Olympics held in PyeongChang, South Korea. Instead the athletes were allowed to compete as Olympic Athletes from Russia (OAR),[37] without the trappings of the other nations' teams. Two OAR athletes, including a bronze medal–winning curler, failed drug tests at the winter games and were suspended.[38]

The IAAF also continued to ban Russia from the 2018 World Indoor Athletics Championships but allowed seven athletes to compete under the ANA designation. These seven athletes won three medals: Danil Lysenko and Mariya Lasitskene swept the gold in the men's and women's high jump, and Anzhelika Sidorova was second in the women's pole vault.[39] The IAAF also authorized thirty-three Russians to compete throughout the 2018 season as neutral athletes.[40]

A couple of drug busts in 2018 are worth noting. Lysenko was stripped of his authorized status in August for refusing to make himself available for drug testing.[41] All international competitors in athletics are required to provide their whereabouts at all times so they can be tested out of competition at any time. Lysenko's failure to do so is a clear case of noncompliance. In September, Zambian 400 meter runner Kabange Mupopo was given a four-year ban from athletics as the result of a positive test for exogenous testosterone at the 2017 World Championships in London. Mupopo claimed that her elevated T levels were a result of her hyperandrogenism "the same condition which affects South African star Caster Semenya."[42] However, it is possible to distinguish exogenous T from endogenous T, so the Zambian's excuse was rejected by the Athletics Integrity Unit. (The old IAAF medical and anti-doping department had been split into the AIU and the Health and Sciences Department). It is amazing to think that the athlete or her coaches apparently thought the 2015 CAS ruling in the Chand case gave athletes license to have unlimited T, when the ruling clearly specified naturally produced testosterone. Or maybe they thought WADA couldn't distinguish injected T from natural T. Either way, the Mupopo case is a head-scratcher.

And what of Yuliya Stepanova and her husband, Vitaly Stepanov? They continue to live in the United States in an undisclosed location. Yuliya testified at a drug inquiry held in June 2018,[43] and I had the opportunity to meet the Stepanovs twice in 2018. Seeing as they are still living in hiding, it would not be appropriate to reveal the locations or the occasions that prompted our meetings. I will say that I enthusiastically expressed my appreciation for the courageous acts they performed on behalf of clean sport. It was truly an honor to meet them, one that I will never forget.

18

TRANSGENDER ATHLETES, 2015–2018

There is clearly a connection between intersex athletes, transgender athletes, and doping athletes. All three of these groups potentially challenge the goal of equitable and meaningful sport, especially among women. Outside of the sport of track and field, transgender athletes are generally considered the biggest threat to the existing playing field; hence it will be a very big deal when the first openly transgender athlete competes in the Olympic Games. I believe that will probably happen in the Tokyo Olympics of 2020, and I will introduce the reader to three potential candidates to be the first to that milestone.

Transgender athletes create headlines at all levels of sport, however, and I'd like to look at some recent trans athletes who have made waves. I can think of no better place to start than with swimmer Schuyler Bailar. According to Schulyer's dad, Gregor Bailar, young Schuyler, assigned female at birth, started to swim before he could walk.[1] Schuyler progressed through the sport until he was setting records as a member of the prestigious Nation's Capital Swim Club. In those days, Schuyler was swimming in the girls' events. In 2013 Schuyler, Katie Ledecky, Janet Hu, and Kylie Jordan combined to break the age group 400 yard medley relay at the national championship meet.[2] Schuyler's excellence in the pool and in the classroom earned him a scholarship to Harvard University, where he was expected to set more records. There was just one tiny problem: Schuyler never wanted to be a girl. Prior to high school he consistently dressed in cargo shorts and baggy shirts, and he wore his hair short. Schuyler was often identified as male in those years, and it brought him happiness—at least until he had to tell someone he was female or use the girls' bathroom.[3] The fact that his gender expression did not conform to expectations brought bullying, so he grew his hair long and started to wear more traditional female attire in high school.[4] He also came out as a lesbian.[5]

Outside the pool, Schuyler was desperately unhappy and, among other things, suffered from an eating disorder. After he graduated high school in the spring of 2014, he took a gap year and checked into a rehab facility, nominally to deal with his eating problems. It was during treatment that a therapist suggested his gender identity might be the cause of his problems. Shortly afterward Schuyler met a trans man, and this encounter gave him the courage to come out as transgender. His family and most of his friends were supportive; the next step was to tell the women's coach at Harvard.[6]

At first, Schulyer considered swimming for the women's team and delaying his hormone therapy, but when he was given the option of joining the men's team, he accepted. He started to take testosterone, and in March 2015 he had top surgery. He surrendered a spot as a star of the women's team at Harvard to be an also-ran for the men. He summed up his choice thusly: "I think it was hard for me to say why I would give up being such a good female athlete for something so [sic] ethereal as happiness."[7] Schuyler has become a media celebrity and is one of the best-known trans men in America. In an interesting twist, Schuyler showed up at my house in Portland one evening in the summer of 2017. My housemate Steve and I were hosting a concert featuring Ryan Cassata, a young transgender singer-songwriter. Schuyler, who was spending the summer completing an internship at the University of Washington in Seattle, is a fan of Ryan's music. Schuyler and his girlfriend arrived at the concert to little fanfare. At one point Ryan, Schuyler, and four or five other trans men posed for a shirtless picture showing off their scarred but masculine chests. It must have been a liberating moment for the young men.

So Schuyler is happy, and famous, and a wonderful role model—but what about his swimming? Initially Schuyler was much slower than almost all Division I male swimmers, but he has made remarkable progress. Schuyler's primary event is the breaststroke, and his best time in high school was 1:03.10 for the 100 yard distance. Although that is terrific time for a girl, it was on the wrong side of one minute, a minimum acceptable time for a Division I male swimmer. Schuyler got back in the pool in November of 2015, and by the end of his freshman season he had reached 59.46 seconds. By the close of his sophomore year, Schuyler swam a 58.58. In February 2018, at the end of his junior year, Schuyler was down to a 57.68, and in his final meet he swan 56.98 at the Harvard versus Princeton and Yale triangular meet in 2019.[8] Schuyler was never a star on the men's team at Harvard, but his progress is a testament to his ability and perseverance, and to the performance-enhancing effects of testosterone. As of the winter of 2019, Schuyler is still the only out transgender athlete to compete after transition in Division I sports in the NCAA. There are, however two trans women who have competed openly in Division III.

The first of these two, Ryan Lavigne, crewed for Lewis and Clark College in Portland, Oregon. Ryan was good enough as a high school rower in Jacksonville, Florida, that Pioneers head coach Sam Taylor recruited her for his men's team. But Ryan had other plans; she enrolled at the college and then started her social and hormonal transition in the fall of 2014.[9] As a sophomore, Ryan returned to the sport that she loves. In the spring of 2016, she made her debut as a part of the women's crew.[10] Lewis and Clark is one of the better teams in Division III rowing, and by the end of her sophomore year Ryan was the second-strongest woman on the women's varsity 8 Pioneer crew. As a junior, Ryan was selected as an All-American second team Division III rower.[11] In Ryan's senior year she and teammate Natalie Stroud won the championship pairs title at the Western Intercollegiate Rowing Championships in a time of 8:37, beating the pair from UC Davis by ten seconds.[12] Once again Ryan was named a Division III All-American.[13] It was a wonderful way for Ryan to finish up her collegiate rowing experience. Although team races are dependent upon eight rowers pulling together, each individual rower's strength is measured on a rowing machine. The time taken to pull 2 kilometers is the standard measure, and Ryan's results on the ergometer are instructive. As a high school senior, she pulled 7:01. In her sophomore year in college, after almost two years of hormone therapy, she pulled 7:25. As a junior she pulled a 7:11, and as a senior she pulled a 7:05—a Pioneer school record, but still slower than she had pulled before transition.[14]

The other trans woman who competed openly at the Division III level is Chloe Anderson, who played volleyball at the University of

California, Santa Cruz (UCSC), during the 2016–2017 season. Prior to playing for the Banana Slugs, Chloe starred at Santa Ana College in Southern California. Chloe also played on the boys' team at Irvine High School prior to her transition. Chloe's height of 6 feet, 1 inch and her vertical leaping ability allowed her to dunk in high school, and she spent endless hours practicing her skills so she could be the best player possible. Unfortunately, her apathy in the classroom limited her opportunities.[15] Chloe started hormone therapy at after graduation, at age nineteen, and within months it had affected her performance in the sport she loved:

> My male muscles that I had developed since puberty were disappearing at an increasingly painful rate. My running slowed down, my swinging got weaker, my vertical jump diminished rapidly. I felt as though all the experience I had accumulated over the years had vanished, as it was like riding a bicycle for the first time. Something I had done so often and had practiced for so long with masculine muscles meant absolutely nothing with the new muscular structure my body was developing.[16]

It took time, but four years later Chloe was playing volleyball for Santa Ana College. And she wasn't just playing—she was a star on the team. "During my time at Santa Ana College, I ended up making it to state playoffs for beach volleyball and made first team all-conference for indoor. My team has been nothing but wonderful and supportive of me, and they have become my family," Chloe told me during our first conversation in 2016.[17]

After two years at Santa Ana, Chloe earned her associate's degree and moved on to bigger things, both academically and athletically. At the time she was feted, scoring an episode on the Olympic Channel and an op-ed for *Outsports*. In the fall of 2016 she transferred to UCSC and began a major in Russian literature. At first she loved her new surroundings, with the redwoods and deer on campus. She even settled into a dorm for transgender students.[18] But unfortunately, her year playing volleyball at UCSC did not go according to the script. Chloe struggled on the court and failed to connect on a personal level with her coach and her teammates. At one point during the season, she attempted suicide and she felt as if "nobody even cared on the team."[19] She quit the team after playing in only six out of twenty-three matches and notching a mere four kills in the whole season.[20] She did not return to the volleyball team for the 2017–2018 season.

Although there are, sadly, no more openly trans athletes competing in NCAA sports as of the end of 2018, there are some who have competed in a more stealthy manner. One of these athletes, Athena Del Rosario, also matriculated at UCSC. Athena was a soccer player on the boys' team at Miro Costa High School in her hometown of Redondo Beach, California, when she started to self-medicate in order to stop her male puberty. She returned to the sport at Los Angeles Valley College (LAVC).[21] Athena played in the fall of 2013 and 2014 at LAVC without telling a soul on the team that she was transgender. In 2013 she was named freshman of the year on her team, and in 2014 she was named team MVP. She also excelled in the classroom, making the dean's list both years at LAVC.[22] Athena then moved to a higher level, and once she was accepted at UCSC, Del Rosario told the athletic department that she was transgender. Her coach allowed Del Rosario to maintain her privacy. Although Athena used the locker room with her teammates, she took showers only when there were private shower stalls.[23]

Del Rosario played for UCSC in the fall of 2015 and 2016. Both years, the team was invited to the NCAA Division III tournament. Halfway through her first season at UCSC, Athena was promoted to the starting keeper spot, leading the Slugs to a conference title and to the NCAA tournament.[24] She was even better in 2016, starting all eighteen games for UCSC and saving a school record eighty-nine shots during the season. Athena had topped out at 5-foot-9, an ideal height for a female keeper. The fact that Athena started hormone therapy so early in life allowed her to "pass" better than many other transgender people, and she was spared the hate she saw leveled at others who were visibly gender nonconforming. Athena was uncomfortable knowing that her life was easier than others who either couldn't "pass" or chose to be out,[25] and so in the spring of 2017, just before she was set to graduate, she came out to her teammates. She then went public in an article published by *Outsports*.[26] Since her very public coming out, Athena has gone on to be a national spokesperson for transgender athletes, a volunteer coach at UCSC, and a willing activist.

Although it is impossible to know how many other stealthy trans athletes compete at the NCAA level, I was told that a Division I conference accepted its first transgender athlete in the 2017–2018 season. If there is only one trans athlete in this major conference, then the total number of trans athletes in the NCAA is still very small. By contrast, there were more than two hundred thousand women playing NCAA sports, and if we assume that transgender people make up at least one half of 1 percent of all Americans,[27] then there should be approximately one thousand trans women in college sports. Seven years after the NCAA first allowed trans women to play, trans women have not only failed to take over, they are still hugely underrepresented.

In addition to college trans athletes, there have also been important recent stories about high school trans athletes. The first of these cases is that of Mack Beggs, who was assigned female at birth but has been living as male since his early teen years. Texas is one of six states in the country that offers wrestling for girls, and Beggs took up the sport. In Beggs's freshman year he won twenty-five of his thirty-nine matches at 110 pounds, but was pinned in both of his matches in the state championship tournament.[28] He started taking testosterone in the fall of his sophomore season—it can take a substantial amount of time for trans men to build muscle—and he improved to 40–9 for the season. At the state meet he won once and lost twice.[29]

In June of 2016, just after the end of Beggs's second season of high school wrestling, the governing body for most of the high schools in Texas decreed that high school athletes would be segregated by gender according to their original birth certificates, meaning that Beggs was stuck wrestling girls for the foreseeable future. In the fall of 2016, Beggs was noticeably more muscular than he had been the previous year. As the season unwound, it became obvious that Beggs was just too strong and too good for the girls he was wrestling. He capped off a stunning 56–0 junior year with a dominating 12–2 win in the finals of the state tourney over Chelsea Sanchez, who had entered the match at 50–3 on the season and had pinned her three previous opponents in the championships.[30] The national media pounced on the story, with many calling out the state of Texas for its misguided policy—a policy that had been put in place to "protect" female athletes from trans girls but had backfired in a huge way in the Beggs case. On the other hand, many people suggested Beggs had cheated by taking T and should be suspended from wrestling altogether.[31] As usual, transgender participation in sports was causing a major divide in public opinion.

Mack Beggs had also been competing with USA Wrestling in Texas in the spring and summer. Until 2017 USA Wrestling did not have a transgender policy, and Beggs chose to wrestle girls in the summer of 2016. Beggs's grandmother explained that he did not think he was ready to wrestle boys. After Beggs's 2016–2017 championship season, USA Wrestling adopted a testosterone-based policy for transgender participation, and Beggs wrestled boys for the first time in his life. He described the experience as "really, really hard."[32] Mack wrestled in the 121-pound division and wrestled both in open and Greco-Roman competition. Although he failed to place in the freestyle division, he did place fourth in the Texas State USA Wrestling Greco-Roman competition, just missing the trip to nationals in Fargo, North Dakota, that was the reward for the top three wrestlers.[33] Texas, however, had not amended its rules at the start of Mack's senior year, and so he was once again wrestling in the girls' division. Mack started the year wrestling in the 119-pound division, but by the time of the state championships he had cut enough weight to reach 110 pounds. He was undefeated for the season, including another state title victory over Sanchez.[34] After his high school wrestling season was over, Mack once again wrestled boys in USA Wrestling, earning a trip to the nationals; had top surgery in August 2018; and started college at Life University in Georgia, where he will wrestle men after taking a redshirt year. Mack's birth certificate was changed in January 2019, and he was the subject of an ESPN film.[35]

The Beggs case was not the only controversy over a trans athlete winning a state championship in girls' sports. During the same season that Beggs was setting Texas alight, a young trans woman was stirring up controversy in the New England state of Connecticut. The rules for transgender athletes could not be more different in the two states. In Texas, all athletes must compete in the gender specified by their birth certificate. In Connecticut, athletes are allowed to compete in the category in which they are identified by their school and their district.[36] Andraya Yearwood had competed in middle school in the boys' division, but when she moved on to high school she decided she was ready to transition socially, if not medically. In the fall of 2016, when Andraya went out for the cheerleading squad, no one complained that she was taking a spot away from another girl. It was a much different story in the spring, when Andraya went out for the girls' track team.[37] Andraya had been one of the fastest boys in middle school, and in the girls' division she won the 100 and 200 meter races in the 2017 Connecticut Class M (smaller schools) State Championships. She later placed third among all girls in the 100 meters at the state open finals. One week later, Yearwood placed second in the New England championships, running 12.22 in the finals after posting a terrific 12.17 in the heats.[38] Yearwood began hormone therapy prior to March 2018.[39] In the spring of 2018 Yearwood was sprinting as fast, or slightly faster, than she had in her freshman year. The difference was that she was no longer the fastest transgender sprinter in the state of Connecticut. That honor went to Terry Miller, who was also a sophomore at a school a mere thirteen miles away from Yearwood's school in suburban Hartford. Miller was running the 100 meter race in less than 12 seconds and also cleaning up in the 200 and 400 meter races. Miller had run in spring of 2017 and in the winter of 2018 on the boys' team but switched to the girls' team in the spring of 2018.[40] Miller set records at the state all-class final, winning the 100 and 200 meter races in 11.72 and 24.17 seconds, respectively. Yearwood finished second in the 100 meter race. Both girls earned the right to compete in the New England championship races. Miller won the 100 and 200 at the New England meet,[41] while Yearwood gave up her spot to another girl. The two sprinters finished first and second in the 55 meter sprint race at the indoor state meet in February 2019 with times of 6.95 and 7.01 seconds, respectively.[42] Yearwood ran in the New Balance Indoor Nationals high school meet, running 7.72 seconds for 60 meters and failing to make the semifinals. Her time was the 31st fastest time of the 36 competitors. Yearwood's entry into the meet is notable, as one year of hormone therapy is required for any trans woman to compete.[43] Miller did not run the meet.

It is both interesting and informative to follow the stories of younger transgender athletes, and the increasing trend toward younger transition is important for both society and sport. It is also true, however, that international-level athletes are going to cause the greatest controversy, so I would like to close this chapter by looking at the lives of three different trans women athletes competing at very high levels in their chosen sports.

Hannah Mouncey is an Australian trans woman who has gone through an almost unimaginable amount of torment ever since her decision to transition in November 2015. Hannah is 6 feet, 2 inches tall and weighs 220 pounds—and if her size is not crime enough, then her audacity to try to play women's sports should condemn her to eternal damnation. At the time of her transition, Hannah was playing on the Australian men's handball team, which was competing in an Olympic qualifying tournament in Qatar. She had first joined the men's national squad in 2012[44] and had subsequently played twenty-two games in her country's uniform.[45] Hannah was a handsome, strapping lad who undoubtedly got lots of attention from the ladies. Why would anyone give up that life for what was about to come next? That question is difficult to answer for anyone who isn't transgender, but the suggestion that Hannah transitioned so she could achieve greater prestige in women's sports is clearly ludicrous. Hannah started hormone therapy, kept her testosterone low, dropped 40 pounds of muscle, and lost a lot of strength during her transition, but she was still going to stand out among other women in her sport because of her residual size and strength. If ever there was a test case for the wisdom of the IOC's testosterone-based policy, Hannah was it. In September of 2016 Hannah petitioned Handball Australia to allow her to play in the Oceania Nations Cup to be played in October in Sydney. At that point Hannah was just short of the twelve months suggested by the IOC guidelines. The officials declined her request,[46] but several months later they allowed her to play. The problem was that because of the schedule of the Olympics and World Championships and a change in the qualifying route for the countries of Oceania, the team was entering a lull period. The Aussie women's handball team wouldn't compete again internationally until December 2018.

Although Hannah's handball career had entered a latent period, another sporting opportunity was soon to open up for her. Australian rules football is a cross between rugby and soccer, with points being scored by kicking the oblong ball through the opposing goal posts. It is the most popular sport in Australia, with average attendance at Australian Football League (AFL) games standing at approximately thirty-five thousand fans per game.[47] The AFL started a women's division in 2017, and the league saw a potential star in Hannah. A league official reached out to Hannah to ask if she was interested in trying out for a position in the fledgling women's league. Hannah had played the game of footy often during her youth, but not at this sort of level. Given the lull in her handball schedule, Hannah agreed to take a crack at footy. In order to blow the rust off of her game, Hannah played for the Ainslee Football Club during the 2017 season in the AFL Canberra League, a minor league located in the state of Canberra. Hannah's height and athleticism helped her in the ruck position. (The ruck is tasked with gaining possession for the team during play stoppages when the ball is tossed in the air by the referee, much like a jump ball in basketball.) Hannah's kicking skills also made her valuable as a full-forward, the primary scoring position, but her lack of speed and quickness in the open field were liabilities. Despite dire warnings, Hannah failed to seriously injure any of her opponents, although she did suffer a couple of cracked ribs herself.[48]

In October 2017 the AFL conducted a draft for the 2018 season. The league initially indicated it would follow the IOC guidelines on transgender players, but at the last minute cited concern over Hannah's size and strength as reasons to exclude her from the draft. The controversy over this decision was one of the largest sports stories in Australia in 2017.[49] Hannah was allowed to play at the state level, implying that she wasn't too big and strong to play against lower-level players. In 2018 Hannah had decided to move to Melbourne for business reasons; there, she opted to play for the Darebin Falcons, historically one of the most successful teams in the Victorian Football League Women's (VFLW).

Despite Hannah's presence, the Falcons had what was for them a dismal season. Hannah finished second in the league in goals scored, but the Falcons finished fifth on the league ladder and failed to make the semifinal round of the playoffs.[50] There was more bad news for Hannah at the end of the season, as the AFL released a transgender policy. In addition to keeping T levels below 5 nmol/L for two years, trans women had to submit data on their size, strength, speed, and stamina, to be compared against the league averages. If a trans woman was deemed too athletic, she would not be allowed to play. The same rules would not apply to cisgender women. After due consideration, Hannah declined to nominate for the draft under the proposed rules.[51] On the bright side, Hannah returned to play handball for her country in December 2018. Hannah was the third-leading scorer for the fifth-place (out of ten) Australian team at the Asian Handball Championships.[52] This qualified the Aussie team for the 2019 World Championships, although the team is unlikely to qualify for the 2020 Olympic

Games, since twenty-four teams qualify for the former, but only twelve for the latter.

Amazingly enough, Hannah Mouncey was not the only tall, strong transgender athlete from Oceania to make waves. New Zealand weightlifter Laurel Hubbard had been a national junior champion and competed at a national level as a senior lifter. Weightlifting competitions are decided by the total weight hoisted in two different lifts, the snatch and the clean and jerk. In the snatch, the athlete must hoist the bar from the floor and over her head in one motion. In the clean and jerk, the athlete first lifts the weight to her shoulders—the clean portion—and then lifts the weight over her head in the jerk phase. Weightlifters are divided by sex and by body mass. The highest weight class has only a minimum body weight but no upper size limit. As a junior in the 105-plus kilogram division, Hubbard had lifted a total of 300 kilograms, a New Zealand record that stood for more than fifteen years.[53] She continued to lift in men's competitions until she was in her thirties and began her transition. After more than two years of hormone therapy, she emerged in 2017 as a force in women's weightlifting. Competing in the newly created 90-plus kilogram class, Hubbard first won the New Zealand title and then captured the Australian International Championship held in Melbourne on March 18. In the latter event she won with a combined total of 268 kilograms.[54] At the Australian competition, Hubbard weighed in at 132 kilograms and towered over her competition. Strength is more a function of body mass than height, however, and Hubbard was only 10 kilograms heavier than the Samoan lifter who placed second in the category that March day.

Hubbard was not finished for the year. She won titles at the Oceania Championships and the World Masters Games, lifting 273 and 280 kilograms, respectively. Hubbard finished out a successful 2017 campaign by placing second in the World Championships in Anaheim, California, in November with a total of 275 kilograms.[55] Hubbard's second place finish should be taken with a grain of salt. The weightlifting federation had recently cracked down on the all-too-apparent doping problem in the sport, banning nine entire national teams from the 2017 World Championships. The winner in Anaheim was American Sarah Robles, who had placed third in the Rio Olympic Games. At 140 kilograms, Robles outweighed Hubbard and the rest of the field and had previously served a two-year ban from the sport due to doping. The gold medalist from Rio, China's Meng Suping, had hoisted a total of 307 kilograms over her head in the 2016 games,[56] but like the rest of her Chinese teammates had been banned from Anaheim. Hubbard was the prohibitive favorite going into the 2018 Commonwealth Games, held in the city of Gold Coast, Australia. The Australian team lodged a protest in order to stop Hubbard from competing, but it was unsuccessful. Hubbard successfully lifted 120 kilograms in her first attempt in the snatch, to lead the competition, but suffered a ruptured tendon in her left elbow when she tried to snatch 132 kilograms.[57] Hubbard had surgery later in April and began her rehab work. By September 2018 Hubbard had progressed far enough that she lifted 110 kilograms in the snatch and 122 kilograms in the clean and jerk in a competition in New Zealand.[58] Her 232 kilogram total would not put her in the top twenty in the world, and she declined to contest the 2018 World Championships. The banned nations, however, did return. The winner of the 87-plus kilogram division, Russian Tatiana Kashirina, lifted 330 kilograms for a new world record.[59] Robles placed fifth, and Hubbard's 2017 total of 275 kilograms would have placed her seventh. In April 2019 Hubbard competed in the Arafura Games in Australia, where she failed in three attempts to snatch 110 kilograms and withdrew from the meet.[60] Hubbard had more luck in July winning the Pacific Games title by lifting 268 kilograms (125 kg in the snatch and 143 kg in the clean and jerk), a total that put her back on track to qualifying for the 2020 Olympic Games. Should Hubbard compete in Tokyo, we can expect a firestorm of protest as evidenced by the number of negative articles that appeared after her July victory.[61]

The other transgender athlete with a realistic shot at Olympic glory in 2020 is Brazilian volleyball player Tifanny Abreu. Tifanny is 6 feet, 3.5 inches tall and played for several years in men's professional leagues across Europe. She stopped playing men's volleyball in 2012 and shortly thereafter began her transition. At first Tifanny thought her volleyball career was over, but after the 2016 IOC transgender guidelines were released, her agent convinced her to return to the sport she loved.[62]

I first had the opportunity to interact with Tifanny in the fall of 2016. At the time she had transitioned socially and had been taking hormones for a couple of years, but was still playing with a men's team in the Netherlands. When I watched video of Tifanny play, I immediately recognized that she was the real deal. Tifanny still had not received permission to play in the women's game, but I knew that once she did, she would make worldwide news. In the spring of 2017 Tifanny got permission to play with a women's club in Italy, and she was both successful and controversial. Tifanny also completed her transition surgically while she was living in Italy. It was very difficult for her to face so much criticism with no support system, so she returned home to the rural state of Goias, northwest of Saõ Paulo. In December 2017 Tifanny first played for Volei Bauru in the Superliga Feminina, the top women's league in Brazil. At the time Tifanny joined the team, roughly halfway through the 2017–2018 season, they were in ninth place in the twelve-team league. Tifanny scored twenty-five points, mostly through her devastating spikes, in her first match and led Volei Bauru to a three-sets-to-one victory that night.[63] Volleyball is the second most popular sport in Brazil, and the scrutiny she faced during the rest of her season rivaled that of Renée Richards forty years earlier.

During the season, Tifanny recorded the highest number of points in a match. The former record holder, Tandara Caixeta, promptly went out and tied Tifanny's record. Many sports stars in Brazil become known by their first name only, and both Tandara and Tifanny have reached that status. I had the opportunity to watch video of the match between the two stars' clubs, and even without speaking Portuguese I could sense the tension in the arena. Tandara's team won the match. Overall, the team record of Volei Bauru was only marginally better in the second half of the season than it had been in the first half. The club eked out the eighth and final playoff spot before getting blown away in the first round of the playoffs in March 2018. Although it is abundantly obvious that Tifanny is very successful at the net, she is also not very quick and is something of a defensive liability. Both her strengths and weaknesses as a volleyball player are influenced by her nature as a transgender player.[64] The club season for volleyball precedes the international season, and the coach of the Brazilian national team said that he was willing to call Tifanny up to the national team. This didn't happen because the Brazilian national and international volleyball federations—the CVB and the FIVB, respectively—formed a group to study the effects of transgender players on the sport of volleyball, requesting that Tifanny be excluded from international play until the group finalized its report.[65]

Tifanny signed a contract to return to the Superliga Feminina for the 2018–2019 season, although she was tagged with a maximum of seven points in the league's parity system. Among other things, each team is allowed only two seven-point players on its roster. Tifanny was one of only two seven-point players who had never won an Olympic gold medal.[66] Given her scoring prowess, it was not unreasonable to assign her seven points, but when viewed as part of the whole, there is clearly an institutional bias against her within the ranks of Brazilian volleyball leaders. Tifanny's club beefed up its roster for the 2018–2019 season by adding other tall, skillful players, including an Italian player who topped out at 6 feet, 7.5 inches.[67] The team finished the 2018–2019 regular season in sixth place in the league but defeated the third-place team in the first round of the playoffs, renewing criticism of Tifanny. Now thirty-four, she is not quite the league sensation she was in her first year. Tifanny did not recover as quickly as other women from the stress of matches, and her team cut back on her playing time to try to help.[68] Once again the Brazilian national team declined to invite Tifanny to play in the summer of 2019, making her selection to the 2020 Olympic team doubtful.

19

TRANSGENDER ATHLETIC RESEARCH UPDATE

There is much to learn from a careful observation of the athletic performance of transgender athletes before and after commencing hormone therapy. The most important data come from those athletes who compete in the so-called CGS sports—that is, those sports whose results can be measured in centimeters, grams, or seconds.[1] Thus, athletes like Schuyler Bailor, Ryan Lavigne, and Laurel Hubbard provide more valuable data than athletes like Hannah Mouncey or Tifanny Abreu. The study I published in 2015 was an important beginning, but it was just the first baby step. I continued to gather retrospective data after 2015, and this process was aided by some of the contacts I made in those years.

In the fall of 2015 I met a doctoral student at the University of Madrid named Jonathan Ospina Betancurt, who was being mentored by María José Martínez-Patiño. I had the opportunity to spend a few enjoyable days with Jonathan and his partner, José, when I visited María in her home in Galicia in November. My connection with Jonathan would prove to be a valuable one for both of us. In the spring of 2016 Jonathan told me about a transgender sprinter from his home country of Colombia. Yanelle Zape was trying to make her country's Olympic team in the 100 or 200 meters.[2] A decade ago she had run 10.7 for the 100 meters when she competed with the men, and now she needed to run 11.3 to make it to Rio. Unfortunately for Zape, she could no longer break 12 seconds.[3] As many others have discovered before her, women's sports are not that easy when one has to compete with female testosterone levels.

Although Zape could not make her dream a reality, her age-graded scores were only slightly lower as a woman than they had been when she was competing in the men's division. Given that she had been back in training only for a few months, it made perfect sense that she wouldn't quite match her earlier performances, but her times indicated that she was still in the same ballpark as an athlete in an age-graded sense. Zape continued to race after she turned forty and she also returned to hurdling as well as sprinting. Prior to transition, she had been best known as a 400 meter hurdler, running 52.88 seconds. In 2017 she ran 1:02.58 in the event; both marks had very similar age grades.[4] In 2018 she decided to try the 80 meter hurdles (the outdoor high hurdles race for women over forty) and she struck bronze at the World Masters Athletics Championships in Malaga, Spain, in September.[5] Then in March 2019, Yanelle moved up a step on the podium, running 9.00 seconds for the 60 meter hurdles to win the silver medal at the World Masters Indoor Athletics Championships.[6] Both of Zape's high hurdles championship races scored age grades significantly above all her other race times. As usual, there was some negative feedback over her performance.

Another elite athlete whose data I mined was an American cyclist named Jillian Bearden. Jillian's data would prove very important to me, but beyond the science, I have grown to be very fond of her on a personal level. I admire her commitment to excellence in her sport, but she also sees the bigger picture and is very committed to integrating trans athletes into women's sport in a manner that is equitable for everyone. Prior to her transition, Jillian was a category 1 cyclist (the highest amateur level) specializing in mountain biking. In 2011 she was tested at a lab in her hometown of Colorado Springs. Bicycle testing consists of attaching a power meter to the bike and then running athletes through increasingly difficult steps in output until they max out. In 2011 Jillian generated 338 Watts of power. In 2015 Jillian started hormone therapy, and she was tested again in the same lab in October 2016, after a year and half of living with female hormone levels. In the latter test, Jillian scored 300 Watts of power, an 11 percent reduction.[7] Jillian also contacted USA Cycling in 2016 and requested to race in the female division. USA Cycling responded by restricting her to road cycling only, telling her that she might be too good at mountain biking and create unfair competition for other women. Jillian placed 11th in her first race in 2016, and no one noticed. After she won her second race, El Tour de Tucson in November 2016, Jillian was inundated with negative press.[8] The race is late in the season and many top cyclists have already packed it in by then, making Jillian's victory less significant than it might have seemed. Jillian did not race again until 2017.

The following year Jillian raced in several smaller races, placing in the top three or four riders in most of them. Then in August, she competed in the Colorado Classic against much higher-level competition. Several of the best North American professional riders were in attendance. The women's portion of the event was a three-day stage race; Jillian was unable to place in the top twenty riders in any individual day, and on her worst day she failed to make the cut that would see her scored in the overall results.[9] Jillian was naturally disappointed about her poor showing, but there was a silver lining. After the race, USA Cycling told her that she would now be allowed to race in women's mountain biking. Jillian tried her hand at a few mountain bike races, but her results were underwhelming.[10] Top mountain bikers are generally smaller than road cyclists, and Jillian was now bigger than most of her rivals. She no longer had the optimal power-to-weight ratio for climbing. Although Jillian continued to compete in mountain biking and added in cyclocross racing too, her main focus was now going to be road cycling. She won her pro card and was eagerly looking forward to 2018. Early in 2018 Jillian suffered a knee injury that sidelined her for much of the spring, but her period of rehab and recovery only made her hungrier for success. It also made her re-evaluate her previous training and racing schedules. Jillian decided that she had been overtraining and racing too much in 2017. Although she trained hard in 2018, she didn't push herself over the edge. She also cut back on her racing and traveling schedules so she could focus on her major goal race for the season. More than anything else, Jillian wanted to atone for her disappointment at the Colorado Classic in 2017.[11] And she did so in a very big manner. The race expanded to four days in 2018, and Jillian crushed the individual time trial, where she was third overall. Over the four days, she placed tenth in the general classification,[12] and she had now reached a new level of success.

Not only was her cycling in ascendency, but she also inked an important sponsorship deal with Specialized, one of the largest makers of quality bikes and components in the world. Specialized was interested in Jillian not just as a rider but also as a spokesperson for greater integration of LGBT cyclists into the mainstream. Both Jillian and Specialized hope their relationship will be a positive one. Jillian did take time away from the sport later in 2018, as she had her vaginoplasty in September. Spending time on a bicycle seat was definitely going to have to wait for a while.[13] Jillian's cycling fortunes show the very complex athletic advantages and disadvantages trans athletes encounter when they switch teams. Jillian is now more successful on the roads than she had previously been, but she is no longer the climbing dynamo she used to be. I have used Jillian's performance data in many presentations, but beyond her value to science, I place a very high value on Jillian's friendship.

The data I gathered from Jillian and from rower Ryan Lavigne were important, as both sets of data were gathered independently and were outside the realm of running. Both of these athletes had reductions in performance in the 10–12 percent range, which was consistent with the results from transgender runners. In November 2016 I presented the data from Bearden, Laivgne, Zape, and other athletes at a scientific meeting in Aliconte, Spain.[14] I also got to spend time with Jonathan and José at their home in suburban Madrid. Jonathan and I met with the leaders of a Madrid-based LGBT sports club one evening to talk about trans issues in sport. That night we met a trans woman volleyball player named Allison who had been playing on the men's club team but wanted to play with other women. I advised the leaders of her club on how they should go about getting her into the women's league. I could see the joy in Allison's eyes when she realized she would be able to play her sport in her true gender. Whenever people imagine trans women competing against other women, they inevitably think that cisgender women can't compete. Allison is about 5 feet, 6 inches tall and played the sport on a recreational level only. She had been on hormone therapy for two years, and it is ludicrous that she should be excluded from women's sport just because of the prejudice of those in charge. In return for my assistance, this Spanish volleyball player put me in touch with Tifanny Abreu before Tifanny achieved her worldwide fame.

Jonathan wasn't the only scientist who was interested in working with me. After a silence of several months following our meeting in Lausanne in November 2015, Yannis Pitsiladis eventually contacted me again. As 2016 came to close, Yannis, María, Jonathan, and I published a paper calling for more scientific study of transgender and intersex athletes.[15] But calling for research and getting it done are two different things. The next step in making trans research a reality was to test transgender athletes as they transitioned. The difficulty was that I needed to find athletes before they started hormone therapy. In 2017 I found two such athletes.

Lauren is a trans distance runner living in the greater Phoenix area. She had not started hormone therapy as 2017 dawned. I wrote to the exercise physiology department at Arizona State University in Phoenix and asked if someone there would test Lauren as she underwent her gender transition. In February 2017 I was connected with a young faculty member named Siddhartha Angadi, who described the chance to test Lauren as the opportunity of a lifetime. Sid and the other people in his lab in Phoenix ran baseline tests on Lauren in the spring of 2017, but Lauren hesitated to start hormone therapy. Gender transition is not to be taken lightly, and Lauren needed to be 100 percent certain before proceeding. Finally, in August, she started to take high-dose estrogen injections, but no testosterone blocker. There are many different strategies employed to reduce T in trans women. In North America it is common to use the drug spironolactone as an anti-androgen drug and add estrogen. In much of the rest of world, birth control pills contain anti-androgen drugs and can be used to lower T, often in conjunction with additional estrogen. Cyproterone acetate is another anti-androgen drug commonly used with estrogen in much of the world. Perhaps most effectively, gonadotropin-releasing hormone agonists (GnRH agonists) can reduce sex hormone levels by 95 percent in both sexes. GnRH agonists are the drug of choice to delay puberty in transgender subjects, and are often combined with cross sex hormones as well. At first Lauren's estrogen injections seemed to be effective; her first bloodwork showed testosterone and estrogen in the normal female range. Within several weeks Lauren's peak VO2 had declined from 58.9 to 53 ml/kg/min.[16] Moreover, she was already putting up age-graded female scores that were almost identical to her male ones from 2016.

But gender transition is a tricky process, and at some point in the fall of 2017 Lauren clearly began to have some second thoughts. She made changes in her hormone regimen (she probably reduced or stopped her meds), her peak VO2 scores began to climb, and her race times got faster. In fact, she ran her lifetime best in the marathon in February 2018. It was not until the spring of 2018 that Lauren went all in on her transition. She began to take the antiandrogen drug spironolactone, started to grow her hair, and began to work in earnest on reducing her facial hair. Lauren also started to run a couple of low-key races in the women's division. At first I was dismayed by Lauren's inconsistent physical transition, but it later occurred to me that her data would be even more important than data from an athlete who underwent a straightforward transition: Lauren's data would give a good indication of what happened in those cases where a trans athlete was either poorly controlled by her medication or was noncompliant in taking her prescribed medication.

The other athlete I found in 2017 who had not started hormone therapy is Charissa, she is a triathlete who was living in rural Kansas at the time. Charissa was traveling to the Denver area one weekend a month for her transition care, and I had her tested on a cycle ergometer quarterly at a private lab in Colorado Springs. When Charissa started hormone therapy in June 2017, her decline in performance was closer to my expectations. Charissa lost 12 percent of her power output within six months, and 15 percent within nine months.[17] Some portion of Charissa's lost aerobic capacity stemmed from a drop in training. She went through relocation, divorce, and transition all at the same time, and it might have been too much to expect her training to stay at previous levels. Charissa resumed racing triathlons in September 2018 and was good but not exceptional on the local level.

I discovered Lauren and Charissa through a transgender runners' Facebook group managed by Amelia Gapin, who was one of the runners in my first study and a pioneering transgender athlete in her own right.[18] If I wanted to find more athletes, I would need an improved method of finding them. University of Michigan endocrinologist Rich Auchus would show me the way forward. Rich and I were among those invited by Duke Law professor and former international-caliber 800 meter runner Doriane Coleman to submit an article for the *Duke Law and Contemporary Problems* journal, as part of an issue she was putting together entitled "Sex in Sport."[19] All of the potential authors met in Durham, North Carolina, in August 2017 as part of a workshop on the issue. During my talk, I mentioned the extreme difficulty in recruiting subjects who had not yet started hormone therapy. Rich piped up and asked me if I had considered collaborating with gender clinics. My first reaction was, why didn't I think of that? For most of the twentieth century, transgender people were considered crazy and were discouraged from transitioning. It wasn't until the latter part of the century that clinics devoted to helping people transition were established. By 2017 most major cities in the United States had one.[20] It would still be necessary to pair up gender clinics with exercise physiologists and to find funding, but Rich had given me a starting point.

Beyond Rich's suggestion, the Duke seminar was important because it gave me the opportunity to meet both Doriane and Rich, who would prove to be important figures in the subsequent Semenya versus IAAF trial at the CAS. Rich's endocrine knowledge and ability to explain concepts cogently would prove crucial in the trial, while Doriane's influence might prove even larger. Doriane's article for the *Duke Law and Contemporary Problems* journal was entitled "Sex in Sport,"[21] and in it she laid out her thesis that the establishment of women's sport inherently required one to discriminate between male and female athletes. This sex-based discrimination is the very foundation for women's sport, and thus Doriane argued that it should be perfectly acceptable to place those athletes with female gender identity but male biology into the male category. At first, I was put off by Doriane's use of the term *biological male* to describe intersex and transgender athletes—after all, sexual biology is complex—but in time I came to appreciate the beauty of her argument and its application to the Semenya case. Doriane also introduced the term sports sex (analogous to my term athletic gender) in her article for the *Duke Law and Contemporary Problems* journal. Sports sex would become the term used by the IAAF and eventually in the CAS decision on the Semenya case.

The next step in my journey happened when I attended the European Federation of Sports Medicine Associations (EFSMA) conference in Lisbon in November 2017.[22] Yannis Pitsiladis, one of the organizers of the meeting, had invited both Maria and me to speak. My talk went well, and I made some important connections as a result. My favorite person I met in Lisbon is a sports medicine physician named Theodora

Papadopoulou. Dora serves on the steering committees for several organizations, including the British Association of Sport & Exercise Medicine (BASEM), and told me that she thought I could speak at the March 2018 BASEM meeting that explored the connection between hormones and sports performance.[23] Yannis, Dora, and I set up an itinerary for me that March that included the BASEM meeting, a public lecture at the University of Brighton, and a meeting with the Tavistock and Portman gender clinic in London. The clinic is one of the largest gender clinics in the world, with more than seven thousand patients and a waiting list that stretches out for approximately two years. James Barrett, the director of the clinic, was very interested in providing subjects for transgender athletic research when I contacted him in January. Yannis, James, and I had an agreeable meeting in March 2018. Yannis has interest in research into muscle myonuclei retention after testosterone reduction,[24] and wants to expand this research into transgender subjects. Yannis also suggested that I could return to school to obtain a PhD using the data from the proposed transgender study for my dissertation at Brighton. Yannis also secured invitations for Sid and for me to the International Federation of Sports Medicine (FIMS) conference in Rio de Janeiro, Brazil, in September 2018.[25] Sid, his partner Stephanie, and I all flew in early to do some sightseeing in this amazingly beautiful city. The conference went well. One highlight was my interaction with a Brazilian endocrinologist named Rogério Friedman, who was part of the panel on transgender and intersex athletes with Sid, Yannis, and me.[26] It was eye-opening for me to see how much respect Rogério has for my work. Dora was also at the meeting, and she and I had the opportunity to spend more bonding time together. Dora is a wonderful person, and our lives were soon to become more entwined.

Unbeknownst to me, Loughborough University—the number one center for sports science in England—had started up a program studying transgender athletes. The program was initiated in the fall of 2018 and headed up by Gemma Whitcomb, who has a psychology PhD and an interest in transgender patients.[27] Given Gemma's educational background, the focus of her program was on a humanities-based approach, although one of her five PhD students was studying the athletic capabilities of transgender athletes, working under the direction of exercise physiologist Emma O'Donnell.[28] Gemma reached out to me in October to offer me a position as a visiting scholar in the 2019–2020 academic year. I quickly accepted Gemma's offer, then told her that I would be in Germany in November for two conferences and had four free days in between my speaking engagements. We made plans for me to visit Loughborough for two of those days. I met Gemma and Emma, gave a talk, met the PhD students, and even got to spend a night with Dora in the nearby charming village of Wymeswold. Dora works at a clinic just outside of Loughborough and spends two nights a week in a five-hundred-year-old cottage in Wymeswold. It came as no surprise to me that Dora is the consummate hostess, and she treated me royally for the twenty-four hours I spent as her guest. Gemma arranged for us to meet for dinner at a spot within walking distance of Dora's cottage. It was halfway though dinner that Gemma asked me if I was interested in becoming a PhD student at Loughborough. In May 2019 I was accepted as a PhD student at the university and I started to make plans to move to England in the fall of 2019.

There was plenty of transgender news in the fall of 2018. In October, Canadian cyclist Rachel McKinnon won the 35–44 age group world championship in the match sprint at the UCI World Masters Championships. McKinnon, standing 6 feet tall and weighing 200 pounds, dwarfed her fellow competitors. Not surprisingly, controversy ensued.[29] McKinnon was a badminton player before transition, took up cycling afterward, and switched her focus to track cycling in 2016. Since McKinnon is fairly new to sprinting, she could conceivably continue to improve for a few years, but it is unlikely that she will make it to the Olympics. McKinnon is an assistant professor in philosophy at the College of Charleston and is an eloquent defender of her right to compete. In fact, McKinnon took advantage of her notoriety, her academic position, and her sustained use of social media to make herself the latest champion of the identity movement as it pertains to sports. It remains to be seen how long-lasting McKinnon's influence will be, but as of early 2019 she is ubiquitous.[30]

Another trans cyclist was making news in the fall of 2018. In December, Portland's own Molly Cameron placed second in the men's 40–44 division of the cyclocross national race in Louisville, Kentucky. That's right, the men's division. How did that happen? you might ask. Molly was born in Wichita Falls, Texas, on August 28, 1976, and assigned male. In her teens she began to question her gender and sexuality, but didn't really have the knowledge of what she was reaching for. Molly moved west and began to transition socially when she was in San Francisco in the late 1990s. She was working as a bike messenger at the time and was heavily involved in the gender-diverse culture of the city. In 2002 she moved to Portland, falling in love with the city and the sport of cyclocross, but being openly transgender meant she couldn't get a job. So Molly opened up her own bike shop, and soon enough she was a successful businesswoman. Molly started racing seriously in 2004, winning some big races in the women's division. She was on hormone therapy at the time, but never really considered surgery. In 2008 her success resulted in complaints against her. At the time the UCI, the IOC, and everyone else required surgery.[31] Molly "didn't really want to race the fucking dudes, you know,"[32] but what choice did she have? It was also around that time that she decided to put more effort into her bike shop and the burgeoning racing team she sponsored. Somewhere along the line—Molly isn't entirely certain when—she stopped taking her hormones. She says it didn't take her long to notice the difference when riding the slopes of Portland's West Hills. And when she got back into racing more seriously a few years later, it turned out that she was now able to beat most of the dudes, too.

Molly and I met for lunch on a cloudy winter's day shortly after her second-place showing. She says that she should have won, but she "fucked up," referring to a slip she suffered late in the race. Molly dropped a lot of F-bombs during the lunch hour, and her rapidfire staccato was tough to keep up with. Molly also said a lot of things I agree with: things like, "Sports aren't really fair, you know, but we have a men's category and a women's category, and somehow you have to shoehorn trans and intersex people into those two categories."[33] Few people understand how difficult it can be to decide who competes in which category better than Molly Cameron.

Her 2008 run-in with gender-based divisions wouldn't be her last. In 2015 Molly was told she couldn't enter the men's division of the cyclocross nationals held in Asheville, North Carolina, because her racing license and her driver's license both listed her as female. At the time Molly said, "This is really kind of hilarious. At first I was forced to race with the dudes and now I'm being forced to race with the women."[34] Molly and USA Cycling worked out their problems, and Molly wound up in the men's race. Jillian Bearden had told me earlier that Molly's case really made USA Cycling think very hard about what was important when deciding who would race in which category. So this is how it came to be that Molly was racing in the men's national cyclocross race on a rainy December day in Louisville. One of the cool things about reading the race report is that Molly's gender never seems to be an issue. The author of the article, and all of Molly's competitors, seemingly have no problem with the fact that Molly is a chick racing the dudes. At several points in the race, Molly opened up a lead on the pack, only to have eventual winner Jake Wells close the gap. Then, in the last lap of the five-lap race, Molly's unfortunate slip allowed Wells to pass her en route to victory.[35] Molly told me that she was considering retiring, but with next year's national championship race being held in nearby Tacoma, Washington, she needed to take one last shot at a national championship. Molly noted that a lot of trans people seem to take delight in being the first trans this or that, but she is probably the first openly transgender woman to medal in a men's masters national championship race. Molly said the words with a little bit of smirk, just so I knew that she really doesn't take any of this trans breakthrough shit that seriously.

December also saw another trans athlete make some noise. His name is Patricio Manuel, his sport is boxing, and he won his first professional fight as 2018 was coming to a close. Patricio's Olympic dream was derailed in 2012 by a shoulder injury, and it was at that time that he decided to transition. In September 2013 he started taking T injections, and he got top surgery in the spring of 2014. Finding trainers, sparring partners, and opponents since his transition has been extremely challenging in the macho boxing world. At least USA Boxing was more accommodating, giving him his men's license after the 2016 IOC transgender guidelines came out.[36] He split his two amateur fights before getting the opportunity to fight as a pro in 2018. In order to get a fight, Manuel needed an opponent, and Golden Boy Promotions, Oscar De La Hoya's company, found him one. Hugo Aguilar, who was 0–5 coming into the bout, had dreamed of fighting in the United States and so was unfazed when he found out two days before the fight that Manuel is transgender. Manuel won the first, third round and fourth rounds of the ensuing bout, but Aguilar won the second round when Manuel tried for a knockout, only to have the Mexican fighter respond with some effective counterpunching.[37] Manuel is planning to fight again in 2019, and hopefully more men will be willing to step into the ring against him.

Other transgender athletes were making sports news at the end of 2018, but the Semenya trial was looming. I had spent much of the year wondering if the IAAF would ask me to be witness at the Semenya trial. The main reason I had been asked to be a witness at the Chand trial was that I had data on changes in athletic capability with changing testosterone levels. The suspension of the hyperandrogenism rules as a result of the Chand case meant that an unknown number of intersex athletes could get off of their testosterone-suppressing medicine, providing an opportunity for the IAAF to gather data on their athletic performance with changing T. In 2017 Stéphane Bermon had published a paper on the reduction in performance observed with testosterone suppression,[38] but surely the IAAF had unpublished data on the improvements intersex athletes experienced after getting off of T-suppressing drugs. The IAAF data on the performance of intersex athletes with changing T levels would be more important to the Semenya case than my data on trans athletes. There were, however, other ways I could contribute. For instance, I had coauthored a paper in 2018 in which I estimated the number of medals won by presumably-intersex athletes in the restricted events over the twenty-five years preceding 2018 and came up with a minimum of thirty medals. (Semenya had six of these.) I was reasonably certain that this number was a valid low-end estimate of the actual medal count, and if true it meant that athletes with these DSDs had been overrepresented at the podium level of global championships in the restricted events by a factor of at least 1,700.[39] The IAAF used similar data in the Semenya trial. After a period of careful deliberation, Jon Taylor asked me to join the IAAF team in December 2018. I was undoubtedly the last person added to the IAAF side. The stage was now set for one of the most important chapters in the long history of gender-variant athletes and, not coincidentally, the last chapter in this book.

20

THE CASTER SEMENYA TRIAL

The Caster Semenya versus the IAAF trial represented a clash of two social phenomena that were pulling the sporting world in opposite directions. On one side, the growing social justice movement was providing support for integrating intersex and transgender athletes into the mainstream of sports. Media outlets around the world were writing supportive articles on athletes like Caster Semenya and Tifanny Abreu,[1] anointing them as heroines in the battle to normalize the lives of those who were different. On the other, there was a growing backlash against athletes who were seen as men invading women's sport.[2] Both Caster and Tifanny were clearly bigger and more athletic looking than the athletes they competed against, igniting the flames of controversy. The IOC, the IAAF, and other international sporting federations were stuck somewhere in the middle, trying to create rules that would allow integration of repressed minorities into women's sport while at the same time preserving the opportunities of cisgender women to reach the pinnacle of their chosen sport. Hence, it was not surprising that the Semenya trial was seen by pundits everywhere as a defining moment in the history of gender-diverse athletes.[3]

The trial would actually pit two claimants against the IAAF: Both Athletics South Africa and Semenya had sued, and in the end both claimants along with their lawyers and expert witnesses shared one side of the table at the CAS hearing.[4] The IAAF took the other side of the table, supported by a team of experts that included Harvard cardiologist Aaron Baggish, David Handelsman, Rich Auchus, Angelica Hirschberg,

Stéphane Bermon, Doriane Coleman, and me.[5] The IAAF legal team included Jon Taylor, Liz Riley, Chris Lavey, and in-house lawyer Frédérique Reynertz. All of the IAAF experts, including me, prepared witness statements and reviewed the statements of the expert witnesses from the Semenya and ASA side. My statement, which came to more than five thousand words, was one of the shorter ones. One of the most important written submissions by the IAAF was a paper signed by more than forty prominent scientists from around the world, which ended as follows: "Therefore, the primary driver of the sex difference in elite athletic performance is exposure in biological males to much higher levels of testosterone during growth, development, and throughout the athletic career."[6]

Once everything was added up, there were somewhere near two hundred thousand words written on this trial, meaning that there was an enormous burden on the judges, Annabelle Bennett and Hans Nater from the Chand case, and newcomer judge Hugh Fraser, a former Olympic sprinter for Canada.[7] The judges had law clerks to assist them, but the task of making sense out of the mountain of evidence was nonetheless daunting.

The IAAF and the CAS had chosen to keep the dates and location of the trial from the public, but someone on the Semenya side had leaked both, along with the suggestion that the IAAF was classifying athletes with XY DSDs as biological males.[8] Although Doriane used the term throughout her witness statement and the IAAF had also done so once or twice, it was clear that the IAAF was taking a more nuanced approach. I have often used the six categories of sex proposed by Katrina Karkazis in the Chand case, and the IAAF did so now. The panel of judges acknowledged the multifaceted nature of sex and gender using nomenclature that was similar to what both the IAAF and I have used.[9]

The IAAF presented a very nice chart in its initial submission showing that those athletes with DSDs such as 5-ARD or 17β-HSD3 were biologically male in most respects, including gonads and testosterone levels, and only biologically female in aspects that had little or nothing to do with sports. The most important endocrine difference between individuals with 5-ARD or 17β-HSD3 and biological men is the low level of dihydrotestosterone possessed by the DSD athletes. DHT is generally considered a tissue-specific androgen that does not affect muscle or other organs responsible for athletic performance; whether or not that was actually true would be one of the key questions of the trial. Another issue concerned the removal of CAH and CAH-variant conditions from the list of relevant DSDs.[10] I had been surprised to see these DSDs on the original list, and I welcomed their removal. Although CAH can cause elevated testosterone levels, the increase in T coincides with a critical reduction in cortisol. The cortisol shortage can lead to a life-threating endocrine imbalance known as salt-wasting disease. An increase in cortisol via injection leads to a reduction in T—and in potential athletic advantage. It is theoretically possible to have an elite athlete with CAH, but the likelihood is extremely low.[11] Although I welcomed the elimination of CAH from the restricted list, the claimants saw it as a deliberate attempt to limit the restricted list to XY DSDs or so-called biological males.

The trial opened up on Monday, and the principal characters plus the lawyers met at the CAS headquarters in the Château de Béthusy, while the rest of us shuffled off to the Association of National Olympic Committees (ANOC) building to watch via closed-circuit television. The lawyers for Caster Semenya were Jim Bunting and Carlos Sayao from Toronto, while the lawyers for the ASA were Norman Arendse and Ncumisa Mayosi from Cape Town.[12] The first order of business was to clear up some housekeeping motions, and it was obvious from the get-go that Bennett was very much in charge. For instance, when Arendse asked to be allowed to submit evidence after the trial, Bennett denied his request with such authority that you could feel the earth move from a kilometer away. After the housekeeping measures were dealt with, the lead counselors gave their opening statements. One of the most important questions to be decided by the panel is whether these regulations are discriminatory or not. Bunting said they are,[13] but Taylor suggested that it is not unlawfully discriminatory to place like with like.[14] Whether or not the DSD rules are discriminatory determines which party bears the burden of proof in the case.

One point emphasized by Bunting during his opening statement is the harm caused to intersex athletes as a result of the DSD regulations.[15] Caster Semenya gave an opening statement and she spoke of the negative ramifications of the DSD regulations on her life. She also spoke of the side effects of the medications used to lower her T including night sweats, weight gain, fever, and abdominal pain.[16] Caster also said that it does not matter how a woman is born; it only matters that she is a woman. It was clear from written statements[17] and from the week's testimony that the claimants did not extend this notion to transgender women. In fact, it was part of their strategy both in this case and in the Chand case to make sharp demarcations between intersex women and transgender women. According to the claimants, the former are women and the latter are men. Moreover, the claimants suggested that any judgment that would allow intersex women to compete in women's sport with male levels of testosterone could not be applied to transgender women.

Dr. Bennett was of another mind. The learned judge, who also holds a PhD in biochemistry, is acutely aware that if she allows all intersex athletes to compete with their natural testosterone levels, transgender athletes will be next.

Stéphane Bermon was up next. He presented data on intersex athletes who had undergone hormone changes, and he also spoke of the impressive levels of overrepresentation of athletes with DSDs in the sport of track and field.[18] Jim Bunting then engaged in in a vigorous cross-examination. Bunting managed to get Bermon partially excluded from some of the hot tubs on Tuesday and Wednesday as a result of his ties to the IAAF. The point that Bunting made was that expert witnesses are supposed to be impartial observers, and since Bermon has a long period of employment with the IAAF, he couldn't possibly be impartial. The implication that the other expert witnesses were impartial was, of course, not entirely true. Witnesses are sought out by each side not just for their expertise but also because their opinions match up with the side bringing them in.

There was also a certain amount of strategic thinking by the lawyers in questioning the validity of their opponent's experts. A lawyer might want to reduce the effectiveness of a given witness by sharp questioning. Both the IAAF and Semenya lawyers used this tactic effectively. Jim Bunting grilled David Handelsman on Tuesday morning over the volatility of his statements in previous trials and over whether he had an unreasonable bias against Richard Holt. In return, Jon Taylor grilled Eric Vilain on Wednesday over his switching views on a protected category for women and his volatile e-mail interactions with the IOC transgender group when we decided to lower the T limit from 10 to 5 nmol/L. In each case the lawyer subjected the expert to combative questioning over a one-hour period, and in each case Bennett was quite unhappy with the time used up for these challenges.

The sessions on Tuesday through Friday were held in the ANOC building, as there were too many of us it fit in the CAS headquarters. Dr. Roger Pielke was questioned on Tuesday morning before the start of the hot tub sessions. Dr. Pielke suggested that it was a "misuse of science" for the IAAF to cite the Bermon and Garnier study.[19] During his testimony, Pielke put forward the suggestion that anyone who was assigned female at birth and who had lived continuously in the female gender until the start of an elite-level sports career was entitled to compete in women's sport.[20] Pielke's suggestion was merely a rewording of the "born female, raised female" argument that has been used by many people, but when it was repeated by all of the witnesses on the Semenya side, it became known as the Pielke consensus.

The hot tubs commenced on Tuesday, and this is when the trial really started to get interesting. The ASA experts serving in the hot tubs were Ross Tucker, Joel Dave, Ariane Spitaels, Marc Blockman, Dankmar Bohning, Mark Engel, Payoshni Mitra, and Lih-Mei Liao; the Semenya hot tub team consisted of Roger Pielke, Eric Vilain, Veronica Gomez-Lobo, Richard Holt, and Anthony Hackney; and the IAAF countered with David Handelsman, Angelica Hirschberg, Rich Auchus, Stéphane Bermon Aaron Baggish, and Jan Kawalski.[21] The hot tub topics included DSDs, the impact of therapy to lower testosterone, the role of testosterone in sports performance, polycystic ovary syndrome, DHT and sports performance, DSDs and sport, the Bermon/Garnier study, and the impact of regulations on women with DSDs.[22] The experts sometimes formed a consensus on a given subtopic and sometimes they split, with the IAAF on one side and the claimants on the other. Bennett asked the experts to meet before each hot tub to work out which points they could agree on and which points would require further discussion by the group. Once the hot tub members got used to this idea, it really saved a lot of time. The pre–hot tub meetings also fostered a degree of collaboration between scientists who had been antagonists prior to the trial. Specifically, Handelsman and Holt did a nice job setting up the DSDs and sport hot tub, while Bermon and Pielke were also effective in delineating the hot tub on the Bermon/Garnier paper. In both of these instances, individuals who had previously been adversaries worked together to make the trial smoother.

The general consensus from the DSD hot tub was that it is difficult to set hard-and-fast rules about the management of DSDs. Rather, it is better to treat the individual patient as opposed to the DSD. Some patients with XY DSDs change gender but again this challenging issue is very much patient specific.[23] There was not agreement on what, if any, sports-related differences there were between individuals with the restricted DSDs and biological males.[24]

The most important disagreement in the hot tub on the role of testosterone in sports performance, was whether or not T was the primary reason for the sports difference in the sexes. All of the IAAF witnesses fully endorsed this proposition, while the claimants' experts offered adjectives other than primary, implying that T was less important than the IAAF claimed. At one point Jon Taylor read an excerpt from a paper written by Ross Tucker in which Tucker had said that the difference in T was primarily responsible for sex differences in athletic performance. Dr. Bennet didn't buy the obfuscation of the claimants' experts, and the verdict states that all sides agreed that T is the "primary, but not the exclusive" cause of sex-related sports differences.[25] Handelsman did a nice job derailing the suggestion that the Y chromosome had some mysterious effect on height, explaining that the extra height of men was due to later puberty and the resultant extra two years of long bone growth. Handelsman was also effective in rebutting Holt's claims of a significant role of growth hormone differences as a factor in sex-specific sports performance. All the experts agreed that T has an erythropoietic effect and that the changes in women's hearts with exercise are smaller than the changes in men. This hot tub closed out the day on Tuesday. One of the truly impressive things about Bennett was that because of her scientific background, she was able to keep up with the experts on complex biological issues. She asked pertinent questions and was able to steer the discussion very well. It would have been extremely difficult to conduct this trial without her at the helm.

Wednesday morning started with PCOS, and everyone agreed that it was a diagnosis of exclusion and that symptoms include irregular periods, hirsutism, acne, multiple cysts on ovaries, and higher T. There was some discussion on how high T could climb for PCOS patients, but everyone agreed that 99.99 percent of women with PCOS had T below 5 nmol/L and that obesity is very common in patients with severe PCOS, meaning that that it is extremely unlikely that an elite athlete would have PCOS and T levels over 5.[26] The session on DHT and sports performance contained little consensus on whether or not DHT was performance enhancing and if so, by how much. Each side brought papers to support its side. While DHT binds to the androgen receptor with 3 to 5 times the potency of T, it is also far less prevalent in the bloodstream, at 10 percent of the concentration of T. Although DHT binds mostly with the prostate, genitals, skin, and hair follicles, there might be lesser binding in other tissues, especially if DHT is introduced exogenously in sufficient concentrations.[27] The Panel ultimately concluded that any effect of DHT on athletic performance was "at most modest compared to the effect of testosterone."[28]

The session on DSDs and sports performance was up after lunch. There was some initial disagreement between Rich Auchus and Eric Vilain over whether or not athletes with DSDs such as 5-ARD or 17β-HSD3 had muscle mass equivalent to typical men; Rich said yes and Eric said no. Bennett stepped in here once again, crafting a statement that while the experts agree that athletes with these DSDs have increased muscle mass over typical women, there is not agreement whether the muscle mass of such athletes reaches male levels. A similar statement covered the question of hemoglobin levels. It was even more difficult to craft a consensus statement on athletes with PAIS, and the IAAF experts stuck with the notion of a case-by-case analysis. Eric contended that the dropping of CAH from the restricted list was motivated by the desire to label intersex athletes as biological men, but Rich spoke of the reasons why CAH athletes are very unlikely to reach elite levels.[29] The last item of note in this hot tub was the list of restricted events. The IAAF experts had suggested that the 800 meter race represented a sweet spot where both strength and aerobic capacity were important. Ross Tucker replied that if the 800 was truly a testosterone-based sweet spot, why wasn't there a larger gap between the men's and women's world records in the event. Tucker's point was soon dubbed the Tucker paradox.[30]

The hot tub on the impact of treatment to lower T yielded agreement that birth control pills or GnRH agonists could be used to lower T, with GnRH agonists as the more effective method, but also the method with more significant side effects. The experts also agreed that some patients with XY DSDs and female gender identity choose to use such methods to lower T.[31] There was however, no agreement as to whether or not the inevitable withdrawal symptoms abate, or whether or not oral medications will consistently maintain T below 5 nmol/L.[32]

The hot tub on the Bermon/Garnier study was allocated two and a half hours on the schedule, reflecting the vision of the ASA group that it was the most important item on the docket. As it turned out, the ability of Bermon and Pielke to reach consensus on some important limitations of the study led to a much shorter and less contentious hot tub than many had imagined. Both men agreed that the study was exploratory in nature, and Bermon explained to the courtroom that he had been directed by Richard McLaren to produce this study during the Chand case. Joel Dave questioned the lack of signed consent by the athletes to use their blood tests for research purposes as the data had been originally intended for anti-doping purposes.[33] Unfortunately, Professor Dave's manner was so aggressive that he was admonished by Dr. Bennett.

Pielke suggested perhaps that the IAAF should do another study, and Angelica Hirschberg mentioned her study detailing the effects of relatively modest testosterone boosting in women that is under review by the *British Journal of Sports Medicine*.[34] Pielke replied that this study was not on elite athletes but could offer no positive alternative. Pielke also suggested that despite the fact that the Bermon/Garnier study showed an association between higher T and performance, the correlation factor was low. Pielke did have to concede that correlation factors are often low in exploratory studies. Amazingly enough, this ended the hot tub after only one hour and relatively little damage to the Bermon/Garnier study.

At this point, the ASA team had to be very disappointed, as they had placed a high priority on discrediting the Bermon/Garnier paper. No sooner had the hot tub session apparently ended then Norman Arendse stood up and claimed that the panel had failed to follow proper procedure because they hadn't discussed all of the talking points that had been initially agreed upon. Bennett wasn't going to allow this to happen, because she knew that the only reasonable grounds for appeal was on a procedural motion. Bennett pointed out that the hot tub experts had come to agreement on some of the talking points prior to the session and that is why they weren't discussed in the session. Furthermore, if Arendse felt that the hot tub session had not been conducted appropriately, then he was welcome to come up to the head of table and lead the session to a more satisfactory conclusion. After taking a five-minute break to talk it over with his team, Arendse withdrew his objection. Once again, Bennett had been masterful in controlling the hearing, averting a potential crisis.

Lastly, there was a very sedate hot tub on the impact of the DSD regulations on the lives of intersex women. Both participants were from the claimants' side and both agreed that intersex women led difficult lives and that the DSD regulations could further add to the misery of the affected athletes. Neither Doriane nor I were involved in the hot tubs, but we had both been present on Tuesday and Wednesday. Doriane had been effective in suggesting ways the IAAF witnesses could be better advocates for their positions. Doriane had also engaged witnesses for the claimants and the panel of judges in casual conversations during lunches and breaks, efforts I think led to a more respectful tone during the actual hot tubs.

With the hot tub sessions over, there were only a few witnesses to examine on Thursday, myself included. My testimony was actually quite anticlimactic. Taylor asked me about my 2:23 marathon from 1982, which was faster than the women's world record at the time, making the point that had I been allowed to compete in women's sports based on gender identity, I would have been a world record holder. Mr. Sayao undertook the cross-examination pointing out the limitations of my study and my lack of academic qualifications,[35] and shortly thereafter my testimony was finished.

Professors Blockman and Coleman also testified Thursday morning. Prof. Coleman made an important clarification of her previous use of the term *biological male*, as she now suggested that XY DSD athletes possessed male gonadal and endocrine sex. She also explained that she had previously intended the term *biologically male* to be used in a reproductive sense, that is, possessing testes.[36] Coleman was cross-examined by Arendse, and this was the last time he took the lead position for the ASA. He was replaced by Ncumisa Mayosi for Friday's closing arguments, and this was a welcome decision. The court finished up all the outstanding testimony by lunchtime on Thursday, and we were given the afternoon off.

The closing arguments were on tap for Friday, and once again both Jim Bunting and Jon Taylor put on quite a display of their skills. Bunting opened by talking about the alleged discriminatory nature of the

DSD regulations and the difficult road the IAAF would face if the CAS panel ruled that discrimination did, in fact, exist. Bunting noted that in the case of a discriminatory rule, the IAAF would need to show that the rules were necessary, proportionate, and reasonable.[37] In particular he claimed that the IAAF would need to prove that DSD athletes possessed a male-like advantage. Bunting admitted that the IAAF evidence on the effect of T was stronger than in the Chand case. Bunting noted the extreme difficulty in deciding whether or not an athlete with PAIS was sufficiently virilized to fall under the DSD regulations, and that both athletes with 5-ARD and 17β-HSD3 had much lower levels of DHT than men did. Bunting claimed that the DHT deficit was decisive in these cases and that they too should be allowed to compete in the women's category.[38] Bunting bought up the Tucker paradox and the Pielke consensus, championing both ideas. He spoke of the undesirable side effects of treatment to lower T and the fluctuations in T levels that can occur when athletes are on such medications. Once again, Bunting did a remarkably good job in his closing statement. Halfway through his arguments, he ran out of water and took the liberty of grabbing the bottle in front of Carlos Sayao. Doriane promptly rose from her seat to get the two Canadian lawyers some more water, displaying her character and the bond between all lawyers.

Ncumisa Mayosi gave the closing argument for the ASA, and while she was much better than Arendse would have been, she still fell short of the brilliance of Bunting and Taylor. The most memorable part of her presentation occurred when she said that the ASA was trying get financial compensation from the IAAF[39] and that the withdrawal of CAH from the DSD list was justification for partial compensation. The ASA had spent lavishly on the trial, bringing an entourage that was at least twice the size of the IAAF or Semenya teams. The South African sports minister had flown to Lausanne "to support Caster Semenya,"[40] although she was not allowed into the trial. All, in all, the South African government had spent approximately $1.5 million (or 25 million Rand),[41] and now it expected to get that money from the IAAF if Caster won. It was a stunning claim, one that contrasted with the decision made by the IAAF and Semenya teams to look after their own finances. Ms. Mayosi's claim triggered a response from the IAAF to ask for compensation from the ASA,[42] and in the end, the ASA was required to give

1500 Swiss Francs to both the IAAF and the Semenya team resulting from "unnecessary and unmeritorious challenges." [43]

Prior to breaking for lunch, Bennett gave both sides the opportunity to accept a verdict somewhere in between a complete yes or no. In the Chand case, both sides had agreed to a possible intermediate verdict, and the result was the two-year suspension of the hyperandrogenism rules and the uncertainty that ensued. Bunting agreed to Bennett's request immediately, but Taylor demurred. During lunch, Jon asked Stef whether he wanted to accept Bennett's proposal, but Stef rolled the dice and said, "Let's go for all or nothing."

After lunch, Taylor was up. He started with the argument that women need a protected class in sports if they are to win anything of importance.[44] Taylor accepted that sex/gender is not entirely binary but said the line between male and female athletes needs to be drawn using performance-based analysis.[45] He said that T is the primary difference between male and female athletes.[46] Taylor claimed that the DSD regulations are not unlawfully discriminatory because they place like with like.[47] In all aspects that matter to sports, athletes with 5-ARD and 17β-HSD3 are like male athletes except for DHT. Taylor later explored the DHT question in detail, claiming that the performance differences between DSD athletes and male athletes as a result of lower DHT levels is minimal. Taylor conceded that PAIS is a more complicated DSD but claimed that an experienced physician could correctly determine whether or not an athlete was sufficiently virilized to require restrictions. Taylor spoke of the extreme overrepresentation of DSD athletes in the restricted events.[48]

In response to the Tucker paradox, Taylor claimed that the world record in the women's 800 is suspect because of doping. If one used the fastest time of a clean female athlete, the gap between the men's and women's 800 meter world records would be larger. He asserted that the Pielke consensus defeated the women's category, and that it would be difficult to determine if a woman had always expressed a female role. The Pielke consensus was also an affront to gender nonconforming people. By way of conclusion, Taylor told the panel that the IAAF was requesting an all-or-nothing verdict. Like Bunting, Taylor was brilliant in closing. Bunting reiterated some of his previous points in a brief response and concluded that he thought the Pielke consensus was a logical way forward. Caster Semenya was up last, and she spoke of a long walk to freedom, echoing Nelson Mandela. She further alluded to the great man by suggesting that sports have the power to unite people. I had been impressed by her quiet presence and dignity throughout the week, and her closing remarks cemented my opinion of her.

Despite Dr. Bennett's earlier prohibition, more evidence was submitted after the close of the trial.[49] On March 21 it was announced that the verdict would be delayed from the original March 26 date to some unspecified date in April. The news release cited the court as stating that "the parties have filed additional submissions and materials."[50] In April, Francine Niyonsaba publicly announced that she was intersex at a news conference[51] and claimed that the IAAF DSD rule was discrimination. It turns out that the CAS panel agreed with her.

On May 1 the CAS panel finally released its verdict. Two of three judges sided with the IAAF: "The Panel found that the DSD Regulations are discriminatory but that, on the basis of the evidence submitted by the parties, such discrimination is a necessary, reasonable and proportionate means of achieving the legitimate objective of ensuring fair competition in female athletics."[52] Furthermore, all three judges agreed with the importance of T in sports performance, stating, "On the basis of the scientific evidence presented by the parties, the Panel unanimously finds that endogenous testosterone is the primary driver of the sex difference in sports performance between males and females."[53] One can only hope that this particular quote from the verdict will quiet those voices that have claimed otherwise for almost ten years. The IAAF and its lawyers and experts had won the day. Additionally, the panel abandoned the notion that legal sex was all-important, stating that "the reason for the separation between male and female categories in competitive athletics is ultimately founded on biology rather than legal status."[54] The panel also rejected the idea that gender identity was important in determining sports categories.

The IAAF set May 8 as the implementation date for the DSD regulations, meaning that intersex athletes had one last opportunity to run the restricted events in the IAAF Diamond League. On May 3 Caster Semenya ran 1:54.98 to win the Diamond League 800 meter race in Doha, with Francie Niyonsaba finishing a distant second in 1:57.75. Earlier in 2019, Semenya had won races in South Africa over distances ranging from 200 meters to 5000 meters, and there was some discussion that she might move up to the latter distance rather than undergo testosterone suppression. She later showed up on the entry list for the 3000 meter race at the Prefontaine Classic.[55] In May, Margaret Wambui acknowledged that she was also affected by the CAS ruling in the Semenya case. Wambui stated that, just like Semenya and Niyonsaba, she too had no intention of lowering her testosterone. Furthermore, the Kenyan star noted that the verdict had reduced her incentive to train hard.[56]

There was a flurry of media activity after the verdict. The general tone of much of the reporting was that Semenya had been wronged, but very few reports noted the fact that athletes with XY DSDs on the restricted list have testes and virtually full male athletic advantage. I gave interviews, engaged in mini-debates with opponents of the ruling, and was swamped with interview requests. The importance of this verdict cannot be overstated. The ruling meant that sports governing bodies are allowed to use biologically based methods to divide their sports into male and female categories. The ruling also acknowledged the reality that testosterone is the most important differentiator between male and female athletes.

On May 13 it was announced that the ASA had decided to appeal the CAS panel verdict, in part because Bennett and Nater were "conflicted" from their involvement in the Chand case.[57] Any appeal by the ASA or by Semenya's lawyers would need to be made by May 31.

As I look back at the trial, there are a few things I would like to emphasize. First off, Annabelle Bennett, Jon Taylor, and Jim Bunting were brilliant throughout the week. Beyond this triplet of legal excellence, I would suggest that the next most important person in the room was David Handelsman. His endocrine knowledge was second to none, and his brilliance was an important key to the verdict. Beyond his scientific knowledge, he had evolved from someone who was widely viewed as hotheaded to a calm and reasoned voice.

And what of my role? I must admit that my presence at the trial seemed superfluous most of the time; but my witness statement was praised by many on both sides of the table. Moreover, I can only hope that the four years of writing, research, and talks that I had undertaken since the Chand trial had some effect on the verdict in the Semenya case. This verdict is congruent with my belief that both inclusion and meaningful sport for all women are important, and I am satisfied that I played some part in the outcome.

EPILOGUE: ONE LAST STORY

There is never going to be universal agreement on the fairest manner in which to divide sport into male and female categories. Although we won't go back to the days of making such determinations based upon external genitalia, there are many who would like to reinstate the use of chromosome patterns to separate the sexes on the playing field. On the other hand, there is also a growing cadre who would allow intersex and/or transgender women to compete without restriction. Lastly, there are people like me, who try to reach some middle ground between the two views. I shall try to summarize my positions briefly here. First, I think that at the level of adult competitive sport, one should try to find some method that maximizes the possibility that all women can enjoy equitable and meaningful sport. I think the method of determining what I have called athletic gender should use evidence-based criteria to separate athletes into male and female divisions. I believe that the best method to do so with the current level of knowledge is to use serum testosterone levels while making allowance for those with androgen insensitivity.

In the future I think that, particularly when assessing transgender women, international sporting federations will make use of data that are not yet available to determine sex/gender policies that are specific to the individual sport. Such policies will require data that do not yet exist. I hope to be one of the scientists involved in the experiments that will make such a system feasible. Most athletes, however, are not all that competitive. For recreational sport among adults, and for all prepubescent athletes, I believe we should allow athletes to choose either male, female, or perhaps some future nonbinary category as they see fit. The most difficult athletes to make decisions about with regard to sex-segregated sports are adolescent athletes. Maturation rates vary largely from one individual to another, as does the level of competitive drive and willingness to train. I think that, for the most part, adolescent athletes should be free to choose whether they want to compete with the boys or the girls, but I do think that higher-achieving adolescent athletes should be subject to restrictions similar to those of adult competitive athletes.

Regardless of what personal beliefs any individual reader might hold, I would hope that this book has made it abundantly clear that the question of what is or is not fair is far from straightforward. If I have opened people's eyes to the complexity of gender and sport issues, while providing some enlightenment about the lives of those athletes who do not fall within the gender binary, then I have accomplished my goal.

I would like to change pace a little bit and leave you with one final story that has nothing to do with women's sport but does have something to do with fairness and sport. It also means that I'll be turning over the closing words to my father, and that has some sentimental value for me.

Much earlier in this book, when I spoke of my high school basketball days, I mentioned two players whom I referred to as the twin towers. The slightly taller of two was named Brian, and although he was not a prolific scorer, he was, without much doubt, the most important player on the team. He was a defensive force, and it was from playing with him that I learned just how important a towering presence in the middle could be to a basketball team. I remember one particular game during my junior year when we played a major rival within our league. One of the opponent's best players, a smooth, small forward whose leaping skills were apparent to anyone who saw him play, penetrated the paint and put up a jump shot that Brian swatted away with ease. The ball fell back into the shooter's hands, and he went right back up with a second jumper. Brian blocked this one too, and again the ball returned to the shooter. The guy took one brief look in Brian's direction, and then, realizing the futility of trying to score on him, turned around and passed the ball out to the perimeter.

Brian and I weren't particularly close off the court. After high school, we went to different universities and never really saw each other, except for maybe an occasional pickup game at Christmastime. A few years later, maybe just before entering graduate school, I was out for a run along the Thames River in southwestern Ontario, and I spied Brian. Back in the day, he had been the best 400 meter runner on our track team; I loved to watch his long legs eat up the track. Brian asked if he could join me, and we ran four or five miles together before I dropped him off. As we ran, we got caught up on each other's lives. It turned out that Brian had dropped out of university; he was in town trying to gain the favor of some girl. Brian had always had some socialization issues, and it was pretty clear that he was a lost soul by this time. He told me he'd love to get together for a run or to shoot hoops some time. I never took him up on his offer, and that was the last time I ever saw him. Brian died by suicide within a year, and I always felt guilty about blowing him off the way I did. Realistically, it probably wouldn't have changed the course of Brian's life, but I should have treated him better.

Many years later, after my transition, Brian appeared to me in a dream. He smiled at me and said that it was good that one of us had turned out happy. I woke up, greatly moved by the vision. Later on, I decided that I probably wasn't really visited by Brian. More than likely it was simply my subconscious that had fabricated Brian out of my need to find some forgiveness. In the end, it doesn't really matter.

Brian and I had gone to different schools prior to meeting in high school, but I remember his name came up one evening during dinner when I was in eighth grade and Brian was a high school freshman. My father, who was the high school basketball coach, was trying to get Brian to come out for the team. Brian had demurred at first, and later, when pressed by dad, confessed that he didn't think the sport was right for him. "Mr. Harper," Brian explained, "It wouldn't be fair for me to play basketball, since I'm taller than everyone else." I can still remember the look of incredulity on my father's face as he turned to the rest of his family gathered around the table and asked, rhetorically, "What the hell does fair have to do with anything?"

RECENT DEVELOPMENTS IN GENDER AND SPORTS

Caster Semenya and her team filed an appeal with the Swiss Federal Tribunal (SFT) on May 29, 2019. On June 3, the court ruled that Semenya (but no other DSD runner) could compete in the restricted events while her appeal is being heard, subject to further submissions from the IAAF. Semenya and Niyonsaba both ran a 2,000 meter race on June 12 near Paris with Semenya winning at 5:38 and Niyonsaba finishing last at 5:43. Subsequently, Semenya won the 800 meter race at the Prefontaine Classic Diamond League meeting on June 30 with a time of 1:55.70, the fastest time ever run on American soil. Semenya did not race again prior to July 30, when the SFT ruled that she could no longer compete in the restricted events prior to their final ruling, meaning that Semenya would not be running the 800 meters in Doha.

There was also news on the transgender front in June as CeCe Telfer became the first openly transgender athlete to capture an NCAA title, winning the 400 hurdles in the Division II meet in a time of 57.53 seconds. Telfer also finished fifth in the 100 meter hurdle race at the same meet. Over the 2019 indoor and outdoor seasons, Telfer competed in sprint and hurdle events from distances of 60 meters up to 400 meters. In contrast to the athletes the author has studied, Telfer's times were not markedly slower in 2019 than those she had posted while competing in men's track prior to her transition. The NCAA requires trans women to undergo one year of hormone therapy but is vague on required hormone levels or enforcement. Telfer's coach stated that she was much more motivated this year than in previous years, a possible explanation for the large relative improvement.

NOTES

1. "PREHISTORIC" WOMEN'S SPORT

1. The talk by Case was part of a symposium sponsored by Duke University as a means of vetting potential articles for its *Law and Contemporary Problems* review. Case would expand upon the ideas she presented at that symposium in an article titled "Heterosexuality as a Factor in the Long History of Women's Sports," *Law and Contemporary Problems* 80, no. 4 (2017): 24–46, https://papers.ssrn.com/sol3/papers.cfm?abstract_id=3138664.

2. Lauren Young, "When Ancient Greece Banned Women From Olympics, They Started Their Own," Atlas Obscura, August 10, 2016, https://www.atlasobscura.com/articles/when-ancient-greece-barred-women-from-even-watching-the-games-they-started-their-own-olympics.

3. "Ancient Heraean Games," Health and Fitness History, https://healthandfitnesshistory.com/historical-athletes/ancient-heraean-games/.

4. "Ancient Olympic Games," Health and Fitness History, https://healthandfitnesshistory.com/historical-athletes/ancient-olympic-games/.

5. "First Modern Olympic Games," History, last updated April 4, 2019, http: //www.history.com/this-day-in-history/first-modern-olympic-games.

6. "Ancient Heraean Games."

7. David Epstein, *The Sports Gene: Inside the Science of Extraordinary Athletic Performance* (New York: Penguin, 2013), 62.

8. Gerry Brown and Mark Zurlo, "Track and Field, First Olympic Appearance: 1896," Infoplease, https://www.infoplease.com/track-field-1.

9. "Athletics at the Summer Olympics," *Wikipedia*, https://en.m.wikipedia.org/wiki/Athletics_at_the_Summer_Olympics.

10. International Association of Athletic Federations, "One Month to Go—IAAF World Cross Country Championships Kampala 2017," press release, February 24, 2017, https://www.iaaf.org/news/press-release/one-month-to-go-world-cross-country-champions.

11. Michelle R. Martinelli, New Events for 2020 Olympics Mean Swimmers Finally Get Pool Equality, *USA Today*, June 9, 2017, https://ftw.usatoday.com/2017/06/2020-tokyo-olympics-swimming-program-equality-katie-ledecky-womens-1500-mens-800-meters-freestyle-international-olympic-committee-announcement.

12. "The Women of Sparta: Athletic, Educated, and Outspoken Radicals," *Ancient History Encyclopedia*, January 18, 2012, https://www.ancient.eu/article/123/the-women-of-sparta-athletic-educated-and-outspoke/.

13. Case, "Heterosexuality as a Factor in the Long History of Women's Sports."

14. "Every Day Life in the Middle Ages," BBC, https://www.bbc.com/bitesize/guides/zm4mn39/revision/6.

15. "Medieval Sports," Medieval Life and Times, http://www.medieval-life-and-times.info/medieval-life/medieval-sports.htm.

16. Jeff Johnston, "Women in Sport and Gaming during Medieval Times," HubPages, March 8, 2018, https://hubpages.com/education/Women-in-Sports-During-Medieval-Times.

17. Ancient Golf, https://ancientgolf.dse.nl/colfuk.htm.

18. "Mary, Queen of Scots," History of Golf, http://www.artsales.com/topics/golf_history/historyofGolf.htm.

19. Sally Jenkins, "Remembering the Mother of Golf, in the Cradle of the Game," *Washington Post*, July 15, 2010, http://www.washingtonpost.com/wp-dyn/content/article/2010/07/14/AR2010071404544.html.

20. "Mary, Queen of Scots," Biography, last updated April 16, 2019, https://www.biography.com/people/mary-queen-of-scots-9401343.

21. "Mary, Queen of Scots," History of Golf.

22. Jenkins, "Remembering the Mother of Golf."

23. "Mary, Queen of Scots," History of Golf.

24. "Mary, Queen of Scots," Biography.

25. David Mathew, "James I," *Britannica*, https://www.britannica.com/biography/James-I-king-of-England-and-Scotland.

26. Barry Steven Lorge and Morys Bruce, "Tennis," *Britannica*, https://www.britannica.com/sports/tennis.

27. Paul Newman, "Maud Watson, the 'First Lady' of Wimbledon," Wimbledon, June 20, 2016, https://www.wimbledon.com/en_GB/news/articles/2016–06–20/maud_watson_the_first_lady_of_wimbledon.html.

28. Mechelle Voepel, "College Athletes Are Already Getting Paid," ESPN, July 18, 2011, http://www.espn.com/college-sports/columns/story? columnist=voepel_mechelle&id=6739971.

29. "First Modern Olympic Games."

30. "Women at the Olympic Games," Topend Sports, http://www.topendsports.com/events/summer/women.htm.

31. Mark Molloy, "How Far Have Women's Rights Advanced in a Century?" *Telegraph* (UK), February 6, 2019, https://www.telegraph.co.uk/women/life/far-have-womens-rights-advanced-century/.

32. Alix Culbertson, "The Suffragettes: The Women Who Risked All to Get the Vote," Sky News, February 6, 2019, https://news.sky.com/story/the-suffragettes-the-women-who-risked-all-in-their-battle-to-vote-11233478.

33. "History of Women's Suffrage," Scholastic, http://teacher.scholastic.com/activities/suffrage/history.htm.

34. Sara Gross, "Alice Milliat and the Women's Olympic Games," Live Feisty, http://livefeisty.com/alice-milliat-and-the-womens-olympic-games/.

35. "Amsterdam 1928 Olympic Games," *Britannica*, https://www.britannica.com/event/Amsterdam-1928-Olympic-Games.

36. Epstein, *The Sports Gene*, 60.

37. Lindsay Parks Pieper, *Sex Testing: Gender Policing in Women's Sports* (Urbana: University of Illinois Press, 2016), 19.

2. THE SCIENCE OF INTERSEX CONDITIONS

1. "Hermaphroditus," Myth Encyclopedia, http://www.mythencyclopedia.com/Go-Hi/Hermaphroditus.html.

2. Michel Foucault, *Abnormal: Lectures at the Collège de France 1974–1975* (London: Verso, 2003), 67.

3. Alice Dreger, *Hermaphrodites and the Medical Invention of Sex* (Cambridge, MA: Harvard University Press, 2000), 139.

4. Ibid., 4, 176.

5. Alice Dreger, *Galileo's Middle Finger: Heretics, Activists, and the Search for Justice in Science* (New York: Penguin, 2015), 51.

6. "Consensus Statement on Management of Intersex Disorders," *Pediatrics* 118, no. 2 (2006), http://pediatrics.aappublications.org/content/118/2/e488.

7. Emi Koyama, "Frequently Asked Questions about the 'DSD' Controversy," Intersex Initiative, last updated June 29, 2008, http://www.intersexinitiative.org/articles/dsdfaq.html.

8. Frank H. Netter and Larry R. Cochard, *Netter's Atlas of Human Embryology* (Teterboro, NJ: Icon Learning Systems, 2002), 159.

9. G. H. Valentine, "Incidence of Chromosome Disorders," *Canadian Family Physician* 25 (1979): 937–39, https://www.ncbi.nlm.nih.gov/pmc/articles/PMC2383192/.

10. Colleen de Bellefonds, "Fetal Development: Your Baby's Sex," What to Expect, https://www.whattoexpect.com/pregnancy/fetal-development/fetal-sex-organs-reproductive-system/.

11. "Anti-Mullerian Hormone," You and Your Hormones, https://www.yourhormones.info/hormones/anti-muellerian-hormone/.

12. "What Are Dominant and Recessive Alleles?" yourgenome, https://www.yourgenome.org/facts/whatare-dominant-and-recessive-alleles.

13. Katrina Karkazis, *Fixing Sex: Intersex, Medical Authority, and Lived Experience* (Durham, NC: Duke University Press, 2008), 56.

14. Dreger, *Hermaphrodites*, 182.

15. Karkazis, *Fixing Sex*, 58.

16. Sara Reardon, "The Spectrum of Sex Development: Eric Vilain and the Intersex Controversy," *Nature*, May 10, 2016, https://www.nature.com/news/the-spectrum-of-sex-development-eric-vilain-and-the-intersex-controversy-1.19873.

17. D. Merke and M. Kabbani, "Congenital Adrenal Hyperplasia: Epidemiology, Management and Practical Drug Treatment," *Paediatric Drugs* 3, no. 8 (2001): 599–611, https://www.ncbi.nlm.nih.gov/pubmed/11577925.

18. Dreger, *Galileo's Middle Finger*, 192.

19. Dreger, *Hermaphrodites*, 38.

20. Dreger, *Galileo's Middle Finger*, 193.

21. "Turner Syndrome," Genetics Home Reference, https://ghr.nlm.nih.gov/condition/turner-syndrome.

22. "Klinefelter syndrome," Genetics Home Reference, https://ghr.nlm.nih.gov/condition/klinefelter-syndrome.

23. Steven M. Carr, "Barr Bodies: Heterochromatized X-chromosomes," Memorial University website, https://www.mun.ca/biology/scarr/Barr_Bodies.html.

24. "Mosaicism," The Chromosome 18 Registry & Research Society, https://www.chromosome18.0rg/other-conditions/mosaicism/.

25. Y. Morel, R. Rey, C. Teinturier, et al., "Aetiological Diagnosis of Male Sex Ambiguity: A Collaborative Study," *European Journal of Pediatrics* 161, no. 1 (2002): 49–59, https://www.ncbi.nlm.nih.gov/pubmed/11808880.

26. "Androgen Insensitivity Syndrome," Genetics Home Reference, https://ghr.nlm.nih.gov/condition/androgen-insensitivity-syndrome.

27. Sharon Kirkey, "Supermodel Comes Out as Intersex: 'My Body Isn't Really Male or Female,' Hanne Gaby Odiele Reveals," *National Post*, January 24, 2017, https://nationalpost.com/news/0125-na-intersex.

28. Malcolm A. Ferguson-Smith and L. Dawn Bavington, "Natural Selection for Genetic Variants in Sport: The Role of Y Chromosome Genes in Elite Female Athletes with 46,XY DSD," *Sports Medicine* 44 (2014): 1629–34, doi: 10.1007/s40279-014-0249-8.https://www.ncbi.nlm.nih.gov/pubmed/25160863.

29. "Androgen Insensitivity Syndrome."

30. "5-alpha Reductase Deficiency," Genetics Home Reference, https://ghr.nlm.nih.gov/condition/5-alpha-reductase-deficiency.

31. Julianne Imperato-McGinley, Luis Guerrero, Teofilo Gautier, and Ralph Edward Peterson, "Steroid 5α-Reductase Deficiency in Man: An Inherited Form of Male Pseudohermaphroditism," *Science* 186, no. 4170 (1974): 1213–15, doi: 10.1126/science.186.4170.1213.PMID4432067. https://www.ncbi.nlm.nih.gov/pubmed/4432067

32. International Association of Athletics Federations, "IAAF Eligibility Regulations for the Female Classification [Athletes with Differences of Sex Development] in Force as from 8 May 2019," May 1, 2019, https://www.iaaf.org/about-iaaf/documents/rules-regulations.

33. "17-beta Hydroxysteroid Dehydrogenase 3 Deficiency," Genetics Home Reference, https://ghr.nlm.nih.gov/condition/17-beta-hydroxysteroid-dehydrogenase-3-deficiency.

34. Heather M. Byers, Lauren H. Mohnach, Patricia Y. Fechner, et al., "Unexpected Ethical Dilemmas in Sex Assignment in 46,XY DSD Due to 5-alpha Reductase Type 2 Deficiency," *American Journal of Medical Genetics, Part C: Seminars in Medical Genetics* 175, no. 2 (2017): 260–67, doi: 10.1002/ajmg.c.31560. https://www.ncbi.nlm.nih.gov/pubmed/28544750.

35. Karkazis, *Fixing Sex*, 268.

3. INTERSEX ATHLETES IN THE 1930s

1. Katherine Harmon, "Charles Darwin's Family Tree Tangled with Inbreeding, Early Death," *Scientific American*, May 3, 2010, https://blogs.scientificamerican.com/observations/charles-darwins-family-tree-tangled-with-inbreeding-early-death/.

2. Melike Bildirici, Özgür Ersin, and Meltem Kökdener, "An Investigation of Hemophilia, Consanguineous Marriages and Economic Growth: Panel MLP and Panel SVR Approach," *Prodecia Economics and Finance* 38 (2016): 294–307, http://www.sciencedirect.com/science/article/pii/S2212567116302039.

3. "Impact of Europe's Royal Inbreeding: Part I," Medical Bag, February 24, 2014, http://www.medicalbag.com/grey-matter/impact-of-europes-royal-inbreeding/article/472405/.

4. "Consanguineous Marriage: Should It Be Discouraged?" *Middle East Health*, June 20, 2012, http://www.middleeasthealthmag.com/may2012/feature2. htm.

5. M. Ellaithi, A. Kamel, and O. Saber, "Consanguinity and Disorders of Sexual Developments in the Sudan," *Sudan Journal of Medical Sciences* 6, no. 4 (2011), https://scholar.google.com.mx/scholar?q=consanguinity+and+disorders+of+sexual+development+in+the+sudan&hl=en&as_sdt=0&as_vis=1&oi=scholart.

6. Sheldon Anderson, *The Forgotten Legacy of Stella Walsh* (Lanham, MD: Rowman & Littlefield, 2017), 6.

7. Ibid., 178, 67.

8. Russell Freedman, *Babe Didrikson Zaharias: The Making of a Champion* (New York: Clarion, 1999), 15.

9. Anderson, *The Forgotten Legacy of Stella Walsh*, 35.

10. Ibid., 38, 41.

11. Lindsay Parks Pieper, *Sex Testing: Gender Policing in Women's Sports* (Urbana: University of Illinois Press, 2016), 19.

12. Freedman, *Babe Didrikson Zaharias*, 35, 41, 44.

13. Anderson, *The Forgotten Legacy of Stella Walsh*, 56.

14. Ibid., 60.

15. Guy Walters, *Berlin Games: How the Nazis Stole the Olympic Dream* (New York: HarperCollins, 2006), 12.

16. Anderson, *The Forgotten Legacy of Stella Walsh*, 70, 68.

17. Freedman, *Babe Didrikson Zaharias*, 62, 64, 65.

18. Ibid., 105.

19. Susan E. Cayleff, *Babe: The Life and Legend of Babe Didrickson Zaharias* (Urbana: University of Illinois Press, 1995), 92.

20. Anderson, *The Forgotten Legacy of Stella Walsh*, 144.

21. Ibid., 83.

22. Sharon Kinney Hanson, *The Life of Helen Stephens: The Fulton Flash* (Carbondale: Southern Illinois University Press, 2004), 4–7.

23. Carol Herkstroeter, "The Fulton Flash Isn't Finished Yet," unidentified newspaper clipping.

24. Hanson, *The Life of Helen Stephens*, 20–22.

25. Ibid., 24–25.

26. Ibid., 26.

27. Anderson, *The Forgotten Legacy of Stella Walsh*, 85.

28. Hanson, *The Life of Helen Stephens*, 53.

29. Anderson, *The Forgotten Legacy of Stella Walsh*, 87.

30. Walters, *Berlin Games*, 62, 138.

31. Anderson, *The Forgotten Legacy of Stella Walsh*, 96.

32. Walters, *Berlin Games*, 211.

33. Hanson, *The Life of Helen Stephens*, 83.

34. Anderson, *The Forgotten Legacy of Stella Walsh*, 104.

35. Hanson, *The Life of Helen Stephens*, 88.

36. Walters, *Berlin Games*, 211.

37. Anderson, *The Forgotten Legacy of Stella Walsh*, 109.

38. Hanson, *The Life of Helen Stephens*, 96.

39. Paul Gallico, *Farewell to Sport*, 2nd ed. (New York: Knopf, 1990), 233–34.

40. Hanson, *The Life of Helen Stephens*, 144, 151, 230.

41. Freedman, *Babe Didrikson Zaharias*, 143, 144, 156.

42. "25 Most Iconic Athletes in the History of Sport," List25, September 20, 2013, https://list25. com/25-most-iconic-athletes-in-the-history-of-sports/.

43. Mike Rowbottom, "Athletics: Only the 'Athlete of the Century' Beat Williamson to Gold," *Independent* (UK), January 31, 2004, https://web.archive.org/web/20070930181530/http: //sport.independent.co.uk/general/article76366. ece.

44. Anderson, *The Forgotten Legacy of Stella Walsh*, 169.

45. Ibid., 175.

46. "Girl Who Became Man Tells of Metamorphosis," *Reading Eagle*, May 28, 1936, https://news.google.com/newspapers?nid=1955&dat=19360528&id=FOUxAAAAIBAJ&sjid=zuIFAAAAIBAJ&pg=4530,6010974.

47. "Mark Weston (athlete)," Revolvy, https://www.revolvy.com/page/Mark-Weston-% 28athlete% 29.

48. Pieper, *Sex Testing*, 30.

49. Hanson, *The Life of Helen Stephens*, 127, 140, 162.

50. Stefan Berg, "How Dora the Man Competed in the Women's High Jump," *Spiegel*, September 15, 2009, http://www.spiegel.de/international/germany/1936-berlin-olympics-how-dora-the-man-competed-in-the-woman-s-high-jump-a-649104. html.

51. Walters, *Berlin Games*, 62.

52. Ibid., 271.

53. Berg, "How Dora the Man Competed in the Women's High Jump."

54. Ibid.

55. Walters, *Berlin Games*, 210.

56. J. D. Watson and F. H. C. Crick, "Molecular Structure of Nucleic Acids: A Structure for Deoxyribose Nucleic Acid," *Nature* 171 (April 25, 1953): 737–38. https://www.nature.com/scitable/content/molecular-structure-of-nucleic-acids-a-structure-13997975.

57. A. H. Bittles, "Consanguineous Marriage and Childhood Health," *Developmental Medicine & Child Neurology* 45 (2003): 571–76, http://onlinelibrary.wiley.com/doi/10.1111/j.1469-8749.2003. tb00959. x/epdf.

4. POSTWAR SEX TESTING

1. Lindsay Parks Pieper, *Sex Testing: Gender Policing in Women's Sports* (Urbana: University of Illinois Press, 2016), 31.

2. Ibid., 30.

3. Metoidioplasty, https://www.metoidioplasty.net/.

4. M. A. Ferguson-Smith and E. A. Ferris, "Gender Verification in Sport: The Need for Change?" *British Journal of Sports Medicine* 25, no. 1 (1991): 17–20, https://www.ncbi.nlm.nih.gov/pmc/articles/PMC1478807/.

5. Democrat and Chronicle (Rochester, New York), December 14, 1952, https://www.newspapers.com/image/137752948/.

6. K. N. Ballantyne, M. Kayser, and J. A. Grootegoed, "Sex and Gender Issues in Competitive Sports: Investigation of a Historical Case Leads to a New Viewpoint," *British Journal of Sports Medicine* 46, no. 8 (2012): 614–17, https://www.ncbi.nlm.nih.gov/pmc/articles/PMC3375582/.

7. "The Incredible Dominance of Fanny Blankers-Koen," International Olympic Committee website, https://www.olympic.org/news/fanny-blankers-koen-athletics.

8. "Foekje Dillema (1928–2007) runner," *A Gender Variance Who's Who*, July 30, 2012, https://zagria.blogspot.com/2012/07/foekje-dillema-1928-2007-runner.html#.W75tNRplChA.

9. "Helsinki 1952 Medal Table," IOC website, https://www.olympic.org/helsinki-1952.

10. Pieper, *Sex Testing*, 48.

11. "Irina Press" [obituary], *Telegraph* (UK), May 31, 2004, https://www.telegraph.co.uk/news/obituaries/1463233/Irina-Press.html.

12. Monica Roberts, "Olympic Gender Drama—The Press Sisters," *TransGriot* (blog), November 9, 2011, https://transgriot.blogspot.com/2011/11/olympic-gender-drama-press-sisters.html.

13. "Irina Press" [obituary].

14. Roberts, "Olympic Gender Drama—The Press Sisters."

15. Pieper, *Sex Testing*, 54.

16. Thomas Murray, *Good Sport: Why Our Games Matter—and How Doping Undermines Them* (New York: Oxford University Press, 2017), 100.

17. Pieper, *Sex Testing*, 52.

18. Arne Ljungqvist and Goran Lager, *Doping's Nemesis* (Cheltenham, UK: Sports Books, 2011), 183.

19. Ferguson-Smith and Ferris, "Gender Verification in Sport."

20. "Ewa Klobukowska," Sports Reference/Olympics, https://www.sports-reference.com/olympics/athletes/kl/ewa-klobukowska-1. html.

21. Ferguson-Smith and Ferris, "Gender Verification in Sport."

22. M. L. Barr and E. G. Bertram, "A Morphological Distinction between Neurones of the Male and Female, and the Behaviour of the Nucleolar Satellite during Accelerated Nucleoprotein Synthesis," *Nature* 163, no. 4148 (1949): 676–77.

23. Murray L. Barr, "Cytological Tests of Sex" [letter to the editor], *Lancet* 267, no. 6906 (1956): 47.

24. "Ewa Klobukowska."

25. Pieper, *Sex Testing*, 56.

26. Ibid., 74.

27. Edith Thys Morgan, "Erik Schinegger: Forgotten World Champion," *Skiing History*, August 9, 2017, https://www.skiinghistory.org/news/erik-schinegger-forgotten-world-champion.

28. John Fry, "Women's Champ Was a Man!" *Ski*, February 15, 2001, https://www.skimag.com/uncategorized/womens-champ-was-a-man.

29. Erik Schinegger and Marco Schenz, *Mein Sieg über mich: Der Mann, der Weltmeisterin wurde* (München: Herbig, 1988).

30. Fry, "Women's Champ Was a Man!"

31. Morgan, "Erik Schinegger."

32. Fry, "Women's Champ Was a Man!"

33. Schinegger, *Mein Sieg über mich*.

34. Fry, "Women's Champ Was a Man!"

35. Morgan, "Erik Schinegger."

36. Fry, "Women's Champ Was a Man!"

37. Morgan, "Erik Schinegger."

38. Fry, "Women's Champ Was a Man!"

39. Morgan, "Erik Schinegger."

40. Fry, "Women's Champ Was a Man!"

41. Pieper, *Sex Testing*, 78.

42. Ibid., 86.

43. Pat Hickey, "Montreal Olympics: East German Swim Cheats Cost Canadians Golden Moment," *Montreal Gazette*, July 18, 2016, https://montrealgazette.com/sports/montreal-olympics-east-german-swim-cheats-cost-canadians-golden-moment.

44. "Montreal 1976 Medal Table," IOC website, https://www.olympic.org/montreal-1976.

45. Ferguson-Smith and Ferris, "Gender Verification in Sport."

5. TRANSGENDER 101

1. Katrina Karkazis has used the first six of these categories, while Josh Safer claims that gender identity is fixed at birth and hence 100 percent biological. Thus, my seven categories are a combination of the collective wisdom of Karkazis and Safer.

2. Richard J. Auchus, "Endocrinology and Women's Sport: The Diagnosis Matters," *Law and Contemporary Problems* 80, no 4 (2017): 132.

3. Lauren Friedman, "Millennials and Gender Fluidity—What Smart Brands Are Doing and Why," *Forbes*, November 28, 2017, https://www.forbes.com/sites/laurenfriedman/2017/11/28/millennials-and-gender-fluidity-what-smart-brands-are-doing-and-why/#785ff425436d.

4. Francine Russo, "Is There Something Unique about the Transgender Brain?" *Scientific American*, January 1, 2016, https://www.scientificamerican.com/article/is-there-something-unique-about-the-transgender-brain/.

5. Joshua Safer and Vin Tangpricha, "Out of the Shadows: It Is Time to Mainstream Treatment for Transgender Patients," *Endocrine Practice* 14, no. 2 (2008): 248–50, https://www.ncbi.nlm.nih.gov/pmc/articles/PMC3105355/.

6. "Hijras—The Third Sex," *I Am Woman, Hear Me Roar* (blog), June 8, 2007, https://nabihameher.wordpress.com/2007/06/08/hijras-—-the-third-sex/.

7. Preeti Sharma, "Historical Background and Legal Status of Third Gender in Indian Society," *International Journal of Research in Economics & Social Sciences* 2, no. 12 (2012): 64–71, https://web.archive.org/web/20140203031618/http:/www.euroasiapub.org/IJRESS/dec2012/7.pdf.

8. Takeshi Ishikawa, "Hijras of India," http://india-hijras.com/ishikawa/hijras/index.html.

9. "Hijras—The Third Sex."

10. Liz Riley, "The Participation of Trans Athletes in Sport—A Transformation in Approach?" LawInSport, February 5, 2016, https://www.lawinsport.com/topics/articles/item/the-participation-of-trans-athletes-in-sport-a-transformation-in-approach.

11. "Fa'afafine—Samoan Boys Brought Up as Girls," *Charting the Pacific*, ABC Radio Australia, http://www.abc.net.au/ra/pacific/people/hazy.htm.

12. Peter Jackson, "Performative Genders, Perverse Desires: A Bio-History of Thailand's Same-Sex and Transgender Cultures," *Intersections: Gender, History and Culture in the Asian Context* 9 (August 2003), sec. 10, http://intersections.anu.edu.au/issue9/jackson.html.

13. Richard Totman, *The Third Sex: Kathoey—Thailand's Ladyboys* (London: Souvenir Press, 2003), 57.

14. Jackson, "Performative Genders, Perverse Desires," sec. 7, 36, 88.

15. Madison Park and Kiki Dhitavat, "Thailand's New Constitution Could Soon Recognize Third Gender," CNN, January 16, 2015, http://edition.cnn.com/2015/01/16/world/third-gender-thailand/index.html. It is not yet clear what rights the 2017 Thai constitution affords to nonbinary individuals.

16. Sam Winter, "Thai Transgenders in Focus: Demographics, Transitions and Identities," *International Journal of Transgenderism* 9, no. 1 (2006): 15–27, doi: 10.1300/J485v09n01_03.

17. John Leland, "A Spirit of Belonging, Inside and Out," *New York Times*, October 8, 2006, https://www.nytimes.com/2006/10/08/fashion/08SPIRIT.html.

18. Walter W. Williams, "The Two-Spirit People of Indigenous North America," First People, https://www.firstpeople.us/articles/the-two-spirit-people-of-indigenous-north-americans.html.

19. Mary Annette Pember, "'Two Spirit' Tradition Far from Ubiquitous among Tribes," *Rewire*, October 13, 2016, https://rewire.news/article/2016/10/13/two-spirit-tradition-far-ubiquitous-among-tribes/.

20. Williams, "The Two-Spirit People of Indigenous North America."

21. Leland, "A Spirit of Belonging."

22. Andrew R. Flores, Jody L. Herman, Gary J. Gates, and Taylor N. T. Brown, *How Many Adults in the US Identify as Transgender?* Williams Institute, June 2016, http://williamsinstitute.law.ucla.edu/wp-content/uploads/How-Many-Adults-Identify-as-Transgender-in-the-United-States.pdf.

23. Steve Hendrix, "A History Lesson for Trump: Transgender Soldiers Served in the Civil War," *Washington Post*, August 25, 2017, https://www.washingtonpost.com/news/retropolis/wp/2017/07/26/a-history-lesson-for-trump-transgender-soldiers-served-in-the-civil-war.

24. Ibid.

25. Jean R. Friedman, "Albert Cashier's Secret," *New York Times*, January 28, 2014, https://opinionator.blogs.nytimes.com/2014/01/28/albert-cashiers-secret/.

26. Linda Paul, "In Civil War, Woman Fought Like a Man for Freedom," *Weekend Edition Sunday*, NPR, May 24, 2009, https://www.npr.org/templates/story/story.php?storyId=104452266.

27. Jean E. Howard, "Crossdressing, the Theatre, and Gender Struggle in Early Modern England," *Shakespeare Quarterly* 39, no. 4 (winter 1988): 418–40.

28. "Lili Elbe," Biography, https://www.biography.com/people/lili-elbe-090815.

29. "Lili Elbe: The Transgender Artist behind The Danish Girl," *The Week*, September 28, 2015, https://www.theweek.co.uk/65324/lili-elbe-the-transgender-artist-behind-the-danish-girl.

30. "Lili Elbe," Biography.

31. Christine Jorgensen, *Christine Joregensen: A Personal Autobiography* (New York: Paul S. Eriksson, 1967), 11.

32. "Christine Jorgensen," Biography, https://www.biography.com/people/christine-jorgensen-262758.

33. Jorgensen, *A Personal Autobiography*, 87.

34. "Christine Jorgensen," Biography.

35. Jorgensen, *A Personal Autobiography*, 120, 126.

36. "Christine Jorgensen," Biography.

37. Jorgensen, *A Personal Autobiography*, 250.

38. Jorgensen, A Personal Autobiography, preface.

39. Jorgensen, *A Personal Autobiography*, 292.

40. "Christine Jorgensen," Biography.

41. Peter Blecha, "Tipton, Billy (1914–1989): Spokane's Secretive Jazzman," HistoryLink, September 17, 2005, http://www.historylink.org/File/7456.

42. Diane Wood Middlebrook, *Suits Me: The Double Life of Billy Tipton*. (Boston: Houghton Miffin, 1998), https://archive.nytimes.com/www.nytimes.com/books/first/m/middlebrook-suits.html.

43. Blecha, "Tipton, Billy (1914–1989)"

44. Middlebrook, *Suits Me*.

6. EARLY TRANSGENDER ATHLETES

1. Renée Richards with John Ames, *Second Serve* (New York: Stein and Day, 1983), 30.

2. Eric Drath, director, *Renée*. ESPN Films, 2011.

3. Richards with Ames, *Second Serve*, 55, 74.

4. Drath, *Renée*.

5. Richards with Ames, *Second Serve*, 305.

6. Ibid., 319, 342.

7. Roger Abrams, *Sports Justice: The Law and the Business of Sports* (Hanover, NH: University Press of New England, 2010).

8. Steve Tignor, "40 Years Later, Renée Richards' Breakthrough Is as Important as Ever," *Tennis*, September 20, 2017, http://www.tennis.com/pro-game/2017/07/40-years-later-renee-richards-breakthrough-important-ever/68064/.

9. Emily Bazelon, "Cross-Court Winner," *Slate*, October 25, 2012, https://slate.com/culture/2012/10/jewish-jocks-and-renee-richards-the-life-of-the-transsexual-tennis-legend.html.

10. Richards with Ames, *Second Serve*, 344.

11. Caitlyn Jenner with Buzz Bissinger, *The Secrets of My Life* (New York: Grand Central, 2017), 51.

12. "The Decathlon," International Association of Athletics Federation website, https://www.iaaf.org/disciplines/combined-events/decathlon.

13. Bruce Jenner and Philip Finch, *Decathlon Challenge. Bruce Jenner's Story* (Englewood Cliffs, NJ: Prentice-Hall, 1977), 42, 46.

14. "Massacre begins at Munich Olympics," History, November 16, 2009, https://www.history.com/this-day-in-history/massacre-begins-at-munich-olympics.

15. Jenner and Finch, *Decathlon Challenge*, 72.

16. Jenner with Bissinger, *The Secrets of My Life*, 81.

17. Jenner and Finch, *Decathlon Challenge*, 77.

18. Phone interview with Caitlyn Jenner, 2017.

19. Ibid.

20. Jenner and Finch, *Decathlon Challenge*, 87.

21. Ibid., 130.

22. Jenner with Bissinger, *The Secrets of My Life*, 249.

23. Jenner and Finch, *Decathlon Challenge*, 183.

24. Emily Yahr, "The Forgotten History of Bruce Jenner: How the 1980s All-American Hero Ended up Here," *Washington Post*, February 4, 2015, https://www.washingtonpost.com/lifestyle/style/the-forgotten-history-of-bruce-jenner-how-the-1970s-all-american-hero-ended-up-here/2015/02/04/3c594ae0-abdf-11e4-ad71–7b9eba0f87d6_story.html.

25. Jenner with Bissinger, *The Secrets of My Life*, 34.

26. Phone interview with Caitlyn Jenner, 2017.

27. Jeremy Wilson, "Exclusive Philippa York Interview—A Life in Three Parts: From Cycling Great Robert Millar to Finding Her True Self," *Telegraph* (UK), April 10, 2018, https://www.telegraph.co.uk/cycling/2018/04/10/exclusive-philippa-york-interview-life-three-parts-cycling/.

28. William Fotheringham, "Philippa York: 'I've Known I Was Different Since I Was a Five-Year-Old," *Guardian* (UK), July 6, 2017, https://www.theguardian.com/sport/2017/jul/06/philippa-york-gender-transition-cyclist-robert-millar.

29. Richard Moore, *In Search of Robert Millar: Unravelling the Mystery Surrounding Britain's Most Successful Tour de France Cyclist* (New York: HarperCollins, 2008).

30. "The All-Time List of British Male Pro Road Cyclists, *Cycling Weekly*, November 28, 2018, https://www.cyclingweekly.com/news/racing/british-racing/cycling-weeklys-all-time-ranking-of-british-pro-riders-70858.

31. "The Enigma Machine," *Herald* (Scotland), May 25, 2007, https://www.heraldscotland.com/news/12778014. the-enigma-machine/.

32. Wilson, "Exclusive Philippa York Interview."

33. Fotherington, "Philippa York."

34. Jenner with Bissinger, *The Secrets of My Life*, 182.

35. Phone interview with Caitlyn Jenner, 2017.

36. Bazelon, "Cross-Court Winner."

7. NOT THE END OF SEX TESTING

1. A. de la Chapelle, "The Use and Misuse of Sex Chromatin Screening for 'Gender Identification' of Female Athletes," *Journal of the American Medical Association* 256, no. 14 (1986): 1920–23, https://www.ncbi.nlm.nih.gov/pubmed/3761498.

2. M. J. Martínez-Patiño, "Personal Account: A Woman Tried and Tested," *Lancet* 366 (2005 supp.): 38–39, https://www.ncbi.nlm.nih.gov/pubmed/16360746.

3. Barbara L. Drinkwater, *Women in Sport* (Malden, MA: Blackwell, 2000): 186.

4. Tibin Kaithappillil Baby, Priya Thomas, Jayanthi Palani, et al., "Sex Determination Efficacy of Papanicolaou and Acriflavine Schiff Stains in Buccal Smears," *Journal of Forensic Dental Science* 9, no. 1 (2017): 46, http://www.jfds.org/article.asp? issn=0975–1475; year=2017; volume=9; issue=1; spage=46; epage=46; aulast=Baby.

5. Barr Body Staining, https://www.slideshare.net/gurya87/barr-body-staining.

6. Lindsay Parks Pieper, *Sex Testing: Gender Policing in Women's Sports* (Urbana: University of Illinois Press, 2016): 134.

7. María José Martínez-Patiño, International Association of Athletics Federations website, https://www.iaaf.org/athletes/spain/maria-jose-martinez-patino-268639.

8. Martínez-Patiño, "Personal Account."

9. Pieper, *Sex Testing*, 142.

10. Arne Ljungqvist and Goran Lager, *Doping's Nemesis* (Cheltenham, UK: Sports Books, 2011), 24, 30.

11. Ibid., 40.

12. Pieper, *Sex Testing*, 146.

13. Ibid., 149.
14. Ibid., 151.
15. P. Fénichel, F. Paris, P. Philibert, et al., "Molecular Diagnosis of 5 alpha-Reductase Deficiency in 4 Elite Young Female Athletes through Hormonal Screening for Hyperandrogenism," *Journal of Clinical Endocrinology & Metabolism* 98, no. 6 (2013): E1055–59, https://www.ncbi.nlm.nih.gov/pubmed/23633205.
16. "Androgen Insensitivity Syndrome," Intersex Society of North America, http://www.isna.org/faq/conditions/ais.
17. Vanessa Heggie, "Testing Sex and Gender in Sports; Reinventing, Reimagining and Reconstructing Histories," *Endeavour* 34, no 4 (2010): 157–63, https://www.sciencedirect.com/science/article/pii/S0160932710000670.
18. Pieper, *Sex Testing*, 152.
19. Ibid., 156.
20. Ibid., 165.
21. L. J. Elsas, R. Hayes, and K. Muralidharan, "Gender Verification at the Centennial Olympic Games," *Journal of the Medical Association of Georgia* 86 (1997): 50–54. https://www.ncbi.nlm.nih.gov/pubmed/9029887.
22. L. J. Elsas, A. Ljungqvist, M. A. Ferguson-Smith, et al., "Gender Verification of Female Athletes," *Genetics in Medicine* 2, no. 4 (2000): 249–54, https://www.ncbi.nlm.nih.gov/pubmed/11252710.
23. C. M. Wiepjes, N. M. Nota, C. J. M. de Blok, et al., "The Amsterdam Cohort of Gender Dysphoria Study (1972–2015): Trends in Prevalence, Treatment, and Regrets," *Journal of Sexual Medicine* 15, no. 4 (2018): 582–90, doi: 10.1016/j.jsxm.2018.01.016. https://www.ncbi.nlm.nih.gov/pubmed/29463477.
24. John Easterbrook, "Transexual Tees Off at Pro Event," CBS News, March 4, 2004. https://www.cbsnews.com/news/transexual-tees-off-at-pro-event/.
25. Will Hodgkinson, "I Don't Think about Gender. I Think about Winning," *Guardian* (UK), August 18, 2005, https://www.theguardian.com/film/2005/aug/19/2.
26. "Nong Thoom," *LGBT Project Wiki*, http://lgbt.wikia.com/wiki/Nong_Thoom.
27. Jahn Westbrook, "Beautiful Boxer," *Transgender Universe*, March 11, 2016, http://archive.transgenderuniverse.com/2016/03/11/beautiful-boxer/.
28. Joseph Kahn, "Bangkok Journal; Was That a Lady I Saw You Boxing?" *New York Times*, April 4, 1998, https://www.nytimes.com/1998/04/04/world/bangkok-journal-was-that-a-lady-i-saw-you-boxing.html.
29. Somporn Suphop, "Sex Change Boxer Is Back in the Ring," *The Nation*, Feb 22, 2006, http://www.nationmultimedia.com/2006/02/22/headlines/headlines_20001353.php.

30. Jon Billman, "Michelle Raises Hell," *Outside*, April 1, 2004, https://www.outsideonline.com/1822371/michelle-raises-hell.

31. "Who Is Michelle Dumaresq? Why Is She So Important?" *Pedal*, http://pedalmag.com/who-is-michelle-dumaresq-why-is-she-so-important/.

32. Michelle Dumaresq, "Michelle's Adventures," letter to Lynn Conway, http://ai.eecs.umich.edu/people/conway/TSsuccesses/MichelleDumaresq.html.

33. Vicki Hall, "Canada's Michelle Dumaresq Upbeat about IOC Change for Transgender Athletes Heading into Rio 2016 Olympics," *National Post*, January 26, 2016, https://nationalpost.com/sports/olympics/canadas-michelle-dumaresq-upbeat-about-ioc-change-for-transgender-athletes-heading-into-rio-2016-olympics.

34. International Olympic Committee, "Statement of the Stockholm Consensus on Sex Reassignment in Sports," November 12, 2003, https://stillmed.olympic.org/Documents/Reports/EN/en_report_905. pdf.

35. Laura Valkovic, "Transgender Athletes in the Winter Olympics," *Liberty Nation*, February 10, 2018, https://www.libertynation.com/transgender-athletes-winter-olympics/.

8. JOANNA'S STORY

1. Frank Deford, "Boston's Savior Bobby Orr Commands Respect, High Price at 18," *Sports Illustrated*, October 17, 1966, https://www.si.com/nhl/2015/06/24/si-vault-feature-bobby-orr-arrives-at-18-to-save-boston-bruins-frank-deford-1966.

2. British statistician Howard Grubb would do most of the early work on the model. H. J. Grubb, "Models for Comparing Athletic Performances," *Statistician* 47 (1998): 509–21. There is an online calculator on his website: http://www.howardgrubb.co.uk/athletics/wmalookup06.html. American mathematician Alan Jones has done much of the more recent work: https://www.runscore.com/Alan/AgeGrade.html.

9. TRANSGENDER AND INTERSEX ATHLETES, 2004–2009

1. Adam Love, Seung-Yup Lim, and Joy T. DeSensi, "Mianne Bagger: A Transitioned Woman's Efforts for Inclusion in Professional Golf," *Women in Sport and Physical Activity Journal* 18, no. 1 (2009): 68–77.

2. "Transgender Golfer Still Faces Barriers," ABC News, July 27, 2005, https://abcnews.go.com/Primetime/Health/story?id=982855&page=1.

3. "Nagl Wins Q-School as Bagger Makes History," November 3, 2004, Ladies European Tour. https://ladieseuropeantour.com/nagl-wins-q-school-as-bagger-makes-history/?cn-reloaded=1.

4. "Ladies European Tour Profile," Ladies European Tour, archived from the original on January 6, 2014, http://www.ladieseuropeantour.com/player_profile.php?id=50058.

5. ALPG Profile," ALPGA Tour, archived from the original on January 6, 2014, http://www.alpg.com.au/default.aspx?s=playerprofile&id=1299.

6. Cyd Zeigler, "30 LGBTQ athletes who showed 'Stonewall Spirt': Mianne Bagger," *Outsports*, June 8, 2019, https://www.outsports.com/2019/6/8/18653434/trans-athlete-mianne-bagger-stonewall-spirit-lgbtq-athlete.

7. Daryl Adair, "Athlete Health and Fair Play: Kristen Worley Case Puts Women's Sport Policy in the Dock," *The Conversation*, July 20, 2017, http://theconversation.com/athlete-health-and-fair-play-kristen-worley-case-puts-womens-sport-policy-in-the-dock-81361.

8. Anne McIlroy, "I'm a Woman on the Move," *Globe and Mail*, September 8, 2007, https://www.theglobeandmail.com/sports/im-a-woman-on-the-move/article1081665/.

9. Teddy Cutler, "Meet the Canadian Athlete Changing Sports' Attitude to Gender," *Newsweek*, February 5, 2016, https://www.newsweek.com/meet-canadian-athlete-changing-sports-attitudes-gender-423405.

10. Cyd Zeigler, "Trans Athlete Wins Policy Changes with Canada Cycling and Others," *Outsports*, August 1, 2017, https://www.outsports.com/2017/8/1/16081592/cycling-canada-trans-athlete-kristen-worley.

11. Samantha Sunrayne, "Profile of a Man: Balian Buschbaum," July 15, 2013, https://samanthasunrayne.wordpress.com/2013/07/15/profile-of-a-man-balian-buschbaum/.

12. "Yvonne Buschbaum Athlete Profile," International Association of Athletics Federations website, https://www.iaaf.org/athletes/germany/yvonne-buschbaum-134467.

13. "Sky's No Limit for Gender-Changed Vaulter," DW, November 23, 2008, https://www.dw.com/en/skys-no-limit-for-gender-changed-vaulter/a-3805970.

14. Monica Roberts, "Balian Buschbaum's New Life," *TransGriot* (blog), February 26, 2009, https://transgriot.blogspot.com/2009/02/balian-buschbaums-new-life.html.

15. A. H. Bittles, "Consanguineous Marriage and Childhood Health," *Developmental Medicine & Child Neurology* 45 (2003): 571–76, http://onlinelibrary.wiley.com/doi/10.1111/j.1469–8749.2003.tb00959.x/epdf/

16. Lindsay Parks Pieper, *Sex Testing: Gender Policing in Women's Sports* (Urbana: University of Illinois Press, 2016), 180.

17. P. Fénichel, F. Paris, P. Philibert, et al., "Molecular Diagnosis of 5 alpha-Reductase Deficiency in 4 Elite Young Female Athletes through Hormonal Screening for Hyperandrogenism," *Journal of Clinical Endocrinology & Metabolism* 98, no. 6 (2013): E1055–59, https://www.ncbi.nlm.nih.gov/pubmed/23633205.

18. Samantha Shapiro, "Caught in the Middle," *ESPN The Magazine*, August 1, 2005, http://www.espn.com/olympics/story/_/id/8192977/failed-gender-test-forces-olympian-redefine-athletic-career-espn-magazine.

19. Sunrita Sen, "AFI to Investigate Santhi Case, Uneven Diet Cited as Possible Reason," *Raw Story*, December 20, 2006, https://www.rawstory.com/news/2006/AFI_to_investigate_Santhi_case_unev_12202006. html.

20. "The Sad Story of Santhi Soundarajan," *Times of India*, January 9, 2007, https://web.archive.org/web/20090112191344/http:/timesofindia.indiatimes.com/articleshow/1109135.cms.

21. Shapiro, "Caught in the Middle."

22. "After Decade Long Struggle, TN Athlete Santhi Soundarajam Given Permanent Post of Athletic Coach," *The News Minute*, October 17, 2016, https://www.thenewsminute.com/article/after-decade-long-struggle-tn-athlete-santhi-soundarajan-given-permanent-post-athletic-coach.

23. "From Police Custody to Podium, Pinki Primed for Higher Glory," *One India*, August 28, 2006, https://www.oneindia.com/2006/08/27/from-police-custody-to-podium-pinki-primed-for-higher-glory-1156748179.html.

24. "Athletics at the 2006 Commonwealth Games," *Wikipedia*, https://en.m.wikipedia.org/wiki/Athletics_at_the_2006_Commonwealth_Games.

25. Ibid.

26. "Jyotirmoyee Sikdar's Husband Asked Me to Frame Pinki Pramanik: Ex-partner," *Times of India*, July 14, 2012, https://timesofindia.indiatimes.com/city/kolkata/Jyotirmoyee-Sikdars-husband-asked-me-to-frame-Pinki-Pramanik-Ex-partner/articleshow/14871486.cms.

27. "Gold Medallist Pinki Pramanik Accused of Being Male, Held for 'Rape,'" Zee News, June 14, 2012, http://zeenews.india.com/sports/others/gold-medallist-pinki-pramanik-accused-of-being-male-held-for-rape_743839.html.

28. "Tests Show Athlete Pinki Pramanik, Charged with Rape, Is Male," NDTV Sports, November 12, 2012, https://sports.ndtv.com/athletics/tests-show-athlete-pinki-pramanik-charged-with-rape-is-male-1545293.

29. "Jyotirmoyee Sikdar's Husband Asked Me to Frame Pinki Pramanik."

10. CASTER SEMENYA

1. David Epstein, "One Year Out: Semenya Remains a Mystery for London Olympics," *Sports Illustrated*, July 27, 2011, https://www.si.com/more-sports/2011/07/27/semenya.

2. Provide Project, *A Profile of the Limpopo Province: Demographics, Poverty, Inequality and Unemployment*, August 2005, http://ageconsearch.umn.edu/bitstream/15607/1/bp050009.pdf.

3. Y. Ganie, C. Aldous, Y. Balakrishna, and R. Wiersma, "Disorders of Sex Development in Children in KwaZulu-Natal Durban South Africa: 20-year Experience in a Tertiary Centre," *Journal of Pediatric Endocrinology & Metabolism* 30, no. 1 (2017), 11–18, https://www.ncbi.nlm.nih.gov/pubmed/27754965.

4. Ariel Levy, "Either/Or: Sports, Sex, and the Case of Caster Semenya," *New Yorker*, November 30, 2008, https://www.newyorker.com/magazine/2009/11/30/eitheror.

5. "Caster Semenya Athlete Profile," International Association of Athletics Federations website, https://www.iaaf.org/athletes/south-africa/caster-semenya-242560.

6. Antoinette Muller, "Caster Semenya Never Signed Informed Consent for Sex Tests, Says Ex-ASA Board Member," *Daily Maverick*, February 12, 2018, https://www.dailymaverick.co.za/article/2018–02–12-caster-semenya-never-signed-informed-consent-for-sex-tests-says-ex-asa-board-member/#.WoYpCqjwbIV.

7. Serena Chaudhry, "South Africa Athletics Chief Admits Lying about Semenya Tests," Reuters, September 19, 2009, https://www.reuters.com/article/us-safrica-semenya-idUSTRE58I0N320090919.

8. Epstein, "One Year Out."

9. Simon Hart, "Caster Semenya 'Is a Hermaphrodite,' Tests Show," *Telegraph* (UK), September 11, 2009, https://www.telegraph.co.uk/sport/othersports/athletics/6170229/Caster-Semenya-is-a-hermaphrodite-tests-show.html.

10. "Athletics Boss Chuene Fired," *Mail & Guardian* (South Africa), February 18, 2011, https://mg.co.za/article/2011–02–18-athletics-boss-chuene-fired/.

11. Anna Kessel, "Caster Semenya to Keep Gold and Decide Own Future, say South Africans," *Guardian* (UK), November 20, 2009, https://www.theguardian.com/sport/2009/nov/20/caster-semenya-gold-medal-gender.

12. Court of Arbitration for Sport, Arbitral Award, June 19, 2019, Section 78, https://www.tas-cas.org/fileadmin/user_upload/CAS_Award_-_redacted_-_Semenya_ASA_IAAF.pdf.

13. M. Morris, "Caster Semenya Wins in Return to Track," *Newser*, July 15, 2010, http://www.newser.com/story/95683/caster-semenya-wins-in-return-to-track.html.

14. "Amended IAAF Rules and New & Updated IAAF Regulations—in Force as of 1 May 2011," IAAF News, May 1, 2011, https://www.iaaf.org/news/iaaf-news/amended-iaaf-rules-and-new-updated-iaaf-regul.

15. Given that the IAAF and the IOC were recommending surgery at the time for intersex athletes, then surely most pre-Semenya intersex athletes wound up having their testes removed. That choice made a very large difference between the career arc of athletes such as the aforementioned Patricia and the career arc of Semenya. Without much doubt, other intersex athletes and their coaches noticed the difference between Semenya's performance after her intervention and the performance of other intersex athletes after surgery. I imagine that few intersex athletes chose surgery much later than around 2012.

16. "Caster Semenya Athlete Profile."

17. The video of the race can be seen at https://www.youtube.com/watch?v=RumxE521dso.

18. International Olympic Committee, "IOC Regulations on Female Hyperandrogenism, Games of the XXX Olympiad in London, 2012," June 22, 2012, https://stillmed.olympic.org/Documents/Commissions_PDFfiles/Medical_commission/2012–06–22-IOC-Regulations-on-Female-Hyperandrogenism-eng.pdf.

19. K. Karkazis, R. Jordan-Young, G. Davis, and S. Camporesi, "Out of bounds? A Critique of the New Policies on Hyperandrogenism in Elite Female Athletes," *American Journal of Bioethics* 12, no. 7 (2012): 3–16, https://www.ncbi.nlm.nih.gov/pubmed/22694023.

20. Toby Selander and Jane Flanagan, "London 2012 Olympics: Caster Semenya Aims for Games Gold in World Record Time after Gender Furore," *Telegraph* (UK), July 14, 2012, https://www.telegraph.co.uk/sport/olympics/athletics/9400529/London-2012-Olympics-Caster-Semenya-aims-for-Games-gold-in-world-record-time-after-gender-furore.html.

21. Amanda Lulham, "Caster Semenya Chosen as South African Flag Bearer for London Olympics," news.com.au, July 19, 2012, https://www.news.com.au/sport/caster-semenya-chosen-as-south-african-flag-bearer-for-london-olympics/news-story/d1e4c6867ce5275e5f68d02b9cbe8d04.

22. The video is here: https://www.youtube.com/watch?v=vHU90FSwmEs.

23. Ross Tucker, "London 2012: Women's 800m // Women's 800m Perplexity, Analyzing Semenya's Race," The Science of Sport, August 11, 2012, https://sportsscientists.com/2012/08/womens-800m-analysing-semenya-other-insights.

24. "Caster Semenya Athlete Profile."

25. The video is also on YouTube. https://www.youtube.com/watch?v=pCbtD0Gm40Q&feature=youtu.be.

26. “Caster Semenya Athlete Profile.”

27. “Caster’s Love Story with Her Wife: She Thought I Was a Boy,” *Times Live*, August 8, 2017, https://www.timeslive.co.za/tshisa-live/tshisa-live/2017–08–08-casters-love-story-with-her-wife-she-thought-i-was-a-boy/.

28. “Caster Semenya Marries Girlfriend in Traditional Ceremony,” Sport24, December 7, 2015, https://www.sport24.co.za/OtherSport/Athletics/South-Africa/caster-semenya-marries-girlfriend-in-tradition-ceremony-20151207.

11. TRANSGENDER AND INTERSEX ATHLETES, 2009–2014

1. Lauren Johnston, “German Tennis Player Sarah Gronert Embroiled in Gender Controversy,” *Daily News*, March 20, 2009, http://www.nydailynews.com/sports/german-tennis-player-sarah-gronert-embroiled-gender-controversy-article-1.370527.

2. “Androgen Insensitivity Syndrome,” Intersex Society of North America, http://www.isna.org/faq/conditions/ais.

3. Mark Hodgkinson, “Sarah Gronert Passes Gender Test to Play on Women’s Circuit,” *Telegraph* (UK), March 27, 2009, https://www.telegraph.co.uk/sport/tennis/wtatour/5063065/Sarah-Gronert-passes-gender-test-to-play-on-womens-circuit.html.

4. “Sarah Gronert,” ITF World Tennis Tour, http://www.itftennis.com/procircuit/players/player/profile.aspx?playerid=100121155.

5. Johnston, “German Tennis Player Sarah Gronert Embroiled in Gender Controversy.”

6. “Sarah Gronert,” ITF World Tennis Tour.

7. Elliot Pohnl, “Lana Lawless: The Story Behind Transgender Trying to Play on LPGA Tour,” Bleacher Report, October 13, 2010, https://bleacherreport.com/articles/490657-lana-lawless-the-story-behind-transgender-trying-to-play-on-lpga-tour#slide2.

8. L. Gooren and M. Bunck, “Transsexuals and Competitive Sports,” *European Journal of Endocrinology* 151, no. 4 (2004): 425–29, https://www.ncbi.nlm.nih.gov/pubmed/15476439.

9. “Fore! Transgender Golfers Get into Catfight over ‘Female at Birth’ Rules,” *Daily Mail* (UK), February 8, 2011, https://www.dailymail.co.uk/news/article-1354617/Transsexual-golfer-Mianne-Bagger-blasts-Lana-Lawless-female-birth-rules.html.

10. Katie Thomas, "Transgender Woman Sues L.P.G.A. over Policy," *New York Times*, October 12, 2010, https://www.nytimes.com/2010/10/13/sports/golf/131awsuit.html.

11. Antonio Gonzalez, "Lana Lawless Gets Chance to Compete on LPGA Tour with Gender Requirement Change," *Christian Science Monitor*, December 2, 2010, https://www.csmonitor.com/USA/Sports/2010/1202/Lana-Lawless-gets-chance-to-compete-on-LPGA-Tour-with-gender-requirement-change.

12. Cyd Zeigler, "Lana Lawless Wins Right to Play on LPGA Tour," *Outsports*, August 24, 2011, https://www.outsports.com/2011/8/24/4051722/moment-42-lana-lawless-wins-right-to-play-on-lpga-tour.

13. Cyd Zeigler, "Kye Allums: First Transgender Man Playing NCAA Women's Basketball," *Outsports*, November 1, 2010, https://www.outsports.com/out-gay-athletes/2013/2/21/4015388/kye-allums-first-transgender-man-playing-ncaa-womens-basketball.

14. Erik Brady, "Transgender Basketball Player Kye Allums of George Washington University Women's Team Talks about His Decision to Come Out," *USA Today*, November 3, 2010, https://usatoday30.usatoday.com/sports/college/womensbasketball/atlantic10/2010-11-03-kye-allums-george-washington-transgender_N.htm.

15. Stephen A. Maglott, "Kye Allums," The Ubuntu Biography Project, October 23, 2017, https: //ubuntubiographyproject.com/2017/10/23/kye-allums/.

16. Katy Stienmetz, "Meet the First Openly Transgender NCAA Division I Athlete," *Time*, October 28, 2014, http://time.com/3537849/meet-the-first-openly-transgender-ncaa-athlete/.

17. Zeigler, "Kye Allums."

18. Katie Thomas, "Transgender Man Is on Women's Team," *New York Times*, November 2, 2010, https://www.nytimes.com/2010/11/02/sports/ncaabasketball/02gender.html.

19. "GW's Kye Allums Reflects on Season," ESPN, March 28, 2011, http://www.espn.com/ncw/news/story?id=6268948.

20. Maglott, "Kye Allums."

21. "GW's Kye Allums Reflects on Season."

22. Pablo S. Torre and David Epstein, "The Transgender Athlete," *Sports Illustrated*, May 28, 2012, https://www.si.com/vault/2012/05/28/106195901/the-transgender-athlete.

23. Maglott, "Kye Allums."

24. Ibid.

25. "Keelin Godsey '06, Alumni Inductee," Bates College Athletics Scholar-Athlete Society, https://www.gobatesbobcats.com/scholar_athlete_society/2015_Keelin_Godsey.

26. "The OutField: Keelin Godsey Has a Hammer," *Rainbow Times*, January 15, 2011, https://www.therainbowtimesmass.com/the-outfield-keelin-godsey-has-a-hammer/.

27. "Keelin Godsey '06, Alumni Inductee."

28. Zolan V. Kanno-Youngs, "NCAA Members Slow to Adopt Transgender Athlete Guidelines," *USA Today*, August 3, 2015, https://www.usatoday.com/story/sports/college/2015/08/03/ncaa-transgender-athlete-guidelines-keelin-godsey-caitlyn-jenner/31055873/.

29. Torre and Epstein, "The Transgender Athlete."

30. Sam Borden, "Transgender Athlete Fails to Qualify," *New York Times*, June 21, 2012, https://london2012. blogs.nytimes.com/2012/06/21/transgender-athlete-fails-to-qualify.

31. "Keelin Godsey '06 Alumni Inductee."

32. Dani Heffernan, "Jaiyah Saelua, the First Transgender Athlete to Play in a World Cup Qualifier," GLAAD, April 30, 2014, https://www.glaad.org/blog/vice-news-interviews-jaiyah-saelua-first-transgender-athlete-play-world-cup-qualifier.

33. Pete Smith, "Jaiyah Saelua: If I Experience Transphobia I Just Tackle Harder," *Guardian* (UK), August 28, 2014, https://www.theguardian.com/football/2014/aug/29/jaiyah-saelua-transgender-footballer-interview.

34. Heffernan, "Jaiyah Saelua, the First Transgender Athlete."

35. Natasha Vargas-Cooper, "Soccer's Fa'afafine Superstar," *Out*, June 26, 2014, https://www.out.com/entertainment/sports/2014/06/26/soccer-trans-jayiah-saelua-american-samoa-third-gender-faafafine.

36. Ibid.

37. Heffernan, "Jaiyah Saelua, the First Transgender Athlete."

38. Ibid.

39. Smith, "Jaiyah Saelua: If I Experience Transphobia."

40. Mike Brett and Steve Jamison, directors, *Next Goal Wins*, Icon Productions, 2014, http://nextgoalwinsmovie.com/.

41. Smith, "Jaiyah Saelua: If I Experience Transphobia."

42. Nick Friend, "'I Wasn't Being Judged on How Well I Could Play': Jaiyah Saelua on Being the First Transgender International Footballer," *Sports Gazette*, November 24, 2017, https://sportsgazette.co.uk/i-wasnt-being-judged-on-how-well-i-could-play-jaiyah-saelua-on-life-as-the-first-transgender-international-footballer/.

43. Rosi Doviverata, "Transgender Athletes at the Pacific Games," *Fiji Sun*, July 18, 2019, https://fijisun.com.fj/2019/07/18/transgender-athletes-at-the-pacific-games/.

44. Eric Prisbell, "Transsexual Gabrielle Ludwig Returns to College Court," *USA Today*, December 4, 2012, https://www.usatoday.com/story/sports/ncaab/

2012/12/04/college-basketball-transgender-player-gabrielle-ludwig-robert-ludwig-mission-college/1744703/.

45. Melissa Isaacson, "Whole New Game for Gabrielle Ludwig," ESPNW, December 20, 2103, http://www.espn.com/espnw/athletes-life/article/10170842/espnw-gabrielle-ludwig-52-year-old-transgender-women-college-basketball-player-enjoying-best-year-life.

46. Cyd Zeigler, "Gabrielle Ludwig Plays Her First College Basketball Game as Trans Woman," *Outsports*, December 7, 2012, https://www.outsports.com/2012/12/7/4054058/gabrielle-ludwig-plays-her-first-college-basketball-game-as-trans.

47. "Gabrielle Ludwig, First Transgender Basketball Player to Play College Ball as Both Man and Woman, Keeps Head High Despite Threats," *Daily News*, December 14, 2012, https://www.nydailynews.com/news/national/transgender-college-hoops-player-head-high-article-1.1220117.

48. Ross Forman, "Transsexual Gabrielle Ludwig: A College Basketball Pioneer," *Windy City Times*, March 19, 2013, http://www.windycitymediagroup.com/lgbt/Transsexual-Gabrielle-Ludwig-A-college-basketball-pioneer/42006.html.

49. Mission College Athletics, Women's Basketball, http://www.missionsaints.com/sports/wbkb/index.

50. Isaacson, "Whole New Game for Gabrielle Ludwig."

51. In 2016 Gabbi and I shared the stage at a Stanford University talk, and I had the chance to speak with her and Coach Cafferata too. I am blessed to have had the opportunity to meet many of the transgender athletes in these pages, and they all have my respect. Few, however, have shown more courage than Gabbi, and she will always be a heroine to me.

12. THE POST-SEMENYA LANDSCAPE

1. Pablo S. Torre and David Epstein, "The Transgender Athlete," *Sports Illustrated*, May 28, 2012, https://www.si.com/vault/2012/05/28/106195901/the-transgender-athlete.

2. David Epstein Archives, *Sports Illustrated*, https://web.archive.org/web/20120503090511/http://sportsillustrated.cnn.com/writers/david_epstein/archive/index.html.

3. Pete's website is no longer online and there is no active link to the former content contained on it. During its time *Younger Legs for Older Runners* was extremely popular among American masters distance runners, and I was happy to contribute. I remember once being asked while running in California, "Aren't you the chick who writes for Pete's blog?"

4. "Who Are We?" The Science of Sport, https: //sportsscientists.com/who-are-we/.

5. Ross Tucker, "Caster Semenya," The Science of Sport, https://sportsscientists.com/thread/caster-semenya/.

6. David Epstein, *The Sports Gene: Inside the Science of Extraordinary Athletic Performance* (New York: Penguin, 2013), 72.

7. International Association of Athletics Federations, *IAAF Regulations Governing Eligibility of Athletes Who Have Undergone Sex Reassignment to Compete in Women's Competition*, https://docs.wixstatic.com/ugd/2bc3fc_476cfbfe00df48c3aa5322a29d5e11b2.pdf.

8. International Olympic Committee, "IOC Regulations on Female Hyperandrogenism, Games of the XXX Olympiad in London, 2012," June 22, 2012, https://stillmed.olympic.org/Documents/Commissions_PDFfiles/Medical_commission/2012-06-22-IOCRegulations-on-Female-Hyperandrogenism-eng.pdf.

9. "Rebecca Jordan-Young," Barnard College, Columbia University, https://barnard.edu/profiles/rebecca-jordan-young.

10. Rebecca M. Jordan-Young, *Brain Storm: The Flaws in the Science of Sex Differences* (Cambridge, MA: Harvard University Press, 2011).

11. Katrina Karkazis on herself, https://www.katrinakarkazis.com/.

12. Katrina Karkazis, *Fixing Sex: Intersex, Medical Authority, and Lived Experience* (Durham, NC: Duke University Press, 2008).

13. K. Karkazis, R. Jordan-Young, G. Davis, and S. Camporesi, "Out of Bounds? A Critique of the New Policies on Hyperandrogenism in Elite Female Athletes," *American Journal of Bioethics* 12, no. 7 (2012): 11–12, https://www.ncbi.nlm.nih.gov/pubmed/22694023.

14. Rebecca Jordan-Young and Katrina Karkazis, "You Say You're a Woman? That Should Be Enough," *New York Times*, June 17, 2012, http://www.nytimes.com/2012/06/18/sports/olympics/olympic-sex-verification-you-say-youre-a-woman-that-should-be-enough.html.

15. Karkazis, Jordan-Young, Davis, and Camporesi, "Out of Bounds?"

16. D. Handelsman, A. Hirschberg, and S. Bermon, "Circulating Testosterone as the Hormonal Basis of Sex Differences in Athletic Performance," *Endocrine Reviews* 39, no. 5 (2018): 803–29, https://doi.org/10.1210/er.2018–00020. https://www.ncbi.nlm.nih.gov/pubmed/30010735.

17. Raquel A. Russell. "Fond Farewells Pour in for Soon-to-Be-Retired Principal Bruce Kidd." University of Toronto Scarborough, May 14, 2018, https://utsc.utoronto.ca/news-events/university-news/fond-farewells-pour-soon-be-retired-principal-bruce-kidd.

18. Jos Truit, "The Olympic Games Are Obsessed with Policing Femininity," Feministing, June 16, 2012, http://feministing.com/2012/06/14/the-olympic-games-are-obsessed-with-policing-femininity/.

19. I had a nice electronic discussion with Bruce and am happy to quote him. He was childhood sports idol of mine, and any disagreement I might have with him will not diminish my admiration for the man.

20. David Epstein and Alice Dreger, "Testosterone in Sports," *New York Times*, April 20, 2014, https://www.nytimes.com/2014/04/21/opinion/testosterone-in-sports.html.

21. Alice Domurat Dreger, www.alicedreger.com.

22. Alice Dreger, *Galileo's Middle Finger: Heretics, Activists, and the Search for Justice in Science* (New York: Penguin, 2015), 27, 50.

23. "Sari van Anders," University of Michigan, http://www.personal.umich.edu/~smva/people.html.

24. I'm not certain if I caught van Anders during a slow week, but I was amazed by the rapid and voluminous responses I got to my queries during our conversation. At the time I was nobody, and I was impressed that she took the time and effort to respond to me in such detail.

25. Arne Ljungqvist and Goran Lager, *Doping's Nemesis* (Cheltenham, UK: Sports Books, 2011), 189.

26. Ibid., 185.

27. Martínez-Patiño would become an important figure in the soon-to-be-discussed 2015 trial.

28. "Dr. Stéphane Bermon, Specialist in Sports Medicine," Eubylon Health Care, http://www.eubylonhealthcare.com/de/spezialisten/st% C3% A9phane-bermon.

29. Stéphane Bermon, LinkedIn, https://www.linkedin.com/in/st% C3% A9phane-bermon-5b996211b.

30. S. Bermon, P. Y. Garnier, A. L. Hirschberg, et al., "Serum Androgen Levels in Elite Female Athletes," *Journal of Clinical Endocrinology and Metabolism* 99, no. 11 (2014): 4328–35.

31. Dr. Bermon was but one of several important people who were kind with their time in 2014. I agreed with him that the public seemed to think that high T was all that it took to get an athlete restricted, and I was grateful for his detailed description of the actual process.

32. P. Fénichel, F. Paris, P. Philibert, et al., "Molecular Diagnosis of 5 alpha-Reductase Deficiency in 4 Elite Young Female Athletes through Hormonal Screening for Hyperandrogenism," *Journal of Clinical Endocrinology & Metabolism* 98, no. 6 (2013): E1055–59. https://www.ncbi.nlm.nih.gov/pubmed/23633205.

33. N. Q. Ha, S. L. Dworkin, M. J. Martínez-Patiño MJ, et al., "Hurdling Over Sex? Sport, Science, and Equity," *Archives of Sexual Behavior* 43, no. 6 (2014): 1035–42, https://www.ncbi.nlm.nih.gov/pubmed/25085349.

34. R. Jordan-Young, P. Sonksen, and K. Karkazis, "Sex, Health, and Athletes," *British Medical Journal* 348 (2014): g2926, doi: 10.1136/bmj.g2926. https://www.bmj.com/content/348/bmj.g2926.

35. S. Bermon, "Androgens and Athletic Performance of Elite Female Athletes," *Current Opinion in Endocrinology Diabetes and Obesity* 24, no. 3 (2017): 246–51, https://www.ncbi.nlm.nih.gov/pubmed/28234801.

36. J. Harper, "Race Times for Transgender Athletes," *Journal of Sporting Cultures and Identities* 6, no. 1 (2015): 1–9, https://pdfs.semanticscholar.org/1e6a/bd2c1e03ba88e9ac8da94ea1d69ff3f4878a.pdf?_ga=2.254440527.659551599.1550520323-1192624875.1550520323.

13. DUTEE CHAND

1. Sujit Kumar Bisoyi, "Sprinter Dutee Chand Set to Realise Olympic Dream," *Times of India*, July 30, 2016, https://timesofindia.indiatimes.com/sports/rio-2016-olympics/india-in-olympics-2016/athletics/Sprinter-Dutee-Chand-set-to-realise-Olympic-dream/articleshow/53461278.cms.

2. Juliet Macur, "Fighting for the Body She Was Born With," *New York Times*, October 6, 2014, https://www.nytimes.com/2014/10/07/sports/sprinter-dutee-chand-fights-ban-over-her-testosterone-level.html.

3. "Dutee Chand," Encyclopedia of Orissa Sports, September 4, 2009, accessed September 9, 2013, http://orisports.com/PersonDetails.aspx?pId=MTgz.

4. "Rousing Welcome to Dutee Chand in KIIT," Odisha Live, September 13, 2013, https://web.archive.org/web/20131004213936/http://odishalive.tv/rousing-welcome-to-dutee-chand-in-kiit/.

5. Macur, "Fighting for the Body She Was Born With."

6. "Rousing Welcome to Dutee Chand in KIIT."

7. Bisoyi, "Sprinter Dutee Chand Set to Realise Olympic Dream."

8. Macur, "Fighting for the Body She Was Born With."

9. Benjamin Riley, "Commonwealth Games Sprinter's Disqualification Shows Australian Athletes Could Face 'Gender Testing,'" *Star Observer*, August 1, 2014, http://www.starobserver.com.au/news/national-news/commonwealth-games-sprinters-disqualification-shows-australian-athletes-could-face-gender-testing/126004.

10. Manu Joseph, "The Definition of a Female Athlete," *Hindustan Times*, July 21, 2014, https://www.hindustantimes.com/columns/the-definition-of-a-female-athlete/story-Si0bkalblOjjJJHP1HudRO.html.

11. "Embodied," Kindle, February 2, 2014, http://kindlemag.in/embodied/.

12. "Interview: Dr. Payoshni Mitra," *In Plainspeak*, September 1, 2014, http://www.tarshi.net/inplainspeak/interview-dr-payoshni-mitra/.

13. "Embodied."

14. Macur, "Fighting for the Body She Was Born With."

15. Ross Murray, Indian Advocates Appeal Sports Authorities to "Let Dutee Run!" GLAAD, September 11, 2014, https://www.glaad.org/blog/indian-advocates-appeal-sports-authorities-let-dutee-run.

16. Macur, "Fighting for the Body She Was Born With."

17. Katrina Karkaizs, *Fixing Sex: Intersex, Medical Authority, and Lived Experience* (Durham, NC: Duke University Press, 2008); see, for example, page 268.

18. Rudraneil Sengupta, "Why Dutee Chand Can Change Sports," *Live Mint*, November 24, 2014, https://www.livemint.com/Leisure/9P3jbOG2G0ppTVB7Xvwj0K/Why-Dutee-Chand-can-change-sports.html.

19. Macur, "Fighting for the Body She Was Born With."

20. Ibid.

21. AFP, "Athletics: Kenya Drops Two Sprinters from World Relay Championship Team over High Testosterone Levels," Scroll, May, 9, 2019, https://scroll.in/field/923086/athletics-kenya-drop-two-sprinters-from-world-relay-championship-team-over-high-testosterone-levels.

22. Ayumba Ayodi, "Athlete Rose from the Slopes of Mt Kenya to World Prominence," *Daily Nation* (Kenya), October 28, 2018, https://www.nation.co.ke/sports/talkup/Nyairera-rose-from-slopes-of-Mt-Kenya-to-world-prominence-/441392-4825506-bqtpi4z/index.html.

23. Javier Clavelo Robinson, "Report: Women's 800M—IAAF World Junior Championships, Oregon 2014," International Association of Athetics Federations website, July 25, 2014, https://www.iaaf.org/news/report/report-women-800m-iaaf-world-junior-champions.

24. "W 800/M 1500: Margaret Wambui and Jonathan Sawe Claim Two Golds for Kenya," *LetsRun*, July 24, 2014, http://www.letsrun.com/news/2014/07/w-800m-1500-margaret-wambui-jonathan-sawe-claim-two-golds-kenya/.

25. J. Harper, "A Brief History of Intersex Athletes," *LetsRun*, September 19, 2014, http://www.letsrun.com/news/2014/09/brief-history-intersex-athletes-sport/.

26. 2015 Results, Prefontaine Classic, https://preclassic.runnerspace.com/eprofile.php?event_id=120&title_id=143&do=title&pg=1&folder_id=190&page_id=13359.

27. Kate Fagan, "Fair? The IOC's Gender Testing Policy Is the Exact Opposite," ESPNW, September 9, 2014, http://www.espn.com/espnw/news-commentary/article/11494007/fair-ioc-gender-testing-policy-exact-opposite.

28. Marc Naimark, "A New Study Supports Female Athletes Unfairly Excluded from Sport," *Slate*, September 12, 2014, https://slate.com/human-interest/2014/09/sex-verification-in-sports-a-new-study-supports-unfairly-excluded-female-athletes.html.

29. Fagan, "Fair?"

30. Naimark, "A New Study Supports Female Athletes Unfairly Excluded from Sport."

31. Thomas Murray, *Good Sport: Why Our Games Matter—and How Doping Undermines Them* (New York: Oxford University Press, 2018), 107.

32. Sarah Fecht, "Science Is Still Trying to Figure out What Makes a Female Athlete," *Popular Science*, May 22, 2015, https://www.popsci.com/scientists-still-trying-figure-out-what-female-athlete.

33. "Son of IAAF President Lamine Diack and Two Others Step Down," *Irish Times*, December 11, 2014, https://www.irishtimes.com/sport/other-sports/son-of-iaaf-president-lamine-diack-and-two-others-step-down-1.2034059.

34. Philip Olterman, "Russia Accused of Athletics Doping Cover-Up on German TV," *Guardian* (UK), December 3, 2014, https://www.theguardian.com/sport/2014/dec/03/russia-accused-athletics-doping-cover-up-olympics.

35. Ibid.

36. Simon Turnbull, "Marilyn Okoro Set for Belated Bronze," *Independent* (UK), February 26, 2013, https://www.independent.co.uk/sport/general/athletics/marilyn-okoro-set-for-belated-bronze-8512259.html.

37. Olterman, "Russia Accused of Athletics Doping Cover-Up on German TV."

38. The Independent Commission Report #1, Final Report, November 9, 2015, https://www.wada-ama.org/sites/default/files/resources/files/wada_independent_commission_report_1_en.pdf.

39. Rebecca R. Ruiz and Michael Schwirtz, (12 May 2016). "Russian Insider Says State-Run Doping Fueled Olympic Gold," *New York Times*, May 12, 2016, https://www.nytimes.com/2016/05/13/sports/russia-doping-sochi-olympics-2014.html.

40. "Russia Responds to Sochi Games Doping Accusations," CBS News, May 16, 2016, https://www.cbsnews.com/news/russia-retesting-sochi-olympics-doping-samples/.

41. James Ellingworth, "Nikita Kamaev, Leading Russian Anti-Doping Official, Was Planning on Writing a Book before Sudden Death," CBC Sports, February 21, 2016, https://www.cbc.ca/sports/nikita-kamaev-leading-russian-

anti-doping-official-was-planning-on-writing-a-book-before-sudden-death-1. 3457433.

42. "Son of IAAF President Lamine Diack and Two Others Step Down."

43. J. Harper, "Race Times for Transgender Athletes," *Journal of Sporting Cultures and Identities* 6, no. 1 (2015): 1–9, https://pdfs.semanticscholar.org/1e6a/bd2c1e03ba88e9ac8da94ea1d69ff3f4878a.pdf?_ga=2.254440527.659551599.1550520323-1192624875.1550520323.

44. Paul Lewis and Julian Borger, "Iranian Nuclear Talks Resume in Lausanne as Deadline Approaches," *Guardian* (UK), March 16, 2015, https://www.theguardian.com/world/2015/mar/16/iranian-nuclear-talks-resume-lausanne-deadline-john-kerry.

14. DUTEE CHAND VERSUS THE IAAF IN THE CAS

1. As noted in the Interim Arbitral Award Delivered by the Court of Arbitration for Sport, CAS 2014/A/3 759 Dutee Chand v. Athletics Federation of India (AFI) & the International Association of Athletics Federations (IAAF), http://www.tas-cas.org/fileadmin/user_upload/award_internet.pdf. https://www.doping.nl/media/kb/3317/CAS%202014_A_3759%20Dutee%20Chand%20vs.%20AFI%20%26%20IAAF%20%28S%29.pdf. Hereafter cited as Chand decision.
2. Ibid.
3. Ibid., para. 10.
4. Ibid., para. 17.
5. Ibid., para. 219.
6. Ibid., para. 174, 266.
7. Ibid., para. 323–25.
8. Ibid., para. 339.
9. Ibid., para. 190–92.
10. "Martin Ritzen," ResearchGate, https://www.researchgate.net/profile/Martin_Ritzen.
11. "Angelica Hirschberg," Karolinski University, https://staff.ki.se/people/anghir?_ga=2.132644684.313828449.1562692902-1125333219.1562692902.
12. "Professor Richard Holt," University of Southhampton, https://www.southampton.ac.uk/medicine/about/staff/righ.page.
13. Chand decision, para. 124.
14. Ibid., para. 490.

15. These ranges were established using immunoassay methods and were soon to change based on an improved testing method known as liquid chromatography/mass spectrometry (LC/MS).

16. M. L. Healy, R. Gibney, C. Pentecost, et al. "Endocrine Profiles in 693 Elite Athletes in the Post-Competition Setting," *Clinical Endocrinology* 81, no. 2 (2014): 294–305.

17. S. Bermon and P. Y. Garnier, "Serum Androgen Levels and Their Relation to Performance in Track and Field: Mass Spectrometry Results from 2127 Observations in Male and Female Elite Athletes," *British Journal of Sports Medicine* 51 (2017): 1309–14, doi: 10.1136/bjsports-2017-097792. https://bjsm.bmj.com/content/51/17/1309.

18. R. Ulrich, H. G. Pope Jr., L. Cléret, et al., "Doping in Two Elite Athletics Competitions Assessed by Randomized-Response Surveys," *Sports Medicine* 48, no. 1 (2018): 211, https://doi.org/10.1007/s40279-017-0765-4.

19. IAAF Regulations Governing Eligibility of Females with Hyperandrogenism to Compete in Women's Competition, IAAF 2011 Section 6.5, https://www.iaaf.org/news/iaaf-news/amended-iaaf-rules-and-new-updated-iaaf-regul.

20. Chand decision, para. 109.

21. McLaren's suggestions were noted in paragraph 538 of the Chand decision and would eventually form the basis for the 2017 Bermon and Garnier study that is referenced above in n. 17.

22. The panel of judges would agree that the overlap issue was unimportant, as noted in paragraph 494 of the Chand decision.

23. Ibid., para. 85.

24. "Dutee Chand Athlete Profile," International Association of Athletics Foundations website, https://www.iaaf.org/athletes/india/dutee-chand-275950.

25. International Olympic Committee, "IOC Consensus Meeting on Sex Reassignment and Hyperandrogenism, November 2015," https://stillmed.olympic.org/Documents/Commissions_PDFfiles/Medical_commission/2015-11_ioc_consensus_meeting_on_sex_reassignment_and_hyperandrogenism-en.pdf.

26. Joanna Harper, "Do Transgender Athletes Have an Edge? I Sure Don't," *Washington Post*, April 1, 2015, https://www.washingtonpost.com/opinions/do-transgender-athletes-have-an-edge-i-sure-dont/2015/04/01/ccacb1da-c68e-11e4-b2a1-bed1aaea2816_story.html?utm_term=.b2e095c13098.

27. Chand decision, para. 490.

28. Ibid., para. 500.

29. Ibid., para. 510.

30. Ibid., para. 528.

31. Ibid., para. 526.

32. Ibid., para. 548.

15. TRANSGENDER ATHLETES, 2013–2017

1. Loretta Hunt, "How Fallon Fox Became the First Known Transgender Athlete in MMA," *Sports Illustrated*, March 7, 2013, https://www.si.com/mma/2013/03/07/fallon-fox-profile.

2. Cyd Zeigler, "Fallon Fox Comes Out as Trans Pro MMA Fighter," *Outsports*, March 5, 2013, https://www.outsports.com/2013/3/5/4068840/fallon-fox-trans-pro-mma-fighter.

3. Greg Bishop and Jack Begg, "A Pioneer, Reluctantly," *New York Times*, May 13, 2013, https://www.nytimes.com/2013/05/13/sports/for-transgender-fighter.

4. Hunt, "How Fallon Fox Became the First Known Transgender Athlete in MMA."

5. "Mitrione Calls Fox 'Disgusting Freak,'" Fox Sports, April 8, 2013, https://www.foxsports.com/ufc/story/matt-mitrione-suspended-indefinitely-calls-transgendered-fighter-fallon-fox-lying-sick-sociopathic-disgusting-freak-040813.

6. Hunt, "How Fallon Fox Became the First Known Transgender Athlete in MMA."

7. Jonathan Snowden, "Transgender Fighter Fallon Fox and Her Slowly Fading 15 Minutes of Fame," *Bleacher Report*, April 22, 2014, https://bleacherreport.com/articles/2038764-transgender-fighter-fallon-fox-and-her-slowly-fading-fifteen-minutes-of-fame.

8. Monica Roberts, "Fallon Fox Wins Semifinal Bout vs. Allanna Jones!" *TransGirot*, May 25, 2013, https://transgriot.blogspot.com/2013/05/fallon-fox-wins-semifinal-bout-vs.html.

9. "Ashlee Evans-Smith Finishes Fallon Fox . . . Twice in One Fight," *AKA Thailand*, June 27, 2017, https://akathailand.com/news/ashlee-evans-smith-finishes-fallon-fox-twice-one-fight/.

10. Fallon Fox, "Fallon Fox Responds to Ashlee Evans-Smith, Who Says Trans Fighters Should Be Barred from Women's MMA," *Outsports*, November 20, 2013, https://www.outsports.com/2013/11/20/5123442/fallon-fox-ashlee-evans-smith-trans-mma.

11. Snowden, "Transgender Fighter Fallon Fox and Her Slowly Fading 15 Minutes of Fame."

12. "Here's the Fallon Fox Fight That Left Tamikka Brents with a Concussion, Broken Orbital and 7 Staples in Her Head," *MiddleEasy*, September 17,

2014, https://middleeasy.com/mma-news/here-s-the-fallon-fox-fight-that-left-tamikka-brents-with-a-concussion-broken-orbital-and-7-staples-in-her-head/.

13. "Fallon Fox: The Queen of Swords," Sherdog: The Global Authority on Mixed Martial Arts, https://www.sherdog.com/fighter/Fallon-Fox-100599?_escaped_fragment_=#!.

14. "Ashley Evans-Smith: Rebel Girl," Sherdog: The Global Authority on Mixed Martial Arts, https://www.sherdog.com/fighter/Ashlee-EvansSmith-75021.

15. Snowden, "Transgender Fighter Fallon Fox and Her Slowly Fading 15 Minutes of Fame."

16. Helen Pidd, "Jailed Transgender Fell Tunner thought UK Athletics Was 'Trying to Kill Her,'" *Guardian* (UK), March 17, 2017, https://www.theguardian.com/sport/2017/mar/17/jailed-transgender-fell-runner-thought-uk-athletics-was-trying-to-kill-her.

17. "Results: Holme Moss Fell Race July 18th 2010," Holmfirth Harriers Athletics Club website, https://www.holmfirthharriers.com/archive2/results/holme_moss10.html.

18. Paula and I would later connect through a private transgender runner Facebook group. Paula has continued to race after her transition.

19. Race Results, Lauren Jeska, Athlinks, https://www.athlinks.com/search/unclaimed/?term=lauren%20jeska.

20. The IAAF and Stéphane Bermon in particular were always careful about maintaining confidentiality up until the end of 2018. I did learn confidential information as part of my role in the Caster Semenya trial.

21. Pidd, "Jailed Transgender Fell Runner Thought UK Athletics Was 'Trying to Kill Her.'"

22. "Lauren Jeska Jailed for Alexander Stadium Stabbings," BBC News, March 14, 2017, https://www.bbc.com/news/uk-england-birmingham-39266777.

23. Richard Spillett, "Champion Fell Runner Is Jailed for 18 Years," *Daily Mail*, March 14, 2017, http://www.dailymail.co.uk/news/article-4312594/Fell-runner-jailed-trying-murder-athletics-official.html.

24. Paola Boivin, "Transgender Golfer Dreams of Playing in LPGA," *USA Today*, March 12, 2013, https://www.usatoday.com/story/sports/golf/2013/03/12/lpga-transgender-bobbi-lancaster/1983171/.

25. Bobbi Lancaster, *The Red Light Runner* (San Bernardino: CreateSpace, 2017), 44.

26. Randy Boswell, "Trailblazing Transgender Golfer from Canada Vies for Place in LPGA Tour—at 62," Canada.com, March 17, 2013, https://o.canada.com/news/trailblazing-transgender-golfer-from-canada-vies-for-place-in-lpga-tour-at-62.

27. Lancaster, *The Red Light Runner*, 82.

28. Boswell, "Trailblazing Transgender Golfer from Canada Vies for Place in LPGA Tour."

29. Lancaster, *The Red Light Runner*, 120, 131.

30. "Meet Bobbi Lancaster," *Morning Drive*, Golf Channel, December 18, 2014, https://www.golfchannel.com/video/meet-bobbi-lancaster.

31. Ibid.

32. Paola Boivin, "Transgender Golfer Bobbi Lancaster Aims for LPGA Tour in 2014," *USA Today*, December 13, 2013, https://www.usatoday.com/story/sports/golf/2013/12/30/lpga-2014-bobbi-lancaster-transgender-golfer/4247307/.

33. Lancaster, *The Red Light Runner*, 198.

34. Athletes, Sports Law, and Policy: An Interdisciplinary Symposium, Stanford University School of Law, May 6, 2107, https://www.sportslaw.org/events/SymposiumFlyer.pdf.

35. Christina Kahrl, "Chris Mosier: I Finally Feel Very Comfortable with My Body," *ESPN The Magazine*, June, 26, 2016, http://www.espn.com/olympics/story/_/page/bodychrismosier/duathlete-chris-mosier-breaking-barriers-repping-team-usa-body-issue-2016.

36. Kinley Preston, "Chris Mosier," *Go Pride*, August 1, 2011, http://chicago.gopride.com/news/interview.cfm/articleid/269776.

37. Chris Mosier, "2014 in Review," Chris Mosier: Athlete, Coach, Cool Dude, January 1, 2015, https://thechrismosier.wordpress.com/2015/01/01/2014-in-review/.

38. Janae and I communicated via e-mail and Skype for several months in 2017.

39. Cyd Zeigler, "Trans Endurance Athlete Chris Mosier Earns Spot on Team USA," *Outsports*, June 7, 2015, https://www.outsports.com/2015/6/7/8743157/chris-mosier-trans-duathlon-team-usa.

40. 2016 Aviles ITU Duathlon World Championships: 35–39 Male AG Sprint, https://wts.triathlon.org/results/result/2016_aviles_itu_duathlon_world_championships/281070.

41. Lauren Steele, "Chris Mosier on Making History as First Trans Member of Team USA," *Rolling Stone*, August 2, 2016, https://www.rollingstone.com/culture/culture-sports/chris-mosier-on-making-history-as-first-trans-member-of-team-usa-250971/.

42. Kahrl, "Chris Mosier."

43. "Team USA Athlete and LGBTQ Advocate Chris Mosier Joins the You Can Play Team as Vice President," You Can Play website, August 15, 2016, http://www.youcanplayproject.org/news/entry/team-usa-athlete-and-lgbtq-advocate-chris-mosier-joins-the-you-can-play-tea.

44. Matt Tuthill, "Transgender Powerlifter Janae Marie Kroc Shares Unbelievable Story," *Muscle and Fitness*, October 2015, https://www.muscleandfitness.com/athletes-celebrities/interviews/transgender-powerlifter-matt-kroczaleski-janae-marie-kroc-shares-unbelievable-story.

45. James Michael Nichols, "Meet Janae Marie Kroc, Recently Out Transgender World Record Bodybuilder," *Huffington Post*, August 1, 2015, https://www.huffingtonpost.com/entry/meet-janae-marie-kroc-recently-out-transgender-world-record-bodybuilder_us_55bbc03de4b0b23e3ce2b451.

46. Nate Green, "Matt Kroc Is More Man than You," *T Nation*, May 24, 2010, https://www.t-nation.com/training/matt-kroc-is-more-man-than-you.

47. "Matt Kroczaleski Breaks Shawn Frankl's All-Time Record," Powerlifting Watch, April 25, 2009, http://www.powerliftingwatch.com/node/11221.

48. Chris Colucci, "Kroc: From Matt to Janae," *T Nation*, March 7, 2016, https://www.t-nation.com/living/kroc-from-matt-to-janae.

49. Ibid.

50. Rover Radio Interview with Kroc, http://www.roverradio.com/watch/interviews/item/2734-transgender-champion-bodybuilder-janae-marie-kroc-full-interview.

51. Tuthill, "Transgender Powerlifter Janae Marie Kroc Shares Unbelievable Story."

52. Colucci, "Kroc."

53. Tuthill, "Transgender Powerlifter Janae Marie Kroc Shares Unbelievable Story."

54. Colucci, "Kroc."

55. Janae first reached out to me in 2017, and I really enjoyed our back-and-forth conversations at the time. I am grateful for her candor and for the fact that so many trans athletes have been a part of my life.

56. "Janae Marie Kroc Talks about Her Movie *Transformer*," queerguru tv, April 17, 2018, https://www.youtube.com/watch?v=Oj-hvqYKY5Y.

57. Caitlyn Jenner with Buzz Bissinger, *The Secrets of My Life* (New York: Grand Central, 2017), 167, 201.

58. Ibid., 9, 270.

59. Ibid., 302.

60. Katy Steinmetz, "The Transgender Tipping Point," *Time*. May 28, 2014, http://time.com/135480/transgender-tipping-point/.

61. Sarah Begley, "Time Announces Shortlist for 2015 Person of the Year," *Time*, December 7, 2015, http://time.com/4136910/person-of-the-year-shortlist-2015/.

62. Jenner, *The Secrets of My Life*, 61, 72.

63. Ivan Levington, "Caitlyn Jenner Says It Was Harder to Come Out as Republican than Transgender," CNBC, July 20, 2016, https://www.cnbc.com/

2016/07/20/caitlyn-jenner-says-it-was-harder-to-come-out-as-republican-than-transgender.html.

64. Scott Gleeson, "Caitlyn Jenner a Force on the Golf Course," *USA Today*, June 14, 2017, https://www.usatoday.com/story/sports/golf/2017/06/13/caitlyn-jenner-golf-sherwood-country-club-donald-trump/102650116/.

65. Caitlyn was wonderful with her time and answered questions that she has probably been asked many times before.

66. Jeremy Wilson, "Exclusive Philippa York Interview—A Life in Three Parts: From Cycling Great Robert Millar to Finding Her True Self," *Telegraph* (UK), April 10, 2018, https://www.telegraph.co.uk/cycling/2018/04/10/exclusive-philippa-york-interview-life-three-parts-cycling/.

67. Richard Moore, "In Search of Scotland's Unsocial Climber Who Conquered Mounatains and Then Fell off the Map," *Guardian* (UK), July 5, 2007, https://www.theguardian.com/sport/2007/jul/06/cycling.tourdefrance.

68. Philippa York, "A Statement from Cyclingnews Contributor Philippa York," *cyclingnews*, July 8, 2017, http://www.cyclingnews.com/news/a-statement-from-cyclingnews-contributor-philippa-york/.

69. Wilson, "Exclusive Philippa York Interview."

16. THE 2016 IOC TRANSGENDER GUIDELINES

1. "800 Metres Women Discipline Overview." 2015 IAAF World Championships, https://www.iaaf.org/competitions/iaaf-world-championships/15th-iaaf-world-championships-4875/800-metres/women.

2. "Francine Niyonsaba Athlete Profile," International Association of Athletics Federations website, https://www.iaaf.org/athletes/burundi/francine-niyonsaba-273769.

3. "Lamine Diack: Ex-Athletics Chief Investigated in Corruption Inquiry," BBC Sport, November 5, 2015, https://www.bbc.com/sport/athletics/34721317.

4. As part of the IAAF submissions in the Caster Semenya trial, Liz Reilly updated the legal gender status of various countries around the world. The number of countries with nonbinary legal status laws are taken from this report.

5. Ibid.

6. "Eric Vilain, M.D., Ph.D.," Intersex Society of North America, http://www.isna.org/about/vilain.

7. "Eric Villain, MD, PhD," Children's National Health System, https://childrensnational.org/research-and-education/about-cri/faculty-and-leadership-directory/vilian-eric.

8. Mike had attended the very first IAAF-sponsored meeting in 1990.

9. Others not mentioned in this chapter were Ugur Erdener, Michael Beloff, Gerard Conway, Robin Mitchel, Rania Elwani, Vidya Mohamed-Ali, Richard Budgett, Lars Engebretsen, and Christian Thill.

10. A few months after the meeting Liz published the following paper: "The Participation of Trans Athletes in Sport—A Transformation in Approach?" Law in Sport, February 5, 2016, https://www.lawinsport.com/topics/articles/item/the-participation-of-trans-athletes-insport-a-transformation-in-approach.Liz continued to update the list she used for her paper, and the most recent version was presented at the Semenya trial and referenced in nn. 4 and 5 above.

11. After attending many conferences, I have noticed that when a speaker is surrounded after his or her talk it is always a good sign. This was not the first time it happened to me, but given the context, my reception was exceedingly gratifying.

12. Over the past few years I have been called Dr. Harper many times. I am not always as good as I should be about correcting people, but I have never claimed to have either a PhD or an MD.

13. Sean Ingle, "Lamine Diack, Former IAAF Head, under Investigation in Corruption and Doping Inquiry," Guardian (UK), November 4, 2015, https://www.theguardian.com/sport/2015/nov/04/lamine-diack-investigation-iaaf-corruption-doping.

14. "IAAF Provisionally Suspends Russian Member Federation ARAF," press release, IAAF website, November 13, 2015, https://www.iaaf.org/news/press-release/iaaf-araf-suspended.

15. Ingle, "IAAF Deputy General Secretary Nick Davies Stands Down over Leaked Email."

16. Owen Gibson, "IAAF Bans Four Senior Officials over Alleged Doping Cover-ups," *Guardian* (UK), January 7, 2016, https://www.theguardian.com/sport/2016/jan/07/iaaf-bans-four-officials-doping-papa-massata-diack.

17. International Olympic Committee, "IOC Consensus Meeting on Sex Reassignment and Hyperandrogenism," https://stillmed.olympic.org/Documents/Commissions_PDFfiles/Medical_commission/201511_ioc_consensus_meeting_on_sex_reassignment_and_hyperandrogenism-en.pdf.

18. Cyd Zeigler, "Trans Triathlete Chris Mosier May Be Banned from Competing at World Championships," *Outsports*, January 21, 2016, https://www.outsports.com/2016/1/21/10802088/chris-mosier-trans-athlete-duathlon-world-championship.

19. Cyd Zeigler, "Exclusive: Read the Olympics' New Transgender Guidelines That Will Not Mandate Surgery," *Outsports*, January 21, 2016, https://

www.outsports.com/2016/1/21/10812404/transgender-ioc-policy-new-olympics.

20. William Bigelow, "Olympics Loosen Rules to Allow Pre-Op M-to-F Transsexuals to Compete with Women," *Breitbart*, January 22, 2016, https://www.breitbart.com/sports/2016/01/22/olympics-allow-transsexuals-to-compete-under-gender-they-identify-with/.

21. The Report from the 2015 US Transgender Survey states that 8% of trans people de-transitioned at some point with 62% of those who de-transition re-transitioning at some point. http://www.ustranssurvey.org/.

22. The NCAA data base is huge with approximately two hundred thousand athletes. Statistically speaking, there should be approximately one thousand trans women competing in the NCAA, yet even in 2019 the numbers are much smaller.

23. One of the weightlifters was undoubtedly Laurel Hubbard, who would become infamous in 2017. I'm not certain who the other athlete was. A month or so after the meeting, a source in England claimed there were two British trans women who were on the verge of competing. The two sets of supposed athletes would become conflated via leaks from our meeting and I had to answer questions about these theoretical trans athletes all summer.

24. Those of us in the larger committee weren't told about the subcommittee until 2017.

17. AFTERMATH OF THE CAS DECISION IN THE CHAND CASE

1. "House of Track," *Inside Track*, December 2015, https://www.gotracktownusa.com/inside_track/2015/12/portlands-house-of-track-to-host-indoor-competition/.

2. Summary, IAAF 2016 World Indoor Track Championships 800 Metres Women—Round 1, http://media.aws.iaaf.org/competitiondocuments/pdf/5681/AT-800-W-h----.RS4.pdf.

3. "Report: Women's 800m Final—IAAF World Indoor Championships Portland 2016," March 20, 2016, International Association of Athletics Federations website, https://www.iaaf.org/news/report/world-indoor-portland-2016-women-800m-final.

4. One of the women in my running club worked as a physical therapist for some of the world-class athletes who make their home in Portland.

5. "Semenya Makes History at Nationals," Sport 24, April 16, 2016, https://www.sport24.co.za/OtherSport/Athletics/South-Africa/semenya-makes-history-at-nationals-20160416.

6. "2016 IAAF Doha Diamond League Diamond League Results," *LetsRun*, May 6, 2016, http://www.letsrun.com/news/2016/05/schedule-entries-results-2016-iaaf-doha-diamond-league/.

7. "Full Results for Rabat Diamond League—2016 Meeting International Mohammed VI d'Atlétisme," *LetsRun*, May 19, 2016, http://www.letsrun.com/news/2016/05/schedule-entries-results-2016-meeting-international-mohammed-vi-datletisme-rabat-diamond-league/.

8. Sarah Barker, "Should There Be Testosterone Limits for Women in Athletics?" *Deadspin*, May 27, 2016, https://deadspin.com/should-there-be-testosterone-limits-for-women-in-athlet-1778330172.

9. Ross Tucker, "Hyperandrogenism and Women vs Women vs Men in Sport: A Q&A with Joanna Harper," The Science of Sport, May 23, 2016, https://sportsscientists.com/2016/05/hyperandrogenism-women-vs-women-vs-men-sport-qa-joanna-harper/?doing_wp_cron=1551563263.8498969078063964843750.

10. Sanchez Manning and Ian Gallagher, "Transgender British Athletes Born Male Set to Make Olympic History by Competing in the Games as Women," *Daily Mail*, July 2, 2016, https://www.dailymail.co.uk/news/article-3671937/Transgender-British-athletes-born-men-set-make-Olympic-history-competing-games-women.html.

11. "2016 IAAF Monaco Diamond League Results—2016 Herculis Results," *LetsRun*, July 15, 2016, http://www.letsrun.com/news/2016/07/2016-iaaf-monaco-diamond-league-results-2016-herculis-results/.

12. Women's 800m—Standings, Rio Olympic Games, August 18, 2016, https://web.archive.org/web/20160831125140/https:/www.rio2016.com/en/athletics-standings-at-womens-800m.

13. Ibid.

14. Andy Bull, "Caster Semenya Wins Olympic Gold but Faces More Scrutiny as IAAF Presses Case," *Guardian* (UK), August 21, 2016, https://www.theguardian.com/sport/2016/aug/21/caster-semenya-wins-gold-but-faces-scrutiny.

15. "Schedule, Entries & Results for 2016 Weltklasse Zürich—Zürich Diamond League," *LetsRun*, September 1, 2016, http://www.letsrun.com/news/2016/08/schedule-entries-results-2016-weltklasse-zurich-zurich-diamond-league/.

16. L. J. Elsas, R. Hayes, and K. Muralidharan. "Gender Verification at the Centennial Olympic Games." *Journal of the Medical Association of Georgia* 86 (1997): 50–54, https://www.ncbi.nlm.nih.gov/pubmed/9029887.

17. S. Bermon, P. Y. Garnier, A. L. Hirschberg, et al. "Serum Androgen Levels in Elite Female Athletes," *Journal of Clinical Endocrinology and*

Metabolism 99, no. 11 (2014): 4328–35, https://www.ncbi.nlm.nih.gov/pubmed/25137421.

18. S. Bermon, "Androgens and Athletic Performance of Elite Female Athletes," *Current Opinion in Endocrinology Diabetes and Obesity* 24, no. 3 (2017): 246–51, https://www.ncbi.nlm.nih.gov/pubmed/28234801.

19. S. Bermon and P. Y. Garnier, "Serum Androgen Levels and Their Relation to Performance in Track and Field: Mass Spectrometry Results from 2127 Observations in Male and Female Elite Athletes," *British Journal of Sports Medicine* 51 (2017): 1309–14, doi: 10.1136/bjsports-2017-097792. https://bjsm.bmj.com/content/51/17/1309.

20. "Dutee Chand's Case against IAAF Hyperandrogenism Regulations Gets Suspended till September," *Scroll*, July 29, 2017, https://scroll.in/field/845439/dutee-chands-case-against-iaaf-hyperandrogenism-regulations-gets-suspended-till-september-end.

21. 2017 Results—Prefontaine Classic, RunnerSpace, May 27, 2017, https://www.runnerspace.com/eprofile.php?event_id=120&do=news&news_id=479678.

22. Results—1000m Herculis, Monaco Diamond League, July 21, 2017, https://monaco.diamondleague.com/fileadmin/IDL_Monaco/user_upload/2017-RESULTATS_1000m_Herculis_Modifiés.pdf.

23. Results, 2017 IAAF World Championships 800 Metres Women—Final, IAAF website, August 13, 2017, https://media.aws.iaaf.org/competitiondocuments/pdf/5151/AT-800-W-f----.RS6.pdf.

24. "Dutee Chand Athlete Profile," IAAF website, https://www.iaaf.org/athletes/india/dutee-chand-275950.

25. Obviously such comments are not proof of anything, but the notion that Chand has some form of androgen insensitivity has become so pervasive that I recently reviewed a proposed scientific paper that claimed it as fact and did not feel the need to cite a reference.

26. Liz Riley, "The Participation of Trans Athletes in Sport—A Transformation in Approach?" Law in Sport, February 5, 2016, https://www.lawinsport.com/topics/articles/item/the-participation-of-trans-athletes-in-sport-a-transformation-in-approach.

27. Court of Arbitration for Sport, "The Application of the IAAF Hyperandrogenism Regulations Remain Suspended," press release, January 19, 2018, https://www.tas-cas.org/fileadmin/user_upload/Media_Release_3759_Jan_2018.pdf.

28. IAAF, "IAAF Introduces New Eligibility Regulations for Female Classification," press release, April 26, 2018, https://www.iaaf.org/news/press-release/eligibility-regulations-for-female-classifica.

29. "Birmingham Diary: IAAF Council Meeting Day 2: Hyperandrogenism, Transfer of Allegiance, RUSAF Suspension Extended, plus Global Calendar Update," *RunBlogRun* (blog), March 10, 2018, http://www.runblogrun.com/2018/03/birmingham-diary-iaaf-council-meeting-day-2-hyperandrogenism-transfer-of-allegiance-rusaf-suspension.html.

30. N. Q. Ha, S. L. Dworkin, M. J. Martínez-Patiño, et al., "Hurdling Over Sex? Sport, Science, and Equity," *Archives of Sexual Behavior* 43, no. 6 (2014): 1035–42, https://www.ncbi.nlm.nih.gov/pubmed/25085349.

31. J. Harper, G. Lima, A. Kolliari-Turner, et al., "The Fluidity of Gender and Implications for the Biology of Inclusion for Transgender and Intersex Athletes," *Current Sports Medicine Reports* 17, no. 2 (2018): 467–72, https://www.ncbi.nlm.nih.gov/pubmed/30531465.

32. "Norton Rose Fulbright Advises Olympic Champion Caster Semenya to Challenge IAAF Rules as Discriminatory," news release, Norton Rose Fulbright website, June 18, 2018, https://www.nortonrosefulbright.com/en/news/115e61b6/norton-rose-fulbright-advises-olympic-champion-caster-semenya-to-challenge-iaaf-rules-as-discriminatory.

33. Richard H. McLaren, Independent Person Report to Sir Craig Reedie, President, World Anti-Doping Agency, in WADA Investigation of Sochi Allegations, July 18, 2016, https://www.wada-ama.org/sites/default/files/resources/files/20160718_ip_report_newfinal.pdf.

34. James Masters, "Russia's Darya Klishina Feeling 'Alone' at Rio Olympics," CNN, August 16, 2016, https://www.cnn.com/2016/08/16/sport/darya-klishina-russia-rio-2016/index.html.

35. Richard H. McLaren, Independent Person 2nd Report to Sir Craig Reedie, President, World Anti-Doping Agency, in WADA Investigation of Sochi Allegations, December 9, 2016, https://www.wada-ama.org/sites/default/files/resources/files/mclaren_report_part_ii_2.pdf.

36. "IAAF Approves the Application of Seven Russians to Compete Internationally as Neutral Athletes," press release, IAAF, April 11, 2017, https://www.iaaf.org/news/press-release/russians-neutral-athletes-2017.

37. Tara John, "No, 'OAR' Isn't a New Country. Here's the Story behind the OAR Winter Olympics Team." *Time*, February 15, 2018, http://time.com/5141549/oar-team-winter-olympics-2018-russia/.

38. Bill Chappell, "2nd Russian Olympian Fails a Doping Test at Pyeongchang Winter Olympics," NPR, February 23, 2018, https://www.npr.org/sections/thetorch/2018/02/23/588211762/second-russian-olympian-fails-a-doping-test-at-pyeongchang-winter-olympics.

39. Thomas Giles, "IAAF Invite Seven Russian Athletes to World Indoor Championships," *Inside the Games*, February 22, 2018, https://www.

insidethegames.biz/articles/1061811/iaaf-invite-seven-russian-athletes-to-world-indoor-championships.

40. "IAAF Approves the Application of 33 Russian Athletes to Compete Internationally s Neutral Athletes," press release, IAAF, June 22, 2018, https://www.iaaf.org/news/press-release/russian-authorised-neutral-athletes-2018-u20.

41. "Authorised Neutral Athlete Status of Danil Lysenko Revoked," press release, IAAF, August 3, 2018, https://www.iaaf.org/news/press-release/authorised-neutral-athlete-status-danil-lysen.

42. Liam Morgan, "Zambian 400m Runner Mupopo Given Four-Year Ban after Positive Drugs Test at 2017 World Championships," *Inside the Games*, September 5, 2018, https://www.insidethegames.biz/articles/1069626/zambian-400m-runner-mupopo-given-four-year-ban-after-positive-drugs-test-at-2017-world-championships.

43. Ben Nuckols, "Hearing Points to Putin's Role in Russian Doping Scandal," AP News, June 25, 2018, https://www.apnews.com/6bc6805ca91548dbbf22501ed9f0fe37.

18. TRANSGENDER ATHLETES, 2015–2018

1. Emma K. Talkoff, "Breaking the Surface with Schuyler Bailar," *Harvard Crimson*, November 10, 2016, https://www.thecrimson.com/article/2016/11/10/schuyler-bailar-underwater/.

2. Jared Anderson, "Schuyler Bailar to Debut with Harvard Men Friday vs. Bryant," *SwimSwam*, November 6, 2015, https://swimswam.com/schuyler-bailar-to-debut-with-harvard-men-friday-vs-bryant/.

3. Talkoff, "Breaking the Surface with Schuyler Bailar."

4. Julie Compton, "OutFront: Harvard Swimmer Sets Example for Other Transgender Athletes," NBC News, October 5, 2017, https://www.nbcnews.com/feature/nbc-out/outfront-harvard-swimmer-sets-example-other-transgender-athletes-n807986.

5. Talkoff, "Breaking the Surface with Schuyler Bailar."

6. Ibid.

7. Ibid.

8. "Schuyler Bailar," CollegeSwimming, https://www.collegeswimming.com/swimmer/216547/.

9. Erik Dresser, "Lewis and Clark's Ryan Lavigne," row2k, March 22, 2016, http://www.row2k.com/features/967/Lewis---Clark-s-Ryan-LaVigne/.

10. Art Edwards, "Lewis and Clark Transgender Rower Returns to Competition," KGW-TV (Portland, OR), March 15, 2016, https://www.kgw.com/

article/news/local/lewis-and-clark-transgender-rower-returns-to-competition/283-84220780.

11. Erik Hall, "College Roundup: Transgender Athlete Makes All-Conference Team," *Outsports*, April 27, 2017, https://www.outsports.com/2017/4/27/15453310/trans-athlete-college-track-lgbt-sports.

12. "Lavigne and Stroud Win Women's Pair, Pios Take Third in Women's Double at WIRA," press release, Lewis and Clark Pioneers, April 29, 2018, https://www.lcpioneers.com/sports/rowing/2017-18/releases/20180429gexmqd.

13. "LaVigne Closes out Pios Career with Second Straight All-American Selection," press release, Lewis and Clark Pioneers, July 27, 2018, https://www.lcpioneers.com/sports/rowing/2017-18/releases/20180717ikn419.

14. Data obtained from Sam Taylor, head coach for Lewis and Clark rowing team.

15. Jeff Miller, "How a Transgender Athlete Became the Person She Already Was," *Orange County Register*, June 29, 2015, https://www.ocregister.com/2015/06/29/miller-how-a-transgender-athlete-became-the-person-she-already-was/.

16. Chloe Psyche Anderson, "This College Volleyball Player Is Headed to the NCAA," *Outsports*, June 1, 2016, https://www.outsports.com/2016/6/1/11814342/transgender-ncaa-volleyball-chloe-psyche-anderson.

17. Interview with Chloe Anderson, May 2016.

18. Nicole Freeling, "Student Challenges Assumptions about Transgender Athletes," UC Santa Cruz Newscenter, September 8, 2016, https://news.ucsc.edu/2016/09/challenging-assumptions.html.

19. Tylah Silva, "Chloe Psyche Anderson Sheds Light on the Experience of Transgender Athletes," *Study Breaks*, May 18, 2017, https://studybreaks.com/students/chloe-psyche-anderson/.

20. "Chloe Anderson," Women's Volleyball, UC Santa Cruz, http://www.goslugs.com/sports/wvball/2016-17/bios/anderson_chloe_a73b?view=profile.

21. Athena Del Rosario, "This Transgender NCAA Goalie Has Competed the Last Two Years and Is Now Coming Out," *Outsports*, May 31, 2017, https://www.outsports.com/2017/5/31/15722952/transgender-ncaa-soccer-athena-del-rosario.

22. "Athena Del Rosario," Women's Soccer, UC Santa Cruz, http://www.goslugs.com/sports/wsoc/2016-17/bios/del_rosario_athena_cy88.

23. Del Rosario, "This Transgender NCAA Goalie Has Competed the Last Two Years and Is Now Coming Out."

24. "Athena Del Rosario," Women's Soccer, UC Santa Cruz.

25. Brittany Sodic, "This Trans NCAA Soccer Player Kept Her Gender a Secret for Years," *Study Breaks*, July 10, 2017, https://studybreaks.com/students/athena-del-rosario/.

26. Del Rosario, "This Transgender NCAA Goalie Has Competed the Last Two Years and Is Now Coming Out."

27. Andrew R. Flores, Jody L. Herman, Gary J. Gates, and Taylor N. T. Brown, *How Many Adults Identify as Transgender in the United States?* June 2016, https://williamsinstitute.law.ucla.edu/wp-content/uploads/How-Many-Adults-Identify-as-Transgender-in-the-United-States.pdf.

28. 2014–2015 Girls Wrestling State Results, University Interscholastic League Texas, https://www.uiltexas.org/wrestling/state-results/2014-2015-girls-wrestling-state-results.

29. 2015–2016 Girls Wrestling State Results, University Interscholastic League Texas, https://www.uiltexas.org/wrestling/state-results/2015-2016-girls-wrestling-state-results.

30. "Transgender Boy Mack Beggs Wins Texas State Girls' Wrestling Title," ESPNW, February 26, 2017, http://www.espn.com/espnw/sports/article/18767310/transgender-wrestler-mack-beggs-euless-trinity-wins-texas-state-girls-wrestling-title.

31. Matt Howerton, "Transgender Wrestler Mack Beggs Booed after Winning State Title," *USA Today*, February 25, 2018, https://usatodayhss.com/2018/mack-beggs-transgender-wrestler-booed.

32. Brad Townsend, "With UIL Days behind Him, Transgender Wrestler Mack Beggs Looks ahead to College, Competing against Men," *Dallas News*, February 22, 2018, https://sportsday.dallasnews.com/high-school/high-schools/2018/06/11/transgender-wrestler-mack-beggs-one-year-later-difficulty-defiance-new-uil-drama.

33. Ibid.

34. "Transgender Wrestler Mack Beggs Wins Texas Girls Title Again," *Guardian* (UK), February 25, 2018, https://www.theguardian.com/society/2018/feb/25/transgender-wrestler-mack-beggs-wins-texas-girls-title.

35. Randy Sachs, "Transgender Wrestler Has 'Top Surgery' and Sex Changed to 'Male' on Birth Certificate," *Fort Worth Star-Telegram*, February 21, 2019, https://www.star-telegram.com/sports/dfwvarsity/article226444165.html.

36. Transathlete.com, State by State High School Transgender Policies, https://www.transathlete.com/k-12.

37. Matthew Conyers, "At Cromwell High, Transgender Athlete Competes with Girls for First Time," *Hartford Currant*, April 7, 2017, https://www.courant.com/sports/high-schools/hc-hs-cromwell-track-andraya-yearwood-0407-20170406-story.html.

38. "Andraya Yearwood Track & Field Bio," Athletic Net, https://www.athletic.net/TrackAndField/Athlete.aspx?AID=11884190.

39. Catherine Thorbecke, "Transgender Athletes Speak Out as Parents Petition to Change Policy that Allows Them to Compete as Girls," ABC news, June 22 2018, https://abcnews.go.com/GMA/News/transgender-athletes-speak-parents-petition-change-policy-compete/story?id=56071191.

40. Jeff Jacobs, "No Easy Answers When It Comes to Transgender Athletes," *Connecticut Post*, June 4, 2018, https://www.ctpost.com/highschool/article/Jeff-Jacobs-No-easy-answers-when-it-comes-to-12967306.php.

41. "Terry Miller Track & Field Bio," Athletic Net, https://www.athletic.net/TrackAndField/Athlete.aspx?AID=14046370.

42. Pat Eaton-Robb, "Transgender Sprinters Finish 1st, 2nd at Connecticut Girls Indoor Track Championships," *Washington Times*, February 7, 2019, https://www.washingtontimes.com/news/2019/feb/24/terry-miller-andraya-yearwood-transgender-sprinter/.

43. Results, 2019 New Balance National Indoor Meet, https://results.armorytrack.com/meets/1724/events/69780/results.

44. Fleta Page, "Mouncey to Make His Debut for Australia," *Canberra Times*, June 17, 2012, https://www.canberratimes.com.au/sport/mouncey-to-make-his-debut-for-australia-20120616-20h49.html.

45. Danielle Gusmaroli, "Hannah Mouncey: Trans Handball Player Sidelined over Height Fears," *Daily Telegraph*. October 16, 2016.

46. Ibid.

47. Glenda Kwek, "AFL Leaves Other Codes in the Dust," *Sydney Morning Herald*, March 26, 2013, https://www.smh.com.au/business/afl-leaves-other-codes-in-the-dust-20130326-2grkp.html.

48. Interview with Hannah Mouncey, January 2018.

49. Richard Harris, "Hannah Mouncey Deserved More Than the AFL's Policy on the Run," ABC News (Australia), October 20, 2017, https://www.abc.net.au/news/2017-10-20/hinds-afl-exclusion-of-hannah-mouncey-from-aflw-highly-damaging/9067542.

50. Sarah Black, "AFLW: Duffin Takes out Top VFLW Honour," Australian Football League, September 10, 2018, https://www.afl.com.au/news/2018-09-10/aflw-duffin-takes-out-top-vflw-honour.

51. Melissa Coulton Ryan, "Hannah Mouncey Withdraws from AFLW Draft Nomination, Hits out at AFL," *The Age* (Australia), September 10, 2018, https://www.theage.com.au/sport/afl/hannah-mouncey-withdraws-aflw-draft-nomination-hits-out-at-afl-20180910-p502r4.html.

52. Nancy Gillen, "Australia Qualify for 2019 IHF World Championships with Fifth-Place Finish at Women's Asian Handball Championships," *Inside the Games*, December 8, 2018, https://www.insidethegames.biz/index.php/articles/1073110/australia-qualify-for-2019-ihf-world-championships-with-fifth-place-fifth-at-womens-asian-handball-championships.

53. Results, New Zealand Interschool's Weightlifting Championship 2014, https://www.sporty.co.nz/asset/downloadasset?id=58b9b97e-f4ab-4e94-a2fe-507c024cb178.

54. Results, 2017 Australian International & Australian Open, https://www.awf.com.au/Portals/0/news/2017/2017%20Australian%20International%20-%20Australian%20Open.pdf?ver=2017-03-20-001039-810.

55. "Hubbard, Laurel, Biography," International Weightlifting Federation, https://www.iwf.net/results/athletes/?athlete=hubbard-laurel-1978-02-09&id=13974.

56. "Rio Olympic Weightlifting Championships," *Wikipedia*, https://en.m.wikipedia.org/wiki/Weightlifting_at_the_2016_Summer_Olympics_–_Women%27s_%2B75_kg.

57. Helen Davidson, "Transgender Weightlifter Laurel Hubbard's Eligibility under Scrutiny," *Guardian* (UK), April 9, 2018, https://www.theguardian.com/sport/2018/apr/09/transgender-weightlifter-laurel-hubbards-eligibility-under-scrutiny.

58. 2018 National Championship Results, Olympic Weightlifting New Zealand, http://olympicweightlifting.nz/wp-content/uploads/2018/09/Official-results-2018-Junior-Senior-National-Championships_.xlsx.

59. International Weightlifting Federation, *Ashgabat 2018 World Weightlifting Championships Start Book*, https://www.iwf.net/wp-content/uploads/downloads/2018/10/Start_Book_Ashgabat.pdf.

60. "Transgender Weightlifter Laurel Hubbard Fails to Make a Lift at Arafura Games," *Stuff*, April 30, 2019, https://www.stuff.co.nz/sport/other-sports/112334560/transgender-weightlifter-laurel-hubbard-fails-to-make-a-lift-at-arafura-games.

61. Rosi Doviverata, "Transgender Athletes at the Pacific Games." *Fiji Sun* July 18, 2019. https://fijisun.com.fj/2019/07/18/transgender-athletes-at-the-pacific-games/

62. Pete Blackburn, "Transgender Volleyball Player Excelling in Brazil, Eyeing 2020 Tokyo Olympics," CBS Sports, December 21, 2017, https://www.cbssports.com/olympics/news/transgender-volleyball-player-excelling-in-brazil-eyeing-2020-tokyo-olympics/.

63. Ibid.

64. Shasta Darlington, "Transgender Volleyball Star in Brazil Eyes Olympics and Stirs Debate," *New York Times*, March 17, 2018, https://www.nytimes.com/2018/03/17/world/americas/brazil-transgender-volleyball-tifanny-abreu.html.

65. Although it is challenging to find detailed reports on Tifanny in English, I found some Brazilian contacts who help me keep up with Tifanny's career. They both verified the information on the 2018 national team selections.

66. "Tiffany Abreu Joins Superliga '7 Points' Player Club," *Volleywood* (blog), March 7, 2018, http://www.volleywood.net/volleyball-related-news/volleyball-news-south-america/brazil-volleyball-news-south-america/tiffany-abreu-joins-superligas-7-points-player-club/.

67. Volei Bauru team website, http://www.voleibauru.com.br/voleibauru/pt/equipe/visualizar/codcategoria/1/adulto.html.

68. Interview with Tifanny Abreu, March 2019.

19. TRANSGENDER ATHLETIC RESEARCH UPDATE

1. K. Moesch, A. M. Elbe, M. L. Hauge, and J. M. Wikman, "Late Specialization: The Key to Success in Centimeters, Grams or Seconds (cgs) Sports," *Scandinavian Journal of Medicine & Science in Sports* 21 (2011): e282–e290, https://www.ncbi.nlm.nih.gov/pubmed/21401722.

2. Ken Stone, "Colombian W40 Transgender Hurdler Claims Bronze in 80H at Malaga Worlds," *Masters Track & Field News* (blog), September 16, 2018, https://masterstrack.blog/2018/09/colombian-w40-transgender-hurdler-claims-bronze-in-80h-at-malaga-worlds/.

3. "Yanelle del Mar Zape Athlete Profile," International Association of Athletics Federations website, https://www.iaaf.org/athletes/colombia/yanelle-del-mar-zape-014750795.

4. Ibid.

5. "XXIII World Masters Athletics Championships, Malaga, 4–16 September 2018," World Masters Athletics, https://world-masters-athletics.com/championships/results-championships-outdoor/.

6. World Masters Athletics Championships Indoor, Torun (Pol), March 24–30, 2019, https://wmaci2019.domtel-sport.pl/.

7. J. Harper, J. Ospina-Betancurt, M. J. Martínez-Patiño, "Analysis of the Performance of Transgender Athletes," *Sports Science* 20 (2016), https://www.sportsci.org/2016/WCPASabstracts/ID-1699.pdf.

8. Tim Stellar, "Transgender Cyclist's Win in Tucson Was Fairer Than It Seemed," *Arizona Daily Star*, November 26, 2016, https://tucson.com/news/local/columnists/steller/steller-transgender-cyclist-s-win-in-tucson-was-fairer-than/article_0851e258-2eb6-540a-8e60-1875e7bc836d.html.

9. 2017 Colorado Classic results, https://www.coloradoclassic.com/2017-colorado-classic-race-results.

10. Interview with Jillian Bearden, October 2017.

11. Ibid.

12. 2018 Colorado Classic results, https://www.coloradoclassic.com/2018-colorado-classic-results.

13. Interview with Bearden.

14. Harper, Ospina-Betancurt, and Marténez-Patiño, "Analysis of the Performance of Transgender Athletes."

15. Y. Pitsiladis, J. Harper, J. Ospina-Betancurt, and M. J. Martínez-Patiño, "Beyond Fairness: The Biology of Inclusion for Transgender and Intersex Athletes," Current Sports Medicine Reports 15, no. 6 (2016): 386–88, https://www.ncbi.nlm.nih.gov/pubmed/27841808.

16. S. Angadi, "Cardiovascular Adaptations in a Male to Female Transgender Athlete before and during Estrogen Therapy," Presented at the 35th FIMS World Congress of Sports Medicine, September 13, 2018, http://fimsrio2018.com/evento/30cbmee/programacao/palestrante/3018.

17. J. Harper, "Analysis of the Performance of Transgender and Intersex Athletes," Presented at the 35th FIMS World Congress of Sports Medicine, September 13, 2018, http://fimsrio2018.com/evento/30cbmee/programacao/palestrante/3017.

18. Nicole Lyn Pesce, "Transgender Woman Becomes the First to Land 'Women's Running' Magazine Cover," *New York Daily News*, June 14, 2016, https://www.nydailynews.com/life-style/trans-woman-land-women-running-cover-article-1.2673093.

19. Law and Contemporary Problems 80, no. 4 (2017).

20. "Interactive Map: Clinical Care Programs for Gender-Expansive Children and Adolescents," Human Rights Campaign, https://www.hrc.org/resources/interactive-map-clinical-care-programs-for-gender-nonconforming-childr.

21. Doriane Lambelet Coleman, "Sex in Sport," *Law and Contemporary Problems* 80, no. 4 (2017): 63–126.

22. 10th Sports Medicine—European Federation of Sports Medicine Associations, Lisbon, Portugal, November16–18, 2017, https://www.emedevents.com/c/medical-conferences-2017/10th-european-sport-medicine-congress-of-european-federation-of-sports-medicine-associations-efsma.

23. "Health, Hormones and Human Performance: BASEM Spring Conference 22 March 2018," *British Journal of Sports Medicine* (blog), December 6, 2017, https://blogs.bmj.com/bjsm/2017/12/06/health-hormones-human-performance-basem-spring-conference-22-march-2018/.

24. Sara Rigby, "Can Transgender Athletes Be Fairly Integrated into Women's Sports?" *Science Focus*, March 29, 2019, https://www.sciencefocus.com/the-human-body/can-transgender-athletes-be-fairly-integrated-into-womens-sports/.

25. 35th FIMS World Congress of Sports Medicine, http://www.fimsrio2018.com/.

26. R. Friedman, "Endocrine and Clinical Aspects of Transgender Athletes," Presented at the 35th FIMS World Congress of Sports Medicine, http://www.fimsrio2018.com/evento/30cbmee/programacao/palestrante/2780.

27. "Gemma Whitcomb," Loughborough University, https://www.lboro.ac.uk/departments/ssehs/staff/gemma-witcomb/.

28. "Emma O'Donnell," Loughborough University, https://www.lboro.ac.uk/departments/ssehs/staff/emma-odonnell/.

29. Fred Dreler, "The Complicated Case of Transgender Cyclist Dr. Rachel McKinnon," *Velo News*, October 18, 2018, https://www.velonews.com/2018/10/news/commentary-the-complicated-case-of-transgender-cyclist-dr-rachel-mckinnon_480285.

30. A. C. Shilton, "Transgender Track World Champion Defends Her Human Right—to Race," *Bicycling*, January 4, 2019, https://www.bicycling.com/culture/a25736012/transgender-world-champion-track-cycling-race/.

31. Sarah Mirk, "Molly Cameron: Bike Racer and Owner of Veloshop," *Portland Mercury*, June 10, 2010, https://www.portlandmercury.com/portland/molly-cameron-cyclocross-racer-veloshop-and-portland-bicycle-studio-owner/Content?oid=2594005.

32. Interview with Molly Cameron, January 2019.

33. Ibid.

34. Jonathan Maus, "Local Transgender Racer Told She Can't Enter Men's Championship Event—Updated," *Bike Portland*, December 10, 2015, https://bikeportland.org/2015/12/10/local-transgender-racer-told-she-cant-race-mens-championship-event-170078.

35. Zachary Schuster, "Wells Defends Masters 40–44 Title with Perfect Final Lap," *Cyclocross*, December 14, 2018, https://www.cxmagazine.com/report-jake-wells-defends-men-masters-40-44-2018-louisville-cyclocross-nationals.

36. Kevin Baxter, "The First U.S. Boxer to Fight as a Woman, and Then as a Man," *Los Angeles Times*, August 4, 2017, https://www.latimes.com/sports/boxing/la-sp-pat-manuel-20170804-htmlstory.html.

37. Kevin Baxter, "Transgender Male Boxer Patricio Manuel Makes History with a Win in His Pro Debut, *Los Angeles Times*, December 8, 2018, https://www.latimes.com/sports/boxing/la-sp-pat-manuel-fight-20181208-story.html.

38. S. Bermon, "Androgens and Athletic Performance of Elite Female Athletes," *Current Opinion in Endocrinology Diabetes and Obesity* 24, no. 3 (2017): 246–51, https://www.ncbi.nlm.nih.gov/pubmed/28234801.

39. J. Harper, G Lima, A. Kolliari-Turner, et al., "The Fluidity of Gender and Implications for the Biology of Inclusion for Transgender and Intersex

Athletes," *Current Sports Medicine Reports* 17, no. 12 (2018): 467–72, https://www.ncbi.nlm.nih.gov/pubmed/30531465.

20. THE CASTER SEMENYA TRIAL

1. Edwin Moses, "Caster Semenya," *Time*, April 16, 2019, http://time.com/collection/100-most-influential-people-2019/5567679/caster-semenya/.

2. Fair Play for Women is a group that was particularly active in late 2018 and early 2019 using both social media and more traditional media to oppose transgender women in sport. It can be found online at https://fairplayforwomen.com/.

3. Associated Press, "Semenya Arrives for Landmark Case at Swiss Sports Tribunal," *Wild about Trial*, February 18, 2019, https://wildabouttrial.com/tag/caster-semenya/.

4. AFP, "IAAF Delays New Gender Rules over Caster Semenya's CAS Case," Eyewitness News, October 16, 2018, https://ewn.co.za/2018/10/16/iaaf-delays-new-gender-rules-over-semenya-s-cas-case.

5. "World Experts Supporting IAAF's Eligibility Regulations for Athletes with DSD at the Court of Arbitration for Sport This Week," press release, International Association of Athletics Federations, February 18, 2019, https://www.iaaf.org/news/press-release/cas-dsd-experts.

6. Ben Levine, Michael Joyner, Nicole L Keith, et al. The Role of Testosterone in Athletic Performance. January 2019. https://law.duke.edu/sites/default/files/centers/sportslaw/Experts_T_Statement_2019.pdf

7. Court of Arbitration for Sport, Executive Summary, ASA and Caster Semenya vs. IAAF, April 30, 2019, sec. 11, https://www.tas-cas.org/fileadmin/user_upload/CAS_Executive_Summary__5794_.pdf.

8. Martyn Ziegler, "Caster Semenya: Olympic Champion Is 'Biological Male,' IAAF Lawyers Will Argue," *Times* (UK), February 13, 2019, https://www.thetimes.co.uk/article/caster-semenya-olympic-champion-is-biological-male-iaaf-lawyers-will-argue-n52dsmsnv.

9. Court of Arbitration for Sport. Arbitral Award. June 19, 2019. Section 463. https://www.tas-cas.org/fileadmin/user_upload/CAS_Award_-_redacted_-_Semenya_ASA_IAAF.pdf.

10. Court of Arbitration for Sport, Executive Summary, sec. 6.

11. Court of Arbitration for Sport. Arbitral Award. June 19, 2019. Section 484. https://www.tas-cas.org/fileadmin/user_upload/CAS_Award_-_redacted_-_Semenya_ASA_IAAF.pdf.

12. Court of Arbitration for Sport, Executive Summary, sec. 6.

13. Court of Arbitration for Sport. Arbitral Award. June 19, 2019. Section 51. https://www.tas-cas.org/fileadmin/user_upload/CAS_Award_-_redacted_-_Semenya_ASA_IAAF.pdf.

14. Court of Arbitration for Sport. Arbitral Award. June 19, 2019. Section 286. https://www.tas-cas.org/fileadmin/user_upload/CAS_Award_-_redacted_-_Semenya_ASA_IAAF.pdf.

15. Court of Arbitration for Sport. Arbitral Award. June 19, 2019. Sections 64 and 65. https://www.tas-cas.org/fileadmin/user_upload/CAS_Award_-_redacted_-_Semenya_ASA_IAAF.pdf.

16. Court of Arbitration for Sport. Arbitral Award. June 19, 2019. Section 78. https://www.tas-cas.org/fileadmin/user_upload/CAS_Award_-_redacted_-_Semenya_ASA_IAAF.pdf.

17. Court of Arbitration for Sport. Arbitral Award. June 19, 2019. Section 67. https://www.tas-cas.org/fileadmin/user_upload/CAS_Award_-_redacted_-_Semenya_ASA_IAAF.pdf.

18. Court of Arbitration for Sport. Arbitral Award. June 19, 2019. Sections 320–322. https://www.tas-cas.org/fileadmin/user_upload/CAS_Award_-_redacted_-_Semenya_ASA_IAAF.pdf.

19. Court of Arbitration for Sport. Arbitral Award. June 19, 2019. Section 138. https://www.tas-cas.org/fileadmin/user_upload/CAS_Award_-_redacted_-_Semenya_ASA_IAAF.pdf.

20. Court of Arbitration for Sport. Arbitral Award. June 19, 2019. Sections 139 and 140. https://www.tas-cas.org/fileadmin/user_upload/CAS_Award_-_redacted_-_Semenya_ASA_IAAF.pdf.

21. Court of Arbitration for Sport. Arbitral Award. June 19, 2019. Sections 477, 479, 481, 482, 484, and 486. https://www.tas-cas.org/fileadmin/user_upload/CAS_Award_-_redacted_-_Semenya_ASA_IAAF.pdf.

22. Ibid.

23. Court of Arbitration for Sport. Arbitral Award. June 19, 2019. Section 477. https://www.tas-cas.org/fileadmin/user_upload/CAS_Award_-_redacted_-_Semenya_ASA_IAAF.pdf.

24. Court of Arbitration for Sport. Arbitral Award. June 19, 2019. Section 478. https://www.tas-cas.org/fileadmin/user_upload/CAS_Award_-_redacted_-_Semenya_ASA_IAAF.pdf.

25. Court of Arbitration for Sport. Arbitral Award. June 19, 2019. Section 479. https://www.tas-cas.org/fileadmin/user_upload/CAS_Award_-_redacted_-_Semenya_ASA_IAAF.pdf.

26. Court of Arbitration for Sport. Arbitral Award. June 19, 2019. Section 481. https://www.tas-cas.org/fileadmin/user_upload/CAS_Award_-_redacted_-_Semenya_ASA_IAAF.pdf.

27. Court of Arbitration for Sport. Arbitral Award. June 19, 2019. Sections 482 and 483. https://www.tas-cas.org/fileadmin/user_upload/CAS_Award_-_redacted_-_Semenya_ASA_IAAF.pdf.
28. Court of Arbitration for Sport. Arbitral Award. June 19, 2019. Section 495. https://www.tas-cas.org/fileadmin/user_upload/CAS_Award_-_redacted_-_Semenya_ASA_IAAF.pdf.
29. Court of Arbitration for Sport. Arbitral Award. June 19, 2019. Sections 484 and 485. https://www.tas-cas.org/fileadmin/user_upload/CAS_Award_-_redacted_-_Semenya_ASA_IAAF.pdf.
30. Court of Arbitration for Sport. Arbitral Award. June 19, 2019. Section 480. https://www.tas-cas.org/fileadmin/user_upload/CAS_Award_-_redacted_-_Semenya_ASA_IAAF.pdf.
31. Court of Arbitration for Sport. Arbitral Award. June 19, 2019. Section 486. https://www.tas-cas.org/fileadmin/user_upload/CAS_Award_-_redacted_-_Semenya_ASA_IAAF.pdf.
32. Court of Arbitration for Sport. Arbitral Award. June 19, 2019. Section 487. https://www.tas-cas.org/fileadmin/user_upload/CAS_Award_-_redacted_-_Semenya_ASA_IAAF.pdf.
33. Court of Arbitration for Sport. Arbitral Award. June 19, 2019. Section 503. https://www.tas-cas.org/fileadmin/user_upload/CAS_Award_-_redacted_-_Semenya_ASA_IAAF.pdf.
34. Court of Arbitration for Sport. Arbitral Award. June 19, 2019. Section 371. https://www.tas-cas.org/fileadmin/user_upload/CAS_Award_-_redacted_-_Semenya_ASA_IAAF.pdf.
35. Court of Arbitration for Sport. Arbitral Award. June 19, 2019. Section 409. https://www.tas-cas.org/fileadmin/user_upload/CAS_Award_-_redacted_-_Semenya_ASA_IAAF.pdf.
36. Court of Arbitration for Sport. Arbitral Award. June 19, 2019. Section 398. https://www.tas-cas.org/fileadmin/user_upload/CAS_Award_-_redacted_-_Semenya_ASA_IAAF.pdf.
37. Court of Arbitration for Sport. Arbitral Award. June 19, 2019. Sections 52–61. https://www.tas-cas.org/fileadmin/user_upload/CAS_Award_-_redacted_-_Semenya_ASA_IAAF.pdf.
38. Court of Arbitration for Sport. Arbitral Award. June 19, 2019. Section 68. https://www.tas-cas.org/fileadmin/user_upload/CAS_Award_-_redacted_-_Semenya_ASA_IAAF.pdf.
39. Ibid.
40. AFP, "South Africa Sports Minister to Back Semenya at Hearing," *Daily Mail* (UK), February 20, 2019, https://www.dailymail.co.uk/wires/afp/article-6726239/South-Africa-sports-minister-Semenya-hearing.html.

41. Daniel Mothowagae, "Semenya vs IAAF: State Prepared to Spend R25m on Legal Battle," *City Press* (South Africa), February 15, 2019, https://city-press.news24.com/Sport/semenya-vs-iaaf-state-prepared-to-spend-r25m-in-legal-battle-20190215.

42. Court of Arbitration for Sport. Arbitral Award. June 19, 2019. Section 628. https://www.tas-cas.org/fileadmin/user_upload/CAS_Award_-_redacted_-_Semenya_ASA_IAAF.pdf.

43. Court of Arbitration for Sport. Arbitral Award. June 19, 2019. Section 632. https://www.tas-cas.org/fileadmin/user_upload/CAS_Award_-_redacted_-_Semenya_ASA_IAAF.pdf.

44. Court of Arbitration for Sport. Arbitral Award. June 19, 2019. Section 287. https://www.tas-cas.org/fileadmin/user_upload/CAS_Award_-_redacted_-_Semenya_ASA_IAAF.pdf.

45. Ibid.

46. Court of Arbitration for Sport. Arbitral Award. June 19, 2019. Sections 290 and 291. https://www.tas-cas.org/fileadmin/user_upload/CAS_Award_-_redacted_-_Semenya_ASA_IAAF.pdf.

47. Court of Arbitration for Sport. Arbitral Award. June 19, 2019. Section 295. https://www.tas-cas.org/fileadmin/user_upload/CAS_Award_-_redacted_-_Semenya_ASA_IAAF.pdf.

48. Court of Arbitration for Sport. Arbitral Award. June 19, 2019. Section 289. https://www.tas-cas.org/fileadmin/user_upload/CAS_Award_-_redacted_-_Semenya_ASA_IAAF.pdf.

49. Ibid.

50. Associated Press, "Decision in Caster Semenya Case Delayed until End of April," CBC Sports, March 21, 2019, https://www.cbc.ca/sports/olympics/caster-semenya-verdict-delayed-1.5065963.

51. Gerald Imray, "Olympic Silver Medalist Also Has Testosterone Condition," CTV News, April 17, 2019, https://www.ctvnews.ca/sports/olympic-silver-medallist-also-has-testosterone-condition-1.4383568.

52. Court of Arbitration for Sport, Executive Summary, sec. 1.

53. Ibid., sec. 21.

54. Ibid., sec. 18.

55. Thomson Reuters, "Caster Semenya to Avoid Testosterone Test Running 3,000m at Prefontaine Classic," CBC Sports, May 22, 2019, https://www.cbc.ca/sports/olympics/trackandfield/caster-semenya-prefontaine-classic-1.5144667.

56. "Margaret Nyairera Wambui Punished for Defying IAAF Ruling," *Kenyan*, May 20, 2019, https://www.kenyans.co.ke/news/39831-kenyan-athlete-punished-defying-iaaf-ruling.

57. Gerald Imray, "South African Government Says Appeal Coming in Semenya Case," NBC Montana, May 13, 2019, https://nbcmontana.com/sports/south-african-government-says-appeal-coming-in-semenya-case.

BIBLIOGRAPHY

BOOKS

Anderson, Sheldon. *The Forgotten Legacy of Stella Walsh*. Lanham, MD: Rowman & Littlefield, 2017.

Cayleff, Susan E. *Babe: The Life and Legend of Babe Didrickson Zaharias*. Urbana: University of Illinois Press, 1995.

Dreger, Alice. *Galileo's Middle Finger: Heretics, Activists, and the Search for Justice in Science*. New York: Penguin, 2015.

———. *Hermaphrodites and the Medical Invention of Sex*. Cambridge, MA: Harvard University Press, 2000.

Drinkwater, Barbara L. *Women in Sport*. Malden, MA: Blackwell, 2000.

Epstein, David. *The Sports Gene: Inside the Science of Extraordinary Athletic Performance*. New York: Penguin, 2013.

Freedman, Russell. *Babe Didrikson Zaharias: The Making of a Champion*. New York: Clarion, 1999.

Gallico, Paul. *Farewell to Sport*. 2nd ed. New York: Knopf, 1990.

Hanson, Sharon Kinney. *The Life of Helen Stephens: The Fulton Flash*. Carbondale: Southern Illinois University Press, 2004.

Hoyer, Niels. *Man into Woman: The First Sex Change, a Portrait of Lili Elbe*. Blue Boat, 1933.

Jenner, Bruce, and Finch, Philip. *Decathlon Challenge: Bruce Jenner's Story*. Englewood Cliffs, NJ: Prentice-Hall, 1977.

Jenner, Caitlyn, with Buzz Bissinger. *The Secrets of My Life*. New York: Grand Central, 2017.

Jorgensen, Christine. *Christine Jorgensen: A Personal Autobiography*. New York: Paul S. Eriksson, 1967.

Karkazis, Katrina. *Fixing Sex: Intersex, Medical Authority, and Lived Experience*. Durham, NC: Duke University Press, 2008.

Lancaster, Bobbi. *The Red Light Runner*. San Bernardino: CreateSpace, 2017.

Ljungqvist, Arne, and Goran Lager. *Doping's Nemesis*. Cheltenham, UK: Sports Books, 2011.

Moore, Richard. *In Search of Robert Millar: Unravelling the Mystery Surrounding Britain's Most Successful Tour de France Cyclist*. New York: HarperCollins, 2008.

Murray, Thomas. *Good Sport: Why Our Games Matter—and How Doping Undermines Them*. New York: Oxford University Press, 2017.

Pieper, Lindsay Parks. *Sex Testing: Gender Policing in Women's Sports*. Urbana: University of Illinois Press, 2016.

Richards, Renée, with John Ames. *Second Serve*. New York: Stein and Day, 1983.

Schinegger, Erik, and Marco Schenz. *Mein Sieg über mich: Der Mann, der Weltmeisterin wurde*. München: Herbig, 1988.

Totman, Richard. *The Third Sex: Kathoey—Thailand's Ladyboys*. London: Souvenir Press, 2003.

Walters, Guy. *Berlin Games: How the Nazis Stole the Olympic Dream*. New York: HarperCollins, 2006.

SCHOLARLY ARTICLES

Auchus, Richard J. "Endocrinology and Women's Sport: The Diagnosis Matters." *Law and Contempory Problems* 80, no. 4 (2017): 127–38. https://lcp.law.duke.edu/article/endocrinology-and-womens-sports-auchus-vol80-iss4/

Baby,T. K., Thomas,P., Palani, J., et al., "Sex Determination Efficacy of Papanicolaou and Acriflavine Schiff Stains in Buccal Smears," *Journal of Forensic Dental Science* 9, no. 1 (2017): 46. http://www.jfds.org/article.asp? issn=0975–1475; year=2017; volume=9; issue=1; spage=46; epage=46; aulast=Baby

Ballantyne, K., N. M. Kayser, and J. A. Grootegoed. "Sex and Gender Issues in Competitive Sports: Investigation of a Historical Case Leads to a New Viewpoint." *British Journal of Sports Medicine* 46, no. 8 (2012): 614–17. https://www.ncbi.nlm.nih.gov/pubmed/21540190

Barr, M. L., and E. G. Bertram. "A Morphological Distinction between Neurones of the Male and Female, and the Behaviour of the Nucleolar Satellite during Accelerated Nucleoprotein Synthesis." *Nature* 163, no. 4148 (1949): 676–77. https://www.nature.com/articles/163676a0

Barr, Murray L. "Cytological Tests of Sex" [letter to the editor]. *Lancet* 267, no. 6906 (1956): 47. https://www.thelancet.com/journals/lancet/article/PIIS0140-6736(56)91883-9/fulltext

Bermon, S. "Androgens and Athletic Performance of Elite Female Athletes." *Current Opinion in Endocrinology Diabetes and Obesity* 24, no. 3 (2017): 246–51. https://www.ncbi.nlm.nih.gov/pubmed/28234801

Bermon, S., and P. Y. Garnier. "Serum Androgen Levels and Their Relation to Performance in Track and Field: Mass Spectrometry Results from 2127 Observations in Male and Female Elite Athletes." *British Journal of Sports Medicine* 51 (2017): 1309–14. https://bjsm.bmj.com/content/51/17/1309

Bermon, S., P. Y. Garnier, A. L. Hirschberg, et al. "Serum Androgen Levels in Elite Female Athletes." *Journal of Clinical Endocrinology and Metabolism* 99, no. 11 (2014): 4328–35. https://www.ncbi.nlm.nih.gov/pubmed/25137421

Bittles, A. H. "Consanguineous Marriage and Childhood Health." *Developmental Medicine & Child Neurology* 45 (2003): 571–76. http://onlinelibrary.wiley.com/doi/10.1111/j.1469–8749.2003. tb00959. x/epdf

Byers, H. M, Mohnach, L. H., Fechner, P. Y., et al. "Unexpected Ethical Dilemmas in Sex Assignment in 46,XY DSD Due to 5-alpha Reductase Type 2 Deficiency." *American Journal of Medical Genetics, Part C: Seminars in Medical Genetics* 175, no. 2 (2017): 260–67. doi: 10.1002/ajmg.c.31560. https://www.ncbi.nlm.nih.gov/pubmed/28544750

Case, Mary Anne. "Heterosexuality as a Factor in the Long History of Women's Sports." *Law and Contemporary Problems* 80, no. 4 (2017): 25–46. https://papers.ssrn.com/sol3/papers.cfm?abstract_id=3138664

Coleman, Doriane Lambelet. "Sex in Sport." *Law and Contemporary Problems* 80, no. 4 (2017): 63–126. https://scholarship.law.duke.edu/lcp/vol80/iss4/5/

de la Chapelle, A. "The Use and Misuse of Sex Chromatin Screening for 'Gender Identification' of Female Athletes." *Journal of the American Medical Association* 256, no. 14 (1986): 1920–23. https://www.ncbi.nlm.nih.gov/pubmed/3761498

Ellaithi, M., A. Kamel, and O. Saber. "Consanguinity and Disorders of Sexual Developments in the Sudan." *Sudan Journal of Medical Sciences* 6, no. 4 (2011): 267–70. https://scholar.google.com.mx/scholar?q=consanguinity+and+disorders+of+sexual+development+in+the+sudan&hl=en&as_sdt=0&as_vis=1&oi=scholart

Elsas, L. J., A. Ljungqvist, M. A. Ferguson-Smith, et al. "Gender Verification of Female Athletes." *Genetics in Medicine* 2, no. 4 (2000): 249–54. https://www.ncbi.nlm.nih.gov/pubmed/11252710

Elsas, L. J., R. Hayes, and K. Muralidharan. "Gender Verification at the Centennial Olympic Games." *Journal of the Medical Association of Georgia* 86 (1997): 50–54. https://www.ncbi.nlm.nih.gov/pubmed/9029887

Fénichel, P., F. Paris, P. Philibert, et al. "Molecular Diagnosis of 5 alpha-Reductase Deficiency in 4 Elite Young Female Athletes through Hormonal Screening for Hyperandrogenism." *Journal of Clinical Endocrinology & Metabolism* 98, no. 6 (2013): E1055–59. https://www.ncbi.nlm.nih.gov/pubmed/23633205

Ferguson-Smith, M. A., and E. A. Ferris. "Gender Verification in Sport: The Need for Change?" *British Journal of Sports Medicine* 25, no. 1 (1991): 17–20. https://bjsm.bmj.com/content/25/1/17

Ferguson-Smith, M. A., and L. D. Bavington. "Natural Selection for Genetic Variants in Sport: The Role of Y Chromosome Genes in Elite Female Athletes with 46,XY DSD." Sports Medicine 44, no. 12 (2014): 1629–34. https://www.ncbi.nlm.nih.gov/pubmed/25160863

Ganie, Y., C. Aldous, Y. Balakrishna, and R. Wiersma. "Disorders of Sex Development in Children in KwaZulu-Natal Durban South Africa: 20-Year Experience in a Tertiary Centre." *Journal of Pediatric Endocrinology & Metabolism* 30, no. 1 (2017): 11–18. https://www.ncbi.nlm.nih.gov/pubmed/27754965

Gooren, L., and M. Bunck. "Transsexuals and Competitive Sports." *European Journal of Endocrinology* 151, no. 4 (2004): 425–29. https://www.ncbi.nlm.nih.gov/pubmed/15476439

Ha, N. Q., S. L. Dworkin, M. J. Martínez-Patiño, et al. "Hurdling Over Sex? Sport, Science, and Equity." *Archives of Sexual Behavior* 43, no. 6 (2014): 1035–42. https://www.ncbi.nlm.nih.gov/pubmed/25085349

Handelsman, D., A. Hirschberg, and S. Bermon. "Circulating Testosterone as the Hormonal Basis of Sex Differences in Athletic Performance." *Endocrine Reviews* 39, no. 5 (2018): 803–29. https://www.ncbi.nlm.nih.gov/pubmed/30010735

Harper, J. "Race Times for Transgender Athletes." *Journal of Sporting Cultures and Identities* 6, no. 1 (2015): 1–9. https://pdfs.semanticscholar.org/1e6a/bd2c1e03ba88e9ac8da94ea1d69ff3f4878a.pdf?_ga=2.254440527.659551599.1550520323-1192624875.1550520323

Harper, J., G. Lima, A. Kolliari-Turner, et al. "The Fluidity of Gender and Implications for the Biology of Inclusion for Transgender and Intersex Athletes." *Current Sports Medicine Reports* 17, no. 12 (2018): 467–72. https://www.ncbi.nlm.nih.gov/pubmed/30531465

Harper, J., J. Ospina-Betancurt, and M. J. Martínez-Patiño. "Analysis of the Performance of Transgender Athletes." *Sports Science* 20 (2016). https://www.sportsci.org/2016/WCPASabstracts/ID-1699.pdf

Healy, M. L., R. Gibney, C. Pentecost, M. J. Wheeler, and P. H. Sonksen. "Endocrine Profiles in 693 Elite Athletes in the Post-Competition Setting." *Clinical Endocrinology* 81, no. 2 (2014): 294–305. https://www.ncbi.nlm.nih.gov/pubmed/24593684

Imperato-McGinley, J., L. Guerrero, T. Gautier, and R. E. Peterson, "Steroid 5α-Reductase Deficiency in Man: An Inherited Form of Male Pseudohermaphroditism," Science 186, no. 4170 (1974): 1213–15. doi: 10.1126/science.186.4170.1213.PMID4432067. https://www.ncbi.nlm.nih.gov/pubmed/4432067

Jordan-Young, R., P. Sonksen, and K. Karkazis. "Sex, Health, and Athletes." *British Medical Journal* 348 (2014): g2926. https://www.bmj.com/content/348/bmj.g2926

Karkazis, K., R. Jordan-Young, G. Davis, and S. Camporesi. "Out of Bounds? A Critique of the New Policies on Hyperandrogenism in Elite Female Athletes." *American Journal of Bioethics* 12, no. 7 (2012): 3–16. https://www.ncbi.nlm.nih.gov/pubmed/22694023

Love, Adam, Seung-Yup Lim, and Joy T. DeSensi. "Mianne Bagger: A Transitioned Woman's Efforts for Inclusion in Professional Golf." *Women in Sport and Physical Activity Journal* 18 no. 1 (2009): 68–77. https://www.academia.edu/1999129/Mianne_Bagger_A_transitioned_womans_efforts_for_inclusion_in_professional_golf

Martínez-Patiño, M. J. "Personal Account: A Woman Tried and Tested." *Lancet* 366 (2005 supp.): 38–39. https://www.ncbi.nlm.nih.gov/pubmed/16360746

Moesch K., A. M. Elbe, M. L. Hauge, and J. M. Wikman. "Late Specialization: The Key to Success in Centimeters, Grams, or Seconds (cgs) Sports." *Scandinavian Journal of Medicine & Science in Sports* 21 (2011): e282–e290. https://www.ncbi.nlm.nih.gov/pubmed/21401722

Morel Y., R. Rey, C. Teinturier, et al. "Aetiological Diagnosis of Male Sex Ambiguity: A Collaborative Study." *European Journal of Pediatrics* 161, no. 1 (2002): 49–59. https://www.ncbi.nlm.nih.gov/pubmed/11808880

Pitsiladis Y., J. Harper, J. Ospina-Betancurt, and M. J. Martinez-Patino. "Beyond Fairness: The Biology of Inclusion for Transgender and Intersex Athletes." *Current Sports Medicine Reports* 15, no. 6 (2016): 386–88. https://www.ncbi.nlm.nih.gov/pubmed/27841808

Reardon, Sara. "The Spectrum of Sex Development: Eric Vilain and the Intersex Controversy." *Nature*, May 10, 2016. https://www.nature.com/news/the-spectrum-of-sex-development-eric-vilain-and-the-intersex-controversy-1.19873

Riley, L. "The Participation of Trans Athletes in Sport—A Transformation in Approach?" Law in Sport, February 5, 2016. https://www.lawinsport.com/topics/articles/item/the-participation-of-trans-athletes-insport-a-transformation-in-approach

Russo, Francine. "Is There Something Unique about the Transgender Brain?" *Scientific American*, January 1, 2016. https://www.scientificamerican.com/article/is-there-something-unique-about-the-transgender-brain/

Safer, J., and V. Tangpricha, "Out of the Shadows: It Is Time to Mainstream Treatment for Transgender Patients." *Endocrine Practice* 14, no. 2 (2008): 248–50. https://www.ncbi.nlm.nih.gov/pmc/articles/PMC3105355/

Ulrich, R., H. G. Pope Jr., L. Cléret, et al., "Doping in Two Elite Athletics Competitions Assessed by Randomized-Response Surveys." Sports Medicine 48, no. 1 (2018): 211. https://doi.org/10.1007/s40279-017-0765-4

Watson, J. D., and F. H. C. Crick. "Molecular Structure of Nucleic Acids: A Structure for Deoxyribose Nucleic Acid." *Nature* 171 (April 25, 1953): 737–38. https://www.nature.com/scitable/content/molecular-structure-of-nucleic-acids-a-structure-13997975

Wiepjes, C. M., N. M. Nota, C. J. M. de Blok, et al. "The Amsterdam Cohort of Gender Dysphoria Study (1972–2015): Trends in Prevalence, Treatment, and Regrets." *Journal of Sexual Medicine* 15, no. 4 (2018): 582–90. https://www.ncbi.nlm.nih.gov/pubmed/29463477

DOCUMENTS

Barr Body Staining, https://www.slideshare.net/gurya87/barr-body-staining.

"Consensus Statement on Management of Intersex Disorders." *Pediatrics* 118, no. 2 (2006). http://pediatrics.aappublications.org/content/118/2/e488

Court of Arbitration for Sport. The Arbitral Award Delivered by the Court of Arbitration for Sport. CAS 2018/O/5794 Mokgadi Caster Semenya v. International Association of Athletics Federations and CAS 2018/O/5798 Athletics South Africa v International Association of Athletics Federations. https://www.tas-cas.org/fileadmin/user_upload/CAS_Award_-_redacted_-_Semenya_ASA_IAAF.pdf

———. Executive Summary. ASA and Caster Semenya vs. IAAF. April 30, 2019. https://www.tas-cas.org/fileadmin/user_upload/CAS_Executive_Summary__5794_.pdf

———. The Interim Arbitral Award Delivered by the Court of Arbitration for Sport. CAS 2014/A/3759 Dutee Chand v. Athletics Federation of India (AFI) & the International Association of Athletics Federations (IAAF). https://www.doping.nl/media/kb/3317/CAS%202014_A_3759%20Dutee%20Chand%20vs.%20AFI%20%26%20IAAF%20%28S%29.pdf

Flores, Andrew R., Jody L. Herman, Gary J. Gates, and Taylor N. T. Brown. *How Many Adults Identify as Transgender in the United States?* June 2016. https://williamsinstitute.law.ucla.edu/wp-content/uploads/How-Many-Adults-Identify-as-Transgender-in-the-United-States.pdf

International Association of Athletics Federations. "IAAF Eligibility Regulations for the Female Classification [Athletes with Differences of Sex Development] in Force as from 8 May 2019." May 1 2019. https://www.iaaf.org/about-iaaf/documents/rules-regulations

———. *IAAF Regulations Governing Eligibility of Athletes Who Have Undergone Sex Reassignment to Compete in Women's Competition*. https://docs.wixstatic.com/ugd/2bc3fc_476cfbfe00df48c3aa5322a29d5e11b2.pdf

International Olympic Committee. "IOC Consensus Meeting on Sex Reassignment and Hyperandrogenism, November 2015." https://stillmed.olympic.org/Documents/Commissions_PDFfiles/Medical_commission/2015-11_ioc_consensus_meeting_on_sex_reassignment_and_hyperandrogenism-en.pdf

———. "IOC Regulations on Female Hyperandrogenism, Games of the XXX Olympiad in London, 2012," June 22, 2012. https://stillmed.olympic.org/Documents/Commissions_PDFfiles/Medical_commission/2012-06-22-IOC-Regulations-on-Female-Hyperandrogenism-eng.pdf

———. "Statement of the Stockholm Consensus on Sex Reassignment in Sports," November 12, 2003. https://stillmed.olympic.org/Documents/Reports/EN/en_report_905.pdf

McLaren, Richard H. Independent Person Report to Sir Craig Reedie, President, World Anti-Doping Agency, in WADA Investigation of Sochi Allegations, July 18, 2016. https://www.wada-ama.org/sites/default/files/resources/files/20160718_ip_report_newfinal.pdf

———. Independent Person 2nd Report to Sir Craig Reedie, President, World Anti-Doping Agency, in WADA Investigation of Sochi Allegations, December 9, 2016. https://www.wada-ama.org/sites/default/files/resources/files/mclaren_report_part_ii_2.pdf

Transathlete.com. State by State High School Transgender Policies. https://www.transathlete.com/k-12

FILMS

Brett, Mike, and Steve Jamison, Directors. *Next Goal Wins*. Icon Productions. http://nextgoalwinsmovie.com/

Drath, Eric, Director. *Renée*. ESPN Films, 2011.

Uekrongtham, Ekachai, Director. *Beautiful Boxer*. GMM Grammy. 2005.

SELECTED NEWS ARTICLES

The following news articles are only a small sample of the ones used in the text of the book, but are some of the more important ones. Other news articles referenced can be found in the chapter endnotes.

Anderson, Chloe Psyche. "This College Volleyball Player Is Headed to the NCAA." Outsports, June 1, 2016. https://www.outsports.com/2016/6/1/11814342/transgender-ncaa-volleyball-chloe-psyche-anderson

Ayodi, Ayumba. "Athlete Rose from the Slopes of Mt. Kenya to World Prominence." *Daily Nation*, October 28, 2018. https://www.nation.co.ke/sports/talkup/Nyairera-rose-from-slopes-of-Mt-Kenya-to-world-prominence-/441392-4825506-bqtpi4z/index.html

Barker, Sarah. "Should There Be Testosterone Limits for Women in Athletics?" *Deadspin*, May 27, 2016. https://deadspin.com/should-there-be-testosterone-limits-for-women-in-athlet-1778330172

Baxter, Kevin. "Transgender Male Boxer Patricio Manuel Makes History with a Win in His Pro Debut." *Los Angeles Times*, December 8, 2018. https://www.latimes.com/sports/boxing/la-sp-pat-manuel-fight-20181208-story.html

Berg, Stefan. "How Dora the Man Competed in the Women's High Jump." *Spiegal*, September 15, 2009. http://www.spiegel.de/international/germany/1936-berlin-olympics-how-dora-the-man-competed-in-the-woman-s-high-jump-a-649104.html

Chaudhry, Serena. "South Africa Athletics Chief Admits Lying about Semenya Tests." Reuters, September 19, 2009. https://www.reuters.com/article/us-safrica-semenya-idUSTRE58I0N320090919

Dreler, Fred. "The Complicated Case of Transgender Cyclist Dr. Rachel McKinnon." *Velo News*, October 18, 2018. https://www.velonews.com/2018/10/news/commentary-the-complicated-case-of-transgender-cyclist-dr-rachel-mckinnon_480285

Epstein, David, and Alice Dreger. "Testosterone in Sports." *New York Times*, April 20, 2014. https://www.nytimes.com/2014/04/21/opinion/testosterone-in-sports.html

Fox, Fallon. "Fallon Fox Responds to Ashlee Evans-Smith, Who Says Trans Fighters Should Be Barred from Women's MMA." *Outsports*, November 20, 2013. https://www.outsports.com/2013/11/20/5123442/fallon-fox-ashlee-evans-smith-trans-mma

Harper, Joanna. "A Brief History of Intersex Athletes." LetsRun.com, September 19, 2014. http://www.letsrun.com/news/2014/09/brief-history-intersex-athletes-sport/

———. "Do Transgender Athletes Have an Edge? I Sure Don't." *Washington Post*, April 1, 2015. https://www.washingtonpost.com/opinions/do-transgender-athletes-have-an-edge-i-sure-dont/2015/04/01/ccacb1da-c68e-11e4-b2a1-bed1aaea2816_story.html?utm_term=.b2e095c13098

Hart, Simon. "Caster Semenya 'Is a Hermaphrodite,' Tests Show." *Telegraph* (UK), September 11, 2009. https://www.telegraph.co.uk/sport/othersports/athletics/6170229/Caster-Semenya-is-a-hermaphrodite-tests-show.html

Imray, Gerald. "Olympic Silver Medalist Also Has Testosterone Condition." CTV News, April 17, 2019. https://www.ctvnews.ca/sports/olympic-silver-medallist-also-has-testosterone-condition-1.4383568

———. "South African Government Says Appeal Coming in Semenya Case." NBC Montana, May 13, 2019. https://nbcmontana.com/sports/south-african-government-says-appeal-coming-in-semenya-case

Ingle, Sean. "Caster Semenya v IAAF: The Inside Story of Sporting Trail of the Century." *Guardian* (UK), May 1, 2019. https://www.theguardian.com/sport/2019/may/01/caster-semenya-iaaf-behind-scenes-sporting-trial-of-the-century

———. "Lamine Diack, Former IAAF Head, under Investigation in Corruption and Doping Inquiry." *Guardian* (UK), November 4, 2015. https://www.theguardian.com/sport/2015/nov/04/lamine-diack-investigation-iaaf-corruption-doping

International Association of Athletics Federations. "IAAF Introduces New Eligibility Regulations for Female Classification." Press release, April 26, 2018. https://www.iaaf.org/news/press-release/eligibility-regulations-for-female-classifica

Jacobs, Jeff. "No Easy Answers When It Comes to Transgender Athletes." *Connecticut Post*, June 4, 2018. https://www.ctpost.com/highschool/article/Jeff-Jacobs-No-easy-answers-when-it-comes-to-12967306.php

Jordan-Young, Rebecaa, and Katrina Karkazis. "You Say You're a Woman? That Should Be Enough." *New York Times*, June 17, 2012. http://www.nytimes.com/2012/06/18/sports/olympics/olympic-sex-verification-you-say-youre-a-woman-that-should-be-enough.html

Joseph, Manu. "The Definition of a Female Athlete." *Hindustan Times*, July 21, 2014. https://www.hindustantimes.com/columns/the-definition-of-a-female-athlete/story-Si0bkalblOjjJJHP1HudRO.html

Kahrl, Christina. "Chris Mosier: 'I Finally Feel Very Comfortable with My Body.'" ESPN, June 26, 2016. http://www.espn.com/olympics/story/_/page/bodychrismosier/duathlete-chris-mosier-breaking-barriers-repping-team-usa-body-issue-2016

Levy, Ariel. "Either/Or: Sports, Sex, and the Case of Caster Semenya." *New Yorker*, November 19, 2009. https://www.newyorker.com/magazine/2009/11/30/eitheror

Macur, Juliet. "Fighting for the Body She Was Born With." *New York Times*, October 6, 2014. https://www.nytimes.com/2014/10/07/sports/sprinter-dutee-chand-fights-ban-over-her-testosterone-level.html

"Margaret Nyairera Wambui Punished for Defying IAAF Ruling." *Kenyan*, May 20, 2019. https://www.kenyans.co.ke/news/39831-kenyan-athlete-punished-defying-iaaf-ruling

Maus, Jonathan. "Local Transgender Racer Told She Can't Enter Men's Championship Event—Updated." Bike Portland, December 10, 2015. https://bikeportland.org/2015/12/10/local-transgender-racer-told-she-cant-race-mens-championship-event-170078

Morgan, Edith Thys. "Erik Schinegger: Forgotten World Champion." *Skiing History*, August 9, 2017. https://www.skiinghistory.org/news/erik-schinegger-forgotten-world-champion

Muller, Antoinette. "Caster Semenya Never Signed Informed Consent for Sex Tests, Says Ex-ASA Board Member." *Daily Maverick*, February 12, 2018. https://www.dailymaverick.co.za/article/2018-02-12-caster-semenya-never-signed-informed-consent-for-sex-tests-says-ex-asa-board-member/#.WoYpCqjwbIV

"Norton Rose Fulbright Advises Olympic Champion Caster Semenya to Challenge IAAF Rules as Discriminatory." Press release, June 18, 2018. https://www.nortonrosefulbright.com/en/news/115e61b6/norton-rose-fulbright-advises-olympic-champion-caster-semenya-to-challenge-iaaf-rules-as-discriminatory

Olterman, Philip. "Russia Accused of Athletics Doping Cover-up on German TV." *Guardian* (UK), December 3, 2014. https://www.theguardian.com/sport/2014/dec/03/russia-accused-athletics-doping-cover-up-olympics

Rigby, Sara. "Can Transgender Athletes Be Fairly Integrated into Women's Sports?" *Science Focus*, March 29, 2019. https://www.sciencefocus.com/the-human-body/can-transgender-athletes-be-fairly-integrated-into-womens-sports/

"Semenya Makes History at Nationals." Sport 24, April 16, 2016. https://www.sport24.co.za/OtherSport/Athletics/South-Africa/semenya-makes-history-at-nationals-20160416

Snowden, Jonathan. "Transgender Fighter Fallon Fox and Her Slowly Fading 15 Minutes of Fame." *Bleacher Report*, April 22, 2014. https://bleacherreport.com/articles/2038764-transgender-fighter-fallon-fox-and-her-slowly-fading-fifteen-minutes-of-fame

Spillett, Richard. "Champion Fell Runner Is Jailed for 18 Years." *Daily Mail* (UK), March 14, 2017. http://www.dailymail.co.uk/news/article-4312594/Fell-runner-jailed-trying-murder-athletics-official.html

Steinmetz, Katie. "The Transgender Tipping Point." *Time*, May 28, 2014. http://time.com/135480/transgender-tipping-point/

Stellar, Tim. "Transgender Cyclist's Win in Tucson Was Fairer Than It Seemed." *Arizona Daily Star*, November 26, 2016. https://tucson.com/news/local/columnists/steller/steller-transgender-cyclist-s-win-in-tucson-was-fairer-than/article_0851e258-2eb6-540a-8e60-1875e7bc836d.html

Stone, Ken. "Colombian W40 Transgender Hurdler Claims Bronze in 80H at Malaga Worlds." *Masterstrack* (blog), September 16, 2018. https://masterstrack.blog/2018/09/colombian-w40-transgender-hurdler-claims-bronze-in-80h-at-malaga-worlds/

Talkoff, Emma K. "Breaking the Surface with Schuyler Bailar." *Harvard Crimson*, November 10, 2016. https://www.thecrimson.com/article/2016/11/10/schuyler-bailar-underwater

Thomas, Katie. "Transgender Woman Sues LPGA over Policy." *New York Times*, October 12, 2010. https://www.nytimes.com/2010/10/13/sports/golf/13lawsuit.html

Thomson Reuters. "Caster Semenya to Avoid Testosterone Test Running 3,000m at Prefontaine Classic." CBC News, May 22, 2019. https://www.cbc.ca/sports/olympics/trackandfield/caster-semenya-prefontaine-classic-1.5144667

Torre, Pablo S., and David Epstein. "The Transgender Athlete." *Sports Illustrated*, May 28, 2012. https://www.si.com/vault/2012/05/28/106195901/the-transgender-athlete

Tucker, Ross. "Hyperandrogenism and Women vs Women vs Men in Sport: A Q&A with Joanna Harper." The Science of Sport, May 23, 2016. https://sportsscientists.com/2016/05/hyperandrogenism-women-vs-women-vs-men-sport-qa-joanna-harper/?doing_wp_cron=1551563263.8498969078063964843750

———. "London 2012: Women's 800m // Women's 800m Perplexity, Analyzing Semenya's Race." The Science of Sport, August 11, 2012. https://sportsscientists.com/2012/08/womens-800m-analysing-semenya-other-insights/

Tuthill, Matt. "Transgender Powerlifter Janae Marie Kroc Shares Unbelievable Story." *Muscle and Fitness*, October 2015. https://www.muscleandfitness.com/athletes-celebrities/interviews/transgender-powerlifter-matt-kroczaleski-janae-marie-kroc-shares-unbelievable-story

Zeigler, Cyd. "Exclusive: Read the Olympics' New Transgender Guidelines That Will Not Mandate Surgery." *Outsports*, January 21, 2016. https://www.outsports.com/2016/1/21/10812404/transgender-ioc-policy-new-olympics

———. "Trans Endurance Athlete Chris Mosier Earns Spot on Team USA." *Outsports*, June 7, 2015. https://www.outsports.com/2015/6/7/8743157/chris-mosier-trans-duathlon-team-usa

Ziegler, Martyn. "Caster Semenya: Olympic Champion Is 'Biological Male' IAAF Lawyers Will Argue." *Times* (UK), February 13, 2019. https://www.thetimes.co.uk/article/caster-semenya-olympic-champion-is-biological-male-iaaf-lawyers-will-argue-n52dsmsnv

INDEX

ABOUT THE AUTHOR

Joanna Harper grew up in Canada and studied at the University of Western Ontario, where she earned an undergraduate degree in physics and a master's degree in medical physics. She was also a successful cross-country and track runner, whose best distance was the marathon. Her 2:23 personal best put her among the top twenty men in the country. After graduation, Harper moved to the United States, and she found a long-term home in Portland, Oregon.

Harper's gender transition began in 2004, and her sharp decline in performance once on suppressive hormone therapy led her to study other transgender athletes. In 2015 Harper published the first peer-reviewed paper analyzing transgender athletic performance. Since then she has continued to study transgender athletes, and a second paper on transgender athletic performance is in the works. Harper has published scholarly articles proposing the use of biological markers to separate male athletes from female athletes, and opinion articles in the mainstream press on matters concerning transgender and intersex athletes. In September 2019 Harper moved to Loughborough, England, to join the nascent program at Loughborough University devoted to transgender athletic research.

Harper was a member of the working group that helped develop the 2016 IOC transgender guidelines. She has served as witness for the IAAF in the Chand and Semenya trials. Harper continues to run competitively and has won numerous age group awards at the national level. *Sporting Gender* is her first book.